All-Star

1

Teacher's Edition

Linda Lee

★ Stephen Sloan ★ Grace Tanaka ★ Shirley Velasco

★ Teacher's Edition by Kristin Sherman

All-Star 1, Teacher's Edition

Published by McGraw-Hill ESL/ELT, a business unit of The McGraw-Hill Companies, Inc. 1221 Avenue of the Americas, New York, NY 10020. Copyright © 2005 by The McGraw-Hill Companies, Inc. All rights reserved. Permission is granted to reproduce these materials as needed for classroom use or for use by individual students. Distribution for sale is prohibited.

2 3 4 5 6 7 8 9 10   QPD   09 08 07 06 05

ISBN 0-07-284666-6

Editorial director: Tina B. Carver
Executive editor: Erik Gundersen
Senior developmental editor: Mari Vargo
Developmental editor: Terre Passero
Director of North American marketing: Thomas P. Dare
Director of international marketing and sales: Kate Oakes
Production manager: Juanita Thompson
Interior designer: Wanda Espana of Wee Design Group

Contents

WELCOME TO THE TEACHER'S EDITION

The *All-Star* Teacher's Edition provides support to teachers using the *All-Star* Student Book. Each unit of the Teacher's Edition begins with a list of the unit's lesson titles, the objective for each lesson, and the Big Picture Expansion Activities that may be used with the Color Overhead Transparencies. Hundreds of additional activities are suggested throughout the Teacher's Edition to expand the use of the target language and life skills in the Student Book.

The *All-Star* Teacher's Edition offers step-by-step procedures for each lesson. Seasoned teachers can use the instructions as a quick refresher, while newer teachers, or substitute teachers, can use the step-by-step instructions as a helpful guide for conducting the Student Book activities in the classroom.

The Teacher's Edition provides:

- Step-by-step procedural notes for each *All-Star* Student Book activity

- 250 Expansion Activities that offer creative, life-skill tasks tied to the "big picture" scenes and the activities in each unit

- "Big Picture" Expansion Activities that focus on speaking, reading, grammar, and writing

- Worksheets for corresponding "Big Picture" Expansion Activities

- Culture, Grammar, and Pronunciation Notes

- Two-page achievement tests for each unit assess listening, reading, vocabulary, writing and grammar skills. Listening passages for the tests are provided on the Student Book Audio CD and Audiocassette programs.

- Listening scripts for all audio program materials

- Answer keys for Student Book, Workbook, and Tests

- Step-by-step procedural notes for the Equipped for the Future (EFF) application lessons found in the Workbook

All-Star is a four-level, standards-based series for English learners featuring a picture-dictionary approach to vocabulary building. "Big picture" scenes in each unit provide springboards to a wealth of activities developing all of the language skills.

An accessible and predictable sequence of lessons in each unit systematically builds language and math skills around life-skill topics. *All-Star* presents family, work, and community topics in each unit, and provides alternate application lessons in its Workbooks, giving teachers the flexibility to customize the series for a variety of student needs and curricular objectives. *All-Star* is tightly correlated to all of the major national and state standards for adult instruction.

Features

★ **Accessible "big picture" scenes** present life-skills vocabulary and provide engaging contexts for all-skills language development.

★ **Predictable sequence of eight, two-page lessons** in each unit reduces prep time for teachers and helps students get comfortable with the pattern of each lesson type.

★ **Flexible structure** allows teachers to customize each unit to meet a variety of student needs and curricular objectives, with application lessons addressing family, work, and community topics in both the Student Book and Workbook.

★ **Comprehensive coverage of key standards, such as CASAS, SCANS, EFF, and LCPs,** prepares students to master a broad range of critical competencies.

★ **Multiple assessment measures** like CASAS-style tests and performance-based assessment offer a broad range of options for monitoring and assessing learner progress.

★ **Dynamic, Interactive CD-ROM program** integrates language, literacy, and numeracy skill building with computer practice.

The Complete *All-Star* Program

★ The **Student Book with Audio Highlights** provides students with audio recordings of all of the dialogues in the Student Book. The audio CD also includes recordings of all of the new vocabulary presented in the "big picture" scenes.

★ The **Student Book** features ten, 16-page units,

integrating listening, speaking, reading, writing, grammar, math, and pronunciation skills with life-skill topics, critical thinking activities, and civics concepts.

★ The **Interactive CD-ROM** incorporates and extends the learning goals of the Student Book by integrating language, literacy, and numeracy skill building with multimedia practice on the computer. A flexible set of activities correlated to each unit builds vocabulary, listening, reading, writing, and test-taking skills.

★ The **Color Overhead Transparencies** encourage teachers to present new vocabulary and concepts in fun and meaningful ways. This component provides a full-color overhead transparency for each of the "big picture" scenes.

★ The **Workbook** includes supplementary practice activities correlated to the Student Book. As a bonus feature, the Workbook also includes alternate application lessons addressing the learner's role as worker, family member, and/or community member. These additional, optional lessons may be used in addition to, or as substitutes for, the application lessons found in Lesson 6 of each Student Book unit.

★ The **Audiocassettes** and **Audio CDs** contain recordings for all listening activities in the Student Book. Listening passages for each unit test are provided at the end of the audio section for that unit.

Overview of the *All-Star* Program
UNIT STRUCTURE

Consult the *Welcome to All-Star* guide on pages xiv–xix of the Student Book. This guide offers teachers and administrators a visual tour of one Student Book unit.

All-Star is designed to maximize accessibility and flexibility. Each unit contains the following sequence of eight, two-page lessons that develop vocabulary and build language, grammar, and math skills around life-skill topics:

★ Lesson 1: Vocabulary
★ Lesson 2: Vocabulary in Action
★ Lesson 3: Talk About It
★ Lesson 4: Reading and Writing
★ Lesson 5: Conversations
★ Lesson 6: Application
★ Lesson 7: Review and Assessment
★ Grammar or Writing Spotlight

Each lesson addresses a key adult standard, and these standards are indicated in the upper right-hand corner of each lesson in a yellow bar.

SPECIAL FEATURES OF EACH UNIT

★ *Window on Grammar.* Grammar is presented and practiced in each unit in blue boxes called *Window on Grammar.* These short presentations offer students small, manageable chunks of grammar that correlate with a variety of national and state standards. *Window on Grammar* boxes provide for written and oral practice of new language structures and functions. Students and teachers will find additional, in-depth grammar practice in a series of two-page lessons called *Spotlight: Grammar* presented throughout the book. A comprehensive *Grammar Reference Guide* at the back of the book summarizes all of the structures and functions presented.

★ *Window on Math.* Learning basic math skills is critically important for success in school, on the job, and at home. As such, national and state standards for adult education mandate instruction in basic math skills. In each unit, a blue box called *Window on Math* is dedicated to helping students develop the functional numeracy skills they need for basic math work.

★ *Window on Pronunciation.* The culminating activity in Lesson 5 (*Conversation*) of each unit is featured in a blue box called *Window on Pronunciation.* This special feature has two major goals: (1) helping students hear and produce specific sounds, words, and minimal pairs of words so they become better listeners and speakers; and (2) addressing issues of stress, rhythm, and intonation so that the students' spoken English becomes more comprehensible.

★ *Spotlight: Grammar* and *Spotlight: Writing.* At the end of each unit, students and teachers will find either a *Grammar Spotlight* or a *Writing Spotlight.* These are optional, two-page lessons that offer a supplementary focus on grammar or writing skill development.

TWO-PAGE LESSON FORMAT

The lessons in *All-Star* are designed as two-page spreads. Lessons 5–7 and the Spotlights employ a standard textbook layout, but Lessons 1–4 follow an innovative format with a list of activities on the left-hand page of the spread and picture-dictionary visuals supporting these activities on the

right-hand page. The list of activities, entitled *Things To Do*, allows students and teachers to take full advantage of the visuals in each lesson, inviting students to achieve a variety of learning goals with them.

"BIG PICTURE" SCENES

Each unit includes one "big picture" scene in either Lesson 2 or Lesson 3. This scene is the visual centerpiece of each unit, and serves as a springboard to a variety of activities provided in the Student Book, Teacher's Edition, Color Overhead Transparencies package, and Interactive CD-ROM program. In the Student Book, the "big picture" scene introduces key vocabulary and serves as a prompt for classroom discussion. The scenes feature characters with distinct personalities for students to enjoy, respond to, and talk about. There are also surprising elements for students to discover in each "big picture" scene.

The Teacher's Edition includes a variety of all-skills "Big Picture Expansion" activities that are tied to the Student Book scenes. For each unit, these expansion activities address listening, speaking, reading, writing, *and* grammar skill development, and allow teachers to customize their instruction to meet the language learning needs of each group of students.

In the Color Overhead Transparencies package, teachers will find transparencies of each "big picture" scene, which they can use to introduce the vocabulary and life-skill concepts in each unit. They can also use these transparencies to facilitate the "Big Picture Expansion" activities in the Teacher's Edition.

Finally, the Interactive CD-ROM program highlights an additional aspect of the "big picture" scenes in its listening activities. Students working with the CD-ROM program listen to a series of new conversations taking place between characters in the "big picture" scenes. They then work through a series of interactive activities based on these conversations and receive immediate feedback on their work.

CIVICS CONCEPTS

Many institutions focus direct attention on the importance of civics instruction for English language learners. Civics instruction encourages students to become active and informed community members. Throughout each *All-Star* unit, students and teachers will encounter *Try This* activities that introduce students to civics concepts and encourage community involvement. In addition, *Application* lessons provide activities that help students develop their roles as workers, parents, and citizens. Those lessons targeting the students' role as citizen encourage learners to become more active and informed members of their communities.

CASAS, SCANS, EFF, LCPS, AND OTHER STANDARDS

Teachers and administrators benchmark student progress against national and/or state standards for adult instruction. With this in mind, *All-Star* carefully integrates instructional elements from a wide range of standards including CASAS, SCANS, EFF, and the Literacy Completion Points (LCPs). Unit-by-unit correlations of these standards appear in the scope and sequence on pages xii–xvii. Here is a brief overview of our approach to meeting the key national and state standards:

★ **CASAS.** Many U.S. states, including California, tie funding for adult education programs to student performance on the Comprehensive Adult Student Assessment System (CASAS). The CASAS (www.casas.org) competencies identify more than 300 essential skills that adults need in order to succeed in the classroom, workplace, and community. Examples of these skills include identifying or using appropriate non-verbal behavior in a variety of settings, responding appropriately to common personal information questions, and comparing price or quality to determine the best buys. *All-Star* comprehensively integrates all of the CASAS Life Skill Competencies throughout the four levels of the series. Level 1 addresses all of the CASAS Level A Life Skills test items on Test Forms 31, 32, 51, and 52.

★ **SCANS.** Developed by the United States Department of Labor, SCANS is an acronym for the Secretary's Commission on Achieving Necessary Skills (wdr.doleta.gov/SCANS/). SCANS competencies are workplace skills that help people compete more effectively in today's global economy. The following are examples of SCANS competencies: works well with others, acquires and evaluates information, and teaches others new skills. A variety of SCANS competencies is threaded throughout the activities in each unit of *All-Star*. The incorporation of these competencies recognizes both the intrinsic importance of teaching workplace skills and the fact that many adult students are already working members of their communities.

★ **EFF.** Equipped for the Future (EFF) is a set of standards for adult literacy and lifelong learning, developed by The National Institute for Literacy (www.nifl.gov). The

organizing principle of EFF is that adults assume responsibilities in three major areas of life — as workers, as parents, and as citizens. These three areas of focus are called "role maps" in the EFF documentation. In the parent role map, for example, EFF highlights these and other responsibilities: participating in children's formal education and forming and maintaining supportive family relationships. Each *All-Star* unit addresses all three of the EFF role maps in its *Application* lessons. Lesson 6 in each Student Book unit includes one of the three application lessons for that unit. The remaining two application lessons are found in the corresponding Workbook unit.

★ **LCPs.** Florida and Texas document the advancement of learners in an adult program through their system of Literacy Completion Points (LCPs). *All-Star* Level 1 incorporates into its instruction the vast majority of standards at LCP Level B.

NUMBER OF HOURS OF INSTRUCTION

The *All-Star* program has been designed to accommodate the needs of adult classes with 70–180 hours of classroom instruction. Here are three recommended ways in which various components in the *All-Star* program can be combined to meet student and teacher needs.

★ **70–100 hours.** Teachers are encouraged to work through all of the Student Book materials, incorporating the *Grammar* and *Writing Spotlights* as time permits. The Color Overhead Transparencies can be used to introduce and/or review materials in each unit. Teachers should also look to the Teacher's Edition for teaching suggestions and testing materials as necessary.
Time per unit: 7–10 hours.

★ **100–140 hours.** In addition to working through all of the Student Book materials, teachers are encouraged to incorporate the Workbook and Interactive CD-ROM activities for supplementary practice.
Time per unit: 10–14 hours.

★ **140–180 hours.** Teachers and students working in an intensive instructional setting can take advantage of the wealth of expansion activities threaded through the Teacher's Edition to supplement the Student Book, Workbook, and Interactive CD-ROM materials.
Time per unit: 14–18 hours.

ASSESSMENT
PURPOSES OF ASSESSMENT

J. Michael O'Malley and Lorraine Valdez-Pierce describe six purposes of assessment in *Authentic Assessment for English Language Learners* (Addison-Wesley, 1966), similar to those listed below.

★ **Screening** determines if the student is at the right level for the English language instruction provided. Some students' language level may be too advanced for an adult ESL program, and their needs better met in an academic program or in adult high school.

★ **Placement** tests determine at what level a student should be placed. Adult ESL programs often give an entrance test of some kind to place the student. Screening and placement can be done with the same instrument. Many programs use CASAS or BEST Plus tests for this purpose.

★ **Monitoring achievement** allows the learner and the instructor to see how well particular information has been learned. An end-of-unit test can demonstrate if the student has been successful in learning specific instructional content.

★ **Measuring performance** involves assessing how well learners accomplish specific tasks using prior knowledge and recent learning. Such tasks are usually productive (speaking/writing) and may involve presentations, reports, or projects.

★ **Program evaluation** can involve a variety of assessments in order to determine the effectiveness of a program as a whole. Programs may look at overall improvement in test scores, examples of student projects, and surveys of students and instructors in evaluating program effectiveness.

★ **Accountability** is required for programs receiving state and federal funds. Federal reporting standards, as described by the National Reporting System (NRS), require that programs demonstrate student progress. This progress is often measured by standardized testing (e.g., CASAS), but may also be substantiated by alternative methods of assessment.

ALL-STAR UNIT TESTS

The Teacher's Edition contains a reproducible unit test for each of the ten units in *All-Star*. Each two-page test assesses students' knowledge of the vocabulary and language structures taught within the unit. Each test is worth 20 points.

Each unit test consists of four sections: Listening, Grammar, Reading/Vocabulary, and Writing. The Listening section includes two short conversations, each followed by multiple-choice questions about the conversation. The Grammar section focuses on structures learned in the unit. Students are asked to choose the correct answer to complete sentences. The Reading/Vocabulary section includes different types of reading passages and multiple-choice questions about those passages. Finally, the Writing section might ask students to write two sentences about a topic introduced in the unit, or to fill out a form or an application similar to one in the unit. The audio portion of each test is provided on the *All-Star* Audio CDs or Audiocassettes.

The Unit Test Listening Script and Unit Test Answer Key are included at the end of the Teacher's Edition.

MULTIPLE FORMS OF ASSESSMENT

The *All-Star* program offers teachers, students, and administrators the following wealth of resources for monitoring and assessing student progress and achievement:

★ **Standardized testing formats.** *All-Star* is correlated to the CASAS competencies and many other national and state standards for adult learning. Students have the opportunity to practice answering CASAS-style listening and reading questions in Lesson 7 of each unit (*What do you know?*), in Lesson 7 of the Workbook (*Practice Test*), and in the Interactive CD-ROM program. Students practice with the same item types and bubble-in answer sheets they encounter on CASAS and other standardized tests.

★ **Achievement tests.** The *All-Star* Teacher's Edition includes end-of-unit tests. These paper-and-pencil tests help students demonstrate how well they have learned the instructional content of the unit. Adult learners often show incremental increases in learning that are not always measured on the standardized tests. The achievement tests may demonstrate learning even in a short amount of instructional time. Twenty percent of each test includes questions that encourage students to apply more academic skills such as determining meaning from context, making inferences, and understanding main ideas. Practice with these question types will help prepare students who may want to enroll in academic classes.

★ **Performance-based assessment.** *All-Star* provides several ways to measure students' performance on productive tasks, including the *Writing Spotlights* and *Conversation Checks* that have corresponding rubrics in the Student Book to facilitate self-assessment. In addition, the Teacher's Edition suggests writing and speaking prompts that teachers can use for performance-based assessment. These prompts derive from the "big picture" scene in each unit and provide rich visual input as the basis for the speaking and writing tasks asked of the students.

★ **Portfolio assessment.** A portfolio is a collection of student work that can be used to show progress. Examples of work that the instructor or the student may submit in the portfolio include writing samples, speaking rubrics, audiotapes, videotapes, or projects. Every Student Book unit includes several *Try This* activities. These activities require critical thinking and small-group project work. As such, they can be included in a student's portfolio. The Teacher's Edition identifies activities that may be used as documentation for the secondary standards defined by the National Reporting System.

★ **Self-assessment.** Self-assessment is an important part of the overall assessment picture, as it promotes student involvement and commitment to the learning process. When encouraged to assess themselves, students take more control of their learning and are better able to connect the instructional content with their own goals. The Student Book includes *Learning Logs* at the end of each unit, which allow students to check off the vocabulary they have learned and skills they have acquired. The Workbook provides self-check boxes in each lesson, encouraging students to monitor their own progress on individual activities and across units.

★ **Other linguistic and non-linguistic outcomes.** Traditional testing often does not account for the progress made by adult learners with limited educational experience or low literacy levels. Such learners tend to take longer to make smaller language gains, so the gains they make in other areas are often more significant. These gains may be in areas such as self-esteem, goal clarification, learning skills, and access to employment, community involvement and further academic studies. The SCANS and EFF standards identify areas of student growth that are not necessarily language based. *All-Star* is correlated with both SCANS and EFF standards. Every

unit in the student book contains a lesson that focuses on one of the EFF role maps (worker, family member, community member), and the Workbook provides alternate lessons that address the other two role maps. Like the Student Book, the Workbook includes activities that may provide documentation that can be added to a student portfolio.

About the authors and series consultants

Linda Lee is lead author on the *All-Star* series. Linda has taught ESL/ELT in the United States, Iran, and China, and has authored or co-authored a variety of successful textbook series for English learners. As a classroom instructor, Linda's most satisfying teaching experiences have been with adult ESL students at Roxbury Community College in Boston, Massachusetts.

Kristin Sherman is the author of *All-Star* Teacher's Edition, Book 1. Kristin has 10 years teaching experience in both credit and non-credit ESL programs. She has taught general ESL, as well as classes focusing on workplace skills and family literacy. She has authored a number of workbooks and teacher's editions for English learners. Her favorite project was the creation of a reading and writing workbook with her ESL students at the Mecklenburg County Jail in North Carolina.

Stephen Sloan is Title One Coordinator at James Monroe High School in the Los Angeles Unified School District. Steve has more than 25 years of teaching and administrative experience with both high school and adult ESL learners. Steve is also the author of McGraw-Hill's *Rights and Responsibilities: Reading and Communication for Civics.*

Grace Tanaka is professor and coordinator of ESL at the Santa Ana College School of Continuing Education, in Santa Ana, California, which serves more than 20,000 students per year. She is also a textbook co-author and series consultant. Grace has 23 years of teaching experience in both credit and non-credit ESL programs.

Shirley Velasco is assistant principal at Palmetto Adult Education Center in Miami, Florida. She has been a classroom instructor and administrator for the past 24 years. At Palmetto, Shirley has created a large adult ESOL program based on a curriculum she developed to help teachers implement the Florida LCPs (Literacy Completion Points).

Teaching Strategies

Repetition: On almost every page of *All-Star*, students have the opportunity to listen to and repeat new vocabulary and structures. They need this structured practice in a low-anxiety environment before they are asked to manipulate this language in reading, writing, listening, or speaking activities. Repetition allows them to learn the pronunciation of individual words, internalize word order, and better approximate the stress and intonation pattern of native speakers. Although the audio program provides for repetition, students may need more frequent repetition drills to reinforce pronunciation or word order. One strategy is to say the new word or phrase and have the class repeat chorally, then call on individual students. You can use the "big picture" color transparencies to introduce or review new language in this way.

When students are practicing conversational structures, you can lead them through a progression of activities. First, you read one role and the students respond chorally. Then, divide the class into two: one half reads one role chorally, and the other half responds chorally. Then model the conversation with a student, or have two students model the conversation for the class. Finally, students can practice with partners. In this way, they acquire confidence as they gradually become more independent in using the new language.

Modeling: Before students are asked to produce language in a new context, they need the opportunity to see it demonstrated and then to practice it in a structured setting. Whenever there is an activity that calls on students to personalize the language, the instructor should model how this is done. For example, if students are asked to talk to a partner and complete the sentence "I'm wearing _____ shoes." You should point to your shoes and say, "I'm wearing . . ." You can then pause and prompt students to say the color of your shoes. Repeat the sentence, including the color of your shoes. After you have modeled the new language, more advanced students can provide additional examples of appropriate responses (e.g., "I'm wearing brown shoes."). Less proficient students can follow their examples.

Elicitation: Elicitation is an effective tool in making the classroom more learner-centered. When students contribute their ideas, they feel more secure about their abilities in the new language, and valued for what they already know. Asking questions and eliciting responses from the class will keep students more actively engaged in learning. More advanced students are often eager to respond, whereas the less proficient may be more reluctant. One way to level the playing field is to provide a sentence stem for the answer (e.g., "My name is _____."), and then have more advanced students model appropriate responses. Less proficient students can follow the pattern set by the students before them. Another strategy is to accept partial or one-word answers and provide the rest of the sentence (e.g., "Tien." "Your name is Tien."). Allowing students to discuss the topic in small groups or pairs before you elicit responses from the whole class is also an effective strategy (see *Modeling*).

Error correction: When and how often to correct students is the subject of much debate. Research suggests that it is repeated exposure to accurate input rather than correction that helps a student internalize new language. Too much correction can cause a learner to feel insecure about his or her language ability and reluctant to take the risks necessary to becoming more fluent in a new language. When accuracy is the goal, as in the repetition of listening activities or completing a multiple-choice assessment, correction should be immediate and constructive. When fluency is the goal, as in Conversation Practice with a partner, correction should be minimized, as it interrupts the conversational flow and can make students more self-conscious. In many cases, students can self-correct if you provide a model of accurate language. For example, if a student says, "Hello. I Carlos," you can respond, "Hi, Carlos. I'm Isabel." By emphasizing the correct form in your response, you can help students monitor their own speech. This technique is often referred to as "counsel correction." Another strategy is to pause before the error, gesturing for students to fill in the correct form.

Pair/group work: Students at a beginning level are often reluctant to work in pairs or small groups, as they are insecure about their own language abilities and may be accustomed to a teacher-centered approach. However, pair and group work activities allow each student more opportunities to engage in conversation in English. To encourage student participation in these activities, walk around and listen to all of the pairs or small groups as they are working. Asking questions or helping with pronunciation makes students feel that the activity is purposeful and personally beneficial. Such monitoring also prepares students to speak in front of the whole group and in authentic situations outside the classroom. To maximize interaction among the students, you can vary the seating arrangements or use strategies such as counting off that match students with different partners each time. Alternatively, you can engineer the groupings so that students complement each other, perhaps placing a more communicative student with one who has stronger literacy skills.

Using the audio program: Every unit in *All-Star* includes substantive listening practice for students on realistic topics. This practice is important not only for assessment purposes, but also to help students become accustomed to listening to and comprehending voices other than that of the instructor. Such activities prepare students to navigate more successfully in the real world with other native speakers. Units are structured so that students first listen to vocabulary or conversational models as they associate the sound with the context, then repeat the new language. When they have mastered the scripted conversation, they are then asked to personalize the new language in describing their own experiences.

Using the interactive CD-ROM: The CD-ROM provides additional language practice and reinforces the learning goals of each unit of the Student Book by integrating language, literacy, and numeracy skill-building with computer practice. The CD-ROM allows students to interact with the language in a variety of ways. The activities support visual learning through pictures and text as well as auditory learning through recorded conversations, monologues, and jazz chants. The drag and drop, and scrambled sentences activities require students' kinesthetic interaction to move words and pictures to appropriate locations on the screen. Students can use the CD-ROM at their own pace and receive instant feedback to their answers. Suggestions for when to use the CD-ROM are included throughout the Teacher's Edition.

Using realia: Adult students attend to and retain information when it is made relevant to their own needs and experience. Using real material such as authentic documents, maps, pictures, and objects not only helps students relate language learning to their own lives, it also appeals to a variety of learning styles. Each unit of *All-Star* includes a form that helps students develop competence with authentic documents. Wherever possible, other realistic diagrams and visuals have been included in the units to help students place the language in real world contexts. Bringing in other authentic materials related to the unit topic can make concepts more tangible and reinforce learning.

How to work with reluctant learners: Sometimes adult students enter literacy and low beginning classes having had little experience in an educational setting. Others may have had negative experiences in school, or may feel that learning English at this stage in their lives is a burden rather than an opportunity. Such students may be reluctant at first to participate in class activities. Recognize that these students have a wealth of experience and knowledge on which to draw, and include activities that are relevant to their everyday lives. For example, in Unit 3, students begin to talk about families. Ask them to bring in photos of the people in their families. In Unit 10, students learn to talk about jobs. Allow them to talk about the kind of work they do. Help them use the language provided in the unit to talk about their own jobs. With every topic, be sensitive to the needs of your students. For example, students who may have lost family members or whose families have been left behind can either tell about their relatives or about the people they live with now.

Scope and Sequence

Unit	Life Skills				
	Listening and Speaking	Reading and Writing	Critical Thinking	Vocabulary	Grammar
Pre-Unit Meeting Your Classmates **Student Book:** *page 2* **Teacher's Edition:** *page 2*	• Listen to introductions • Introduce yourself • Ask for and give spelling of names	• Make a name tag		• Personal information (first name, last name) • Alphabet	
1 Getting Started **Student Book:** *page 4* **Teacher's Edition:** *page 4*	• Exchange personal information • Talk about things in a classroom • Follow classroom instructions • Say and understand numbers (telephone, area code, zip code) • Use appropriate greetings and partings • Ask about occupations • Introduce people **Pronunciation Focus:** Long vowel sounds: *I* and *E*	• Read a world map • Read and write classroom instructions • Read for specific information • Read job ads • Read and complete application forms • Make flashcards	• Classify information • Apply what you know • Interpret information (on an application form) • Interpret a world map	• Classroom vocabulary • Countries • Personal information (name, address, etc.) • Occupations	• Personal pronouns • Imperatives • Punctuation **Spotlight:** Simple present of *be*; possessives
2 Places **Student Book:** *page 20* **Teacher's Edition:** *page 32*	• Describe the location of things in the community • Talk about places on a U.S. map • Ask for clarification • Talk about library services **Pronunciation Focus:** Voiced and voiceless *Th* sounds	• Use a telephone directory • Read a map • Read traffic signs • Complete an application for a library card • Write addresses and phone numbers **Spotlight:** Personal interest stories	• Interpret a map • Classify places (public/private) • Interpret an illustration • Interpret traffic signs	• Geographical directions (N, S, E, W) • Places in the community • People and things in a library • Street signs	• Prepositions of location • *There is/There are* • *Is there/Are there* • Singular and plural nouns • Punctuation
3 Time and Money **Student Book:** *page 36* **Teacher's Edition:** *page 59*	• Ask for and tell the time of day • Ask about business hours • Ask about prices • Ask for a phone number from directory assistance • Listen to an automated phone message **Pronunciation Focus:** Syllable stress in numbers	• Read amounts of money • Read and write personal checks • Read a time schedule • Read signs (in the library) • Write time schedules • Describe a scene • Write amounts of money in words and numbers	• Draw conclusions • Classify information • Compare	• Times of day • Time words • Days of the week • Money: coins and bills • Parts of a personal check	• *Yes/no* questions with *be* • Questions with *how much* **Spotlight:** *Yes/No* questions and answers with be; information questions with *be*

Correlations to National Standards

Civics Concepts	Math Skills	CASAS Life Skill Competencies	SCANS Competencies (Workplace)	EFF Content Standards	Literacy Completion Points (LCPs)
		• 0.1.4, 0.1.6, 0.2.1	• Sociability	• Communicate so that others understand	• 22.02
• Identify countries on a map • Recognize different occupations in the community	• Use numbers 0 to 11 • Understand page references • Read and write telephone numbers and addresses	• 1: 0.1.2, 0.2.1, 1.1.3, 2.7.2, 6.6.5 • 2: 0.1.5, 2.2.1, 6.6.5, 7.1.4, 7.4.1 • 3: 0.1.5, 6.0.2, 7.1.3 • 4: 0.2.2 • 5: 0.1.4, 0.1.1 • 6: 4.1.3, 4.1.8, 4.6.3 • 7: 0.1.2, 7.1.4, 7.4.7, 7.4.8 • GS: 0.1.6	Emphasized are the following: • Know how to learn • See things in the mind's eye • Sociability • Work well with others • Work with people of diverse backgrounds	Emphasized are the following: • Communicate so that others understand • Listen to and learn from others' experiences and ideas	• 1: 30.02, 32.07, 33.09 • 2: 33.02 • 3: 25.01, 32.07 • 4: 22.01, 32.04, 33.07 • 5: 22.02, 22.03, 33.02 • 6: 18.01 • 7: 32.13 • GS: 22.01, 32.02, 33.03
• Identify public services • Locate cities and states in the U.S. • Make a neighborhood map • Identify places in the community • Understand traffic signs • Visit a public library • Complete a library card application	• Understand phone numbers • Read math symbols • Understand spatial relationships	• 1: 0.1.2, 2.1.1, 2.2.5, 6.7.3 • 2: 0.1.2, 0.1.6, 1.1.3, 1.9.4 • 3: 0.1.2, 2.2.1, 2.2.3 • 4: 1.9.4, 2.2.2, 5.2.4, 6.0.3, 6.0.4 • 5: 0.1.2, 0.1.6, 2.5.4, 2.6.1 • 6: 0.1.2, 2.5.5, 2.5.6 • 7: 0.1.2, 7.1.4, 7.4.7, 7.4.8 • WS: 0.2.4, 4.6.1, 7.5.1	Emphasized are the following: • See things in the mind's eye • Understand how systems work	Emphasized are the following: • Get involved in the community and get others involved • Assist others • Find and use community resources and services	• 1: 29.01 • 2: 29.01, 32.01, 32.10 • 3: 26.04, 32.02 • 4: 26.03, 32.01, 32.06 • 5: 26.03, 32.01, 32.02 • 6: 29.01 • 7: 32.08, 32.113 • WS: 32.10, 33.01
• Identify the business hours of places in the community • Distinguish U.S. coins and bills	• Interpret clock time • Use numbers 12 to 90 • Write the time using numbers • Count coins and bills • Read and understand price tags • Write dollar amounts on personal checks • Use addition and subtraction to calculate total costs	• 1: 0.1.2, 2.3.1, 6.0.2 • 2: 0.1.2, 0.1.6, 2.3.2, 2.5.4 • 3: 1.1.2, 1.1.6, 6.0.1 • 4: 1.8.2, 6.1.1, 6.5.1, 7.3.2 • 5: 0.1.3, 0.1.4, 2.1.8 • 6: 1.2.1, 1.2.2, 2.1.1 • 7: 0.1.2, 7.1.4, 7.4.7, 7.4.8 • GS: 7.2.3	Emphasized are the following: • Understand how systems work	Emphasized are the following: • Manage time and resources • Learn new skills	• 1: 25.01, 25.02 • 2: 25.03 • 3: 25.05 • 4: 32.08 • 5: 23.02, 25.04 • 6: 32.07 • 7: 32.13, 34.02 • GS: 33.02, 33.06, 33.07

CASAS and LCP standards: Numbers in bold indicate lesson numbers. • **GS**: Grammar Spotlight • **WS**: Writing Spotlight

Scope and Sequence

	Life Skills				
Unit	**Listening and Speaking**	**Reading and Writing**	**Critical Thinking**	**Vocabulary**	**Grammar**
4 **Calendars** Student Book: *page 52* Teacher's Edition: *page 86*	• Describe the weather • Talk about events on a calendar • Talk about holidays • Talk about appointments • Make, cancel, and reschedule an appointment **Pronunciation Focus:** Short *A* and long *A*	• Read information on a calendar • Read appointment cards • Read and write about holidays • Write appointments and events on a calendar **Spotlight:** Personal interest stories	• Classify information • Evaluate • Interpret information about appointments • Interpret information about a school calendar	• Months of the year • Weather words • Holidays • Ordinal numbers	• *Wh* questions with *be* • Questions with *how many* • Singular and plural nouns • Capitalization
5 **Clothing** Student Book: *page 68* Teacher's Edition: *page 110*	• Ask for information in a store • Ask about sizes and prices • Describe clothing • Listen to a story • Give opinions about clothes • Return something to a store • Talk about appropriate clothing **Pronunciation Focus:** Vowel sounds in *shoes* and *should*	• Add words to a Venn diagram • Describe clothes • Read store signs • Read price tags • Read a store receipt • Write a store receipt • Write a personal check • Read a story • Complete a story chart • Read an office memo	• Make inferences • Classify information • Sequence events • Predict • Summarize	• Clothing names • Colors • Department store people, places, and actions • Sizes • Prices • Descriptive words for clothing	• Present continuous statements • Present continuous questions and answers • Object pronouns **Spotlight:** Present continuous statements; information questions with the present continuous
6 **Food** Student Book: *page 84* Teacher's Edition: *page 133*	• Give opinions about foods • Ask for items in a grocery store • Describe food containers • Ask for price information • Listen to a recorded message **Pronunciation Focus:** Intonation in *yes/no* questions	• Write a shopping list • Read store flyers • Read store receipts • Interpret a food pyramid • Read a recipe • Connect sentences with *and* • Write a recipe **Spotlight:** Recipes	• Classify information • Make comparisons • Choose the best alternative • Sequence events	• Food • Descriptive words for food • Grocery store places, things, and actions • Food containers • Food groups	• Questions and answers with *do* and *don't* • Frequency adverbs
7 **Families** Student Book: *page 100* Teacher's Edition: *page 155*	• Talk about family members and responsibilities • Talk about personal interests and activities • Make telephone calls • Discuss family expenses • Give opinions about expenses **Pronunciation Focus:** Linking consonant to vowel	• Make a family tree • Write about family responsibilities • Read family portraits and take notes • Write about family	• Classify information • Estimate	• Family members • Household activities • Park activities • Family expenses	• *Yes/No* questions + simple present • Simple present statements • *Don't* and *doesn't* **Spotlight:** Simple present statements; information questions with the simple present

Correlations to National Standards

Civics Concepts	Math Skills	CASAS Life Skill Competencies	SCANS Competencies (Workplace)	EFF Content Standards	Literacy Completion Points (LCPs)
• Identify important holidays in the U.S. • Keep community appointments on a calendar • Interpret a child's school calendar	• Use ordinal numbers • Read and write dates • Convert dates to numeric form • Interpret schedules • Understand appointment times and dates	• 1: 0.1.2, 2.3.2, 6.0.2, 2.7.1 • 2: 0.1.4, 0.2.3, 2.6.3, 2.7.3 • 3: 6.0.1, 7.1.2 • 4: 0.1.2, 2.7.1, 2.7.2 • 5: 0.1.4, 2.1.8, 3.1.2 • 6: 2.3.2, 7.1.1, 7.1.4 • 7: 0.1.2, 7.1.4, 7.4.7, 7.4.8 • WS: 2.7.1, 7.5.1	Emphasized are the following: • Problem solving • Self-management • Acquire and evaluate information • Organize and maintain information	Emphasized are the following: • Manage time and resources • Pass on values, ethics, and cultural heritage • Organize, plan, and prioritize work	• 1: 25.03, 29.03, 30.01 • 2: 25.01, 32.01, 32.07 • 3: 24.03, 25.04, 32.02 • 4: 32.07, 32.10 • 5: 24.03, 34.03 • 6: 31.04 • 7: 32.04, 32.13 • WS: 33.06
• Explore a department store • Interpret price tags and receipts • Recognize different occupations in the community	• Understand prices and sales receipts • Use multiplication and division to calculate totals	• 1: 1.1.9, 1.3.9, 6.6.5 • 2: 1.3.1, 1.3.7 • 3: 1.1.4, 1.2.1, 1.2.2, 1.2.4, 4.4.1, 6.1.3 • 4: 7.2.7 • 5: 8.1.2 • 6: 4.4.1, 8.4.1 • 7: 0.1.2, 7.1.4, 7.4.7, 7.4.8 • GS: 7.4.3	Emphasized are the following: • Creative thinking • Reasoning • See things in the mind's eye • Analyze and communicate information	Emphasized are the following: • Provide for physical needs • Reflect on and reevaluate opinions and ideas	• 1: 28.02 • 2: 33.03 • 3: 28.03, 33.03 • 4: 22.03 • 5: 19.01 • 6: 19.01 • 7: 32.13, 32.08, 32.10 • GS: 33.02
• Understand the food groups • Explore a grocery store • Interpret receipts • Understand healthy eating	• Use U.S. measurements: pounds, ounces, and cups • Compare prices • Budget for food • Calculate serving sizes • Read and write measurements for recipes	• 1: 1.3.8 • 2: 0.1.2, 1.3.8 • 3: 1.1.4, 1.1.7, 1.3.8, 6.5.1 • 4: 1.2.2, 1.2.4, 1.2.5 • 5: 1.3.3 • 6: 3.5.1, 3.5.2, 3.5.9 • 7: 0.1.2, 7.1.4, 7.4.7, 7.4.8 • WS: 1.1.1, 8.2.1	Emphasized are the following: • Decision making • Problem solving • See things in the mind's eye • Self-management • Use resources wisely • Teach others new skills • Acquire and evaluate information	Emphasized are the following: • Find and use community resources and services • Find, interpret, and analyze diverse sources of information • Provide for physical needs • Communicate so that others understand	• 1: 24.05 • 2: 32.01 • 3: 28.01 • 4: 25.05, 28.03 • 5: 32.01 • 6: 32.04, 32.07 • 7: 32.08, 32.13 • WS: 32.07
• Discuss community-related activities	• Take messages that include telephone numbers • Create a household budget • Use addition and multiplication to calculate totals	• 1: 0.2.1, 6.6.8 • 2: 8.2.1, 8.2.5, 8.2.6, 8.3.1 • 3: 0.2.4, 2.7.2 • 4: 7.5.1 • 5: 2.1.7, 2.1.8 • 6: 1.5.1, 7.4.9, 7.5.5, 7.5.7 • 7: 0.1.2, 7.1.4, 7.4.7, 7.4.8 • GS: 7.2.2, 7.2.5, 7.3.3	Emphasized are the following: • Self-management • Integrity and honesty • Use resources wisely • Acquire and evaluate information • Organize and maintain information	Emphasized are the following: • Provide a nurturing home environment • Provide for physical needs • Teach children • Establish rules and expectations for children's behavior	• 1: 31.01 • 2: 31.03 • 3: 34.02 • 4: 34.03 • 5: 32.02 • 6: 32.08 • 7: 32.02, 32.13 • GS: 33.07

CASAS and LCP standards: Numbers in bold indicate lesson numbers.   •   **GS**: Grammar Spotlight   •   **WS**: Writing Spotlight

Scope and Sequence

	Life Skills				
Unit	Listening and Speaking	Reading and Writing	Critical Thinking	Vocabulary	Grammar
8 **Health** Student Book: *page 116* Teacher's Edition: *page 176*	• Talk about health problems • Discuss remedies • Listen to and practice 911 calls **Pronunciation Focus:** Linking vowel to vowel with a *Y* or *W* sound	• Read warning labels • Read opinion paragraphs • Read bar graphs • Indent a paragraph • Write an opinion paragraph • Draw a bar graph **Spotlight:** Opinions	• Classify information • Make inferences • Analyze arguments • Make decisions	• Parts of the body • Health problems • Remedies • Safety warnings	• Can for ability • Giving advice with *should* and *shouldn't*
9 **House and Home** Student Book: *page 132* Teacher's Edition: *page 198*	• Describe things in a house • Talk about accidents in the home • Ask for housing information **Pronunciation Focus:** Stress in compound nouns	• Write a comparison of two houses • Read bar graphs • Read classified ads • Write a classified ad • Read bills • Write personal checks	• Compare and contrast • Choose the best alternative • Classify information • Make decisions	• Areas of a house • Household furniture and other items • Features of a house • Types of housing • Classified ad abbreviations • Utility bills	• Comparing past and present • Simple past statements • Negative simple past statements **Spotlight:** Simple past statements; information questions with the simple past
10 **Work** Student Book: *page 148* Teacher's Edition: *page 220*	• Respond to job ads • Listen to a job interview • Give opinions about what to do in an interview • Give reasons **Pronunciation Focus:** Stressing important words in sentences	• Read and write help wanted ads • Read a success story • Write a story • Read for specific information • Complete job applications • Complete an idea list **Spotlight:** Past tense stories	• Classify information • Reason • Sequence events	• Occupations and skills • Help wanted ad abbreviations • Work experience	• *Yes/No* questions with the simple past • Future with *be going to*

Appendices

Correlations to National Standards

Civics Concepts	Math Skills	CASAS Life Skill Competencies	SCANS Competencies (Workplace)	EFF Content Standards	Literacy Completion Points (LCPs)
• Explore a health clinic • Understand safety warnings • Understand when to call 911 • Explore a hospital	• Use U.S. measurements: gallons, quarts, pints, cups and ounces • Interpret bar graphs	• **1**: 3.1.1 • **2**: 3.1.1 • **3**: 3.4.3 • **4**: 3.3.1, 3.4.1, 3.4.2, 6.6.1 • **5**: 2.1.2, 2.5.1 • **6**: 2.2.1, 3.1.3, 2.5.3, 7.4.4 • **7**: 0.1.2, 7.1.4, 7.4.7, 7.4.8 • **WS**: 7.3.4, 7.4.2	Emphasized are the following: • Reasoning • See things in the mind's eye • Integrity and honesty • Organize and maintain information	Emphasized are the following: • Provide for physical needs • Find and use community resources and services • Exercise human and legal rights and civic responsibilities • Help self and others	• **1**: 24.01 • **2**: 32.01 • **3**: 32.10 • **4**: 19.01, 27.02 • **5**: 23.01, 27.01 • **6**: 24.02 • **7**: 32.10, 32.13 • **WS**: 32.05, 32.08
• Recognize different types of housing in a community • Use classified ads as a source of community information	• Interpret bar graphs • Compare rent prices for apartments and houses • Interpret and pay bills	• **1**: 1.4.1 • **2**: 1.4.2 • **3**: 0.1.6, 3.4.2, 6.7.2 • **4**: 1.4.2 • **5**: 2.1.8, 2.2.1, 7.5.5 • **6**: 1.5.1, 1.5.3, 1.8.2, 2.4.1 • **7**: 0.1.2, 7.1.4, 7.4.7, 7.4.8 • **GS**: 0.2.1, 0.2.4	Emphasized are the following: • Decision making • See things in the mind's eye • Acquire and evaluate information	Emphasized are the following: • Find, interpret, and analyze diverse sources of information • Provide for physical needs • Find and use community resources and services	• **1**: 28.04 • **2**: 32.07 • **3**: 32.04 • **4**: 28.04 • **5**: 23.02 • **6**: 25.06, 28.05 • **7**: 31.03, 32.13 • **GS**: 33.07
• Use help wanted ads as a source of community information • Recognize some dos and don'ts of interviewing	• Solve word problems • Understand hourly wages • Use addition and multiplication to calculate totals	• **1**: 4.1.6, 4.4.2, 6.6.5 • **2**: 4.4.4, 4.4.5, 4.4.6, 4.4.7 • **3**: 4.1.2, 4.1.5, 4.1.7 • **4**: 4.1.9 • **5**: 4.1.2, 4.1.7 • **6**: 4.1.2 • **7**: 0.1.2, 7.1.4, 7.4.7, 7.4.8 • **WS**: 7.5.2, 7.5.4	Emphasized are the following: • Problem solving • Self-esteem • Integrity and honesty • Acquire and evaluate information • Analyze and communicate information • Work within the system	Emphasized are the following: • Find and get a job • Plan and renew career goals • Find, interpret, and analyze diverse sources of information	• **1**: 32.01 • **2**: 18.02 • **3**: 20.02 • **4**: 32.02 • **5**: 18.02, 20.02 • **6**: 18.03 • **7**: 32.08, 32.13 • **WS**: 32.01, 32.10

CASAS and LCP standards: Numbers in bold indicate lesson numbers. • **GS**: Grammar Spotlight • **WS**: Writing Spotlight

OBJECTIVE

Introducing Yourself

1. Practice the Conversation 🎧

* Welcome students to the class and introduce yourself. Follow the structure in the conversation: *Hi. My name is* _____. Gesture to yourself.

* Direct students' attention to the picture. Point to the woman in the picture and say *Anna*. Point to the man in the picture and say *Tom*. Pause after each name and have students repeat.

* Ask students to read the conversation while you say it aloud or play the tape or CD.

* Say the conversation or play the tape or CD a second time and pause after each line to have students repeat.

* Read *A's* lines and have students respond as a group with *B's* lines. Or, you can divide the class in half and have one side read *A's* lines and the other read *B's* lines.

* Model the activity with a student. Read *A's* lines and substitute your own name for *Anna's*. Cue the student to respond with his or her name.

* Put the students in pairs to practice the conversation. Have them switch partners and practice again. Walk around the room to monitor the activity and provide help as needed.

LISTENING SCRIPT

Pre-Unit: Practice the Conversation

Listen to the conversation. Then listen and repeat.

A: Hello. My name is Anna.
B: Hi. I'm Tom.
A: Nice to meet you, Tom.
B: Nice to meet you, too.

EXPANSION ACTIVITY: Introductions

* Organize students in two lines facing each other. Tell the two students facing each other to practice the conversation.

* After a bit, move the first person in one line to the other end of the line. Everyone should then be facing a new partner. Practice the conversation again.

* Change partners a few more times to practice the conversation.

2. Say the Alphabet 🎧

* Ask students to look at the alphabet as you say the letters aloud or play the tape or CD.

* Say the letters or play the tape or CD a second time, pausing after each letter to have students repeat.

* Write the letters on the board. Point to letters in random order and prompt the class to name them.

* With students in pairs, have one practice saying each letter while their partner points to the letters they name.

LISTENING SCRIPT

Pre-Unit: Say the Alphabet

Listen to the letters. Then listen and repeat.

A, B, C, D, E, F, G, H, I, J, K, L, M, N, O, P, Q, R, S, T, U, V, W, X, Y, Z

3. Practice the Conversation

* Direct students' attention to the photo and ask, *Who is in the picture?*

* Ask students to read the conversation as you say it aloud or play the tape or CD.

* To check comprehension, ask questions about the conversation: *What is the man's last name? What is his first name?*

* Say the conversation or play the tape or CD a second time. Pause after each line and have students repeat.

* Practice the conversation by having half the class read *A's* lines and the other half read *B's* lines.

★ Ask students to close their books and practice the conversation with a partner.

★ Direct students' attention to the chart. Point out that they will be writing the first and last names for three of their classmates. Model this by copying the chart on the board and filling it in after asking three students their names.

★ Instruct students to interview three classmates and write their answers on the chart. Walk around the room to monitor the activity and provide help as needed. Make sure students are asking for spelling and not just having the other students write their own names on the chart.

LISTENING SCRIPT

Pre-Unit: Practice the Conversation

Listen to the conversation. Then listen and repeat.

A: What's your first name?
B: Sue.
A: What's your last name?
B: Chan.
A: What's your last name?
B: C - h - a - n.

Culture/Civics Note:
★ Explain that we say our given or first name first. We say our family name or last name last.

4. Write

★ Ask students to look at the name tag. Read it and have students repeat.

★ Draw a name tag on the board. Demonstrate how to make a name tag for one of your students.

★ Tell students to make name tags for their partners.

Hi. My name is

_____

EXPANSION ACTIVITY: Name Tags

★ Distribute large index cards and instruct students to write their first and last names on the bottom half of the card.

★ Show the class how to fold the cards in half to make little tents so their name is visible. Also, direct students to write their names on the other half of the card so their names can be seen from the front or the back.

★ Students should use these cards for a few days until everyone knows the names of the people in the class.

★ Collect all the name tags; redistribute them randomly, making sure that no one receives a name tag with their name on it. Ask students to look at the name tag and give it to the correct person.

1 Getting Started

UNIT OVERVIEW

LESSON	OBJECTIVE	STUDENT BOOK PAGE #
1. Where are you from?	Identifying Countries	p. 4
2. Where's your notebook?	In the Classroom	p. 6
3. Read page 6.	Understanding Classroom Instructions	p. 8
4. Application Forms	Reporting Personal Information	p. 10
5. Nice to meet you.	Greeting People	p. 12
6. Occupations	Looking at Job Ads	p. 14
7. What do you know?	Review and Assessment	p. 16
8. Spotlight	Grammar	p. 18

Big Picture Expansion Activities

FOCUS	TITLE	SUGGESTED USE
Speaking	*Yes/No* Memory Game	Lesson 3
Reading	Who is Jane?	Lesson 4
Grammar	Practicing *Is* and *Are*	Lesson 2
Writing	Describing People	Lesson 6
Speaking	Assessment: Talking about the Picture	Lesson 7

Big Picture Expansion Activity Worksheets

WORKSHEET #/FOCUS	TITLE	TEACHER'S EDITION PAGE #
1. Grammar	Practicing *Is* and *Are*	p. 241
2. Reading	Who is Jane?	p. 242

OBJECTIVE

Identifying Countries

VOCABULARY

Brazil	France	Somalia
Canada	Haiti	the United States
China	Mexico	Vietnam
Colombia	Morocco	

WINDOW ON GRAMMAR

Simple Present with *Be*

THINGS TO DO

1. Find the Countries 🎧

★ Hold up the book and point to the map. Have students say *map*.

★ Have students brainstorm the names of countries. Write them on the board and pronounce each one. Have students repeat.

★ Have students look at the maps in their books as you say the words or play the tape or CD.

★ Say the words or play the CD a second time. Pause after each word, and ask the students to repeat the word and point to the country on the map.

★ Have students write the name of one more country on the line next to number 12 and circle it on the map. Have students work in pairs and practice saying each country as the other partner points to that country on the map. Then have partners switch roles.

★ Point to the countries in random order, and have students say the names.

LISTENING SCRIPT

Lesson 1: Find the Countries

Look at the map. Listen to the words. Then listen and repeat.

1. Canada	7. France
2. the United States	8. Morocco
3. Mexico	9. Somalia
4. Haiti	10. China
5. Colombia	11. Vietnam
6. Brazil	

EXPANSION ACTIVITY: Identify Syllables

★ Tell students that all words have a number of syllables or beats. Demonstrate this with your name, clapping as you say each syllable: *San – dra* (two claps).

★ Demonstrate with the names of a few students. Have everyone clap for each syllable.

★ Have students look at the countries listed in the book. Tell them you will say the name of the country, and they should write the number of syllables next to the name. Do the first country together. Say *Chi – na* and ask students how many syllables you pronounced. Have them write 2 next to *China*.

★ Have them continue with all of the country names and then check their answers with a partner.

★ Go over the answers with the class.

ANSWER KEY:

China, 2; Vietnam, 3; Somalia, 4; Morocco, 3; France, 1; Haiti, 2; Brazil, 2; Colombia, 4; Mexico, 3; the United States, 5; Canada, 3

2. Ask Questions 🎧

★ Read the conversation or play the tape or CD as the students listen.

★ Read or play the conversation again. Pause after each item, and ask the students to repeat.

★ Write the conversation on the board, replacing *Victor* and *Mexico* with your name and country. Have the class read *A's* lines and you read *B's*.

★ Model the conversation with a student from another country. Cue the student to say his or her name and country.

★ Have students work in pairs and practice the conversation using their own names and countries. Walk around and provide help if needed.

★ Copy the chart on the board, including the headings: *What's your name? Where are you from?*

Lesson 1: Ask Questions

Listen to the conversation. Then listen and repeat.

A: What's your name?
B: My name is Victor.
A: Where are you from?
B: I am from Mexico.
A: Mexico! That's interesting.

★ Call on a student and ask both questions. Write the information on the chart.

★ Have students stand up, walk around the room, and talk to four classmates, asking the same two questions. They should write the information on the charts in their books. Circulate to make sure they are on task.

★ Have a few students report what they wrote on their chart. Add those students to the list on the board.

Culture/Civics Note:
★ You may want to tell students that in adult classrooms, students usually call other students by their first names. In some classrooms, the teacher may also be called by his or her first name. Teachers will let students know what they like to be called. Because customs vary, some students may feel uncomfortable calling a teacher by his or her first name.

EXPANSION ACTIVITY: Map Skills

★ Have students find the places listed in their chart from Activity 2 on the map. For example, if Marie is from France, they should find France on the map.

★ Have students work in pairs and practice explaining where classmates are from and pointing to these places on the map.

3. Write

★ Write the following sentence format on the board: _____ *is from* _____.

★ Call on a student to tell you someone's name and where that person is from. Cue the student if necessary by pointing to the partial sentence on the chart.

★ Write the student's name and country in the sentence on the board.

★ Write the numbers 1 through 4 on the board under your sentence. Have students write four sentences about four classmates in their books.

_____ *is from* _____.

1.
2.
3.
4.

EXPANSION ACTIVITY: Tally Sheet

★ Copy the list of countries from Activity 1 on the board.

★ Point to *China* and ask: *Who is from China?* Have students stand up if they are from China.

★ Make tally marks next to China for each student standing. If no one is from China, write a zero and move through the list until you find a country someone is from.

★ Call out other countries and have students stand. Ask someone in each group to make tally marks next to the name of their country on the board to represent the number of people from that country.

★ ★

📁 **TRY THIS**

★ ★

★ Review the alphabet and write all the letters on the board.

★ Write *Australia* next to the letter *A*. Underline the first *A* in *Australia*. Repeat with the letters *B* (*Brazil*) and *C* (*China*).

★ Have students work in pairs and write one country that begins with each letter of the alphabet.

★ When students have finished their lists, call on students to name a country for each letter.

★ Have volunteers write the names of the countries on the board next to the appropriate letters.

EXPANSION ACTIVITY: Alphabet Game

★ Write the letters of the alphabet on pieces of paper big enough for the class to see. Give one (or two) to each student, but you keep the letter *A*.

★ Put the piece of paper with the letter *A* on the board and say, *This is A. What comes next?* The student with letter *B* stands and identifies the letter and tapes it on the board. Continue until all the letters are on the board.

★ Then the teacher says, *My name is Teresa, and Teresa begins with T.* Write your name under the letter *T* on the board.

★ Continue around the room until all students have introduced themselves and written their names on the board.

WINDOW ON GRAMMAR: Simple Present with *Be*

A. Read the sentences.

★ Copy the grammar paradigm on the board. Read across the paradigm and have students repeat. As you read, point to the words on the chart. Make sure students understand how the verbs and pronouns match.

★ Make sure students understand the meaning of the pronouns. Gesture toward yourself and others to illustrate *I, you, he, she, they,* and *we.* Write several proper names on the board (*Susan, John, Maria*) and elicit pronouns (*she, he, they*) that would replace those names in a sentence.

★ Practice asking questions from the chart and having students answer.

B. Complete the sentences with *am, is,* or *are.*

★ Go over the first sentence: *Victor _____ from Mexico.* Ask students if *am, is,* or *are* goes on the line. Explain that they should write *is* because *Victor* is singular.

★ Have students complete 2–6 with *am, is,* or *are.* They should look at the chart for help. Have them go over the answers with a partner.

★ Go over the answers with the class.

★ Review contractions. Have them rewrite sentences 1, 3, 4, 5, 6 using contractions.

ANSWER KEY:

1. is; 2. are; 3. is; 4. am; 5. are; 6. is
Contractions: 1. Victor's; 3. Sandra's; 4. I'm; 5. You're; 6. New York's

EXPANSION ACTIVITY: Create Your Own Questions

★ Write a question on the board about one of the students in your class: *Where is Fatima from?* Then write a question about two people in the class: *Where are Luis and Miguel from?* Write students' answers on the board in full sentences.

★ Instruct students to write two of their own questions about people in the class. Tell them their sentences should begin with *Where is* and *Where are.*

★ Have a few volunteers ask the other students their questions. If students respond with the name of the country, but give a single word answer, give a positive response and then restate the answer as a sentence: *Right. Fatima is from Somalia.*

★ Have students work in pairs and practice asking and answering questions. Emphasize that they should respond to questions with full sentences.

 Students can do Unit 1, Section 2, *Listen and Choose* on the Interactive CD-ROM.

OBJECTIVE

In the Classroom

VOCABULARY

PEOPLE	PARTS OF A ROOM	
student	door	
teacher	floor	
	wall	
	window	

THINGS		
board	computer	pen
book	desk	pencil
calendar	map	piece of paper
chair	notebook	table
clock		

GRAMMAR

Possessives

THINGS TO DO

1. Learn New Words 🎧

★ Point to the "big picture" in the book or the color overhead transparency and ask students, *What is this?* Elicit that the picture shows *a classroom.*

★ Ask students to look at the picture and listen while you say the words or play the CD or tape.

★ Say the words or play the CD or tape a second time. Pause after each word and ask the students to repeat it. As the students listen a third time, have them point to each item as the name of that item is spoken.

★ Point to the items in random order, and have students say the name of that item.

★ Tell students to work in pairs. One will practice saying the words as the other points to the items in the book. Have them switch roles and do the exercises again.

EXPANSION ACTIVITY: Alphabetical Order

★ Review the alphabet. Ask students which letter is first in the alphabet. Ask students if any of the new words from this lesson begin with *A* (*no*). Continue by asking which letter is the second in the alphabet, and if any new words begin with *B* (*board*). Write the word *board* on the board.

★ Divide students into small groups and have them write the words from *Learn New Words* in alphabetical order. Have them include the words from all three categories.

★ Ask one person from each group to go to the board and write the words on the board in alphabetical order.

ANSWER KEY:

board, book, calendar, chair, clock, computer, desk, door, floor, map, notebook, pen, pencil, piece of paper, student, table, teacher, wall, window

LISTENING SCRIPT

Lesson 2: Learn New Words

Look at the picture. Listen to the words. Then listen and repeat.

1. teacher	Where's the teacher?
2. wall	What's on the wall?
3. clock	Where's the clock?
4. door	Where's the door?
5. board	Where's the board?
6. table	Where's the table?
7. calendar	Where's the calendar?
8. map	Where's the map?
9. notebook	Where's the notebook?
10. pen	Where's the pen?
11. pencil	Where's the pencil?
12. piece of paper	Where's the piece of paper?
13. book	Where's the book?
14. floor	What's on the floor?
15. chair	Where's the chair?
16. computer	Where's the computer?
17. desk	Where's the desk?
18. student	Where's the student?
19. window	Where's the window?

2. Write

★ Gesture to your classroom and ask students, *What is in our classroom?* Write what they say on the board.

★ Point out that *clock* is written on the first line. If you have a clock, ask students *Where is the clock?* Ask them to point it out to you.

★ Have students write the names of five more things they can see in the classroom.

★ Call on a few students to tell the class about some things they wrote on their lists and ask the class to point to where that object is.

EXPANSION ACTIVITY: Identify the Object

★ Have a group of students stand in various parts of the room—some in the front, a group in back, and others on the sides.

★ Tell the students that you will say the name of something in the classroom and that the students standing closest to that object should touch it. For example, if you say *board,* the students standing at the front of the room should touch the board. If there are still students sitting, they may help by pointing to the object.

★ Call out the names of several items in the room.

★ Repeat the activity with new words and new groups of students. You can also have students call out the words to change the game and involve more students.

---

3. Ask Questions

★ Write these sentences on the board:

> A: Where's the _____?
> B: It's <u>on the</u> _____.

★ Model this activity with a student. Ask a question about an object in the picture and elicit the location. Call on a few students to

answer questions about the location of objects in the picture.

★ Have students work in pairs and practice asking and answering questions about the picture.

★ ★

 TRY THIS

★ ★

★ Make a set of flash cards with index cards or a piece of paper. On one side write each of the vocabulary words from this lesson. On the other side of the card draw a simple picture of the object the vocabulary word represents. You could also distribute one or more index cards to each student and have them create flashcards.

★ Walk around and show the students the picture, asking, *What is this?* Have students say the name of the object.

★ Another option is for students to make their own personal set of flashcards and practice on their own and with a partner.

EXPANSION ACTIVITY: Flash Card Race

★ Make a set of the flashcards described in *Try This.*

★ Have students work in small teams with their books closed. Have one student volunteer to be the scorekeeper.

★ Quickly show a different flashcard to one team at a time, and have the team say the name of the object.

★ Show a different flashcard to a different team and have that team say the name of the object.

★ Each incorrect answer earns the team a point. The team with the lowest number of points wins. This game should move quickly.

★ Small prizes for the winners will probably increase enthusiasm and the energy level of the class for the activity.

BIG PICTURE EXPANSION ACTIVITY:
GRAMMAR—Practicing *Is* and *Are*

★ Make copies of Worksheet # 1 (p. 241) and distribute them to students.

★ Put the color overhead transparency for Unit 1, Lesson 2, on the projector or have students look at the "big picture" in their books.

★ Ask students to complete the sentences with *is* or *are* and then check their answers with a partner.

★ Go over the answers with the class.

ANSWER KEY:

1. are; 2. is; 3. is; 4. are; 5. are; 6. is; 7. is; 8. are; 9. is; 10. are

Students can do Unit 1, Section 1, *Learn New Words* on the Interactive CD-ROM.

OBJECTIVE

Understanding Classroom Instructions

VOCABULARY

ask	open	say
circle	practice	sit down
close	raise	stand up
go to	read	take out
listen	repeat	write

WINDOW ON MATH

Numbers 0 to 11

THINGS TO DO

1. Learn New Words 🎧

★ Hold up the book and point to the pictures.

★ Ask students to listen and look at the picture while you say each sentence or play the tape or CD.

★ Say the sentence or play the tape or CD a second time. Pause after each sentence, and ask the students to repeat.

★ As students listen a third time, have them point to each instruction in the book as they hear it.

Grammar Notes:

★ Students may notice that instructions begin with a verb. Explain that beginning a sentence with a verb can sound forceful or rude.

★ Because of this, we often add *please* to an instruction to make it more polite. *Please* is usually at the beginning or the end of the instruction. (*Please open your book. Open your book, please.*)

EXPANSION ACTIVITY: Charades

★ Write each of the instructions from Activity 1 on separate slips of paper.

★ As an example, write one of the instructions on the board and act it out. Have the class guess the instruction.

★ Ask a volunteer to come to the front of the class. Give the student a slip of paper, and put your finger to your lips to indicate that he or she must not talk.

★ Have the student act out the instruction and prompt the other students to guess what the action is.

★ Repeat with new volunteers until all the instructions have been acted out.

LISTENING SCRIPT

Lesson 3: Learn New Words

Look at the pictures. Listen to the classroom instructions. Then listen and repeat.

1. Read page 10.
2. Listen to the words.
3. Repeat the words.
4. Say *computer*.
5. Ask a partner.
6. Circle your name.
7. Write your name.
8. Practice the conversation with a partner.
9. Take out a piece of paper.
10. Open your book.
11. Close the window.
12. Raise your hand.
13. Stand up.
14. Sit down.
15. Go to the board.

2. Follow Instructions

★ Call on a few students and give them each a different instruction (e.g., *Say computer, Open your book,* etc.) If necessary, mime what they are supposed to do.

★ Have students work in pairs and take turns giving each other instructions.

EXPANSION ACTIVITY: Simon Says

★ Tell students that you are going to play a game called *Simon Says* and explain how the game works. Students should follow any instruction they are given if the person giving the command says *Simon says* before the instruction. They should not follow the instruction if the person does not say *Simon says* before the instruction.

★ Model the activity. Give an instruction, such as, *Simon says, "Stand up."* Gesture for students to stand up. Then say, *Point to the clock.* If students begin to point, shake your head *no.* Exaggerate the action. Give a few more instructions with and without saying *Simon says* to make sure students understand the game. If students make a mistake, tell them they are out of the game for now and should sit down.

★ Ask a volunteer to come to the front of the class to give instructions while the rest of the class follows. Continue with various volunteers.

3. Write

★ Copy the verbs from 1–5 on the board: *Say, Write, Open, Close, Go to.*

★ Brainstorm words that can follow each verb. Ideas might include:

Say hello, notebook, teacher.

Write your name, your address, your city.

Open the door, the window, your book.

Close the door, the window, your book.

Go to the door, the board, the table.

★ Ask students to write their own instructions for doing something and then have them take turns giving instructions to the class. Note that some instructions can be followed by everyone—*Stand up*, for example—while others are best given to just one student: *Close the door.*

EXPANSION ACTIVITY: Read and Follow Instructions

★ Write a list of instructions on the board and ask the students to follow them. Use the instructions below or create your own.

1. Take out a piece of paper.
2. Write your name on the paper.
3. Open your book to page ___?___.
4. Write three words from page ___?___ on the paper.
5. Circle one word on your paper.
6. Ask a partner to read the word.

★ Have students exchange their papers. Read the instructions again and have each partner check and correct the paper. Call on a few students, and ask them what word their partner circled.

★ ★

 TRY THIS

★ ★

★ Copy the cluster diagram from the book on the board. Ask students to read the sentence in the center of the cluster diagram: *Things that open and close.*

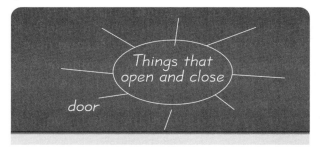

Things that open and close

door

★ Point to the word *door* and ask, *Can you open and close a door?* Elicit the correct response and write *door* on the board.

★ Have students write other things that open and close next to each line in the diagram.

★ Go over the answers with the class. Possible answers include: *door, window, book, notebook, hand.*

EXPANSION ACTIVITY: Cluster Diagram Option

★ Make a cluster diagram of your own on the board. In the center write *Things a student takes out.*

★ Tell students to work in pairs and copy the cluster diagram. Have them complete the diagram adding words that fit the category. Possible answers include: *a piece of paper, a book, a notebook, a pencil, a pen, etc.*

★ Have volunteers come to the board and write words on the cluster diagram.

★ You can repeat this activity using different topics for the center of the diagram: students from Mexico; words that begin with *b*; ways to practice English, etc.

WINDOW ON MATH: Numbers 0–11

A. Listen to the numbers.

★ Say the numbers, or listen to the tape or CD and have the students repeat them.

★ Practice by counting objects around the classroom. For example, pick up five books and cue the students to count to five. Repeat the exercise with other objects and numbers.

B. Listen to the conversation.

★ Say each line of the conversation or listen to the tape or CD and have students repeat.

★ Model the instruction in the conversation: *Open your book to page 5.* Have students respond with *B's* line: *Which page?* Repeat the instruction.

★ Repeat the conversation, replacing the page number with numbers up to 11 in random order. Cue students to ask *Which page?* each time.

★ Have students work in pairs and practice the conversation. Remind them to turn to the page they are instructed to find.

LISTENING SCRIPT

Lesson 3: Window on Math

A. Listen to the numbers. Then listen and repeat.

zero	three	six	nine
one	four	seven	ten
two	five	eight	eleven

B. Listen to the conversation. Then listen and repeat.

A: Open your book to page 5.
B: Which page?
A: Page 5.

BIG PICTURE EXPANSION ACTIVITY: SPEAKING—*Yes/No* Memory Game

★ Put the "big picture" color overhead transparency for Unit 1, Lesson 2, on the projector or have students look at the "big picture" in their books.

★ Give them one minute to memorize as much as they can about the picture. Then turn off the projector or tell students to close their books.

★ Say three sentences about the picture—one that includes correct information and two that include incorrect information: *One teacher is in the classroom* (correct). *Eleven students are in the classroom* (incorrect). *Two maps are in the classroom* (incorrect). Ask students to say *yes* if the sentence is right and *no* if it is wrong.

★ Write the sentences on the board. Ask the students to look at the picture and write three more sentences about the picture using numbers between 0 and 11. The sentences can include correct or incorrect information. More proficient students may not need to write their sentences first; they can simply say three sentences about the picture.

★ After the students have written three sentences, have them close their books. Have them work with a partner and take turns saying sentences about the picture while their partner responds with *yes* or *no*.

 Students can do Unit 1, Section 2, *Listen and Choose* on the Interactive CD-ROM.

OBJECTIVE

Reporting Personal Information

VOCABULARY

address	married
area code	middle name
birthplace	occupation
city	single
divorced	state
female	street
gender	telephone number
male	zip code
marital status	

WINDOW ON GRAMMAR

Punctuation Marks

THINGS TO DO

1. Learn New Words 🎧

★ Point to the picture and make sure the students know it is an application form. Ask the question *Where do you see or use application forms?* Possible answers: *at school, at work, for visas,* and *for credit cards.*

★ Have students listen and look at the picture while you say the words or play the tape or CD.

★ Say the words or play the tape or CD a second time. Pause after each word and ask the students to repeat.

★ Say the words in random order and have students point to the item in the picture.

LISTENING SCRIPT

Lesson 4: Learn New Words

Look at the picture. Listen to the information. Then listen and repeat.

His first name is Paul. His middle name is Richard. His last name is Bridges. His address is 8517 Alvarado Street in Los Angeles, California. The zip code is 91012. Paul's telephone number is area code 310-555-5678. His birthplace is Sacramento, California in the United States. His gender is male. His marital status is married. He's a teacher. That's his occupation.

Listen and repeat.

1. middle name	10. gender
2. address	11. male
3. street	12. female
4. city	13. marital status
5. state	14. single
6. zip code	15. married
7. telephone number	16. divorced
8. area code	17. occupation
9. birthplace	

2. Read

★ Write the first sentence on the board, including the two blanks. Read the sentence, and have students repeat.

★ Have students complete the sentences by looking at the application form. When they are finished, have them compare answers with a partner.

★ Go over the answers with the class.

ANSWER KEY:

Paul's <u>last name</u> is Bridges. His <u>middle name</u> is Richard. His <u>address</u> is 8517 Alverado Street in Los Angeles, California. The <u>zip code</u> is 91012. Paul's <u>telephone number</u> is area code (310) 555-5678. His <u>birthplace</u> is the United States.

Pronunciation Notes: *S* and *D* Endings
★ Consonant endings can be difficult for some students. In English, *s* and *d* sounds are particularly important because they often indicate plurality (*book<u>s</u>*), person (*he eat<u>s</u>*), possessive (*Victor'<u>s</u>*), and past tense (*marrie<u>d</u>*). Make sure students pronounce correctly the *s* and *d* sounds in the new words.

Literacy Note:
★ Eight of the words in the list of *Learn New Words* contain a *vowel-consonant-silent e* combination at the end of the word: *name, state, zip code, area code, telephone, male,* and *female*. Point out this pattern to your students.

★ Note that the silent *e* indicates that the preceding vowel will have a long sound (or will say its own name).

14 Unit 1

EXPANSION ACTIVITY: True or False?

★ Tell students that you are going to read some sentences and that some of them are true, and some are false.

★ Say *Paul's last name is Bridges.* Ask students if it's true (nod your head) or false (shake your head). Elicit that the response is true. Do the same with a statement that is false: *Paul's last name is Richards.*

★ Tell the students to write three sentences about the application form. Two sentences should be true, and one should be false. They should write them in random order.

★ Have students work in pairs and take turns reading their sentences while their partner responds with true or false.

★ Call on a few students to read their sentences aloud. Have the class respond together with true or false.

★ A variation on this exercise is to have the students write two true sentences about themselves and one false sentence. Have volunteers read their sentences to the class and see if the class can guess which sentences are true and which sentence is false.

3. Write

★ Ask students to look at the directions and the example question. Read the question aloud, and pause to let the students repeat.

★ Model the interview with a student. Ask the student the first question, eliciting an answer, then have the student ask you the same first question.

★ Ask the students what other questions they need to ask a partner to complete the application form. Write those questions on the board. Have students write them in their notebook.

★ Put the students in pairs to ask each other the questions. Have them fill out the application form for their partner.

Culture/Civics Notes:

★ Some students may not know that the family name (also called the *surname* or *last name*) is said last in Western culture, even though on forms we sometimes write the last name first. First names are also known as *given names,* or sometimes, *Christian names.* Most people also have middle names or initials.

★ When some women get married, they take the last name of the man that they marry as their own. Their old last name is then known as a *maiden name.* Sometimes their maiden name becomes their middle name after marriage.

EXPANSION ACTIVITY: Inside/Outside Circle

★ Ask students to read the questions they wrote in the interview in Activity 3 and try to remember as many of the questions as they can.

★ Have them form two concentric circles, one circle inside the other, with the students facing each other.

★ Tell students that they will ask and answer one question with the student facing them. Model this with a student, asking one question, *What's your first name?* Elicit the response, *Carlos.* Have that student ask you one question, *What's your zip code?* Answer with *22101* or whatever your zip code is.

★ After each question, have the outer circle move clockwise, or to the left, so that each student is facing a new partner. Have them ask and answer questions again. Repeat this until each student has talked to eight or more students.

WINDOW ON GRAMMAR: Punctuation Marks

A. Circle the punctuation marks.

★ Write two or three sentences on the board that require a period, a question mark, and a comma. (*Where are you from? I'm from Boston, Massachusetts.*) Put a circle in the places where the punctuation belongs, but leave out the punctuation.

★ Ask what belongs in those circles, or ask a volunteer to come up and fill in the circles.

★ Point to each punctuation mark, saying its name, and have students repeat. Explain that we use periods at the end of a statement, question marks after a question, and commas between a city and a state or country.

★ Have students complete the exercises in Part A.

★ Go over the answers with the class.

B. Add the punctuation marks.

★ Have students read the sentences and add the punctuation marks that are required.

★ Have them check their answers with a partner.

★ Go over the answers with the class.

ANSWER KEY:

A. 1. Where are you from⑦
   2. I am from Miami⑦ Florida⊙
   3. Your book is on the floor⊙
   4. Where is Paris⊙ France⑦

B. 1. What's her name?
   2. Listen to your teacher.
   3. He is from San Francisco, California.
   4. His birthplace is Toronto, Canada.

BIG PICTURE EXPANSION ACTIVITY: READING—Who is Jane?

★ Make copies of Worksheet #2 (page 242) and distribute them to students.

★ Put the color overhead transparency for Unit 1, Lesson 2, on the projector or have students look at the "big picture" in their books. Ask students to locate Jane in the picture.

★ Ask students to read the paragraph about Jane and put in the correct punctuation marks. Have them check their answers with a partner.

★ Go over the answers with the class.

ANSWER KEY:

A. Jane is a student. She is from Salzburg, Austria. Her last name is Thiede. Her birthplace is Innsbruck, Austria. Jane is in the United States now. She is in Seattle, Washington. Her address is 23 High Street. Jane is single.
B. 1. Thiede; 2. Innsbruck, Austria; 3. 23 High Street; 4. single; 5. Yes.

 Students can do Unit 1, Section 3, *Read and Write* on the Interactive CD-ROM.

LESSON 5 — Nice to meet you.

STUDENT BOOK PAGES 12–13

OBJECTIVE

Greeting People

WINDOW ON PRONUNCIATION

Long Vowel Sounds: *I* and *E*

1. Practice the Conversation: Greeting Someone 🎧

★ Ask students to look at the picture for Conversation 1. To set the context, ask, *Who is in the picture? Where are they?*

★ Read the conversation or play the tape or CD.

★ Read or play the conversation again. Pause after each sentence and ask students to repeat.

★ Ask comprehension questions: *What's the man's name? What's the woman's name?*

★ Point out the titles *Mr., Ms., Mrs.* and explain their meaning.

★ Introduce yourself using the appropriate title. Call on a few students to introduce themselves by title and last name.

★ Point out that there are two places in the conversation example where it is appropriate to use different words without changing the meaning. First, we can say either *hello* or *hi* to begin a conversation. Second, when we meet people for the first time, it is polite to say either *Nice to meet you,* or *How do you do?*

★ Model the conversation with a student. Have the student read A's lines. Demonstrate how to use both *How do you do?* and *Nice to meet you.*

★ Have students work in pairs and practice the conversation. Walk around to monitor the activity and provide help as needed.

★ Have volunteers practice the conversation in front of the class.

Conversation Note:
★ Another technique for dialogue practice is the disappearing dialogue.

★ Write the dialogue on the board with A and B parts clearly written. As the whole class reads the dialogue aloud, erase a word as they continue to recite. Then erase more words until the students can recreate the whole dialogue from memory.

LISTENING SCRIPT

Lesson 5: Practice the Conversation—Greeting Someone

Listen to the conversation. Then listen and repeat.

A: Hello. I'm Mr. Campos.
B: Nice to meet you, Mr. Campos. I'm Ms. Jones.
A: Nice to meet you.

Listen to the new words and expressions. Listen and repeat.

Hi.	Mr.
How do you do?	Ms.
Hello.	Mrs.

Culture/Civics Notes:
★ You may want to point out that titles are frequently used in formal situations. We often use titles for people we don't know at all, and for teachers, doctors, dentists, and those who are older than we are or who are in a position of authority.

★ As a rule, we use titles until the other person tells us it is okay to use his or her first name. In most situations, after the introduction the speaker will say something like *Please call me John.* Then we know *John* wants to have a less formal conversation. Children, classmates, and coworkers usually call each other by their first names.

★ Both men and women in the United States often shake hands when they meet someone new.

★ *How do you do?* is not really a question that requires a specific answer. It is just a formulaic phrase used to acknowledge an introduction. In some cultures—England for example—people do often still say *Very well, thank you* in response to this question.

★ In Western cultures, it is also important to look into the eyes of the person you are meeting. This conveys confidence, respect, and honesty.

Unit 1   **17**

EXPANSION ACTIVITY: Meet and Greet

★ Tell the students that they are going to introduce themselves using their titles and last names to as many people as they can in three minutes. Remind them to follow the conversation model, to shake hands, and to look into the other person's eyes.

★ Have the students stand up. When you tell them to begin, they should introduce themselves to the person nearest them, and then continue around the room until you say stop.

★ You could also have students practice this conversation in concentric circles, rotating one of the circles after each introduction.

★ Set a time limit of three minutes.

2. Practice the Conversation: Introducing Someone 🎧

★ Repeat the basic procedure introduced in Activity 1.

★ To set the context, ask, *Who is in the picture? Where are they?*

★ Copy the conversation on the board, leaving blanks where more than one phrase is possible. Include blank lines for the names. Model the conversation with two students. Note that one student does not need to talk, but needs to be introduced. If your students are at a higher level, add a line for the third person to say at the end of the conversation. (*Nice to meet you, too.*)

★ To check comprehension, ask, *What's the man's name? What's his friend's name?*

★ Point out three ways to answer the question *How are you?* You can say *fine, good, not bad.* Ask students if they know of other answers, such as *so-so, not so good, great.*

★ Point out three ways to introduce another person. Write them on the board.

> This is _____.
>
> I want to introduce you to _____.
>
> I want you to meet _____.

LISTENING SCRIPT

Lesson 5: Practice the Conversation—Introducing Someone

Listen to the conversation. Then listen and repeat.

A: Hi, Jon. How are you?
B: Fine, thanks. And you?
A: I'm fine. Jon, this is my friend, Gina.
B: Hi, Gina. Nice to meet you.

Listen to the new words and expressions. Listen and repeat.

Good.
Not bad.
OK.
Great.
I want to introduce you to my friend Gina.
I want you to meet Gina.
This is Gina.

Culture/Civics Notes:

★ Students may not realize that *How are you?* is often just another greeting. It is not usually taken as an opportunity to really talk about how you are doing. *Fine, thanks.* is the most common response. It is polite to respond by asking the other person *And how are you?*

★ It is okay for men to introduce women or women to introduce men. It is common for men and women to be equal friends.

★ It is polite to introduce an older person to a younger person and to name the older person first.

3. Practice the Conversation: Saying Goodbye 🎧

★ Repeat the basic procedure from Activity 1.

★ To set the context, ask, *Who is in the picture? Where are they?*

★ To check comprehension, ask, *What are the people's names?*

★ Point out possible ways to say goodbye: *See you later. Nice to see you. Have a nice day.*

LISTENING SCRIPT

Lesson 5: Practice the Conversation: Saying Goodbye

Listen to the conversation. Then listen and repeat.

A: Good-bye, Jon.
B: Bye, David. Have a nice day.
A: You too.

Listen to the new words and expressions. Listen and repeat.

Have a nice day.
See you later.
Nice to see you.
Have a great day.
Have a good day.

Culture/Civics Notes:

★ *Nice to see you* can be used as part of a greeting: *Hi Jon, nice to see you.* Or, it can be a part of a leave-taking: *Bye, David. Nice to see you.* Sometimes when it is part of a leave-taking, we say, *It was nice to see you.*

★ *Bye* is a shortened form of *good-bye*.

EXPANSION ACTIVITY:
Hello and Goodbye

★ Have students work in pairs and create conversations in which they introduce themselves to a new classmate and say goodbye.

★ Suggest that they use first names in both the introduction and the leave-taking. They can use their real name or you can do something fun and ask them to create a new personality and name for themselves. It can be someone famous.

★ Walk around to provide help as needed.

★ Have volunteers practice conversations in front of the class.

WINDOW ON PRONUNCIATION:
Long Vowel Sounds: *I* and *E*

A. Listen to the words.

★ Write an *I* and an *E* with a vertical line between the two letters on the board. Point to each letter and say the sound. Have students repeat.

★ Ask students to brainstorm some words that include these sounds. Write them on the board under the appropriate letter.

★ Read the words or play the tape or CD. Read or play the tape or CD a second time, and have students repeat the words. Have the students write *I* or *E* next to each word in the book to indicate the sound.

★ Tell students to complete the chart in their book. Write all the words that include an *I* sound in the list on the left, and all the words that include an *E* sound in the list on the right.

★ Ask volunteers to write the words in the chart on the board.

LISTENING SCRIPT

Lesson 5: Window on Pronunciation
Long Vowel Sounds: *I* and *E*

Listen to the words. Then listen and repeat.

1. I	7. my	13. we
2. fine	8. try	14. write
3. see	9. three	15. nice
4. me	10. he	16. read
5. meet	11. street	17. bye
6. hi	12. China	18. country

B. Write the words in the correct place.

★ Have students look at the headings and say the words in each column.

★ Ask students to complete the chart by writing the words from Activity A above in the appropriate column.

★ Have them go over their answers with a partner. Encourage them to say the words aloud.

★ Go over the answers with the class.

ANSWER KEY:

Sounds like *I*: I, fine, hi, my, try, China, write, nice, bye

Sounds like *E*: see, me, meet, three, he, street, we, read, country

C. Listen and circle the word you hear.

★ Play the tape or listen to the CD. Have students circle the word they hear for each item.

★ Go over the answers with the class.

★ Tell students to work in pairs and take turns saying one of the words in each pair as their partner circles the word in their book.

LISTENING SCRIPT

Lesson 5: Practice the Conversation

Listen and circle the word you hear.

1. my my
2. he he
3. E E
4. write write
5. bye bye
6. we we

Literacy Notes:

★ In English there are 5 letters that represent the vowels, but there are at least 14 vowel sounds. All five vowels have both long and short sounds. The long sounds actually "say the name" of the vowel. Students are sometimes confused by vowels that make the sound of another letter: *bye—I, Haiti—E*.

★ Both sounds are held for a long time and sound like there is a *y* at the end. If students are having trouble with either, have them exaggerate the length of the vowel sound.

★ The Window on Pronunciation exercises in Lesson 5 use minimal pairs, or words that differ only in one sound, to help students with both pronunciation and listening discrimination.

EXPANSION ACTIVITY: Find the Sounds

★ Have students work in groups of 3 or 4.

★ Ask them to brainstorm a list of other words that include either the long *I* sound or the long *E* sound. Suggest that they think about the names of people in the class, streets, countries, cities, etc.

★ Call on a student in each group to give an example of either sound and make a list of words for each sound on the board.

★ Say each word and have students repeat.

 Students can do Unit 1, Section 2, *Listen and Choose* on the Interactive CD-ROM.

EQUIPPED FOR THE FUTURE ROLE

Work

OBJECTIVE

Looking at Job Ads

VOCABULARY

bus driver	pharmacist
cashier	police officer
dentist	salesclerk
doctor	machinist
nurse	

1. Learn New Words 🎧

★ Ask the students to look at the pictures in the book. Tell them that these are pictures of people at work who have different occupations. *Occupation* is the word we use for the type of work we do. Ask the class, *What is my occupation?* (*teacher*).

★ Ask questions about the names of the people in the pictures: *What is Joan's last name? What is Mr. Brunov's first name?*

★ Have students listen and look at the pictures while you say the words or play the tape or CD.

★ Say the words or play the tape or CD a second time. Pause after each word and ask the students to repeat.

★ Say the words a third time in random order, and tell the students to point at the related photos.

★ Point to the occupations in random order, and have students say the name.

LISTENING SCRIPT

Lesson 6: Learn New Words

Look at the pictures below. Listen to the words. Then listen and repeat.

1. dentist	Joan Baxter is a dentist.
2. bus driver	Larry Fisher is a bus driver.
3. pharmacist	Ken Park is a pharmacist.
4. doctor	Emma Lambert is a doctor.
5. salesclerk	Paul Ming is a salesclerk.
6. machinist	David Campos is a machinist.
7. police officer	Gina Mata is a police officer.
8. nurse	Leo Brunov is a nurse.
9. cashier	Amy Craft is a cashier.

Grammar Note:

★ Many occupations have an *-er, -or,* or *-ist* ending. Point out to students that these endings often mean *the person who does a particular job.* For example: *A bus driver is a person who drives a bus.* Have the students identify as many occupations as they can that have an *-er, -or,* or *-ist* ending.

Culture/Civics Note:

★ Some students may be used to only women or only men performing certain types of jobs. You may want to explain that either men or women can fill all of the occupations in this lesson. More women work in some occupations than men (nurses), and more men than women work in others (machinists or police officers), but all of them can be done by either gender.

EXPANSION ACTIVITY: Discussing Gender and Occupation

★ Draw a chart on the board with three headings: *Male, Female,* and *Male and Female.*

★ Tell students to copy the chart on a piece of paper. Ask them to list occupations under the appropriate headings according to the culture in their home country. For example, if most police officers in their home country are men, they would write *police officer* under *male.*

★ When they are finished, put them in groups of three or four to compare charts and see where there are similarities and differences.

Male	Female	Male and Female

2. Ask Questions

★ Read the questions and responses aloud, pausing to let students repeat.

★ Review *he* and *she*, *he's* and *she's*.

★ Ask students a few questions about other people in the Activity 1 pictures and have the class answer. (*What's Amy's occupation? She's a cashier.*)

★ Have students work in pairs and take turns asking and answering questions about the people in the pictures.

EXPANSION ACTIVITY: Charades

★ Write each occupation on an index card or a piece of paper.

★ Group students in pairs and give each pair a card. They will act out the occupation on the card for the class to guess.

★ To start, model the occupation while the class guesses what you are. For example, if you are a dentist, have a student sit in a chair with an open mouth while you do a check-up. Ask, *What is my occupation?* Have students guess the correct occupation.

★ After students have prepared their charades, ask pairs to come to the front of the room. Give them time to mime their occupation, and then ask the class, *What's his/her occupation?*

3. Read

★ Point to the job ads in the book. Ask questions: *What are they? Where can you see job ads?* (newspapers, boards, windows).

★ Have the students read the ads and circle the occupations. Remind them to look for the words they learned in the Learn New Words section.

★ Go over the ads, asking the class what occupation is listed in each ad.

ANSWER KEY:

1. bus driver; 2. machinist; 3. salesclerk; 4. cashier; 5. pharmacist; 6. driver

EXPANSION ACTIVITY: Rank It

★ Ask students to rank the six job ads in order of desirability. Tell them to write 1 next to the job that they like the best and 6 next to the job they like the least.

★ Pair students and have them compare their rankings. Tell them to give one reason they like one ad the most and one reason they like one ad the least.

4. Write

★ Ask students what they see in the ads. Cue them with questions such as, *Do you see addresses? Do you see names of people?*

★ Have students look at the chart in the book. Copy the chart on the board. Point to the headings and have students say them aloud.

★ Ask students to read the ads and write down the occupations in the left column under the heading *Occupation*.

★ Tell students to look at the ad for a bus driver and go over the information there and in the chart. Ask, *Does the ad have a telephone number? What is it? Does the ad have an address?* Point out that the telephone number is listed in the chart, but that there is no address listed under *street address*.

★ Instruct the students to complete the chart for the other job ads and then compare answers with a partner. Ask a few students to complete the chart on the board.

ANSWER KEY:

Occupation	Street Address	Telephone Number
1. Bus driver	XXX	916-555-0819
2. Machinist	433 Ray Avenue Auburn, California	916-202-1234
3. Salesclerk	11 Alvarado Street	555-7400
4. Cashier	873 Mission Street Livermore, CA	916-682-1414
5. Pharmacist	XXX	916-555-8700
6. Driver	10 Johnson Road	916 555-0612

EXPANSION ACTIVITY:
Using the Newspaper

★ Bring the Help Wanted section of a newspaper to class or ask students to bring it in themselves.

★ Group students in pairs and distribute pages to each pair of students.

★ Have them look for ads for the occupations in Lesson 6. Also invite them to look for ads for other jobs they are interested in.

★ Ask students to add the information from these ads to the chart in Activity 4.

  BIG PICTURE EXPANSION ACTIVITY:
WRITING—Describing People

★ Have students look at the "big picture" or put the color overhead transparency for Unit 1, Lesson 2, on the projector.

★ Have students write three sentences about people in the picture. Encourage them to be creative and imagine where the people might be from and what their occupations might be.

★ Walk around the room to monitor the activity, check punctuation, and provide help as needed.

★ Instruct students to read their sentences to a partner. Have the partner identify who the student wrote about by pointing to that person in the picture.

1. Listening Review 🎧

TESTING FOCUS: Completing Answer Keys
★ Copy the following on the board:

Questions	Answer Key
1. What is his address? A. John B. 1223 Main Street C. teacher	1. Ⓐ Ⓑ Ⓒ

★ Read the question and possible answers aloud. Ask the students which answer is correct (B).
★ Show them how to color in the circle B on the answer key on the board.
★ Point out the Answer Sheet box in the book for the Listening Review.
★ After students have answered the first question, walk around to make sure all the students have marked the answer box correctly. Note that they may have marked the wrong answer, but they should have correctly colored in the corresponding circle.

★ Go over the directions with the class.
★ Read the items or play the tape or CD and have the students mark their answers in the Answer Sheet box in their book.
★ Walk around to monitor the activity and help students stay on task.
★ Have students check their answers with a partner.
★ Go over the answers with the class.

LISTENING SCRIPT

Lesson 7: Listening Review

Listen and choose the correct answer. Use the Answer Sheet below.

1. Open your book.
2. Her book is on the floor.
3. She's a teacher.
4. It's a calendar.
5. What's his telephone number?
6. What's her zip code?
7. What's her occupation?
8. What state is he from?
9. What's their area code?
10. What's her address?

ANSWER KEY:

1. B; 2. C; 3. C; 4. A; 5. B; 6. B; 7. C; 8. B; 9. B; 10. A

2. Conversation Check: Pair Work

★ Go over the directions. Have students work in pairs and remind them that each partner has some information, but that other information is missing. They must ask their partners questions to complete their charts.
★ Walk around to monitor the activity and provide help as needed.

Assessment Note:
★ You can use the Conversation Check Activity as an oral assessment. Ask pairs of students to complete the activity while you note areas of difficulty.

LEARNING LOG

★ Point out the four sections of the Learning Log: *I know these words; I can ask; I can say;* and *I can write.*
★ Have students check what they know and what they can do.
★ Walk around to note what they don't know or can't do. Use this information to review areas of difficulty.

BIG PICTURE EXPANSION ACTIVITY:
SPEAKING Assessment—Talking about the Picture

★ You can use the "big picture" in Unit 1 to place new students in open entry classes, to diagnose difficulties, or to measure progress.

★ Work with one student at a time and show them the big picture. Ask, *What do you see in the picture? Tell me about the picture.* Tell the student you want him or her to speak for as long as possible. Wait a moment for the student to prepare to answer. If the student has difficulty, you can use prompts: *What do you see in the classroom? Who do you see in the classroom? What are the students doing?*

★ You can use a rubric like the one below to rate beginning speakers.

3	Uses sentences, although form may be incorrect Can speak for sustained length of time Responds to prompts, but doesn't need them to begin speaking
2	Can use nouns and verbs Uses phrases Answers informational questions
1	Can name objects Uses single words Can answer yes/no questions
0	Cannot say anything independently May be able to point to objects when prompted

TEACHER NOTES:

Things that students are doing well:

_____

_____

_____

_____

_____

_____

Things students need additional help with:

_____

_____

_____

_____

_____

_____

_____

Ideas for further practice or for the next class:

_____

_____

_____

_____

_____

Students can do Unit 1, Section 5, *Practice Test* on the Interactive CD-ROM.

OBJECTIVE

Simple Present of *Be*; Possessive Adjectives; Possessive of Names

★ Read the sentences in the grammar paradigm and have students repeat.

★ Call on students and say a personal pronoun (*I*), and have the students respond with the correct form of be (*am*).

★ Go over the contractions in the box. With books closed, say a personal pronoun and form of *be* (*You are*). Prompt students to respond with the contraction (*you're*).

★ Ask students if the negative *not* comes before or after the form of *be*.

1. Read the story.

★ Ask students to read the story. For additional literacy and pronunciation practice, read each sentence of the story aloud. Pause and have students repeat each sentence.

★ Ask students what form of *be* they see in the first sentence (*are*). Point out that this word is circled. Tell students to circle the other examples of *be* in the story; there are 15 more examples.

★ Have students check their answers with a partner.

★ Go over the answers with the class.

ANSWER KEY:

There <u>are</u> twenty (20) students in my class. Ten students <u>are</u> from Mexico. Four students <u>are</u> from Russia. Three students <u>are</u> from China. Two students <u>are</u> from Haiti, and one student <u>is</u> from Egypt. Eleven students in my class <u>are</u> married. Nine students <u>are</u> single. I <u>am</u> the student from Egypt. My name <u>is</u> Fatima, and I <u>am</u> married. My teacher <u>is</u> Mr. White. His first name <u>is</u> David, and he <u>is</u> from Canada. Mr. White <u>is</u> not married. He <u>is</u> single.

2. Read the story again.

★ Go over the first question together: *Is Fatima from Russia?* Point out that the phrase *is not* is written as an example on the first line in item 1. Ask the class, *Where is Fatima from?* Ask students what they should write in the second sentence in item 1 (*is*).

★ Ask students to read the story again. Ask them to complete the rest of the sentences with *are, is, are not,* or *is not*. Walk around the room to help as needed.

★ Have students check their answers with a partner.

★ Go over the answers with the class. Ask volunteers to write the sentences on the board.

ANSWER KEY:

1. Fatima <u>*is not*</u> from Russia. She <u>*is*</u> from Egypt.
2. Fatima <u>*is*</u> married. She <u>*is not*</u> single.
3. Eleven students in Fatima's class <u>*are*</u> married.
4. Mr. White <u>*is not*</u> a bus driver. He <u>*is*</u> a teacher.
5. Mr. White and Fatima <u>*are not*</u> from the United States.
6. Mr. White <u>*is not*</u> from Egypt. He <u>*is*</u> from Canada.
7. Two students in Fatima's class <u>*are*</u> from Haiti.

3. Rewrite each sentence above.

★ Go over the example. Ask the question, *What is the contraction for is not?* Point out that *isn't* is in the first sentence. Ask students, *What is the contraction for she is?*

★ You can point out that there are two ways to write the contraction *he/she/it + is not*. *He's not* or *He isn't* are both acceptable forms.

★ Have students work individually to rewrite the sentences in Activity 2 using contractions. Walk around the room to provide help as needed.

★ Group students in pairs to compare their sentences.

★ Go over the sentences with the class.

ANSWER KEY:

1. Fatima __isn't__ from Russia./Fatima __'s not__ from Russia. She __'s__ from Egypt.
2. Fatima __'s__ married. She __isn't__ single./ She __'s not__ single.
3. Eleven students in Fatima's class __are (no contraction)__ married.
4. Mr. White __isn't__ a bus driver./Mr. White __'s not__ a bus driver. He __'s__ a teacher.
5. Mr. White and Fatima __aren't__ from the United States.
6. Mr. White __isn't__ from Egypt./Mr. White __'s not__ from Egypt. He __'s__ from Canada.
7. Two students in Fatima's class __are (no contraction)__ from Haiti.

4. Complete the sentences.

★ Go over the information in the grammar box. Use gestures to indicate the different personal pronouns and elicit the possessive adjectives. For example, point to yourself and say, *This is my book,* stressing the possessive.

★ Walk around the room, and pick up the books of different students. As you pick up the book, say, *This is _____.* And elicit the possessive of that person's name (*Theo's book*).

★ Read the directions to the students. Tell them to work individually to complete the sentences and then check theirs with a partner's.

★ Go over the answers with the class.

ANSWER KEY:

1. Their; 2. Our; 3. His; 4. My; 5. Her; 6. Their/their

5. Write a sentence about each person.

★ As an example, have students look at number 1. Ask what words have been added to complete the sentence. Elicit that *Bob* is now the possessive, *Bob's,* and that *is* is between *telephone number* and *555-9584.*

★ Do number 2 with the class. Ask them to create a sentence with the available information. Elicit that they should make *David* possessive, and add the word *is* between *zip code* and *91012.*

★ Have students work individually to complete the other sentences. Point out that students will use a possessive and a form of *be* in each sentence.

★ Have students compare their sentences with a partner's.

★ Go over the sentences with the class.

ANSWER KEY:

a. Bob's telephone number is 555-9584.
b. David's zip code is 91012.
c. Rose's marital status is married.
d. Anna's area code is 212.
e. Mr. White's first name is David.

EXPANSION ACTIVITY: Personal Information

★ Copy the chart below on the board, and ask students to copy the chart in their notebooks.

First Name	Last Name	Marital Status	Birthplace	Address

★ Tell students that they are going to talk to three other students to complete the chart.

★ Ask students what questions they should ask. Elicit the following questions and write them on the board: *What's your first name? What's your last name? What's your marital status? What's your birthplace? What's your address?*

★ Before the students begin, model the activity with a volunteer. Ask the five questions and write the student's information in the first row of the chart on the board.

★ Have students stand up and walk around the room to complete the chart, talking to three other students.

★ Call on students randomly to report on one of the people they talked to.

EQUIPPED FOR THE FUTURE ROLE

Family

OBJECTIVE

Getting School Supplies

VOCABULARY

binder	grade
child	list
eraser	ruler

A. Look at the box above.

★ Have students look at the three pictures. Ask questions about each picture: *Is the student male or female? What is his name?*

★ Read the sentences in each picture and have the students repeat.

★ Have students evaluate the box with information about the schools. Ask comprehension questions such as, *What school is grade 3 in? Does North High School have Grade 6?*

★ Read the directions for Activity A and have students complete the exercise.

★ Go over the answers with the class.

ANSWER KEY:

1. West Elementary; 2. North High;
3. South Middle

Culture/Civics Notes:

★ The public school system where you are teaching may differ from your students' home country. Most school districts in the United States follow one of two models:

1. In one model, students in grades kindergarten through sixth grade go to an elementary school. Grades 7 and 8, or sometimes 7 through 9, are considered junior high. Grades 9–12 or 10–12 are high school or senior high school.

2. In the model presented in Activity A, grades up through 5 are in an elementary

---

school; grades 6–8 are in a middle school; and grades 9–12 are known as high school.

★ No matter what model the school district follows, students generally go to school through 12th grade. Children go to at least one year of school before first grade (kindergarten) and many children also go to preschool before kindergarten.

B. Learn new words.

★ Read each of the new words and have students repeat.

★ Explain the meaning of the new words. Show examples of *binder, ruler, eraser.* Point to the pictures to illustrate *child.*

★ Tell students to look at the lists of school supplies in the different grades. Explain to students that these are *lists*, and describe generally what a list is (a written series of names, numbers, things, etc., sometimes in order, sometimes random).

★ Have students circle the new words in the reading.

ANSWER KEY:

South Middle School
Grades 6–8
58 Elm Street
Charlotte, North Carolina

Parents: Read the list of school supplies for your child.

Grade 6:
Notebooks (2)	Binder (1)
Pens (4)	Erasers (2)
Pencils (9)	Paper

Grade 7:
Notebooks (3)	Binder (1)
Pens (4)	Erasers (2)
Pencils (10)	Paper
Ruler (1)	

Grade 8:
Notebooks (4)	Binders (2)
Pens (5)	Erasers (3)
Pencils (11)	Paper
Ruler (1)	

Culture/Civics Note:
★ Your students may come from countries where school supplies are provided by the school. You can point out that students in the U.S. usually buy their own school supplies and that the supplies on these lists are fairly standard.

C. Write the numbers.

★ Have students look at the list to find the item. Then write the number next to each item.

★ Go over the answers with the class.

ANSWER KEY:

1. 3; 2. 2; 3. 4; 4. 10; 5. 2; 6. 1

D. Answer the questions.

★ Ask students to read the list again or look at the boxes in Activities A and B to answer the questions.

★ Go over the answers with the class.

★ Have students work in pairs and take turns asking and answering the questions.

ANSWER KEY:

1. South Middle School; 2. 58 Elm Street;
3. Charlotte; 4. 9–12; 5. West Elementary School

E. Read the sentences.

★ Have students read the list again and complete each sentence with the correct number.

★ Read the sentences aloud and go over the answers with the class. Have students repeat the sentences.

ANSWER KEY:

1. 3; 2. 2; 3. 4; 4. 9; 5. 3

Take It Outside

★ Read the questions and have students repeat.

★ Ask students to interview someone they know. If you do this in class, they can ask questions of a classmate. If they do this as an out-of-class assignment, have them ask anyone who has a child in school.

★ When they have completed the interview, have a few students share their answers with the class.

EXPANSION ACTIVITY: What About You?

★ Tell students that you are going to ask the class some questions. For each question, a *yes* answer means individual students should stand up; a *no* answer means students should sit down. If already standing, students who answer *yes* should remain standing.

★ Of course, to facilitate the beginning of the game, the answer to the first question must be *yes* for all students. Ask a question such as, *Are you a student?* Make sure all the students stand up.

★ Ask questions that use the vocabulary from this lesson and from the unit. Create your own or use the ones below. Make sure students understand the meaning of *do you have*, even though they have not yet learned the structure explicitly.

> *Do you have children?*
> *Is your child in elementary school?*
> *Is your child in middle school/junior high school?*
> *Is your child in high school?*
> *Are you in elementary school?*
> *Do you have a binder?*
> *Do you have an eraser?*
> *Do you have a ruler?*
> *Do you have a pen?*

EQUIPPED FOR THE FUTURE ROLE

Community

OBJECTIVE

Sending Letters

VOCABULARY

envelope	return address
letter	send
receive	stamp

A. Learn new words.

★ Ask students to read the directions. Read the new words aloud and have students repeat.

★ Read the letter aloud. Pause after each sentence and have students repeat.

★ To check comprehension, ask, *Who writes the letter? What country is Keiko from? What school does Keiko go to? What is Keiko's occupation?*

★ Have students look at the envelope and ask, *Is this a letter?*

★ To check comprehension, ask, *What is Keiko's address? What is Rosa Lynch's address? What is Keiko's zip code? Does Rosa Lynch live in New York?*

★ Have students underline the new words.

Culture/Civics Note:
★ Point out that we often use *Dear* in our greetings in letters, even when we are not writing to family or close friends. We often use *Sincerely* as a way to end the letter before we sign our names.

B. Answer the questions.

★ Read the questions aloud and have students repeat.

★ Ask students to look at the letter and envelope to answer the questions.

★ After students have answered the questions, have them check their answers with a partner.

★ Go over the answers with the class.

ANSWER KEY:

1. Keiko Ishikawa; 2. Mrs. (Rosa) Lynch; 3. Ishikawa; 4. Rosa; 5. 44 Market Street, Charlotte, NC 28205

C. Check *yes* or *no* about the letter and the envelope.

★ Read the directions and go over the example. Point out that there is a check mark in the box next to *yes* because Keiko does write the letter.

★ Have the students check *yes* or *no* for the other sentences.

★ Go over the answers with the class.

ANSWER KEY:

1. yes; 2. no; 3. yes; 4. yes; 5. no; 6. yes

D. Write your name and address on the envelope.

★ Point to the envelope. Tell students they are going to send a letter to Rosa Lynch and need to finish addressing the envelope. Explain that their address is called the *return address,* and that it goes in the upper left-hand corner of the envelope.

★ Have the students write their names and addresses on the appropriate lines.

★ Walk around the room to provide help as needed.

★ Instruct students to write the words from the box on the lines, identifying the different parts of an envelope.

★ Go over the answers.

ANSWER KEY:

letter, return address, stamp, envelope

Take It Outside

★ Tell students that they are going to practice writing information on an envelope.

★ Have the students write their own names and addresses on the return address lines of the envelope.

★ Write these questions on the board: *What is your name? What is your address? What is your city? What is your state? What is your zip code?*

★ Read the questions and have students repeat them.

★ Ask them to ask a family member, friend, coworker, or classmate the questions outside of class and use the answers to complete the envelope.

EXPANSION ACTIVITY:
Write Your Teacher

★ Bring envelopes to class and give one envelope to each student.

★ Tell students that they are going to write a letter to you.

★ Have them write your home or school address on the envelope. Dictate the address to them. Then write it on the board.

★ Ask students to write their own addresses in the return address area of the envelope.

★ Have the students write you a letter. They should introduce themselves and present some personal information, such as where they are from, what they like to do, and what their occupation is. They can use Keiko's letter as a model.

★ Collect the letters or have students mail them to you.

UNIT OVERVIEW

LESSON	OBJECTIVE	STUDENT BOOK PAGE #
1. Where's the post office?	Identifying Places in the Community	p. 20
2. It's next to the drugstore.	Giving Directions	p. 22
3. Is there an ATM around here?	In Town	p. 24
4. Maps	Reading a U.S. Map	p. 26
5. Is there a restaurant near here?	Asking for Locations	p. 28
6. The Public Library	Using Library Services	p. 30
7. What do you know?	Review and Assessment	p. 32
8. Spotlight	Writing	p. 34

Big Picture Expansion Activities

FOCUS	TITLE	SUGGESTED USE
Speaking	Memory Game	Lesson 3
Reading	A story about Janet	Lesson 2
Grammar	*There is/There are*	Lesson 5
Writing	Describing the Town	Lesson 7
Speaking	Assessment: Talking about the Picture	Lesson 7

Big Picture Expansion Activity Worksheets

WORKSHEET #/FOCUS	TITLE	TEACHER'S EDITION PAGE #
3. Reading	A story about Janet	p. 243
4. Grammar	*There is/There are*	p. 244

OBJECTIVE

Identifying Places in the Community

VOCABULARY

bank	library
bookmobile	movie theater
community center	park
drugstore	police station
fire station	post office
gas station	restaurant
hospital	school
laundromat	supermarket

WINDOW ON GRAMMAR

There Is/There Are

THINGS TO DO

1. Learn New Words 🎧

★ Ask students to look at the pictures and identify the things they recognize.

★ Have them listen while you say the words or play the tape or CD.

★ Say the words or play the tape or CD a second time. Pause after each word and ask the students to repeat the word and point to the correct picture.

★ Group students in pairs and instruct them to take turns pointing to pictures as their partner says the names.

★ Tell students to write the correct names of the places next to the pictures.

★ Ask students questions about the locations near their homes of places in the photos: *Where is the post office? Where is the hospital?*

LISTENING SCRIPT

Lesson 1: Learn New Words

Look at the pictures. Listen to the words. Then listen and repeat.

1. fire station	Where's the fire station?
2. police station	Where's the police station?
3. post office	Where's the post office?
4. community center	Where's the community center?
5. library	Where's the library?
6. bookmobile	Where's the bookmobile?
7. school	Where's the school?
8. park	Where's the park?
9. bank	Where's the bank?
10. drugstore	Where's the drugstore?
11. gas station	Where's the gas station?
12. supermarket	Where's the supermarket?
13. hospital	Where's the hospital?
14. laundromat	Where's the laundromat?
15. movie theater	Where's the movie theater?
16. restaurant	Where's the restaurant?

EXPANSION ACTIVITY:
Literacy Skills—Alphabetizing

★ Make a T chart on the board with the headings *One Word* and *Two Words*.

One Word	Two Words

★ Read and point to the first item in Activity 1, *fire station*. Ask students how many words they see. Then read and point to item 9, *bank*, and ask how many words they see. Write *bank* under *One Word* and *fire station* under *Two Words*.

★ Instruct students to copy the chart and complete it with the remaining words from the list.

★ Ask a student to complete the chart on the board.

★ Have students put the words from each column in alphabetical order. Ask the questions *What is the first letter of the alphabet? Do any of the words begin with A? What is the next letter? Do any words begin with B?* Explain that *bank* comes before *bookmobile* because the second letter, *a*, comes before *o*.

★ Students should work with a partner to finish putting the words in alphabetical order. Go over the answers with the class.

Culture/Civics Notes:

★ A community center is a place in the community that offers services and activities, such as recreation, classes, and meeting space.

★ A bookmobile is a traveling library. People with library cards can check out books from large vehicles that go from community to community in an effort to improve literacy.

2. Practice the Conversation 🎧

★ Read the conversation or play the tape or CD as the students listen.

★ Play the tape or CD or read the conversation again. Pause after each item, and ask the students to repeat.

★ Prompt the class to say *B's* lines as you say *A's* lines, then reverse the roles. Ask students to close their books and practice the conversation again from memory.

★ Instruct students to look at the excerpt from the phone directory. Ask comprehension questions such as *What places do you see in the list? Is there a community center? Is there a police station? What is the phone number for the police station?* Make sure the students notice the addresses and telephone numbers in the listing.

★ Model the conversation with a student, substituting a different place for the community center.

★ Have students work with a partner to practice the conversation using different places on the phone list. Walk around to make sure they understand the activity and provide help if needed.

★ Have volunteers practice the conversation in front of the class, substituting different places from the phone list.

LISTENING SCRIPT

Lesson 1: Practice the Conversation

Look at the Westville telephone book. Listen to the conversation. Then listen and repeat.

A: Where's the community center?
B: It's on Daniel Street.
A: What's the phone number?
B: It's area code (643) 555-1547
A: Thanks.
B: You're welcome.

Culture/Civics Note:

★ It is okay for people to ask strangers, both men and women, for directions or information about places.

★ Whether the person is able to give the information or not, it is always polite to thank the person. We usually say, *thank you*, *thanks*, or *thanks a lot*. We can also say *thanks anyway* if the person was unable to provide the information. The response is usually, *You're welcome*, or *No problem*.

★ ★

📁 **TRY THIS**

★ ★

★ This activity will be most successful if students use real telephone directories. You can bring some directories to class or give this as an out-of-class assignment.

★ Put students in groups of four or five.

★ Ask each group to list five places in the community they might need to contact.

★ Have each student in the group look up one place either in class or at home. Instruct students to share their information, so every student has five listings.

★ Ask a couple of groups to share the five places they looked up with the class and give the information they found.

EXPANSION ACTIVITY:
What's in Your Neighborhood?

★ Ask students to note three interesting or useful businesses in their community.

★ Have them write down the names of the businesses, the addresses, and the phone numbers. They can go to the business to get the information, or they can simply look up the name of the business in the telephone book.

WINDOW ON GRAMMAR:
There Is/There Are

A. Read the sentences.

★ Read the sentences and have students repeat.

★ Ask students what form of the verb *be* is used in the sentences.

★ Point out that when we talk about one place or thing, we use *is*. When we talk about two or more places or things, we use *are*. Ask students questions about the sample sentences: *How many fire stations are on High Street? How many supermarkets are there on Low Street?*

B. Complete the sentences with *is* or *are*.

★ Tell students to write *is* or *are* on the blank lines in the four sentences. Remind them to look at the number of places to determine if the verb is singular or plural.

★ Go over the answers.

ANSWER KEY:

1. are; 2. is; 3. are; 4. is

C. Write 3 sentences about your street or town.

★ Ask students, *What is on your street?* When students respond with the names of places, repeat the information in a complete sentence and write it on the board: *There is a <u>bank</u> on <u>Francisco's</u> street.*

★ Have students write three sentences about their streets and cities.

★ Have students compare their sentences with a partner.

★ Call on a few students to read their sentences aloud.

EXPANSION ACTIVITY:
Classroom Object Review

★ Point to objects in the classroom and ask students to say the name of the object.

★ Write on the board, *There is _____ _____ in the classroom. There are _____ _____ in the classroom.*

★ Explain that you will call on a student and then say the name of something in the classroom. The student should use either of the sentences on the board to say how many of those things are in the classroom. Then that student will choose another student and name an object for him or her to use in one of the sentences.

★ Give an example, such as *teacher*, and elicit the correct sentence from the class: *There is one teacher in the classroom.*

★ Call on a student and name an object. Have the student put it in the correct sentence.

★ Ask that student to choose another object and ask another student. Continue around the room until all the students have responded. You may have to repeat objects.

 Students can do Unit 2, Section 1, *Learn New Words* on the Interactive CD-ROM.

LESSON 2 — It's next to the drugstore.

OBJECTIVE

Giving Directions

VOCABULARY

across from	near
between	next to
in back of	on the corner of
in front of	

WINDOW ON GRAMMAR

Is there/Are there

THINGS TO DO

1. Learn New Words

★ Ask students to look at the words while you say them or play the tape or CD.

★ Say the words or play the tape or CD a second time. Pause after each word and ask the students to repeat the word.

★ As students listen a third time, pause after each word and have them point to the related picture.

★ Demonstrate the words in random order, and have students say each word. For example, stand next to a student, point to the student and then yourself, indicating the relationship, and elicit that you are *next to* the student.

★ Ask students to write the words under the pictures.

LISTENING SCRIPT

Lesson 2: Learn New Words

Look at the pictures. Listen to the words. Then listen and repeat.

1. next to	The post office is next to the drugstore.
2. between	The laundromat is between the drugstore and the supermarket.
3. across from	The bank is across from the post office.
4. in front of	The bookmobile is in front of the library.
5. near	The school is near the park.
6. in back of	There's a park in back of the library.
7. on the corner of	There's a gas station on the corner of State Street and Main Street.

EXPANSION ACTIVITY: Total Physical Response

★ Invite three volunteers to come to the front of the class.

★ Give instructions that include prepositional phrases from Activity 1: *Monica, please stand next to Patrick. Henry, stand between Dipti and Maria.* Encourage the class to provide help. Note that *on the corner of* cannot be used in this activity.

★ Ask questions about where the students are standing: *Who is standing next to Monica?*

★ Repeat with other groups of students until the entire class has participated.

2. Practice the Conversation

★ Tell students to listen with their books closed. Read the conversation aloud or play the tape or CD.

★ Have students open their books and read the conversation or play the tape or CD a second time. Pause after each line and ask the students to repeat.

★ Model the conversation from the book with a student. Read *A's* line and demonstrate how to substitute a different place for the *post office*. Help the student respond with the correct location information and finish the conversation.

★ Point out that *A* repeats what *B* said as a way to confirm the given information. Explain that this is a common way to confirm what someone has said. Note that the listener only repeats the new, potentially unclear or relevant information, not the whole sentence.

★ Group students in pairs to practice the conversation using different places and locations. Have them ask about all seven places in pictures 1–7. Walk around to make sure they understand the activity, and provide help if needed.

LISTENING SCRIPT

Lesson 2: Practice the Conversation

Listen to the conversation. Then listen and repeat.

A: Excuse me. Where's the post office?
B: It's next to the drugstore.
A: Next to the drugstore?
B: That's right.

EXPANSION ACTIVITY:
What did you say?

★ Recycle the vocabulary from Unit 1, and reinforce confirming information using variations on the conversation in Activity 2.

★ Write the following conversations on the board:

1. A: Where's <u>the teacher</u>?
   B: She's <u>next to the board</u>.
   A: <u>Next to the board?</u>
   B: That's right.

2. A: What's his name?
   B: His name is <u>Michael Landon</u>.
   A: <u>Michael Landon?</u>
   B: That's right.

★ Have students work in pairs and practice the new conversations.

★ When the students are finished, tell them to create their own conversations, replacing the underlined text in each sentence with different information.

---

3. Write

★ Instruct students to look at the map. Tell students to use the information in pictures 1–7 to complete the map. They should write the correct names of the places on the map.

★ Have students check their answers with a partner.

★ Go over the answers with the class.

EXPANSION ACTIVITY:
Listen and Sequence

★ Have students look at their maps in Activity 3.

★ Tell the students that you are going to tell a story. They should write a 1 on the map next to the first place they hear, a 2 next to the second new place they hear, and so on.

★ You can read this story or create your own: *My name is Anna. I am a student. I go to school. Our school is near a park. We go to the library or the bookmobile every week. I live near the school. I go to the post office to mail letters. I go to the bank to get money. I go to the laundromat to wash my clothes. We go to the gas station to get gas for our car.*

★ Go over the answers with the class.

★ ★

 TRY THIS

★ ★

★ Draw an outline of the area around your school or building. Include the street the school is on and at least one block. Include your building and write the name of the building.

★ Tell students to copy the map on a piece of paper, and then ask them to draw in the correct locations of at least five other buildings or places (parks, parking lots, etc.).

★ If appropriate, allow students to go outside and write down the names and locations of services and businesses in the area.

★ Put students in groups of three or four to compare maps.

★ Ask volunteers to draw and identify other buildings and places on the map on the board.

EXPANSION ACTIVITY: Complete the Map

★ Model this activity by drawing a map of the area near your home on the board. Include the streets and blank squares to mark the locations of buildings.

★ Ask volunteers to come to the board and write the names of the places on your map according to the directions you give: *There is a school on the corner of Carmel and Johnson streets. The gas station is next to the school on Carmel Street.*

★ Next, have students make a map of five places near their home or a public place. Tell them to draw the places, but that they shouldn't write the names of the places on the map.

★ Have students work in pairs and exchange maps. Have partner *A* give *B* information about the locations of the places. Partner *B* should write the names of the places on the map. Have them switch roles when one map is complete.

ANSWER KEY:

1. no; 2. yes; 3. yes; 4. yes; 5. no

BIG PICTURE EXPANSION ACTIVITY: READING—A Story about Janet

★ Make copies of Worksheet #3 (p. 243) and distribute them to students.

★ Put the "big picture" color overhead transparency for Unit 2, Lesson 3, on the projector or have students look at the "big picture" in their books.

★ Have students read the story or you can read the story aloud line by line and have students repeat. Ask comprehension questions: *Who is in the story? What is her occupation? Where is she?*

★ Instruct students to answer the questions and check their answers with a partner. Go over the answers with the class.

★ Have students practice asking and answering questions with a partner.

WINDOW ON GRAMMAR: *Is there/Are there*

A. Read the sentences.

★ Read the questions and answers in the chart and have students repeat.

★ Ask students how the question form is different from the statement form. Point out that in the question form, the verb *be* comes before *there*. In the answer form, the form of *be* comes after *there*.

B. Complete the sentences with *Is there* or *Are there*.

★ Go over the first question with the class. Elicit that the question should read, *Is there a supermarket near your home?* Ask several students this question, making sure you get at least one *yes* and one *no* response.

★ Ask students to complete the remaining questions. Go over the answers with the class when they are finished.

★ Have students work in pairs and take turns asking and answering the questions.

ANSWER KEY:

1. Is there; 2. Is there; 3. Are there; 4. Is there; 5. Are there; 6. Are there

Grammar Note:

★ Students can be confused by the structure *there is/there are*. *There* is in the subject position, but the verb *is* or *are* actually agrees with the noun phrase that follows it in a statement.

★ Remind students to look at the noun phrase following the verb *be* to determine whether they should use *is* or *are* as the verb. If the noun is singular, they must use *is*; if the noun is plural, they must use *are*.

EXPANSION ACTIVITY:
Sentence Scramble

★ Ask students to write four questions using *Is there* or *Are there*. They will ask another student these questions.

★ Have students write their questions on index cards or pieces of paper, putting one word on each card so the words in the sentence can be mixed up. Make sure they do not capitalize any of the words.

is	there	a
bank	near	here

★ Have them shuffle the cards for one sentence.

★ Working in pairs, tell students to exchange the cards for one sentence.

★ Instruct them to arrange their partner's cards first as questions, and then as statements.

 Students can do Unit 2, Section 1, *Learn New Words* and Section 2, *Listen and Choose* on the Interactive CD-ROM.

OBJECTIVE

In Town

VOCABULARY

VEHICLES	THINGS	SIGNS
ambulance	ATM	do not enter
bus	bus stop	no left turn
car	crosswalk	no parking
taxi	mailbox	no right turn
truck	parking lot	one way
	pay phone	stop
	sidewalk	
	stoplight	

THINGS TO DO

1. Talk About the Picture

★ Put the "big picture" color overhead transparency for Unit 2, Lesson 3, on the projector or have students look at the "big picture" in their books.

★ To review vocabulary, ask questions about the picture such as, *Where's the library? Is there a restaurant in the picture?*

★ Read the two example sentences aloud. Ask students to point to the places in the picture mentioned in the example sentences.

★ Ask students to write five more sentences about the picture. If necessary, write sentence starters on the board, such as, *There's a _____. There are _____. The library is _____. The restaurant is _____.*

★ Group students in pairs and have one student read his or her sentences while the partner points to the places in the picture. Students should then switch roles and do the exercise again.

★ Call on a few students to read their sentences aloud. Elicit enough sentences to demonstrate all the new vocabulary from this unit so far.

EXPANSION ACTIVITY: What's Wrong with the Sentence?

★ Write an inaccurate sentence on the board about the picture: *There's a library on Market Street.*

★ Ask the students what information in the sentence is wrong—(*The library is on Pine Street, not Market Street*).

★ Ask for a volunteer to come to the board and correct the sentence.

★ Have students write three more inaccurate sentences about the picture and exchange these sentences with a partner. The partner should then correct the sentences.

★ For more practice, have a few students write incorrect sentences on the board. Ask the class to correct the sentences on a separate piece of paper.

2. Learn New Words 🎧

★ Put the "big picture" color overhead transparency for Unit 2, Lesson 3, on the projector or have students look at the "big picture" in their books.

★ Point out that the new words for this unit are in three groups: *Vehicles*, *Things*, and *Signs*.

★ Say the words or play the tape or CD. Have students read along.

★ Say the words or play the tape or CD again. Pause and ask students to repeat and point to the picture of each word as they say it.

★ Point to the items on the transparency or in the book in random order and have the students say the names.

★ Note that *ATM* is an acronym for *automated teller machine*. Explain briefly what an acronym is.

Lesson 3: Learn New Words

Look at the picture. Listen to the words. Then listen and repeat.

1. bus stop	There's a bus stop near the laundromat.
2. parking lot	There's a parking lot next to the supermarket.
3. bus	There's a bus near the bus stop.
4. ambulance	There's an ambulance in front of the hospital.
5. crosswalk	There's a crosswalk near the movie theater.
6. sidewalk	There's a sidewalk in front of the movie theater.
7. mailbox	There's a mailbox in front of the post office.
8. stoplight	There's a stoplight on Main Street.
9. truck	There's a truck on Pine Street.
10. taxi	There's a taxi across from the community center.
11. car	There's a car across from the bookmobile.
12. pay phone	There's a pay phone on the corner of Front Street and Main Street.
13. ATM	There's an ATM next to the bank.
14. stop	
15. no parking	
16. do not enter	
17. no right turn	
18. no left turn	
19. one way	

Culture/Civics Notes:

★ You must be 16 years old to drive in the United States.

★ In most states in the United States, new residents must get a driver's license from that state within a specified time period. Drivers can be ticketed if they are driving with an out-of-state license after that period.

★ Although all communities use the same traffic signs, laws may vary from region to region. For example, in many states a driver can turn right on a red light after stopping, but this rule is not universal. It is important for students to know the particular laws and practices in their communities.

BIG PICTURE EXPANSION ACTIVITY: SPEAKING—Memory Game

★ Tell students to look at the "big picture" in the book or put the color overhead transparency for Unit 2, Lesson 3, on the projector.

★ Divide the class into teams. Have each team create *yes/no* or *wh-* questions about the picture: *Is there a supermarket on Pine Street?* Make sure that each team creates enough questions so that each member can ask at least one question. Encourage students to ask about little details in the picture.

★ Remove the transparency from the projector and have students close their books. Within each team, they should then answer the created questions based on their memory of the picture.

★ Next, each team will ask another team their questions about the picture. Every student should ask one question, and the game should continue until each team has had a chance to ask and answer questions about the picture. Each correct answer earns a point.

★ Small prizes for the winning team will probably increase enthusiasm for the game and the energy level of the class.

3. Practice the Conversation

★ Read the conversation aloud or play the tape or CD.

★ Play the tape or CD or read the conversation a second time. Pause after each line and have students repeat.

★ Ask students to look at the pictures below the conversation. Read *A's* line and demonstrate how to substitute an object from the Learn New Words section. Elicit the correct information from the students.

★ Ask a student to read *B's* line and to substitute information that will correspond with that spoken by *A*.

★ Have students work in pairs and practice the conversation, making appropriate substitutions. Walk around to monitor the activity and provide help as needed.

★ Remind students that not all the new words or phrases can be used in the conversation in Activity 3. Students should notice that the signs are really directions for the driver.

LISTENING SCRIPT

Lesson 3: Read the Conversation

Listen to the conversation. Then listen and repeat.

A: Excuse me. Is there a mailbox around here?
B: Yes, there is. There's one on Pine Street. It's in front of the post office.
A: Thanks a lot.

**EXPANSION ACTIVITY:
Sentence Sequencing**

★ Break up the conversation from Activity 3 and write it on strips of paper as indicated below. (*Note:* You can break up the conversation in a way that fits your class size by creating larger or smaller conversation segments on each strip of paper.)

★ Have students look at the conversation again and tell them to try and memorize as much of it as they can.

Excuse me	Is there a mailbox
around here?	Yes, there is.
There's one	on Pine Street.
It's in front	of the library.
Thanks a lot.	

★ Ask for volunteers and give one card or strip of paper to each volunteer. Ask them to memorize their parts.

★ Ask those students to walk around and say their parts to each other and then put themselves in the correct order according to the conversation.

★ Have them say the conversation aloud, with each student reading his or her own portion.

★ Repeat with a new group of students until everyone in class has had the opportunity to participate.

 Students can do Unit 2, Section 2, *Listen and Choose* and Section 4, *Fun and Games* on the Interactive CD-ROM.

OBJECTIVE

Reading a U.S. Map

VOCABULARY

capital	north of	west of
east of	south of	

WINDOW ON MATH

Reading Math Symbols

THINGS TO DO

1. Talk About the Picture

★ Tell students to look at the map. To help them become familiar with the places on the map, ask questions such as, *Where is California? Where is our state?*

★ Ask students to name their city and state. Remind them that the city is *in* the state; the state is the larger geographic entity.

★ Go over item *a* together. Then have students answer questions *b* through *d*. Go over the answers.

★ Ask the students to write three questions about places on the map.

★ Group students in pairs and instruct them to take turns asking and answering questions about the map.

ANSWER KEY:

a. Alabama and Georgia; b. Oregon, Nevada, Arizona; c. New Mexico; d. Georgia

EXPANSION ACTIVITY: World Map

★ Have students look at a world map and ask them questions about countries: *What countries are next to France? What country is between China and India? What is the capital of Bolivia?*

★ Have each student create three questions about countries, and then have them take turns asking and answering the questions in pairs.

2. Learn New Words 🎧

★ Point to the compass rose. Show students that on a map, *north* points to the top of the paper, *south* to the bottom, *east* to the right and *west* to the left.

★ Say the words or play the tape or CD.

★ Say the words or play the tape or CD again. Pause and have students repeat and point to the words in their books.

★ Give students a couple of examples using the new words: *Oregon is north of California. Washington, D.C. is the capital of the United States.*

★ Have students look at the map and complete the sentences using the new words.

★ Go over the answers with the class.

LISTENING SCRIPT

Lesson 4: Learn New Words

Look at the map. Listen to the words. Then listen and repeat.

1. capital	The capital of Florida is Tallahassee.
2. north of	New York is north of Pennsylvania.
3. south of	Texas is south of Oklahoma.
4. east of	Texas is east of New Mexico.
5. west of	Arizona is west of New Mexico.

ANSWER KEY:

1. capital; 2. north; 3. south; 4. east; 5. west

EXPANSION ACTIVITY: Community Map

★ Bring in maps of your city and/or state. You can go to a travel agent for maps or go online and print a map. Make enough copies for all the students.

★ Have students look at the map scale. Ask, *How many miles is it between our city and the state capital? Is the capital north of our city?*

★ Tell students to write five more questions about relationships between places on the map. Then have them ask a partner their questions. Make sure they use the new vocabulary from Activity 2.

★ Ask volunteers to read their questions and instruct the class to answer the questions.

3. Read

★ Have students read the paragraphs and insert the correct states in the blank spaces.

★ To reinforce emerging literacy skills, read each sentence aloud and have students repeat. Ask volunteers to read the whole paragraph aloud and instruct students to underline the new words from Activity 2.

★ Have students check their answers with a partner. Go over the answers with the class.

ANSWER KEY:

1. Tennessee; 2. Colorado

EXPANSION ACTIVITY: 20 Questions

★ Explain that the class is going to play a game. In this game, the students will ask *yes/no* questions to try to guess the name of a state.

★ Demonstrate the activity. First, select a state but don't tell students the name of the state. Then provide examples of *yes/no* questions that the students could ask to identify that state. *Is it in the east? Is it north of Texas? Is it between Florida and Maine? Is it next to Canada?* Tell them the name of the state.

★ Choose another state for the actual game, and call on students to ask questions. Have them guess which state you have chosen.

★ Ask a volunteer to choose a state and answer questions about that state. Have them whisper the name of the state to you so you can monitor accuracy and provide help if needed.

★ Have the other students ask *yes/no* questions until they guess the name of the state or until they've asked 20 questions, whichever comes first.

★ Repeat with other volunteers and different states.

Culture/Civics Notes:

★ Point out that most people in the United States have cars. Because travel between cities is often by car rather than train or bus, people use road maps frequently.

★ Mileage between cities or exits on a highway is usually shown on a road map. Drivers often have to add the mileage between exits to determine travel distance.

EXPANSION ACTIVITY: Write about a City

★ Have students work in pairs to write about a city.

★ Use the following model: *This city is about _____ miles from here. This city is in the country of _____. It's in the state of _____. It is north of _____ and south of _____. What city is it?*

★ An alternative is to have them write about a state or a country.

WINDOW ON MATH: Reading Math Symbols

A. Read the symbols. 🎧

★ Copy the symbols on the board.

+ plus	− minus	= equals
> is more than		< is less than

★ Point to each symbol and say the name or play the tape or CD. Have students repeat.

★ Demonstrate the meaning of the symbols with classroom objects. For example, take three pencils in your right hand and ask students how many you are holding. Then, take three pencils in your left hand and ask the same question. Tell students that 3 plus 3 equals 6 and write $3 + 3 = 6$ on the board. Put one more pencil in your right hand and say 4 is more than 3. Write $4 > 3$ next to the > sign. Demonstrate the meanings of the remaining signs using similar images and examples.

B. Read the sentences.

★ Read the sentences aloud and have students repeat.

★ Ask individual students to read the sentences as well.

C. Add the missing symbols.

★ Ask the students to read example 1 aloud: $5 + 1 = 6$

★ Tell students to write in the missing symbols for the other equations and then check their answers with a partner.

★ Go over the answers with the class. Have different students read the sentences aloud.

ANSWER KEY:

1. $5 + 1 = 6$
2. $3 + 2 = 5$
3. $7 > 3$
4. $2 < 4$
5. $1 − 1 = 0$
6. $4 + 2 = 6$

EXPANSION ACTIVITY: Word Problems

★ Using a local map, write simple word problems on the board. See examples below:

Monticello, Georgia is between Jackson and Eatonton. It is 21 miles from Monticello to Eatonton. It is 16 miles from Monticello to Jackson. How many miles is it from Jackson to Eatonton? Answer: $21 + 16 = 37$

Lafayette is between Lake Charles and Baton Rouge. It is 60 miles from Lafayette to Baton Rouge. It is 72 miles from Lafayette to Lake Charles. How many miles is it from Lake Charles to Baton Rouge? Answer: $60 + 72 = 132$

★ Have students write down and solve the equations you create.

★ Have students create their own word problems using state or local road maps. Each student should create three of their own word problems.

★ You can introduce the concept of *and back*. Say, *It is 16 miles from Monticello to Jackson. How many miles is it from Monticello to Jackson and back?* (32)

★ Have students create their own word problems using *and back*.

 Students can do Unit 2, Section 3, *Read and Write* and Section 4, *Fun and Games* on the Interactive CD-ROM.

┌┄ **LISTENING SCRIPT** ┄┐

Lesson 4: Window on Math—
Reading Math Symbols

A. Listen to the symbols.

+ plus (and)   = equals   > is less than
− minus   < is more than

OBJECTIVE

Asking for Locations

WINDOW ON PRONUNCIATION

Voiced and voiceless *th* sound

1. Practice the Conversation: Asking for Repetition 🎧

★ Have students look at the picture for Activity 1. Ask questions such as, *Who is in the picture? Where are they?*

★ Read the conversation aloud or play the tape or CD.

★ Play the tape or CD or read the conversation a second time. Pause after each line and have students repeat.

★ Ask comprehension questions such as, *What are they looking for? Where is Zorro's Pizzeria?*

★ Point out that there are different ways to ask for repetition: *Excuse me? I'm sorry? What was that?* or *Please say that again*. Say each of these phrases and have students repeat.

★ Model the conversation with a student. Have the student read *A's* lines. Demonstrate how to substitute one of the other ways to ask for repetition.

★ Have students work in pairs to practice the conversation and use the different ways to ask for repetition. Walk around to monitor the activity and provide help as needed.

LISTENING SCRIPT

Lesson 5: Practice the Conversation— Asking for Repetition

Listen to the conversation. Then listen and repeat.

A: Is there a restaurant near here?
B: Excuse me?
A: Is there a restaurant near here?
B: Yes, there is. There's one on Pine.
A: Thanks.

Listen to the new expressions. Listen and repeat.

I'm sorry. What was that?
Please say that again.
What was that?

EXPANSION ACTIVITY: What's Near the School?

★ Instruct students to create their own conversations about places near the school.

★ First, have the class brainstorm places they might ask about: *library*, *supermarket*, *bookstore*. Remind them that they need to know the location of the place they use in the conversation.

★ Have students work in pairs and create a conversation. Walk around the room to provide help as needed.

★ Ask some students to role-play the conversation in front of the class.

---

2. Practice the Conversation: Saying You Don't Know

★ Repeat the basic procedure from Activity 1.

★ To set the context, have students look at the picture, asking them, *Who is in the picture? Where are they?*

★ To check comprehension, ask, *What is the woman looking for? Does the man know where the drugstore is?*

★ Point out that when we don't know where some place is, we can say, *I'm not sure. Sorry. I don't know.* or *Sorry, I'm new in town*.

★ Have students work in pairs to practice the conversation and use the different ways of expressing lack of knowledge. Walk around to monitor the activity and provide help as needed.

LISTENING SCRIPT

Lesson 5: Practice the Conversation—
Saying You Don't Know

Listen to the conversation. Then listen and repeat.

A: Excuse me. Is there a drugstore near here?
B: I'm not sure.
A: Okay. Thanks anyway.

Listen to the new words and expressions. Listen and repeat.

Sorry, I don't know.
Sorry, I'm new in town.
Sorry, I'm not sure.

EXPANSION ACTIVITY: Dictation

★ Tell students that you are going to read or dictate a conversation similar to the one in Activity 2.

★ Tell them you will read everything three times. They should write down the sentences.

★ Use the following conversation or create your own. Pause after each line.

   A: Excuse me. Is there a hospital near here?
   B: I don't know.
   A: Okay. Thanks anyway.

---

3. Practice the Conversation: Asking a Follow-Up Question 🎧

★ Repeat the basic procedure from Activity 1.

★ To set the context, have students look at the picture and ask, *What are they looking at? Why do you think they are looking at the map?*

★ To check comprehension, ask, *What are they trying to find out? Is Sacramento in the north or south of California?*

★ Group students in pairs to practice the conversation and use different types of follow-up questions. Walk around to monitor the activity and provide help as needed.

LISTENING SCRIPT

Lesson 5: Practice the Conversation—
Asking a Follow-Up Question

Listen to the conversation. Then listen and repeat.

A: Where's Sacramento?
B: It's in California.
A: In the north or the south of the state?
B: In the north.

Listen and repeat.

Atlanta	Florida
Georgia	Lansing
Tallahassee	Michigan

EXPANSION ACTIVITY: Team Challenge

★ Instruct each student to create two questions about a city like those in Activity 3: *Where's Boston? In the east or in the west of the United States?*

★ Divide the class into teams. Tell each team member to read their two questions and have the other team members guess the answer.

★ Ask a member of one team to then read their questions to another team. If the answers to both questions are correct, the team answering the questions earns a point.

★ Continue the game until everyone has had a chance to ask and answer questions about a place.

★ The team with the most points wins.

Pronunciation Expansion:
Voiced and Voiceless *TH* Sound

★ Write *th-* on the board as the heading for each of two columns. Write *thanks* in one column and *the* in the other column.

Th-	Th-
thanks	the

★ Demonstrate how the voiceless *th* sound in *thanks* is made: Put your tongue between your teeth and blow out. Have students do the same. Have them put their hands on their throats and form the *th* sound without using their voices. Explain that they shouldn't feel vibrations in their throats. Write *voiceless* next to the *Th* in the first column.

★ Tell students to form the *th* sound in *the* using their voices. Their tongues should be sticking out between their teeth, and make sure they feel the vibrations in their throats when they make the sound. Write *voiced* next to the *Th* in the second column.

WINDOW ON PRONUNCIATION: Voiced and Voiceless *Th* Sounds

A. Listen to the words. 🎧

★ Read the words or play the tape or CD.

★ Play the tape or CD or read the words a second time. Pause and have students repeat.

★ Play the tape or CD or read the words a third time. Have students underline the voiced *th* sound in the words as they listen.

★ Tell students to write the words from the first part of Exercise A in the correct place in the chart and then check their answers with a partner.

★ Go over the answers with the class and complete the chart on the board or have two students complete the chart.

LISTENING SCRIPT

Lesson 5: Window on Pronunciation—Voiced and Voiceless *Th* Sounds

Listen to the words. Then listen and repeat.

1. thanks	7. three
2. then	8. this
3. there	9. the
4. third	10. north
5. theater	11. they
6. that	12. south

ANSWER KEY:

Th sounds like *thanks*	*Th* sounds like *the*
1. thanks 6. birth	1. the
2. third 7. south	2. then
3. theater	3. there
4. three	4. that
5. north	5. this

B. Work with a partner. Ask and answer the questions.

★ Read the questions aloud and have students repeat.

★ Have students work in pairs and take turns asking and answering the questions. Explain that all the answers will include a *th* sound.

★ Go over the answers with the class, focusing on voiced or voiceless *th* sounds.

ANSWER KEY:

1. three; 2. Yes, there is/no, there isn't.
3. north; 4. south; 5. the theater is _____

📽 BIG PICTURE EXPANSION ACTIVITY: GRAMMAR—*There is/There are*

★ Make copies of Worksheet #4 (p. 244) and distribute them to students.

★ Put the "big picture" color overhead transparency for Unit 2, Lesson 3, on the projector or have students look at the "big picture" in their books.

★ Instruct students to read and answer the questions and then check their answers with a partner.

★ Go over the answers with the class.

ANSWER KEY:

A. 1. B; 2. A; 3. B; 4. A; 5. B;
B. 1. is; 2. is; 3. are. 4. are; 5. are

 Students can do Unit 2, Section 2, *Listen and Choose* on the Interactive CD-ROM.

EQUIPPED FOR THE FUTURE ROLE

Community

OBJECTIVE

Using Library Services

VOCABULARY

audiobooks	library card
checkout desk	magazines
children's books	videos
librarian	

THINGS TO DO

1. Learn New Words 🎧

★ Have students look at the pictures. Ask, *Where is this? Do you go to the library?* Ask students to name the things they know in the pictures: *books, people, computers, etc.*

★ Say the words or play the tape or CD.

★ Say the words or play the tape or CD a second time. Pause after each word and ask the students to repeat the word and point to the correct picture.

★ Have students write each word next to the correct picture.

★ Read the sentences in each picture about library procedures and have the students repeat. Then have students work in pairs and take turns asking and answering the questions about the library.

LISTENING SCRIPT

Lesson 6: Learn New Words

Look at the pictures. Listen to the words. Then listen and repeat.

1. librarian	Where's the librarian?
2. checkout desk	Where's the checkout desk?
3. library card	Where's your library card?
4. magazines	Where are the magazines?
5. audiobooks	Where are the audiobooks?
6. videos	Where are the videos?
7. children's books	Where are the children's books?

Culture/Civics Notes:

★ Most libraries require some proof of address —a utility bill, for example—before they will issue you a card. Others require applicants to write their address on an envelope, and the library sends the new card in the mail.

★ Library cards are usually free, but many libraries charge a fee to replace a lost or stolen card.

★ Many libraries have free story-telling programs for children and some offer bilingual story hours. Many libraries also offer continuing education programs for adults, including computer classes.

Pronunciation Notes:

★ Items in a series, except for the final item, are read with constant or continuous intonation. The final item receives falling intonation. An example of this is the answer to the question: *What can I take out from the library?* The answer contains a list: *books, magazines, books on tape, and videos.*

★ Instruct students to practice reading the list of items with the appropriate intonation.

EXPANSION ACTIVITY: Alphabetical Order

★ Remind students that in some sections of the library, the books are kept in alphabetical order according to the author's last name, so it's important to review and understand alphabetizing words.

★ Ask students to write their names on the board, last name first, with a comma in between their first and last names: *West, Michael.*

★ Working with a partner, have students alphabetize the names. Cue them if necessary by asking, *Do any of the names begin with A? with B?* and so on.

★ Remind them that if two last names are the same, they should use the first name to alphabetize.

2. Write

★ Go over the directions and the information asked for in the application. Tell students that this application asks for information common to most libraries.

★ Ask students to complete the sample library card application form.

★ Have them go over the information with a partner and compare answers.

**EXPANSION ACTIVITY:
Completing a Real Application**

★ Pick up library card applications for your students or have the students each pick one up from their local library.

★ Instruct the students to complete the applications. They can drop the application forms off at their local libraries if they don't yet have cards.

★ ★

 **TRY THIS**

★ ★

★ Go to the library on a field trip or have students do this as an out-of-class assignment.

★ Have them write five things they see in the library.

★ When students have returned from the library, ask them to tell the class about five things they saw during their visit.

1. Listening Review 🎧

★ Go over the directions with the class.

★ Read the items or play the tape or CD, and have the students mark their answers in the Answer Sheet.

★ Walk around to monitor activity and help students stay on task.

★ Tell students to check their answers with a partner.

★ Go over the answers with the class.

LISTENING SCRIPT

Lesson 7: Listening Review

Listen and choose the correct place. Use the Answer Sheet.

1. What's next to the gas station?
2. What's across from the police station?
3. What's between the library and the hospital?
4. What's on the corner of Main Street and Pine Street?
5. What's west of the bank?
6. What's north of the supermarket?

ANSWER KEY:

1. A; 2. C; 3. A; 4. B; 5. B; 6. A

2. Dictation 🎧

TESTING FOCUS: Dictation Strategies

★ Tell students that because they will hear the following conversations three times, they can focus on something different each time they listen. Explain that the first time, they should just listen for the meaning and not write anything down. The second time they should write down what they hear. The third time they should add to or correct their sentences as they listen.

★ Instruct students to look at the three conversations. Tell them again that they will hear each conversation three times. Remind them to keep the dictation strategies in mind as they listen.

★ Have them read the partial conversations before they listen so they know what information to listen for.

★ Read the conversations or play the tape or CD three times.

★ Tell the students to write in the missing words. Go over the answers.

LISTENING SCRIPT

Lesson 7: Dictation

Listen and write the words you hear.

1. A: Excuse me. Where's the post office?
   B: It's on Front Street.
2. A: Excuse me. Is there a mailbox near here?
   B: Yes, there is. It's in front of the library.
3. A: What's the capital of New Mexico?
   B: I'm not sure.

3. Conversation Check: Pair Work

★ Go over the directions. Have students work in pairs and remind them that each partner has some information, but that other information is missing. They must ask their partners questions to complete their charts.

★ Walk around to monitor the activity and provide help as needed.

Assessment Note:
★ You can use the Conversation Check Activity as an oral assessment. Ask pairs of students to complete the activity while you note areas of difficulty.

LEARNING LOG

★ Point out the four sections of the *Learning Log*: *I know these words*, *I can ask*, *I can say*, and *I can write*.

★ Have students check what they know and what they can do.

★ Walk around to note what they don't know or can't do. Use this information to review areas of difficulty.

BIG PICTURE EXPANSION ACTIVITY: WRITING—Describing the Town

★ Put the "big picture" color overhead transparency for Unit 2, Lesson 3, on the projector or have students look at the "big picture" in their books.

★ Ask questions about the picture: *Where's the post office? Where is Gould's Drugstore? Is the police station near the library?*

★ Instruct students to write 3–5 sentences about the picture, describing where places are. Have students read their sentences to a partner.

★ Ask a few volunteers to read their sentences to the class.

BIG PICTURE EXPANSION ACTIVITY: SPEAKING Assessment—Talking about the Big Picture

★ You can use the "big picture" in Lesson 3 to assess placement in open-entry classes, to diagnose difficulties, or to measure progress.

★ Work with one student at a time. Show the "big picture" to the student and say, *What do you see in the picture?* or, *Tell me about the picture.* Instruct the student to speak for as long as possible. Wait a moment for the student to prepare to answer. If the student has difficulty, you can use prompts: *What buildings do you see in the picture? What streets do you see? Who do you see?*

★ You can use a rubric like the one below to rate beginning speakers.

3	Uses sentences, although form may be incorrect Can speak for sustained length of time Responds to prompts, but doesn't need them to begin speaking
2	Can use nouns and verbs Uses phrases Answers informational questions
1	Can name objects Uses single words Can answer yes/no questions
0	Cannot say anything independently May be able to point to objects when prompted

TEACHER'S NOTES:

Things that students are doing well:

_____

_____

_____

_____

_____

Things students need additional help with:

_____

_____

_____

_____

_____

_____

_____

Ideas for further practice or for the next class:

_____

_____

_____

_____

_____

 Students can do Unit 2, Section 5, *Practice Test* on the Interactive CD-ROM.

OBJECTIVE

Writing Stories

FOCUS ON WRITING

Punctuation Marks

1. Read stories A and B.

★ Ask students to look at the pictures and identify the names of things they know. Write the names of the objects and the actions they can identify on the board.

★ Have students read stories A and B. Alternatively, read them aloud, pausing after each line to have students repeat.

★ Instruct students to look at the two columns at the top of the page. Ask them to find all the words in the paragraphs that begin with *C* and *R* and to write each under the correct heading. Have students check their answers with a partner. Go over the answers with the class.

★ Discuss the paragraphs. Ask comprehension questions such as, *Who is Story A about? What does she like to do? Where is she from?* Ask similar questions about Story B.

LISTENING SCRIPT

Spotlight: Writing—Stories

Listen and write the words you hear.

A: Hi! My name is Carol. I'm from Colorado. I like to read, talk on the telephone, and go to the movies. I don't like to watch TV.

B: My name is David. I'm from Reno, Nevada. I like to drive my car, listen to the radio, and go to parties. I don't like to clean my room.

ANSWER KEY:

C: Carol, Colorado, car, clean
R: read, Reno, radio, room

2. Correct the story.

★ Instruct students to look at the *Focus on Writing* box. Read the rules aloud.

★ Write the examples on the board. Point out the periods used at the end of the two sentences and the commas between the words in a series.

★ Have students read the paragraph and correct it by adding five punctuation marks. Remind them to look at stories A and B if they need a model.

★ Walk around to monitor student progress and provide help as needed.

★ Go over the answers with the class.

ANSWER KEY:

My name is Ann. I like to watch TV, read books, and go to school. I don't like to go to the supermarket.

3. Complete the chart about you.

★ Ask students to look at the pictures in the circles and name the activities they see: *dance, relax, eat, wash dishes, go to the dentist.*

★ Copy the chart on the board. Model the activity with information about something you like. For example, nod your head and say, *I like to dance.* Write that activity under *I like to.* Then model talking about something you don't like. Shake your head and say, *I don't like to wash dishes.* Write that activity under the heading *I don't like to.*

★ Help students brainstorm other activities they may like or dislike doing and write them on the board: *cook, study, work, listen to music, go to the library, eat at a restaurant, etc.*

★ Tell students to complete the chart with their own information and then share the information with a partner. Walk around the room to monitor the activity and provide help as needed.

★ Have a few volunteers read their lists, practicing the pronunciation focus mentioned earlier—intonation of words in lists remains constant except for the last word of the list, which falls.

4. Write your own story.

★ Have students look at the lined area and tell them they will write their own stories in that space.

★ Remind students to look at stories A and B and the chart in Activity 3 to write their own stories. Walk around to monitor the activity and provide help as needed.

★ Have students draw a picture that shows what they like to do in the space on the right.

★ Ask a few volunteers to read their stories to the class.

**EXPANSION ACTIVITY:
Interview a Partner**

★ Use the list of activities that you brainstormed in Activity 3, or elicit suggestions from the students again. Write them on the board.

★ Write the question on the board: *Do you like to _____?*

★ Tell students that they are going to interview a partner. Model the activity with a student. First, ask questions using the form on the board and some of the activity ideas: *Do you like to dance? Do you like to eat in a restaurant? Do you like to drive?* Write a few sentences on the board based on the interview. *Laura likes to dance and eat in restaurants. She doesn't like to drive. She doesn't have a driver's license.*

★ Have students work in pairs and take turns interviewing each other. Have each of them write a story about their partner that describes the other person but doesn't include a name.

★ Collect the stories and read them aloud. Have the class guess who is being described in the story.

EQUIPPED FOR THE FUTURE ROLE

Family

OBJECTIVE

Reading School Maps

VOCABULARY

cafeteria
gym
main office
nurse's office
playground

Culture/Civics Notes:
★ Students who are new to this culture may not know about transportation options for public schools. In most communities, children can take a school bus to and from school. Sometimes parents drive the children to school, and sometimes children walk.
★ Small children should be accompanied to and from the bus stop every day.
★ Parents who drive children to school are usually given a map and instructions on exactly where in front of the school to drop off and pick up their children.

A. Learn new words.

★ Say the new words aloud while students read them in their books. Say the words a second time, pausing after each to have students repeat.
★ Tell students that this is the kind of map that parents sometimes get from their children's school.
★ Instruct students to circle the new words on the map.
★ Go over the meanings of the new words.

B. Complete the sentences.

★ Read the words in the box aloud and have students repeat.
★ Tell students to complete the sentences using the words in the box. Explain that each word or phrase should be used only once. Although

more than one answer may be possible, have them choose the best response.
★ Go over the answers with the class.
★ Remind students to keep track of their answers in the self-correct box following the exercise.

ANSWER KEY:

1. near/in front of; 2. next to; 3. in front of/next to; 4. across from; 5. between

C. Match the questions and answers.

★ For extra practice with reading and pronunciation, read each question aloud. Then read the questions again, pausing after each to have students repeat. Next, read each answer aloud. Then read them again, pausing to have students repeat.
★ Go over the example. Read question 1 aloud. Look at the map and locate the nurses office. Point out to students that they should write the letter of the correct response on the line next to the question.
★ Ask students to finish the exercise.
★ Go over the answers with the class.
★ Have students take turns asking and answering the questions with a partner.

ANSWER KEY:

1. F; 2. B; 3. E; 4. C; 5. D; 6. A

D. Answer the questions.

★ Go over the example. Read the question and have students read the response.
★ Have students answer the questions. Remind them that some of the answers may be found in Exercise C.
★ Go over the answers with the class.
★ Have students work in pairs, taking turns asking and answering the questions.

ANSWER KEY:
(More than one answer may be correct.)

1. It's near the gym.
2. It's in front of the cafeteria.
3. It's between the cafeteria and the main office.
4. It's next to the nurse's office.
5. It's in front of the gym.
6. It's across from the nurse's office.

E. Check *yes* or *no* about the picture.

★ Read the sentences. Pause after each one and have students repeat.

★ Read the first sentence in a questioning tone. Elicit the response *yes*. Have students check the box next to *yes*.

★ Have the students check *yes* or *no* in response to the other sentences.

★ Go over the answers with the class.

ANSWER KEY:

1. yes; 2. no; 3. yes; 4. no; 5. no

 Take It Outside

★ Have students interview someone they know. If you do this in class, they can ask a classmate. If they do this as an out-of-class assignment, have them ask anyone who has a child in school.

★ Read the questions and pause after each to have students repeat.

★ When they have completed the interview, ask a few students to share their answers with the class.

EXPANSION ACTIVITY:
Is It True or False?

★ Divide the class into two teams. Have each team write ten sentences about your school. Five of them should be correct and five should be incorrect.

★ Have the teams to take turns reading sentences. The opposing team should determine if each sentence is true or false and respond with *yes* or *no*. Each correct answer earns a point.

★ Small prizes for the winning team will probably raise the energy level in class and increase enthusiasm for the game.

EQUIPPED FOR THE FUTURE ROLE

Work

OBJECTIVE

Completing Mileage Logs

VOCABULARY

drive/drives   odometer
mileage log   work/works

Culture/Civics Note:

★ Students may be unfamiliar with mileage logs. Explain that mileage logs are used for regularly scheduled maintenance, which makes sure a vehicle is kept in good condition by regularly changing parts and fluids. They are also used for reimbursement—employees who use their own cars on work-related trips sometimes get money to pay for gas.

A. Learn new words.

★ Say the new words aloud, then say them a second time, pausing after each to have students repeat.

★ For extra practice with reading and pronunciation, read the story aloud. Pause after each sentence and have students repeat.

★ Tell students to circle the new words on the map. Walk around to monitor the activity and provide help as needed.

★ Ask comprehension questions such as, *What is Marco's last name? What is the name of the school?* This will prepare students to complete Activities B and C.

B. Complete the sentences.

★ Go over the directions.

★ Read the first item and elicit that Marco is a bus driver. Instruct the students to write *bus driver* on the line provided.

★ Tell students to complete the other sentences and check their answers with a partner.

★ Go over the answers with the class.

ANSWER KEY:

1. a bus driver; 2. Hoover Elementary School;
3. mileage log; 4. cities/gas station;
5. Highway 321

C. Answer questions about Marco.

★ Draw part of a dashboard from a car on the board, making sure to include the speedometer and odometer. Point to the odometer and explain to students that it records how many miles the car has gone.

★ Ask students to look at the mileage log. Point to the headings and elicit the kind of information that is contained in the log: *date; destination/reason for travel; starting odometer; ending odometer; miles; driver.* Go over each term.

★ Ask comprehension questions such as, *What is the date? How many miles is it to Locke and back?* Make sure students understand the concept of *to a place and back.*

★ Ask the first question: *What is Marco's occupation?* Elicit the answer *bus driver.* Have students write the answer on the line. Note that students may also write a complete sentence: *Marco is a bus driver.* Have students answer the remaining questions.

★ Go over the answers.

★ Group students in pairs, and have them take turns asking and answering the questions.

ANSWER KEY:

1. bus driver; 2. Hoover Elementary School; 3. 3.0; 4. 10; 5. Santori; 6. Highway 321, in Washington

D. Complete the table with information about where you go today.

★ Copy the table on the board.

★ Read the directions and go over the example.

★ Model the activity with information about you. For example, tell the students that you go from home to school and back home, and then write in the number of miles on the board. Then write one other place that you go to and write the mileage on the board.

★ Have students complete the table for themselves. Walk around to monitor the activity and provide help as needed.

★ Call on a few students to talk about their chart.

E. Answer the questions.

★ Ask the students to answer the questions. Remind them that the information is in the table above.

F. Write a story about yourself.

★ Copy the story on the board, filling in the blanks with information about yourself.

★ Have students complete the story, including information about themselves. Walk around to monitor the activity and provide help as needed.

★ Call on a few students to read their stories to the class.

📁 Take It Outside

★ Ask students who have a job if their workplace has a mileage log. If you have students who work at a place with mileage logs, ask them to bring in a copy. Alternatively, have students copy the table in Activity D on a piece of paper.

★ Read the questions, pausing after each to have students repeat.

★ Instruct students to interview someone they know using the questions they practiced. If you do this in class, they can interview a classmate.

★ Afterward, tell the students to complete the table (or real mileage log) with the information from the interview.

★ Call on a few students to talk about the person they interviewed.

EXPANSION ACTIVITY: Word Problem

★ Copy the following mileage log on the board.

MILEAGE LOG					
Date	Destination /reason	Starting Odometer	Ending Odometer	Miles	Driver
		150			

★ Copy the story on a transparency and put the sheet on the overhead projector, but don't turn the machine on yet.

★ Read the story below two times and have students fill in the mileage log as they listen.

Today is October 5. Cindy McCarthy goes to the supermarket and back. It is 15 miles. Cindy goes to the gas station and back. It is 8 miles. She goes to school and back. It is 16 miles.

★ Put the story on the overhead projector, or write it on the board. Have students check the mileage log they completed.

★ Ask volunteers to write the information in the table on the board.

ANSWER KEY:

MILEAGE LOG					
Date	Destination /reason	Starting Odometer	Ending Odometer	Miles	Driver
10/5	Supermarket and back	150	165	15	Cindy McCarthy
10/5	Gas Station and back	165	173	8	Cindy McCarthy
10/5	School and back	173	199	16	Cindy McCarthy

UNIT 3 Time and Money

UNIT OVERVIEW

LESSON	OBJECTIVE	STUDENT BOOK PAGE #
1. What time is it?	Telling Time	p. 36
2. Is the library open on Monday?	At the Library	p. 38
3. It's five cents.	Counting Money	p. 40
4. Checks	Reading and Writing Checks	p. 42
5. Thank you for calling.	Making Phone Calls	p. 44
6. Business Hours	Reading Time Schedules	p. 46
7. What do you know?	Review and Assessment	p. 48
8. Spotlight	Grammar	p. 50

Big Picture Expansion Activities

FOCUS	TITLE	SUGGESTED USE
Speaking	Asking about the Hours	Lesson 5
Reading	Pablo and his Son	Lesson 2
Grammar	Questions and Answers about the Library	Lesson 3
Writing	Writing about the Library	Lesson 7
Speaking	Assessment: Talking about the Picture	Lesson 7

Big Picture Expansion Activity Worksheets

WORKSHEET #/FOCUS	TITLE	TEACHER'S EDITION PAGE #
5. Reading	Pablo and his Son	p. 245
6. Grammar	Questions and Answers about the Library	p. 246

OBJECTIVE

Telling Time

VOCABULARY

twelve	after
thirteen	at night
fourteen	before
fifteen	in the afternoon
sixteen	in the evening
seventeen	in the morning
eighteen	midnight
nineteen	minutes
twenty	noon
twenty-one	six o'clock
twenty-two	9:00 A.M.
thirty	9:00 P.M.
thirty-one	
thirty-two	
forty	
fifty	

WINDOW ON GRAMMAR

Yes/ No Questions with *Be*

THINGS TO DO

1. Learn Numbers 🎧

★ Ask students to listen and look at the numbers while you say them or play the tape or CD.

★ Say the numbers or play the tape or CD a second time. Pause after each number and ask the students to repeat and point to the number.

★ Write other numbers on the board and ask students to say the numbers and write them as words: *twenty-one, thirty-one, forty-one, fifty-one, twenty-seven, thirty-seven, forty-seven, fifty-seven, twenty-six, thirty-five, forty-two, fifty-three.*

```
21, 31, 41, 51
27, 37, 47, 57
26, 35, 42, 53
```

★ Go over the answers with the class. Make sure students see the pattern—that a number between one and nine is added to twenty, thirty, etc., after a hyphen to create symbols or words with different numerical values.

LISTENING SCRIPT

Lesson 1: Learn Numbers

Listen to the numbers. Then listen and repeat.

twelve	twenty
thirteen	twenty-one
fourteen	thirty
fifteen	thirty-one
sixteen	thirty-five
seventeen	forty
eighteen	fifty
nineteen	

2. Learn New Words 🎧

★ Have students look at the pictures. Ask what they see in the pictures: *clocks, a man in a park, a man sleeping, people in a cafeteria.*

★ Have students listen and look at the new words while you say the words or play the tape or CD.

★ Say the words or play the tape or CD a second time. Pause after each word or phrase and ask the students to repeat and point to the picture that reflects the word or words.

★ Walk around the classroom with the book open. Point to the pictures in random order and have students say the word or phrase that goes with each picture.

★ Have them write the word or phrase under the appropriate picture.

LISTENING SCRIPT

Lesson 1: Learn New Words

Look at the pictures. Listen to the words. Then listen and repeat.

Times
1. six o'clock   It's six o'clock.
2. noon   It's noon.
3. midnight   It's midnight.
4. 9:00 A.M.   It's 9:00 A.M.
5. 9:00 P.M.   It's 9:00 P.M.

Time of Day
6. in the morning   It's eight o'clock in the morning.
7. in the afternoon   It's 2:15 in the afternoon.
8. in the evening   It's 7:30 in the evening.
9. at night   It's 11:45 at night.

Other Words
10. before   It's ten before three.
11. after   It's ten after three.
12. minutes   It's fifteen minutes after four.

Language Notes:

★ Only two times on the clock have special names: noon and midnight.

★ *O'clock* is only used when the minute hand is on twelve. We do not say: *It is five before two o'clock.*

★ We use other expressions to talk about time: *It's half past five. It's a quarter to one.* But it's not important to teach those expressions in this lesson.

★ *Before* is usually used when the minute hand is between the six and the twelve, or for times that are less than a half an hour before the next hour. *After* is usually used when the minute hand is after twelve and before six, or for times that are less than half an hour after the hour.

EXPANSION ACTIVITY: Beanbag Toss

★ Make sure students understand what times are considered *in the morning, in the afternoon, in the evening,* and *at night.*

★ Explain that you are going to toss the beanbag to a student and say a time. They will have to respond with the part of the day in which that time exists. For example, if you say *9 A.M.,* the student should say *in the morning.*

★ Continue tossing the beanbag until all students have had a chance to respond. Remember to use *A.M.* and *P.M.* in your times.

---

3. Practice the Conversation 🎧

★ Have students listen to and read the conversation while you read it or play the tape or CD.

★ Say the conversation or play the tape or CD a second time. Pause after each line and ask the students to repeat.

★ Have the class read *A's* lines and you read *B's* lines. Demonstrate how to substitute a different time for *B's* scripted answer: *It's ten forty-five.* Make sure the students repeat the time you said. Remind students that repeating information as a question is a way to confirm information.

★ Ask students to tell you the time on the eight clocks below the conversation. Write the times on the board: *4:00, 3:15, 4:30, 10:15, 7:05, 10:30, 8:10, 9:45*

★ Have students practice the conversation using the times on the clocks. Walk around to make sure they understand the activity and provide help if needed.

LISTENING SCRIPT

Lesson 1: Practice the Conversation

Listen to the conversation. Then listen and repeat.

A: Excuse me. What time is it?
B: It's two o'clock.
A: Two o'clock?
B: That's right.

Culture/Civics Notes:

★ You may want to tell your students it is okay to ask a stranger of either gender for the time.

★ Usually, when we approach a stranger, we stand about an arm's length away. Personal space is an important and often subconscious value in Western culture.

EXPANSION ACTIVITY: Telephone Game

★ Put students in groups of 10 or more.

★ Tell them that you will walk around to each group and whisper a time to one of the students in that group: *It's four in the afternoon.* That student will whisper the time to another student, and so on. The last student to hear the time should say it aloud.

★ Have students play a few rounds of the game in their groups.

WINDOW ON GRAMMAR: *Yes/No* Questions with *Be*

A. Read the questions and answers.

★ Read the questions and answers, pausing to let students repeat after each.

★ Call on individual students and ask one of the sample questions, and elicit affirmative and negative responses.

B. Complete the questions with *is* or *are*.

★ Instruct students to look at item 1. Ask them if they should write *Is* or *Are* on the line. Point out that *Is* is correct because it's followed by *your school*, which is singular.

★ Tell students to complete the questions with *Is* or *Are*. Go over the answers with the class. Have students work in pairs and take turns asking and answering questions 1–5.

ANSWER KEY:

1. Is; 2. Are; 3. Is; 4. Are; 5. Are

C. Write 4 questions. Then ask a partner.

★ Tell students to write four additional questions about when places are open.

★ Have them take turns asking and answering questions with a partner.

EXPANSION ACTIVITY: Dictation

★ Dictate several sentences about when places are open. Create your own sentences or use these: *1. The park is open at 8:00 A.M. 2. The school is not open at night. 3. Most gas stations are open in the evening. 4. The library is open in the afternoon.* Read each sentence three times.

★ Have some students write the sentences on the board while others correct their own papers.

★ Ask questions using the information in the sentences: *Is the park open in the morning? Is the library open at 3:00 P.M.?* Elicit answers from individual students.

 Students can do Unit 3, Section 1, *Learn New Words* on the Interactive CD-ROM.

OBJECTIVE

At the Library

VOCABULARY

Days of the week	Signs
Sunday	No eating.
Monday	No smoking.
Tuesday	
Wednesday	
Thursday	
Friday	
Saturday	

THINGS TO DO

1. Talk About the Picture

★ Put the "big picture" color overhead transparency for Unit 3, Lesson 2, on the projector or have students look at the "big picture" in their books.

★ Ask questions about the picture such as, *What do you see? What's on the desk? What time is it?*

★ Go over the example sentences and have students write five additional sentences about the picture.

★ After checking their work, ask volunteers to write sentences on the board as a model for less proficient students.

2. Learn New Words 🎧

★ Ask students to look at the Library Hours sign in the picture.

★ Have them listen and look at the picture while you say the words or play the tape or CD. Pause after each word to have students repeat and point to the word in the picture.

★ Point to the words on the transparency in random order, and have students say each word.

★ Instruct students to circle the words in the picture.

LISTENING SCRIPT

Lesson 2: Learn New Words

Listen and repeat the words.

1. Sunday
2. Monday
3. Tuesday
4. Wednesday
5. Thursday
6. Friday
7. Saturday
8. no smoking
9. no eating

Culture/Civics Notes:

★ Some of your students may never have been to a library in this country. They may not know that many activities are not allowed in most libraries, including eating, drinking, listening to music, loud talking, smoking, and talking on cell phones.

★ As a class, brainstorm a list of other places where some activities may not be allowed. Your list may include *movie theaters, restaurants, work, school,* and *stores*. Have students work in groups to list activities that are not allowed in those places.

EXPANSION ACTIVITY: Sequencing Drill

★ Ask the students to stand in a circle.

★ Toss a beanbag to or point to a student and say a day of the week, *Tuesday*. That student should repeat the day. The person to his or her right should then say the day before, *Monday*. After that, the first student chosen repeats the day you first said, *Tuesday*. Finally, the person to the left of the *Tuesday* student says the day after, *Wednesday*.

★ This is a quick drill. The pattern should sound like this. The teacher says: *Tuesday*. Then the students say, *Tuesday, Monday, Tuesday, Wednesday*.

★ The student with the beanbag then throws the beanbag to or points to another student, says a different day of the week, and the students repeat the drill. Continue this until all students have participated.

3. Practice the Conversation

★ Instruct the students to listen and look at the conversation while you read it or play the tape or CD.

★ Say the conversation or play the tape or CD a second time. Pause after each line and ask the students to repeat.

★ Model the conversation with a student. Ask the student to read *A's* lines while you read *B's*. Demonstrate how to substitute different times for *B's* scripted answers. Make sure the student repeats the time you said. Remind students that repeating information as a question is a way to confirm information.

★ Group students in pairs to practice the conversation using the times on the schedule. Walk around to make sure they understand the activity and to provide help if needed.

LISTENING SCRIPT

Lesson 2: Practice the Conversation

Listen to the conversation. Then listen and repeat.

A: Is the library open on Monday?
B: Yes, it's open from noon to 9:00.
A: From noon to 9:00?
B: Right.

★ ★

 TRY THIS

★ ★

★ Go over the directions and the examples with the students.

★ This activity is best done using a place that has posted hours. If your school has a library or snack bar, students can go and write down the hours it is open or they can write down the hours of their own local library, bookstore, school, or supermarket.

 BIG PICTURE EXPANSION ACTIVITY: READING—Pablo and His Son

★ Make copies of Worksheet #5 (p. 245) and distribute them to students.

★ Put the "big picture" color overhead transparency for Unit 3, Lesson 2, on the projector or have students look at the "big picture" in their books.

★ Ask the students to read the story or read it yourself aloud line by line, pausing to have the students repeat after each line.

★ Have them answer the questions and check their answers with a partner.

★ Go over the answers with the class.

ANSWER KEY

1. no; 2. yes; 3. yes; 4. no; 5. no; 6. no; 7. yes; 8. yes; 9. yes; 10. no

---

EXPANSION ACTIVITY: What else has posted hours?

★ As a class, brainstorm a list of places with posted hours. The list may include *a bank, a restaurant, a store, a park,* and *a post office*.

★ Ask students to write down the hours of one of these places if they can remember them, or tell them to notice the hours and write them down before the next class.

Students can do Unit 3, Section 2, *Listen and Choose and Read* and Section 3, *Write* on the Interactive CD-ROM.

OBJECTIVE

Counting Money

VOCABULARY

COINS	BILLS
dime	a dollar
half-dollar	five dollars
nickel	fifty dollars
penny	one hundred dollars
quarter	one thousand dollars
	ten dollars
	twenty dollars

WINDOW ON GRAMMAR

Questions with *How much*

THINGS TO DO

1. Learn New Words 🎧

★ Have students look at the pictures. Ask them what all these words have in common. (*They are all money.*)

★ Ask students to listen and look at the pictures of money while you say the words or play the tape or CD.

★ Say the words or play the tape or CD a second time. Pause after each word and ask the students to repeat and point to the correct picture.

★ Instruct students to write each word under the correct picture.

LISTENING SCRIPT

Lesson 3: Learn New Words

Look at the pictures. Listen to the words. Then listen and repeat.

1. penny	A penny equals one cent.
2. nickel	A nickel equals five cents.
3. dime	A dime equals ten cents.
4. quarter	A quarter equals twenty-five cents.
5. half-dollar	A half-dollar equals fifty cents.
6. dollar	How much is the pen? It's a dollar.
7. five dollars	How much is the magazine? It's five dollars.
8. ten dollars	How much is the calendar? It's ten dollars.
9. twenty dollars	How much is the clock? It's twenty dollars.
10. fifty dollars	How much is the chair? It's fifty dollars.
11. one hundred dollars	How much is the table? It's one hundred dollars.
12. one thousand dollars	How much is the computer? It's one thousand dollars.

EXPANSION ACTIVITY: Matching Game

★ Have students work in groups of two to three. Give each group 24 index cards or pieces of paper. Tell them to write the new words on twelve of the cards—one word on each card (*penny*). Then, write the numbers that represent the new words on the other twelve index cards (*1¢*).

★ Instruct the students to shuffle all the index cards together and then lay them face down on the desk in four rows of six cards each.

★ Tell them to take turns turning over two cards at a time. If they turn over a matching numeral and word, they keep the two cards. The person in the group with the most cards wins.

★ Small prizes for the winners will probably increase enthusiasm for the game and raise the energy level in the classroom.

---

2. Write

★ Look at number 1. Ask students what coins they see in the picture: *a quarter and a dime*. Ask how much a quarter and a dime are when added together. Write on the board *25¢ + 10¢ = ?* Elicit that the total is *35¢*.

★ Have students add up the coins in each picture in 2–4.

★ Have students check their answers with a partner.

★ Go over the answers with the class.

EXPANSION ACTIVITY: What's in your pocket?

★ Ask students to get all the coins (or bills, if you want to work with greater amounts) from their pockets and/or wallets.

★ Have them add up the coins and write down the total value.

★ Group students in pairs and have them take turns showing combinations of coins and stating the amount. For example, if one partner shows two nickels, the other partner should say *10 cents.* Walk around to monitor the activity and provide help as needed.

★ Pretend to sell classroom objects for specific prices. For example, hold up a pencil and say *10 cents.* Have students separate out on their desks the money necessary to buy the objects.

★ Make sure they check their amounts with a partner or with you.

3. Practice the Conversation 🎧

★ Have students listen to and look at the conversation while you read it or play the tape or CD.

★ Read the conversation or play the tape or CD a second time. Pause after each line and ask the students to repeat.

★ Tell the class to read *A's* lines and you read *B's* lines. Demonstrate how to substitute different amounts for *B's* scripted answer (*ten cents*). As you make substitutions, point out the photos of coins in different amounts below the conversation.

★ Have students work in pairs and practice the conversation using the amounts listed below the conversation. Walk around to make sure they understand the activity. Provide help if needed.

LISTENING SCRIPT

Lesson 3: Practice the Conversation

Listen to the conversation. Then listen and repeat.

A: How much is it?
B: Thirty cents.
A: Are you sure?
B: Yes.

EXPANSION ACTIVITY: Snack Machine

★ If your building or school has a snack machine, you can make a list of items the machine actually sells. If not, make up the items and the prices.

★ Help the students brainstorm a list of snack items, real or imagined, found in the machine: *potato chips, pretzels, gum, nuts.*

★ Group students in pairs and assign each student three items to get the prices of (or to create the prices of).

★ Tell them to practice the conversation again, this time asking about the snack items. For example, *A's* first line might be, *How much is it for the potato chips?* Partner *B* must respond with the price indicated on the machine.

WINDOW ON GRAMMAR: Questions with *How much*

A. Read the questions and answers.

★ Read each question and answer and pause after each to let students repeat.

★ Call on individual students to ask one of the sample questions. Elicit a response from another student.

B. Work with a partner. Ask and answer the questions.

★ Model how to read the questions: *How much is a penny and a penny? How much is a nickel and a penny?* Make sure students understand that they can substitute any other items, as long as they are asking about two coins.

★ Have students work in pairs and have them take turns asking and answering the questions. Walk around the room and help as needed.

★ Call on a few partners to ask and answer questions in front of the class.

BIG PICTURE EXPANSION ACTIVITY: GRAMMAR—Questions and Answers about the Library

★ Make copies of Worksheet #6 (p. 246) and distribute them to students.

★ Put the "big picture" color overhead transparency for Unit 3, Lesson 2, on the projector or have students look at the "big picture" in their books.

★ Have students answer the questions and check their answers with a partner.

★ Go over the answers with the class.

★ Instruct students to practice asking and answering the questions with a partner.

ANSWER KEY:

A. 1. No, it isn't; 2. No, it isn't; 3. Yes, it is; 4. Yes, it is; 5. Yes, it is; 6. No, it isn't.
B. 1. $3; 2. $2; 3. $.15 or 15¢; 4. $.25 or 25¢

EXPANSION ACTIVITY: Add up the Money

★ Tell the students that in this activity, they are going to practice adding coins and bills together. They will repeat the amounts that were said by the person before them and then add a new coin or bill.

★ Model the activity with a group of students. Write the following question on the board and instruct a student to ask you the question: *How much is a penny and a dime?* Answer the question: *11 cents.* Turn to the next student and ask a question, adding one coin: *How much is a penny and a dime and a quarter?* Elicit the correct answer and have that student repeat your question with one additional coin to the next student in the group.

★ Have the students practice this chain addition in groups of five or more people. They can use pencil and paper to add the coins. Walk around to monitor the activity and help as needed.

 Students can do Unit 3, Section 1, *Learn New Words,* Section 2, *Listen and Choose*, and Section 4 *Fun and Games* on the Interactive CD-ROM.

OBJECTIVE

Reading and writing checks

VOCABULARY

amount
check
check number
signature

WINDOW ON MATH

Adding and Subtracting

THINGS TO DO

1. Learn New Words 🎧

★ Ask students to look at the pictures of checks. Have them listen and look at the words while you say the words or play the tape or CD.

★ Say the words or play the tape or CD a second time. Pause after each word and ask the students to repeat and point to the part of the picture that illustrates the word.

LISTENING SCRIPT

Lesson 4: Learn New Words

Look at the pictures. Listen to the words.

1. check	It's a check.
2. check number	The check number is one twenty four.
3. amount	The check amount is twelve dollars.
4. signature	It's David's signature.

2. Read

★ Copy the following chart on the board. Have students look at the chart.

Check #	To	Amount	For
124	Coral Beach Library	$12.00	books
___	___	___	___
___	___	___	___

★ Ask students what information they need to complete the chart. Point out that the information is identified by the chart headings. Elicit *check number, who the check is made out to, the amount*, and *what the check is for*.

★ Go over the example. Ask questions such as, *Who or what is check number 124 made out to? What is the amount of check 124?*

★ Have students complete the chart with information about the other two checks. Walk around the room and provide help as needed.

★ After checking their charts, ask volunteers to complete the chart on the board.

★ Go over the answers with the class.

ANSWER KEY:

Check#	To	Amount	For
124	Coral Beach Library	$12.00	late books
125	CASH	$50.00	food

EXPANSION ACTIVITY: Fractions to Decimals

★ Write several fractions on the board that have 100 as a denominator: *25/100, 50/100, 32/100, 90/100, 45/100, etc.*

★ Change two of the fractions into decimals or cents (*$.25,.50*) and instruct students to change the rest of them.

★ Have them compare answers with a partner and ask volunteers to write the correct answers on the board.

3. Write

★ Ask students to look at the checks. Identify how the amount is written on the three checks—the dollar amount is written numerically in the box, and it's also written out as words on the line.

★ Look at the numbers in the activity and go over item *1: $25.00.* Point out that the way the amount is written is how the students would write it on a check. Have students write out the other amounts in the same manner. Walk around the room and provide help as needed.

★ Ask volunteers to write the amounts on the board.

ANSWER KEY:

1. Twenty-five and 00/100 dollars; 2. Thirty-one and 50/100 dollars; 3. Fifty-six and 34/100 dollars.

★ Copy check #127 on the board.

★ Ask questions such as, *What is the date today? Where do you write "Ace Drugstore"? What do you put on the last line?*

★ Ask students to write a check to Ace Drugstore for $53.10.

★ Walk around the room and provide help as needed.

★ Ask a volunteer to complete the check on the board.

EXPANSION ACTIVITY: Meet Your Match

★ Give each student an index card.

★ Group students in pairs. Have them write any numerical amount on one card (*$15.35*) and that same amount written out on the other card (*Fifteen and 35/100 dollars*).

★ Collect all the cards and shuffle them.

★ Give one card to each student. Instruct them to walk around the room until they find the student who has the matching card.

★ Have the partners stand together and say the amount to the class.

★ ★

📁 TRY THIS
★ ★

★ Ask students if they write checks and what they write checks for. Write their answers on the board: *rent, telephone bill, books.*

★ Distribute blank pieces of paper and have students draw a check. Ask them to follow the format for the check in Activity 3.

★ Walk around the class to make sure students are drawing the check accurately.

★ Tell students to write this check for something they want or need.

★ Call on a few students to talk about their checks: *who it is to, what the amount is, what it is for.*

EXPANSION ACTIVITY: What do we want?

★ Bring in advertisements for furniture, electronics, or other household goods. Put students in small groups and give each group a few advertisements. Tell them that they are a family, that they must choose one or two things they want to buy from the advertisements, and that they have $200 to spend.

★ Have each person suggest one thing and give a reason why they think the "family" should buy it. Tell each group to discuss the suggested purchases. The group must agree on what they are going to buy and then write a check for the total amount.

★ Call on someone in each group to explain what they decided to buy.

WINDOW ON MATH: Adding and Subtracting

A. Listen to the sentences.

★ Ask the students to look at the sentences.

★ Read each sentence, or play the tape or CD. Pause after each sentence and have students repeat: *Ten cents plus twenty-five cents equals thirty-five cents.*

B. Write the missing numbers.

★ Ask students to write the answer for the first equation. Elicit that the answer is *$1.50*.

★ Have students complete the rest of the equations.

★ Group them in pairs and have them take turns reading the equations to each other to check their answers.

★ Go over the answers with the class.

EXPANSION ACTIVITY: Number Dictation

★ Tell students that you are going to say some monetary amounts and they are going to write the amounts down.

★ Go over an example: *Twenty-three dollars and nineteen cents.* Ask a volunteer to write the amount on the board as a number: *$23.19.*

★ Dictate ten numbers and read each number three times.

★ Ask volunteers to write them on the board and check the answers.

Students can do Unit 3, Section 4, *Fun and Games* on the Interactive CD-ROM.

LISTENING SCRIPT

Lesson 4: Window on Math
Adding and Subtracting

Listen to the sentences. Then listen and repeat.

$10¢ + 25¢ = 35¢$	$\$1.00 + 50¢ = \$1.50$
$50¢ + 25¢ = 75¢$	$\$5.00 + \$2.00 = \$7.00$
$5¢ - 1¢ = 4¢$	$\$10.00 - \$1.00 = \$9.00$
$60¢ - 10¢ = 50¢$	$\$50.00 - \$30.00 = \$20.00$

ANSWER KEY:

1. $1.50; 2. $.50 or 50¢; 3. $.60 or 60¢;
4. $22.00; 5. $15.00; 6. $21.50; 7. $80.00;
8. $150.00

OBJECTIVE

Making Phone Calls

WINDOW ON PRONUNCIATION

Thirteen or Thirty? Syllable Stress in Numbers

1. Practice the Conversation: Asking about Business Hours 🎧

★ Have students look at the picture for Conversation 1. To set the context, ask, *Who is in the picture? Where are they?*

★ Read the conversation aloud or play the tape or CD.

★ Read or play the tape or CD a second time. Pause after each statement and have students repeat.

★ To check comprehension, ask, *Where does speaker A work? What does speaker B want to know? When is the drugstore open on Thursday?*

★ Point out that there are two places in the conversation in which to make a substitution: Speaker *B* can ask about other days; Speaker *A* will answer with the correct hours.

★ Brainstorm as a class other days and times and have students write their ideas next to the light bulb.

★ Model the conversation with a student. Have the student read *A's* lines. Demonstrate how to substitute for *B's* scripted answers by using a different day. Make sure the student answers with different times.

★ Have students work in pairs to practice the conversation. Walk around to monitor the activity and provide help as needed.

★ Ask volunteers to act out the conversation in front of the class.

Culture/Civics Notes:

★ Beginning students are often uncomfortable calling businesses for information. It may help them to know that although some businesses answer the phone with a greeting—*hello, good morning*—others may answer with the name of the business, such as *Joy's Supermarket*. And many businesses use answering machines to give information to callers, so students can call back as many times as necessary if they don't understand something.

★ Remind students to make sure they know the name of the place they are calling so they can recognize it if the person who answers the phone uses it. Or they can say, *Is this . . .* and name the business.

LISTENING SCRIPT

Lesson 5: Practice the Conversation—Asking about Business Hours

Listen to the conversation. Then listen and repeat.

A: Hello. Anderson's Drugstore. Can I help you?
B: Yes. What are your hours on Thursday?
A: We're open from eight to six.
B: Thank you.

📋 BIG PICTURE EXPANSION ACTIVITY: SPEAKING—Asking about the Hours

★ Put the "big picture" color overhead transparency for Unit 3, Lesson 2, on the projector or have students look at the "big picture" in their books.

★ Tell students to look at the sign for the library hours and ask comprehension questions: *Is the library open on Sunday? What are the hours on Monday?*

★ Copy Conversation 1 on the board, making these changes:

A: *Hello. Hale Library. Can I help you?*
B: *Yes. What are your hours on <u>Monday</u>?*
A: *We're open from <u>12 to 3</u>.*

★ As a class, brainstorm other questions about the library and write them on the board: *What time is Story Hour? How much is a video? What is the address?*

★ Have students work in pairs to practice asking for information about the library.

EXPANSION ACTIVITY:
Make a Phone Call

★ Tell students to use the telephone book to find the number for a business, public service or movie theater.

★ Have them call that place and find out their hours of business. Remind students that many business phones use an automated answering system, so they can call back many times if they don't understand the message. This is certainly true for a movie theater. If they call a movie theater, they can get the name of a particular movie and the times it's showing.

★ Call on students to share their information with the class.

2. Practice the Conversation: Calling Directory Assistance

★ Repeat the basic procedure from Activity 1.

★ To set the context, ask, *Who is in the picture? Where are they?*

★ To check comprehension, ask, *What is the name of the telephone company? What does the caller want to know? What city does Rafael Hernandez live in?*

★ As a class, brainstorm ideas for substituting different information in the conversation and have students write them in the space provided.

★ Group students in pairs to practice the conversation and make substitutions. Walk around to monitor the activity and provide help as needed.

★ Ask volunteers to act out the conversation in front of the class.

LISTENING SCRIPT

Lesson 5: Practice the Conversation—Calling Directory Assistance

Listen to the conversation. Then listen and repeat.

A: Welcome to Horizon. What city and state?
B: Miami, Florida.
A: What listing?
B: Rafael Hernandez.
A: The number is area code 305-555-5938.

Culture/Civics Notes:

★ Some of your students may come from countries that have only one telephone service provider. They may find our system confusing. Telephone service providers give customers information as a service. Customers can call a special number and find out a telephone number or an address for a specific person. Usually, there is a charge for the call.

★ Telephone listings are organized by city and state. Often, a recorded message greets the customer and asks first for the city and state. Once the customer has responded, he or she will probably get a second question asking for the listing (the person's or business' name). At this point, a recording may provide the telephone number, or an operator may come on the line.

★ Remind students to say the city, state, and listing very clearly so the automated answering system can process the information.

EXPANSION ACTIVITY:
What's the area code?

★ To reinforce map skills as well as the ability to use the telephone book, bring in old telephone books or photocopy the pages of the telephone book that show the breakdown of area codes on a map and in a listing.

★ Have students work in pairs and create questions that ask about the area code for different cities and states: *What's the area code for Allentown, Pennsylvania?*

★ Each pair of students should exchange their questions with another pair and use the information in the telephone book to answer the questions.

3. Listen and Write: Listening to a Recorded Message 🎧

★ Instruct students to look at the picture. Explain that this activity is not a conversation. Instead, the students will hear an automated voice answering system.

★ Read the information or play the tape or CD and have students write in the missing numbers.

★ Read or play the tape or CD a second time so students may check their answers.

★ Go over the answers with the class.

LISTENING SCRIPT

Lesson 5: Listen and Write—Listen to a Recorded Message

Listen and write the missing numbers. Then listen and check.

Thank you for calling the Coral Beach Public Library. For hours, press 1.
The library is open Monday through Thursday from eleven to nine. On Friday and Saturday, the library is open from nine to five. Good-bye.

ANSWER KEY:

The library is open Monday through Thursday from 11:00 to 9:00. On Friday and Saturday, the library is open from 9:00 to 5:00. Good-bye.

WINDOW ON PRONUNCIATION: *Thirteen* or *Thirty*? Syllable Stress in Numbers

A. Listen to the words. Then listen and repeat. 🎧

★ Tell students to listen and look at the numbers while you say the words or play the tape or CD. Tell students that the part of the word with a dot over it is the syllable that is stressed. Stress means that part is pronounced more strongly than the other parts.

★ Say the words or play the tape or CD a second time. Pause after each word and ask the students to repeat.

LISTENING SCRIPT

Lesson 5: Window on Pronunciation

A. Listen to the words. Then listen and repeat.

thirteen	thirty
fourteen	forty
fifteen	fifty
sixteen	sixty
seventeen	seventy
eighteen	eighty
nineteen	ninety

B. Listen and circle the numbers you hear. 🎧

★ Go over the directions and do the first item together. Write *13* and *30* on the board. Say either number and ask the class which one you said. Circle that number on the board.

★ Say the words or play the tape or CD. Pause after item 1 and make sure students have circled a number.

★ Continue saying the words or playing the tape or CD and have students circle the numbers they hear.

★ Tell students to check their answers with a partner.

★ Go over the answers with the class.

LISTENING SCRIPT

Lesson 5: Window on Pronunciation

B. Listen and circle the numbers you hear.

1. 13	5. 17
2. 40	6. 80
3. 50	7. 90
4. 16	

C. Listen and point to the numbers you hear. 🎧

★ Read both options for each item: *It's six-fifty. It's six-fifteen.* Pause and have students repeat.

★ Say the sentences or play the tape or CD and have students point to the number they hear.

★ Go over the answers with the class.

★ Have the students practice reading the sentences with a partner. They can say either of the two numbers. Their partners should circle the correct numbers in the book.

★ Walk around to monitor the activity and provide help as needed.

LISTENING SCRIPT

Lesson 5: Window on Pronunciation

C. Listen and point to the numbers you hear.

1. It's six-fifteen.
2. It's fifty cents.
3. From 9:30 A.M. to 6:00 P.M.
4. The price is $3.18.

EXPANSION ACTIVITY:
Label the Syllables

★ Bring to class candies of different sizes or round stickers of different sizes. Give several to each student.

★ Write your name on the board. Put a big circle over the stressed syllables, and a small circle over the unstressed syllables.

★ Have students write their names on a piece of paper and then indicate stress with the markers (candies or stickers) of the appropriate size.

★ Tell students you are going to dictate a series of numbers and have them write the letters A–J on a piece of paper. As you dictate, they should write out the numbers and then place the candies or stickers over certain syllables to indicate stress.

★ Do the first item with the class as an example. Write A on the board and say *fourteen* three times.

★ Have students write *fourteen* for item A and place their stress markers over the syllables in the word. Ask a volunteer to come to board and draw circles to indicate the syllable stress in *fourteen* (•●). Walk around to make sure students have placed their markers correctly.

★ Dictate nine other numbers and instruct students to place their stress markers over each.

★ Have students check their answers with a partner.

★ Go over the answers with the class.

EQUIPPED FOR THE FUTURE ROLE

Community

OBJECTIVE

Reading Time Schedules

1. Read

★ Have students look at the four business signs. Ask the class, *What places are these hours for?* (*bank, drugstore, post office, hospital*).

★ Ask comprehension questions such as, *What time does the bank open on Monday?* (*9:00 A.M.*) *What time does the post office close on Saturday?* (*2:00 P.M.*) *What times can you visit someone in the hospital in the evening?* (*7–9*)

★ Go over question 1 with the class, asking, *What's open on Sunday morning?* Elicit that the drugstore is open, and that you can visit the hospital on Sunday morning.

★ Have the students write down the answers to the rest of the questions and check their answers with a partner.

★ Go over the answers with the class.

ANSWER KEY

1. The drugstore and the hospital are.
2. They're open from 9:00 to 3:00 on Monday through Friday.
3. The drugstore and the hospital are.
4. The bank and the post office are closed on Sunday.
5. It's open from 9:00 to 2:00.
6. The drugstore and the hospital are.
7. No, the bank isn't open on Sunday.

EXPANSION ACTIVITY: Memory Game

★ Divide the class into teams. Instruct the students to look at the signs and try to remember as much as they can.

★ Have the students close their books, then ask each team questions about the signs. You can use the questions in the book, create your own, or use the questions below. Continue until every student has answered a question.

> *Is the bank open at 7:00 A.M.?* (no)
> *Can you visit the hospital at 2:00 P.M?* (no)
> *What is open on Saturday at 11:00 A.M.?* (drugstore, post office and hospital)
> *How many visiting hours does the hospital have a week?* (28)
> *What time does the post office/ drugstore/bank open on _____?*
> *What time does the post office/drugstore/bank close on _____?*
> *Which place is open for the least number of hours?*

★ Each correct answer earns a point. The team with the most points wins.

2. How much is it?

★ Ask students to look at the four pictures and ask them what they see: *pay phone, parking lot, parking meter, washing machine*. Write the words on the board.

★ Have students answer the questions by looking at the pictures.

★ Go over the answers with the class.

★ Have students work in pairs to practice asking and answering the questions.

ANSWER KEY:

1. 35 cents; 2. $10, $15; 3. $.50, $.75; 4. $3, $4.50

EXPANSION ACTIVITY: Scavenger Hunt

★ Prepare this activity before coming to class.

★ First, note the prices of things you see around the school (candy in the snack machine, water in the drink machine, the student parking lot, a parking meter on the street, a chicken sandwich at the snack bar, copies in the library, pencils at the bookstore, coffee at a nearby cafe).

★ Next, create questions about these items: *How much are candy bars in the snack machine on the first floor?*

★ Write the questions on the board or on a transparency. Alternatively, you can dictate the questions to the students and then show them the sentences afterward so they can check their answers. Either way, have the students copy the questions.

★ Put the students in small groups to answer the questions. Some members of the group should start at the beginning of the list, some in the middle, and some at the bottom of the list so they won't all be in the same place at the same time. The first group to return with correct answers for all the questions wins.

EXPANSION ACTIVITY: Compare Businesses

★ Ask students to state the types of places they researched in Activity 3: *banks, supermarkets, bookstores.* Write these categories on the board as headings on a chart. Have the students list the information they gathered for each business under the correct heading. The listing for banks might look something like this:

BANKS

Name	Address	Telephone number	Hours
First Center	990 Center St.	555-7999	M–F 8–3, Sat. 9–12
BankUnited	50 Main St.	555-8000	M–F 9–5
National Bank	11510 North St.	555-1212	M–F 9–4, Sat. 9–1

★ Put students in small groups to discuss and decide which place they would go to in each category and why: *I would go to First Center Bank because it opens at 8:00 A.M.*

3. Write

★ Assign this as an out-of-class activity. Ask students to notice the information needed in the chart—*name, address, telephone number,* and *hours* for a few different places.

★ Have students complete the chart by adding information for three additional businesses. Then have them work in pairs to share the information with a partner.

★ Call on a few students and ask them to talk about one place that they researched.

1. Listening Review 🎧

★ Go over the directions with the class.

★ Read the four items or play the tape or CD and have the students mark their answers on the Answer Sheet.

★ Walk around to monitor activity and help students stay on task.

★ Have students check their answers with a partner.

★ Go over the answers with the class.

LISTENING SCRIPT

Lesson 7: Listening Review

Listen and choose the time you hear. Use the Answer Sheet.

1.
A: Excuse me. What time is it?
B: It's five o'clock.
A: Okay. Thanks.

2.
A: CTS Drugstore.
B: Yes. When do you open tomorrow?
A: At eight.
B: Thanks.

3.
A: When's the next bus?
B: It's at 8:45.
A: Thanks.

4.
A: When's your class today?
B: It's at noon.
A: Are you sure?
B: Yes, of course.

Listen and choose the correct answer. Use the Answer Sheet.

5. What are your hours on Monday?
6. What time is it?
7. How much is it?
8. When's the party?
9. What day is it?
10. How much is it?

ANSWER KEY:

1. A; 2. C; 3. B; 4. A; 5. B; 6. A; 7. B; 8. A; 9. C; 10. A

2. Conversation Check: Pair Work

★ Group students in pairs. Go over the directions and have them complete the activity.

★ Remind students that each partner has some information, but that other information is missing. They must each ask their partner questions to complete the chart.

★ Walk around to monitor the activity and provide help as needed.

Assessment Note:

★ You can use the Conversation Check as an oral assessment. Ask pairs of students to complete the activity while you note areas of difficulty.

LEARNING LOG

★ Point out the four sections of the Learning Log: *I know these words, I can ask, I can say,* and *I can write.*

★ Ask students to check what they know and what they can do.

★ Walk around to note what they don't know or can't do. Use this information to review areas of difficulty.

 BIG PICTURE EXPANSION ACTIVITY: WRITING—Writing about the Library

★ Put the "big picture" color overhead transparency for Unit 3, Lesson 2, on the projector or have students look at the "big picture" in their books.

★ Ask the class, *What is at the library? Where is the sign for the library hours? Where is the clock?* Call on a few students to share their observations with the class.

★ Tell the students to write three sentences about the library. Remind them to look at the "big picture" for ideas. They can begin sentences with *There is/There are* and use language from Unit 2 to describe location: *near, next to, in front of, behind,* and *between.* Ask students to read their sentences to a partner.

★ Invite a few volunteers read their sentences to the class.

 BIG PICTURE EXPANSION ACTIVITY: SPEAKING Assessment—Talking about the Big Picture

★ You can use the "big picture" to assess placement of new students in open-entry classes, to diagnose difficulties, or to measure progress.

★ Work with one student at a time. Show the "big picture" to the student and ask, *What do you see in the picture?* or, *Tell me about the picture.* Tell the student to speak for as long as possible. Wait a moment for the student to prepare an answer. If the student has difficulty, you can use prompts: *Where are they? What do you see in the library? Who do you see in the library? What are the people doing?*

★ You can use a rubric like the one below to rate beginning speakers.

3	Uses sentences, although form may be incorrect Can speak for sustained length of time Responds to prompts, but doesn't need them to begin speaking
2	Can use nouns and verbs Uses phrases Answers informational questions
1	Can name objects Uses single words Can answer yes/no questions
0	Cannot say anything independently May be able to point to objects when prompted

TEACHER'S NOTES:

Things that students are doing well:

_____

_____

_____

_____

_____

_____

Things students need additional help with:

_____

_____

_____

_____

_____

_____

_____

Ideas for further practice or for the next class:

_____

_____

_____

_____

_____

_____

Students can do Unit 3, Section 5, _Practice Test_ on the Interactive CD-ROM.

OBJECTIVE

Yes/No Questions and Answers with *Be*

Yes/No Questions and Answers with *Be*

★ Read the sentences in the grammar paradigm and have students repeat.

★ Call on students and ask a question: *Are you from Mexico?* Elicit answers that include information about themselves: *No, I'm not. / Yes, I am.*

★ Go over the contractions in the box with the class.

1. Write the words in the correct order.

★ Have students look at the first *A/B* conversation. Look at the question and the words in parentheses. Point out that the scrambled words have been rearranged to form a question. Note that the first word begins with a capital letter.

★ Ask the question, *Are you from Mexico?* Instruct students to write their answers on the line next to *B*.

★ Ask students to complete the other conversations. Have them use the words in parentheses to form a question and then answer the question.

★ Go over the answers with the class orally, or have the students write the questions on the board.

★ Group students in pairs to practice asking and answering the questions.

ANSWER KEY:

Answers for A: 1. Are you from Mexico? 2. Is your school near a restaurant? 3. Is your class in the morning? 4. Is five dollars/ten dollars more than five dollars/ten dollars? 5. Are Don and Daisy in your class?
Answers for B: will vary.

EXPANSION ACTIVITY: Scrambled Sentences

★ Tell students to write two questions on strips of paper and then cut them up into several pieces.

★ Students should exchange their cut-up questions with a partner and then reconstruct the questions they were given, arranging the slips of paper in the correct order.

★ Have them write down the questions and answers, then practice asking and answering the questions in pairs.

2. Complete the conversations.

★ Have students look at the sentences and ask them what is missing (a form of *be*). Point out that *Is* is written as an example on the first line. Elicit the missing word(s) for *B* in the first conversation (*is*) and have students write *is* on the correct line.

★ Instruct the students to complete the other conversations.

★ Go over the answers with the class.

★ Group the students in pairs to practice the conversations.

ANSWER KEY:

A: <u>Is</u> your signature on the check?
B: Yes, it <u>is</u>.
A: <u>Is</u> the library open in the evening?
B: Yes, it <u>is</u>.
A: <u>Is</u> the bank on State Street?
B: No, it <u>isn't</u>.
A: <u>Am</u> I near the bank?
B: Yes, you <u>are</u>.

Information Questions with *Be*

★ Read the sentences in the grammar paradigm and pause after each so the students can repeat.

★ Call on individual students and ask a question: *What is your name?* They should answer with information about themselves.

★ Go over the contractions in the box.

3. Match the questions and answers.

★ Go over the first example and ask, *What is on your chair?* Students should look at the possible answers on the right and choose the best answer: *my book and my notebook.* Point out that *a* has been written on the line next to 1.

★ Tell students to finish the exercise. Walk around the room to monitor the activity and provide help as needed.

★ Students should check their answers in pairs.

★ Go over the answers with the class.

★ Tell students to practice asking and answering the questions in pairs, once with their books open and once with their books closed. The answers don't have to match the exact answers in the book, but the contexts should be correct.

4. Complete the conversations.

★ Go over the example with the class.

★ Instruct students to complete the conversations. Walk around the room to monitor the activity and provide help as needed.

★ Go over the answers with the class.

★ Have students practice the conversations in pairs and encourage them to try closing their books before they answer.

EQUIPPED FOR THE FUTURE ROLE

Work

OBJECTIVE

Understanding Vacation Leave

VOCABULARY

full-time
get/gets
salary
vacation
vacation leave

Culture/Civics Note:
★ Students may be unfamiliar with work benefits in this country. Many full-time jobs offer vacation leave. Explain that this is time off with pay.

A. Learn new words.

★ Read the words in the box. Pause after each so that students can repeat.

★ Tell the students to read the story and underline the new words. Alternatively, read the story aloud to reinforce developing literacy skills. Pause after each sentence and have students repeat.

★ Allow students time to check their answers with a partner.

★ Go over the answers with the class.

ANSWER KEY:

Paul is a salesclerk. He works in a supermarket. He is a <u>full-time</u> worker. His <u>salary</u> is $10.00 an hour. He works 40 hours in a week. Paul <u>gets</u> <u>vacation leave</u>. He can go on <u>vacation</u> for 80 hours, or 10 working days, every year. He gets $10.00 an hour on <u>vacation</u>!

B. Circle the correct answer.

★ Read the questions about the paragraph aloud or ask students to read them. Instruct students to circle the correct answers.

★ Group students in pairs to compare their answers.

★ Go over the answers with the class.

★ Have each pair take turns asking and answering the questions.

ANSWER KEY:

1. a; 2. b; 3. b; 4. a; 5. b

C. Complete the sentences.

★ Ask the students to look again at the new words in the box. Instruct them to write one of the words on each line to complete each sentence. Walk around the room and provide help as needed.

★ Have students check their answers with a partner.

★ Ask volunteers to read the sentences aloud to the class.

ANSWER KEY:

1. full-time; 2. salary; 3. vacation;
4. vacation leave

D. Talk to Paul about his job.

★ Read the questions aloud. Pause after each and have students repeat.

★ Read Paul's answers aloud. Pause after each and have students repeat.

★ Go over the example and ask the students to match the rest of the questions and answers, drawing lines between them to create correct pairs.

★ Go over the answers with the class.

★ Have students work in pairs and take turns asking and answering the questions.

ANSWER KEY:

1. b; 2. a; 3. d; 4. e; 5. f; 6. c

E. Read the information for Paul.

★ Have students look at Paul's pay stub. Elicit that this is a form that is attached to most paychecks, and it provides information about the period for which a person receives his or her wages.

★ Ask students what kinds of information is on the paystub: *pay period, employee name, salary, hours worked, money earned in that pay period, money earned for that year, how much vacation leave the employee has.* Note that there is usually other information on paystubs such as federal income tax, FICA, health payments and state income tax.

★ Ask comprehension questions such as, *Who is the employee? (Paul Ming) How much money does he get an hour? ($10) How much money does he get in one week? ($400.00) How much vacation leave does Paul have at this point? (6 days or 48 hours).*

★ Tell students to complete the sentences with information from the paystub.

★ Go over the answers with the class.

ANSWER KEY:

1. $10; 2. 40; 3. $400; 4. 6

 Take It Outside

★ Read the questions, pausing after each to have students repeat.

★ Instruct students to interview someone they know who works. If they do this in class, they can speak with a classmate. If they do this as an out-of-class assignment, they can interview anyone who holds a job.

★ After they have completed the interview, call on a few students to share their answers with the class.

★ Read the example paragraph and tell students to write a paragraph about the person they interviewed. Use the example paragraph as a model.

★ Have students work in pairs and have them read their paragraphs to each other.

★ Ask volunteers to read their paragraphs to the class.

EXPANSION ACTIVITY: Compare Jobs

★ Put students in pairs or small groups.

★ Copy the chart below on the board and have students copy the chart on paper.

★ Explain the headings and go over the example in the chart.

JOB	GOOD THINGS +	BAD THINGS –
supermarket salesclerk	vacation leave	not much money

★ Each student should tell their group about the person they interviewed in the Take It Outside Activity. Each team member should complete the chart with information provided by all team members and the team should discuss what are the "Good Things" and the "Bad Things" about each job.

★ Ask volunteers to explain which job they would want and why.

EQUIPPED FOR THE FUTURE ROLE

Family

OBJECTIVE

Planning a Family Vacation

VOCABULARY

beach
car
hotel

A. Learn new words.

★ Have students read the two ads. Ask the students what these ads are for; instruct them to find the words *hotel, beach*, and *car* in the ads and circle them. Ask about their experiences and preferences: *Do you like the beach? Do you like hotels?*

★ Ask comprehension questions such as, *Where is the hotel? What is the name of the hotel? What is the hotel near? How much is a car? What is the name of the car place?*

B. Complete the sentences.

★ Have students complete the sentences. Remind them to look at the ads to find the words they need. Walk around the room to provide help as needed.

★ Have students check their answers with a partner.

★ Go over the answers with the class.

ANSWER KEY:

1. hotel; 2. $69; 3. $30; 4. car; 5. 1300 South Street; 6. 1-800-555-3211

C. Check the things that are in the ads.

★ Read the list of items from each column. Pause after each item and have students repeat.

★ Ask students to read the ads again and check the box next to each word or phrase if that information is given in the ad.

★ As an example, look at the first item in the column under *Sand Castle Beach Hotel*. Ask the class, *Is there an address for the hotel?* Since the answer is *no*, the students should not check the box next to *address*.

★ Tell the students to complete the exercise. Walk around the room and provide help as needed.

★ Go over the answers with the class.

ANSWER KEY:

Sand Castle Beach Hotel	**Martin Autos**
☐ address	☑ address
☑ telephone number	☐ telephone number
☑ amount of money for a room	☑ amount of money for a car
☑ name of the hotel	☑ name of car company
☐ days of the week	☑ days of the week

D. Read the story.

★ Have the students read the story or read it aloud. Pause after each sentence and have students repeat.

★ Ask comprehension questions such as, *Where is Paul? Where is his room? Where did he get the car?*

★ Go over the example.

★ Have students look at the ads and write the amount of money Paul will spend in each scenario. Students should check their answers with a partner.

★ Go over the answers with the class.

ANSWER KEY:

1. $198; 2. $426; 3. $129; 4. $237

 Take It Outside

* You can assign this as an out-of-class assignment. Instruct students to plan a vacation with family or friends. They can use maps, ads, or other resources to get the information to answer the questions.

* Group students in pairs to describe to each other the vacation they planned with their family, friends, or with other classmates.

* Call on a few students to tell the class about the vacation they planned.

* Alternatively, you can make it an in-class assignment and put students in small groups to plan a hypothetical vacation together. Bring in road atlases or other maps, newspaper ads from the travel section, or brochures to help the students in their planning.

EXPANSION ACTIVITY: Ad Agency

* Have students work in pairs or small groups to make an ad for a hotel.

* Brainstorm with the students what information should be in the ad: *name, location, address, telephone number, cost per night, good things nearby.* Help students brainstorm any additional vocabulary they might need to complete the ad: *mountains, lake, airport.*

* Students should decide on the details about their hotel and then create the ad. Provide paper and crayons or markers. Walk around to monitor the activity and provide help as needed.

* Call on a representative from each group to present their hotel ad. Ask the class to vote on the best ad. Display them in the room.

Calendars

UNIT OVERVIEW

LESSON	OBJECTIVE	STUDENT BOOK PAGE #
1. When is your birthday?	Identifying Months	p. 52
2. The party is on Sunday.	Events on a Calendar	p. 54
3. What's the date?	Keeping Track of Appointments	p. 56
4. Holidays	Identifying Holidays	p. 58
5. I need to cancel my appointment.	Scheduling Appointments	p. 60
6. School Calendars	Interpreting a School Calendar	p. 62
7. What do you know?	Review and Assessment	p. 64
8. Spotlight	Writing	p. 66

Big Picture Expansion Activities

FOCUS	TITLE	SUGGESTED USE
Speaking	Making an Appointment	Lesson 5
Reading	A Story about Alice	Lesson 2
Grammar	Singular and Plural Nouns	Lesson 4
Writing	Write about Your Schedule	Lesson 7
Speaking	Assessment: Talking about the Picture	Lesson 7

Big Picture Expansion Activity Worksheets

WORKSHEET #/FOCUS	TITLE	TEACHER'S EDITION PAGE #
7. Reading	A Story about Alice	p. 247
8. Grammar	Singular and Plural Nouns	p. 248

OBJECTIVE

Identifying Months

VOCABULARY

MONTHS OF THE YEAR	WEATHER WORDS
January	cloudy
February	cold
March	hot
April	rainy
May	sunny
June	warm
July	
August	
September	
October	
November	
December	

WINDOW ON GRAMMAR

Questions with *How many*

THINGS TO DO

1. Learn New Words 🎧

★ Ask students to look at the pictures and identify the words they know. Write the words on the board.

★ Tell students to listen and read the words while you say them or play the tape or CD.

★ Say the words or play the tape or CD a second time. Pause after each word and ask the students to repeat the word and point to the picture that illustrates that word.

★ Have students work in pairs to practice saying the words as their partners point to the pictures. Then have students switch roles and do the exercise again.

★ Instruct the students to write the words under the correct pictures.

LISTENING SCRIPT

Lesson 1: Learn New Words

Look at the pictures. Listen to the words. Then listen and repeat.

1.	January	It's January.
2.	February	It's February.
3.	March	It's March.
4.	April	It's April.
5.	May	It's May.
6.	June	It's June.
7.	July	It's July.
8.	August	It's August.
9.	September	It's September.
10.	October	It's October.
11.	November	It's November.
12.	December	It's December.
13.	cold	It's cold here.
14.	warm	It's warm here.
15.	hot	It's hot here.
16.	rainy	It's rainy here.
17.	sunny	It's sunny here.
18.	cloudy	It's cloudy here.

EXPANSION ACTIVITY: Beanbag Toss

★ Practice the months by playing beanbag toss. Tell the class that you will toss the beanbag to a student and say a number from 1 to 12. Explain that the student should answer with the name of the month that corresponds to the number. Then the student should toss the beanbag to another student and say a different number.

★ Model the activity. Call the name of a student and toss them the beanbag. Say *one*. Elicit from the student that the first month is *January*.

★ Once students understand the activity, continue the beanbag toss until all the students have had an opportunity to respond.

2. Write

★ Have students look at the incomplete sentences.

★ Ask a volunteer to read the first sentence, and then ask the class the name of the month you are in currently. Tell the class to write the month on the line.

★ Have students complete the rest of the sentences.

★ Have them work in pairs and take turns reading the completed sentences.

★ Call on students to read their sentences aloud.

ANSWER KEY:

Answers will vary.

Grammar Note:
★ Point out to students that we use *in* when talking about months: *School starts in September.*

EXPANSION ACTIVITY: *Yes/No* Flashcards

★ Give each student two cards of different colors (*red* and *green*). Have them write *yes* on one card and *no* on the other.

★ Read the sentences from Activity 2 aloud. When you read them, make some accurate and some inaccurate: *It's hot here in January. It's hot here in August.*

★ Have students hold up one card after you read each sentence to tell you *yes* or *no*.

3. Interview

★ Model the activity for the class. Have a student ask you A's question: *When is your birthday?* Answer the question with, *It's in _____.* Then, fill in the appropriate month on the chart.

★ Have students copy the chart in the book on a piece of paper and include the headings *Name* and *Birthday*.

★ Invite students to stand up and ask five classmates the question. They should record the answers on their charts.

★ Call on a few students to talk about their classmates.

★ Write the names of the months on the board (or have volunteers do this). Call out each month and have students raise their hands if their birthday is in that month. Make tally marks to show how many people have birthdays in each month.

January	//	July	/
February	LHT	August	//
March	/	September	
April	//	October	///
May		November	/
June	///	December	//

EXPANSION ACTIVITY: Bar Graph

★ Draw a graph on the board with the months on the horizontal axis and number of students on the vertical axis.

★ Have students copy the graph on a piece of paper.

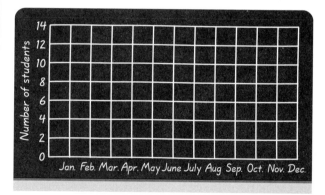

★ Look at January on the tally chart you did for the interview in Activity 3 or ask how many students have birthdays in January. Point to the tally marks and elicit the number. Make a circle on the graph on the board to indicate the number of students with birthdays in January.

★ Tell students to complete the graph.

★ Ask volunteers to draw the circles for the other eleven months in the graph on the board.

WINDOW ON GRAMMAR: Questions with *How Many*

A. Read the questions.

★ Read the questions in the paradigm. Pause after each and have students repeat.

★ Read them a second time and ask students to answer them. (*12, 52, 365*)

B. Complete the questions.

★ Review with the class the words in the yellow box. Say each of them and have students repeat.

★ Group students in pairs to fill in the blanks and practice asking and answering the questions.

★ Invite a few pairs of students to ask and answer the questions in front of the class.

EXPANSION ACTIVITY: Jeopardy Game

★ Write five questions for each of the following categories: *our classroom, our city, our country, personal facts*. Use the ones below or create your own.

Our Classroom
How many students are in our class?
How many teachers are in our class?
How many desks are in our classroom?
How many boards are in our classroom?
How many chairs are in our classroom?

The Calendar
How many days are in January?
How many days are in February?
How many months are after July?
How many months are before September?
How many months is this class?

Our Country
How many states are in the United States?
How many states are touching this one?
How many people live in this country?
How many capitals does the United States have?
How many presidents does the United States have?

Personal Facts
How many children do you have?
How many people live with you?
How many classmates do you have?
How many books are on your desk?
How many dollars are in your pocket?
How many hours a day do you study English?

★ Divide the class into teams. Tell the teams to take turns naming a category. Ask each team a question from the category named. Each correct answer earns a point. The team with the most points wins.

★ Small prizes for the winners will probably increase enthusiasm for the game and raise the energy level of the class.

 Students can do Unit 4, Section 1, *Learn New Words* and Section 4, *Fun and Games* on the Interactive CD-ROM.

OBJECTIVE

Events on a Calendar

VOCABULARY

ORDINAL NUMBERS	OTHER WORDS
1st first	basketball game
2nd second	birthday party
3rd third	dentist's appointment
4th fourth	doctor's appointment
5th fifth	job interview
6th sixth	PTO meeting
7th seventh	
8th eighth	
9th ninth	
10th tenth	
11th eleventh	
12th twelfth	
13th thirteenth	
14th fourteenth	
15th fifteenth	
16th sixteenth	

THINGS TO DO

1. Learn Ordinal Numbers 🎧

★ Put the "big picture" color overhead transparency for Unit 4, Lesson 2, on the projector or have students look at the "big picture" in their books. Ask, *What is this?* Elicit that the picture shows *a calendar with events scheduled on it.*

★ Ask the students to look at the numbers in each box on the calendar. Explain that these are dates. Tell students that when we say dates we use the *ordinal* form of the number, as in *January fifth.* But we write *January 5.*

★ Have students look at the numbers and listen while you say them or play the tape or CD.

★ Say the numbers or play the tape or CD a second time. Pause after each number and ask the students to repeat and point to each number as they say it.

★ Call out cardinal numbers (*15*) and have students respond with the corresponding ordinal number (*15th*).

★ Have students work in pairs and have one practice saying the ordinal numbers as his or her partner points to the number in the book. Reverse roles and do the exercise again.

LISTENING SCRIPT

Lesson 2: Learn Ordinal Numbers

Listen to the numbers. Then listen and repeat.

first	ninth
second	tenth
third	eleventh
fourth	twelfth
fifth	thirteenth
sixth	fourteenth
seventh	fifteenth
eighth	sixteenth

EXPANSION ACTIVITY: Numbered Heads

★ Have students work in groups of five. Give each student in each group a number.

★ Tell students that you are going to give instructions to one member of each group.

★ Model the activity. Call out an ordinal number and give a direction: *Third person, stand up.* Make sure the person who is number 3 in each group stands up. Or, *Second person, write your name on the board.*

★ Continue the activity until everyone has followed a direction. Change the students' numbers and continue.

2. Learn New Words 🎧

★ Point to the pictures in the book or display the color overhead transparency.

★ Have students look at the pictures and listen while you say the words or play the tape or CD.

★ Explain that *PTO* is an abbreviation for *Parent Teacher Organization.*

★ Say the words or play the tape or CD a second time. Pause after each phrase and ask the students to repeat and point to the picture that illustrates the phrase as it is said.

★ Point to the pictures in random order, and have students say the name of the items pictured.

LISTENING SCRIPT

Lesson 2: Learn New Words

Look at the pictures. Listen to the words. Then listen and repeat.

1. doctor's appointment	Her doctor's appointment is on May first.
2. computer class	Her computer class is on May third.
3. birthday party	Her birthday party is on May sixth.
4. PTO meeting	Her PTO meeting is on May eighth.
5. job interview	Her job interview is on May ninth.
6. basketball game	Her basketball game is on May eleventh.
7. dentist's appointment	Her dentist's appointment is on May fifteenth.

★ Ask students to look at the conversation. Read the conversation, pausing after each line to have students repeat.

★ Model the activity with a student. Have the student read *A's* lines and you read *B's*. Cue the student to substitute another activity—*a birthday party*—for the scripted response. Demonstrate how to answer *A's* questions: *sixth, Sunday.*

★ Have students work in pairs to ask and answer questions about the calendar. Walk around the room to monitor the activity and provide help as needed.

★ Call on a few students and ask about events on the calendar.

3. Practice the Conversation 🎧

★ Ask students to look at the conversation. Read the conversation or play the tape or CD as the students listen.

★ Read or play the conversation again. Pause after each sentence and ask the students to repeat.

★ For additional practice, have the students read the conversation together. You read *A's* lines and have the class respond with *B's* lines, then reverse roles.

★ Model the conversation with a student. Have the student read *A's* lines. Cue the student to

substitute one of the dates listed below the conversation for the scripted answer. Demonstrate how to give an excuse, using the activity that is scheduled on the date the student substituted.

★ Tell students to add a date from Alice's calendar next to the light bulb.

★ Have pairs practice the conversation. Walk around to monitor the activity and provide help as needed.

LISTENING SCRIPT

Lesson 2: Practice the Conversation

Listen to the conversation. Then listen and repeat.

A: Alice, do you want to meet on the first?
B: What day is that?
A: Tuesday.
B: Oh, sorry. I have a doctor's appointment on the first.

EXPANSION ACTIVITY: Beanbag Toss

★ Put the "big picture" color overhead transparency for Unit 4, Lesson 2, on the projector or have students look at the big picture in their books.

★ Write these sentences on the board: A: *Do you want to meet on the first?* / B: *Is that a Tuesday?* / A: *Yes.*

★ Tell the class that you will toss the beanbag to a student; ask the first question and name a date. The student should respond with the second question and name a day of the week. Remind them to look at the calendar so they can name the correct day.

★ Throw the beanbag to a student and ask the first question, replacing the *first* with a different date. The student should determine whether they're free on that day or not. If they are free, they can respond with, *Yes, I'm free on Tuesday.*

★ When students understand the activity, have the student you modeled the activity with throw the beanbag to another student and ask the first question, choosing a different date. Continue tossing the beanbag around the room until all students have had a chance to participate.

TRY THIS

★ Distribute paper to the class or have students write in their notebooks.

★ Draw a weekly calendar for next week on the board. Make sure to include the dates and the days of the week.

★ Model the activity for students by talking about yourself: *I teach on Monday and Wednesday from 7:00 to 9:00. I have a meeting on Tuesday at 2*. Write your activities on the calendar you created on the board.

★ Tell students to copy the calendar on their papers and to complete the calendars with at least five activities, either real or imagined.

★ Call on students and ask each one to tell the class about one activity they wrote on their calendar. They should explain what the activity is, the date or day, and the time.

EXPANSION ACTIVITY: Information Gap

★ Put students in pairs and have them use the personal calendars that they completed in the Try This activity.

★ Instruct them to make an appointment with their partner for next week. Remind them to look at the conversations in activities 2 and 3 for ideas: *Do you want to meet on _____? When is your meeting?*

★ They should refer to their personal calendars to see if they are available on the day and at the time suggested.

★ Walk around the room to monitor the activity and provide help as needed.

★ Tell students to repeat the activity a few times with new partners. Explain that it will get more challenging as they add appointments to their calendars.

BIG PICTURE EXPANSION ACTIVITY: READING—A Story about Alice

★ Make copies of Worksheet #7 (p. 247) and distribute them to students.

★ Put the "big picture" color overhead transparency for Unit 4, Lesson 2, on the projector or have students look at the "big picture" in their books.

★ Ask students to read the story about the other things Alice has to do in May.

★ Have students look at the picture to answer the questions.

★ Go over the answers with the class.

★ Tell students to add the new events to Alice's calendar on the "big picture."

ANSWER KEY:

A. English class is on May 2nd and 4th.
Lunch on May 10th.
Library meeting on May 13th.
Dancing on the 5th and the 12th.
B. 1. c; 2. b; 3. c

Students can do Unit 4, Section 2, *Listen and Choose* and Section 4 *Fun and Games* on the Interactive CD-ROM.

OBJECTIVE

Keeping Track of Appointments

VOCABULARY

17th seventeenth
18th eighteenth
19th nineteenth
20th twentieth
21st twenty-first
22nd twenty-second
23th twenty-third
24th twenty-fourth
25th twenty-fifth
26th twenty-sixth
27th twenty-seventh
28th twenty-eighth

WINDOW ON MATH

Writing Dates

THINGS TO DO

1. Learn Ordinal Numbers 🎧

★ Ask students to look at the pictures in the book. Ask questions about the pictures and elicit that these are appointment cards. Ask students where they get appointment cards: *doctor, dentist, hair salon, car service centers.*

★ Have them look at the numbers and listen while you say the numbers or play the tape or CD. Remind them that these are ordinal numbers.

★ Say the numbers or play the tape or CD a second time. Pause after each number and ask the students to repeat and point to each number as it is said.

★ Call out cardinal numbers (*25*) and have students respond with the corresponding ordinal number (*twenty-fifth*).

★ Put students in pairs and have one practice saying the ordinal numbers as their partner points to the number in the book. Reverse roles and do the exercise again.

LISTENING SCRIPT

Lesson 3: Learn Ordinal Numbers

Listen to the numbers. Then listen and repeat.

seventeenth	The seventeenth of June is a Sunday.
eighteenth	The eighteenth of June is a Monday.
nineteenth	The nineteenth of June is a Tuesday.
twentieth	The twentieth of June is a Wednesday.
twenty-first	The twenty-first of June is a Thursday.
twenty-second	The twenty-second of June is a Friday.
twenty-third	The twenty-third of June is a Saturday.
twenty-fourth	The twenty-fourth of June is a Sunday.
twenty-fifth	The twenty-fifth of June is a Monday.
twenty-sixth	The twenty-sixth of June is a Tuesday.
twenty-seventh	The twenty-seventh of June is a Wednesday.
twenty-eighth	The twenty-eighth of June is a Thursday.

EXPANSION ACTIVITY: Review

★ Copy a calendar for the current month on the board.

★ Call on students and ask several questions about the calendar: *What day is the nineteenth? What date is the third Friday of this month?*

2. Write

★ Instruct students to look at the appointment cards. Ask the class, *What information is on the appointment cards?* Answer: *name, date, day, time, type of appointment.*

★ Tell the students to look at Henry's appointment card and ask, *When is Henry's appointment?* Point out that the correct answer is spoken as *June 22nd,* but is written in the example as *June 22.*

★ Ask students to look at the chart in the book. Point out that the information about Henry is written on the chart.

★ Have students complete the chart with information from the other appointment cards. Remind them to look at the names on the cards as they complete the chart.

★ Walk around the room to monitor the students' progress and provide help as needed.

★ Copy the chart on the board. Ask volunteers to fill in the information. Go over the answers with the class.

ANSWER KEY:

NAME	DATE	TIME	DAY
Henry	June 22	10 A.M.	Friday
Sue	June 22	4 P.M.	Friday
Alice	June 28	11 A.M.	Thursday
Sam	June 22	9 A.M.	Friday

EXPANSION ACTIVITY:
Dictation and Correction

★ Dictate to the class five sentences about the appointment cards and have students write them in their notebook or on a piece of paper. Read each sentence three times. Use the sentences below or create your own. Note that some of the sentences should be false.

Sam has an appointment on Friday.

Lisa's appointment is at 9:00 A.M.

Nancy's appointment is on June 25.

Chris's appointment is on Monday.

Henry's appointment is at 10:00 P.M.

★ Ask students to read their sentences, look in the book, and write *True* or *False* after each sentence. If the sentence is false, have them correct it.

★ Go over the answers with the class.

3. Practice the Conversation 🎧

★ Have students look at the conversation. Ask them to tell you what are the three questions being asked: *When's _____ appointment? What time? What day is that?* Write the questions on the board.

★ Have students close their books. Read the conversation aloud or play the tape or CD.

★ Read the questions about Henry and elicit answers from the class.

★ Read or play the conversation again with books open. Pause after each sentence and ask students to repeat.

★ Have students work in pairs to practice asking and answering questions about the other appointment cards.

LISTENING SCRIPT

Lesson 3: Ask Questions

Listen to the conversation. Then listen and repeat.

A: When's Henry's appointment?
B: It's on June twenty-second.
A: What time?
B: At 10:00 A.M.
A: What day is that?
B: Friday.

WINDOW ON MATH:
Writing Dates

A. Read these dates.

★ Go over the examples in the book. Point out to students that we always write the month first, then the day, then the year. Some students may be used to writing the day, the month, and the year, as that is the custom in many countries.

★ Ask students to read the dates. Remind them that we say dates as ordinal numbers even though they are written as cardinal numbers.

B. Write the dates another way.

★ Point out to students that sometimes they will need to write the date as all numerals, and sometimes they will need to write out the month.

★ Have students complete Exercise B and check their answers with a partner.

★ Go over the answers with the class.

ANSWER KEY:

3/16/80 = March 16, 1980
5/19/01 = May 19, 2001
April 11, 1944 = 4/11/44
February 17, 2002 = 2/17/02

C. What's the date today?

★ Ask students to write today's date in two different ways on the lines.

★ Go over their answers.

Grammar Notes:

★ Students may not be familiar with the punctuation we use in dates. Point out that slashes are usually used in numerical dates, although sometimes dashes are used. A comma separates the day from the year in dates when the month is written as a word. No punctuation separates the month and year without a day, even when the month is spelled out (*January 2000*)

★ Because we have recently entered a new century, sometimes four digits are required when stating a date (*7/18/2004*).

★ Remind students that dates are written with the month first, then the day, then the year, not the day, the month, and the year as some students might be accustomed to.

Pronunciation Notes:

★ Years beginning with *19* (1956) are usually read as two separate two-digit numbers: *nineteen, fifty-six*.

★ Years beginning with *20* (2006), are usually read as the whole number: *two thousand and six* or *two thousand six*.

Students can do Unit 4, Section 2, *Listen and Choose* and Section 4, *Fun and Games* on the Interactive CD-ROM.

OBJECTIVE

Identifying Holidays

VOCABULARY

Election Day
Independence Day
Labor Day
New Year's Day
Thanksgiving
Valentine's Day

WINDOW ON GRAMMAR

Singular and Plural Nouns

THINGS TO DO

1. Read 🎧

★ Have students look at the pictures. Ask them comprehension questions such as, *What holiday is in February? Which holiday is always on a Thursday? Which holiday is the first one of the year?*

★ Have students look at the chart and ask them what information they need to complete the chart: *name of the holiday* and *when it is.*

★ Have students read about the holidays and complete the chart.

★ Ask students to compare answers with a partner.

★ To go over the answers, ask about the holidays: *When is Valentine's Day?*

LISTENING SCRIPT

Lesson 4: Read

1. For people in the United States, New Year's Day is on January first. That's the first day of the new year.
2. Valentine's Day is on February 14.
3. In the United States, Independence Day is on the fourth of July.
4. Labor Day is on the first Monday in September. This holiday is for workers in the United States.

5. Election Day in the United States is on the first Tuesday after the first Monday in November.
6. Thanksgiving is a big holiday in the United States. It's on the fourth Thursday in November.

EXPANSION ACTIVITY: Calendar Group Work

★ Bring in or ask students to bring in calendars for the current (or next) year. You need enough so that each group of four can work with one calendar.

★ Divide the class into groups of four.

★ Have each group find on the calendar the holidays they just learned about and then create sentences about those holidays and dates as well as other details about the year. Some sentences can be true and some can be false.

★ When the students are finished, have each group read its sentences to another group. That group must decide if the sentences are true or false. They can refer to their calendar for help. Continue until each group has read all of its sentences.

★ Each correct answer earns the team a point.

2. Write

★ Instruct students to look at the questions in each column. Read the questions aloud and pause after each to have students repeat.

★ Ask students to write their responses to the questions on a piece of paper or in their book and share their answers with a partner.

★ Have a few volunteers answer the questions aloud.

EXPANSION ACTIVITY: Small Group Discussion and Drawing

★ Have students draw a picture of one thing they like about their favorite holiday.

★ Have students share their ideas and their pictures in small groups. They may not have all the vocabulary necessary to explain their ideas, but they should be able to communicate visually. Walk around to monitor the activity and provide help as needed.

★ You can then have students form new groups with people who share the same favorite holiday. This can only be done if the same favorite holiday is shared by at least two people. Have those groups compare their pictures.

★ Ask a representative from each group to tell the class the name and date of their favorite holiday.

★ As a variation, you can have each group make a poster of the holiday similar to the holiday pictures in the lesson and post them in the classroom.

3. Interview

★ Have students look at the example and copy the headings—*Name, Holiday,* and *Month*—on a piece of paper or in their notebooks. Write the headings on the board.

★ Read the lines in the example interview, pausing after each to have students repeat.

★ Model the activity. Call on several students and ask the two questions: *What's your favorite holiday? When is it?* Write the information under the headings on the board.

★ Have students walk around the room to ask five classmates the questions and record their answers.

★ Call on a few students to talk about one of their classmates: *Jaime's favorite holiday is New Year's Day. It's in January.*

EXPANSION ACTIVITY: Guessing Game

★ Write several clues about each holiday on slips of paper and distribute them to the class, focusing on only one holiday at a time. Have students read the clues aloud. Elicit the name of the holiday from the class.

★ Create your own clues or use the ones below.

New Year's Day
It's on a different day every year.
It's usually cold in New York on this day.
The month and the day are the same number.
It's before Valentine's Day.

Valentine's Day
It's two weeks after the first of the month.
It's in the month that has 28 days.
It's after New Year's Day.
It's in the second month.

Independence Day
It's always on the same date.
It's in the first week of the month.
It's on a different day every year.
It's between Valentine's Day and Labor Day.

Labor Day
It's on a different date every year.
It's in the ninth month.
It's always on a Monday.
It's a day for workers.

Election Day
It's after Labor Day.
It's in the eleventh month.
It's before Thanksgiving.
It's on a Tuesday.

Thanksgiving
It's before December.
It's in the eleventh month.
It's on a Thursday.
It's always on the fourth Thursday.

★ As a variation, have students work in small groups to create their own holiday clues. Have groups exchange clues and guess the holiday. Make sure the students don't make the clues too easy.

WINDOW ON GRAMMAR: Singular and Plural Nouns

A. Read the words.

★ Ask students to look at the chart in the yellow box.

★ Go over the meanings of *singular* and *plural*. Tell students that when we are talking about two or more of something, the noun is plural. We usually add -s to a noun to make it plural.

★ Make sure students understand how the plurals of *family* and *library* are formed.

B. Write the missing singular or plural form.

★ Tell students to write the missing singular or plural forms for each of the nouns.

★ Go over the answers with the class.

ANSWER KEY:

two families; two schools; two cities; one state; one hour; one post office

Grammar Notes:

★ This is an introduction to plurals, and students should not be expected to be experts.

★ If helpful, you can explain to students the rule for words ending in *consonant + y*: the *y* changes to *i*, and then *we* add *es*. You may need to review what vowels and consonants are. Note that holiday, a word ending in a *vowel + y*, does not change.

★ Although not addressed in this activity, students may ask about other types of plurals. We add -es to words ending in *ss, x, ch, sh,* and *z*. Many words have irregular plurals, such as *men, women, children*.

EXPANSION ACTIVITY: How many?

★ Group students in pairs to write down how many of each type of classroom object there is/are in your classroom: *15 desks, 1 clock, 20 chairs*.

★ When they are finished, ask questions beginning with *How many* _____ ? (*How many chairs are there in the classroom?*)

BIG PICTURE EXPANSION ACTIVITY: GRAMMAR—Singular and Plural Nouns

★ Make copies of Worksheet #8 (p. 248) and distribute them to students.

★ Put the "big picture" color overhead transparency for Unit 4, Lesson 2, on the projector or have students look at the "big picture" in their books.

★ Review the activities on Alice's schedule.

★ Review the formation of plurals from singular nouns.

★ Go over the directions for parts A and B of the Worksheet and have students complete both parts. Go over the answers.

ANSWER KEY:

A. 1. basketballs; 2. parents; 3. dentists; 4. doctors; 5. computers; 6. hours

B. 1. doctors; 2. computers; 3. parents; 4. hours; 5. basketballs; 6. dentists

Students can do Unit 4, Section 3, *Read and Write* and Section 4, *Fun and Games* on the Interactive CD-ROM.

OBJECTIVE

Scheduling Appointments

WINDOW ON PRONUNCIATION

Short *A* and Long *A*

1. Practice the Conversation: Making an Appointment 🎧

★ Have students look at the picture for Conversation 1. To set the context, ask the class, *Who is in the picture? What are they doing?*

★ Read the conversation or play the tape or CD.

★ Read or play the conversation again. Pause after each sentence and ask students to repeat.

★ To check comprehension, ask the class, *What is the caller's name? When is the appointment?*

★ Point out that there are two places in the conversation to substitute information: *the caller's name* and *the date and time of the appointment.*

★ Point out that when people answer the phone in an office, they usually identify the office in the greeting.

★ Model the conversation with a student. Have the student read *B's* lines. Cue the student to substitute *Gina Mata* for the scripted name in the conversation. Demonstrate how to substitute a different date and time—*March 10th at 2*—for the scripted information.

★ Have students practice the conversation in pairs. Walk around to monitor the activity and provide help as needed. Encourage them to use their own names in the conversation and a date that is in the near future.

LISTENING SCRIPT

Lesson 5: Practice the Conversation—Making an Appointment

Listen to the conversation. Then listen and repeat.

A: Dr. Lambert's office.
B: Yes, this is Jim Brown. I'd like to make an appointment.
A: Okay. Our next opening is on March 6th at 11:00.
B: Great. I'll take it.

BIG PICTURE EXPANSION ACTIVITY: SPEAKING—Making an Appointment

★ Put the "big picture" color overhead transparency for Unit 4, Lesson 2, on the projector or have students look at the "big picture" in their books.

★ Copy on the board this variation for Lesson 5, Conversation 1:

A: Dr. Lambert's office.

B: This is Alice Chen. I'd like to make an appointment.

A: Okay. Our next opening is on <u>May 1st at 11</u>.

B: <u>That's not good for me. I have a doctor's appointment on May 1st.</u>

A: <u>What day is good for you?</u>

B: <u>May 2nd.</u>

A: Okay, I do have several times available that day.

★ Explain the meaning of "*That's not good for me.*" This gives students another way to say "*Oh, sorry.*" which they learned in Lesson 2. This is a way to say they are busy on a certain day.

★ Model the conversation with the students. Have the students read *A* and you read *B*. Group students in pairs to practice making appointments. Remind them to use the calendar in Lesson 2. Walk around to monitor the activity and provide help as needed.

2. Practice the Conversation: Canceling an Appointment 🎧

★ Repeat the basic procedure from Activity 1.

★ To set the context, ask the class, *Who is in the picture? Where are they?*

★ To check comprehension, ask students, *Who is calling? What does he want? When is the next opening?*

Lesson 5: Practice the Conversation—Cancelling an Appointment

Listen to the conversation. Then listen and repeat.

A: Dr. Lambert's office.
B: This is Jim Brown. I need to cancel my appointment.
A: When is it?
B: It's on March 6th at 11:00.
A: Okay. Thanks for calling.

3. Practice the Conversation: Rescheduling an Appointment 🎧

★ Repeat the basic procedure from Activity 1.

★ To set the context, ask the class, *What do you think they're talking about?*

★ To check comprehension, ask students, *Who is the caller? Why did he call? When is his new appointment?*

Lesson 5: Practice the Conversation—Rescheduling an Appointment

Listen to the conversation. Then listen and repeat.

A: Dr. Lambert's office.
B: This is Jim Brown. I need to reschedule my appointment.
A: Okay. I have an opening on May 5th at 2:00.
B: That's good. Thank you.

**EXPANSION ACTIVITY:
Conversation Scramble**

★ Photocopy and enlarge the sentences in the conversation. Make enough copies so that each pair of students will have a set.

★ Group students in pairs and give a set to each pair; have them put the sentences in order.

★ When they're done, have them cut the sentences up so that each word is on a separate slip of paper. Mix the words up.

★ Tell the students to unscramble the words and reconstruct the conversation. Walk around the room to monitor the activity and provide help as needed.

★ The students should look in their books to check the sentences.

WINDOW ON PRONUNCIATION: Short *A* and Long *A*

A. Listen to the words. Then listen and repeat. 🎧

★ Say the short *A* sound (as in *map*) and have students repeat. Point out that the mouth opens fairly wide when making this sound and that the sound is made near the back of the throat.

★ Say the long *A* sound (as in *make*) and have students repeat. Instruct students to say the sound and feel the shape of their mouths. Elicit that the mouth begins open when the long *A* sound is made, but then closes a bit so that it is open more horizontally than vertically, like when we smile. Explain that the long *A* sound is really two sounds /ey/.

★ Read the words or play the tape or CD. Read or play the words a second time, pausing after each to have students repeat.

★ Ask the students to write the words on the chart. Remind them to write the words with the long *A* sound in the first column, and the words with the short *A* sound in the second column.

★ Have them check their answers with a partner.

★ Go over the answers with the class.

★ Write the names *Dave* and *Sam* on the board. Ask students if they think these words will have a short or long *A* sound. Elicit that *Dave* has a long sound and *Sam* has a short sound. Point out that all the words that end in an *e*, specifically a silent *e*, have a long *A* sound.

Lesson 5: Window on Pronunciation

Listen to the words. Then listen and repeat.

1. male	8. cashier	15. table
2. gas	9. map	16. okay
3. date	10. back	17. state
4. that	11. May	18. day
5. make	12. rainy	19. April
6. magazine	13. raise	20. sale
7. basketball	14. after	

ANSWER KEY:

Sounds like letter A (long A)	Sounds like a in map (short a)
April	after
date	back
day	basketball
make	cashier
male	gas
May	magazine
okay	map
rainy	that
raise	
sale	
state	
table	

B. Work with a partner.

★ Have students work in pairs to practice asking and answering the questions. Point out that all the answers will have either a short or long *A* sound.

★ Walk around the room to monitor the activity and provide help as needed.

★ Go over the answers with the class.

ANSWER KEY:

1. state; 2. Today's date is _____; 3. May;
4. Answers will vary.; 5. after

Literacy Note:

★ Your students may not have learned the rule about silent *E* making a letter say its name. Point out that when we have a word that ends in the pattern *vowel-consonant-silent e*, the vowel will usually have the long sound, or sound like the name of the letter.

★ Help students brainstorm words that end in this pattern. Suggest they look at previous lessons for ideas: *phone, home, note, nice, fine, code, fire, five, dime*. Point out that this is a good guideline but it is not always true: *have, one*.

EXPANSION ACTIVITY: Create Questions

★ Have students create three questions, each of which will use one of the words from the previous Window on Pronunciation exercise in the answer: *What is the fifth month? What do you buy at a gas station?*

★ Have students work in pairs to practice asking and answering the questions.

EQUIPPED FOR THE FUTURE ROLE

Family

OBJECTIVE

Interpreting a School Calendar

THINGS TO DO

1. Read

★ Instruct students to look at the school calendar. Help them develop skimming skills by asking questions such as, *What is this?* (a school calendar) *How do you know?* (it tells the first day of school, when schools are closed, etc.).

★ Ask students if they have children in school and if they've received a school calendar. Ask the class why school calendars are important (*so parents know important dates such as holidays, when report cards are issued, etc.*).

★ Ask students to read the questions at the bottom of the page. Tell them that reading the questions first can help them find the information they need. Have the students read the calendar carefully and answer the questions.

★ Students should check their answers with a partner.

★ Go over the answers with the class.

ANSWER KEY:

1. September 3; 2. Labor Day; 3. November 11, 28, 29; 4. 4; 5. Oct. 4; 6. Jan. 2

EXPANSION ACTIVITY: Find the Mistake

★ Write on the board or dictate to the class ten statements about the South Beach City School Schedule, each of which contains one inaccuracy. Use the sentences below or create your own. The correct word or phrase appears in brackets.

The first day of school is September 2 [September 3].

The first holiday is National Day of Remembrance [Labor Day].

Schools are closed [open] on September 11.

September 19 is a Tuesday [Thursday].

Report cards are issued before [after] Veterans' Day.

Winter holidays begin on November 28 [December 23].

Thanksgiving is on November 29 [28].

There are seven [4] holidays before December 1.

There are three [4] holidays on Mondays.

Progress reports are issued in October and November [December].

★ Ask the students to rewrite the sentences and correct the mistakes.

★ Ask volunteers to write the correct sentences on the board.

2. Mark the Calendar

★ Help students brainstorm ways to write school holidays on the calendar (*no school, holiday, school closed*).

★ Have them write the South Beach school holidays on the November calendar.

★ Walk around to make sure they have written the dates correctly.

3. Write

★ Help students brainstorm a list of things that are important to write on a calendar. The list might include events from Lesson 2, as well as holidays, meetings, tests, and social activities. Write the ideas on the board.

★ Ask students to look at the calendar. Have them write in the name of the current month (or the next month if you are near the end of the current one) and the dates.

★ Tell students to write important dates on their calendars and explain the dates on their calendars to a partner.

★ Ask a few volunteers to tell the class about something on their calendars.

1. Listening Review 🎧

> **TESTING FOCUS:**
> **Listening Discrimination—Minimal Pairs**
>
> ★ To prepare students for items 1–8, tell them that they will listen for a discrete sound (the *s* ending that indicates plurality).
> ★ Give the class a few examples of this exercise: *students, teachers, book, paper, copies.* Pause after each word. Have students raise their hands if they hear the *s* sound.

★ Go over the directions with the class. Point out that they are listening for the *s* sound in questions 1–8.

★ Read the items or play the tape or CD and have the students mark their answers on the Answer Sheet.

★ Walk around to monitor the activity and help students stay on task.

★ Have students check their answers with a partner.

★ Go over the answers with the class.

LISTENING SCRIPT

Lesson 7: Listening Review

Listen and choose the word you hear. Use the Answer Sheet.

1. country	5. dollars
2. months	6. cents
3. holidays	7. state
4. family	8. cities

Listen and choose the best answer. Use the Answer Sheet.

9. How many days are in a week?
10. What's the first month of the year?
11. What day is the twenty-first?
12. What day is between Monday and Wednesday?
13. What month is between July and September?
14. When's Thanksgiving in the United States?

Listen and choose the correct appointment card. Use the Answer Sheet.

15. His appointment is on Wednesday.
16. Her appointment is on Friday.

ANSWER KEY:

1. country; 2. months; 3. holidays; 4. family; 5. dollars; 6. cents; 7. state; 8. cities; 9.C; 10. B; 11. C; 12. B; 13. A; 14. B; 15. B; 16. A

2. Conversation Check: Pair Work

★ Go over the directions. Have the students work in pairs and remind them that each partner has some information, but other information is missing. They must ask their partner questions to complete the appointment cards.

★ Walk around to monitor the activity and provide help as needed.

> **Assessment Note:**
> ★ You can use the Conversation Check Activity as an oral assessment. Ask pairs of students to complete the activity while you note areas of difficulty.

LEARNING LOG

★ Point out the four sections of the Learning Log: *I know these words, I can ask, I can say,* and *I can write.*

★ Have students check what they know and what they can do.

★ Walk around to note what they don't know or can't do. Use this information to review areas of difficulty.

BIG PICTURE EXPANSION ACTIVITY: WRITING—Write about Your Schedule

★ Put the "big picture" color overhead transparency for Unit 4, Lesson 2, on the projector or have students look at the "big picture" in their books.

★ Tell students to write a sentence about three of Alice's events and read them to a partner. Write a few of their sentences on the board: *She has a basketball game on the 11th. Alice has a dentist's appointment on Monday, the 14th.*

★ Refer students back to the weekly schedule they wrote for themselves in the Try This exercise in Lesson 2. From that, students should write a paragraph and include a sentence about each of their activities.

★ Ask students to read their paragraphs to a partner. Have the partner make a list of the things that the student will do. Have partners switch tasks and do the exercise again.

BIG PICTURE EXPANSION ACTIVITY: SPEAKING Assessment—Talking about the Big Picture

★ You can use the "big picture" as an individual assessment to place new students in open entry classes, to diagnose difficulties, or to measure progress.

★ Work with one student at a time. Show the "big picture" to the student. Ask, *What do you see in the picture?* or, *Tell me about the picture.* Tell the student you want him or her to speak for as long as possible. Wait a moment for the student to prepare to answer. If the student has difficulty, you can use prompts: *What is this? Why are there numbers? Who do you see in the picture? What are the people doing?*

★ You can use a rubric like the one below to rate beginning speakers.

3	Uses sentences, although form may be incorrect Can speak for sustained length of time Responds to prompts, but doesn't need them to begin speaking
2	Can use nouns and verbs Uses phrases Answers informational questions
1	Can name objects Uses single words Can answer yes/no questions
0	Cannot say anything independently May be able to point to objects when prompted

 Students can do Unit 4, Section 5, *Practice Test* on the Interactive CD-ROM.

OBJECTIVE

Singular and Plural Nouns
Writing about Holidays

FOCUS ON WRITING

Capital Letters

1. Read stories A and B. Find these words.

★ Instruct students to look at the pictures in the book and identify the names of things they know. Write them on the board.

★ Have students read paragraphs A and B. Alternatively, read them aloud to the class, pausing after each line to have students repeat.

★ To check comprehension for each story, ask: *Who is the story about? What holiday does he/she like? Why does she like it? What do they do on that holiday?*

★ Ask students to look at the two columns at the top of the page. Tell them to find in the paragraphs all the singular nouns that begin with the letters in the column on the left and write them there. Also, find the plural nouns and write them in the column on the right.

★ Have students check their answers with a partner. Go over the answers with the class.

ANSWER KEY:

Singular Nouns: holiday, mother, father, family, church
Plural Nouns: parades, fireworks, parties, presents

2. Correct the punctuation.

★ Ask students to look at the *Focus on Writing* box. Read the rules aloud and go over the examples.

★ Instruct students to correct the paragraph by adding ten capital letters. Remind them to look at stories A and B if they need a model.

★ Walk around to monitor student progress and provide help as needed.

★ Go over the answers with the class. Ask them why they capitalized the letters they did. Make sure they realize that the pronoun *I* is always capitalized.

ANSWER KEY:

My name is Fatima. My favorite holiday is Ramadan. This year it is in March. I like this holiday because I visit with my family. We go to Egypt to see them.

3. Write your own story.

★ Point out to students the lined area in the book and tell them they are going to write a story about their favorite holiday in that space.

★ Remind students to include details about when the holiday is, what they do, and why they like it. Have them look at the other stories in this section to help them write their own stories. Walk around to monitor the activity and provide help as needed.

★ Ask students to draw a picture in the space on the right that shows something about their favorite holiday.

★ Have students read their stories to a partner.

★ Ask a few volunteers to read their stories to the class.

EXPANSION ACTIVITY:
Find Someone Who

★ Write *Find someone who likes _____.* on the board. Then brainstorm a list of things associated with holidays. Your list might look like this:

fireworks	*turkey*
parades	*dumplings*
presents	*go to church*
flowers	*candles*

★ Students should copy the list from the board on a piece of paper.

★ Have students stand up and walk around the room, asking classmates about the different items: *Do you like fireworks?* Point out that they can only write each person's name on the list once.

★ When students have completed the activity, ask the class questions such as, *Who likes fireworks? Who likes turkey?*

EQUIPPED FOR THE FUTURE ROLE

Community

OBJECTIVE

Learning about Community Events

A. Read the newspaper below.

★ Have students look at the reading and ask them questions such as, *What is this?* or *Where do you see this?* Ask them to raise their hands if they read a newspaper.

★ To help students practice skimming skills, tell them to look at all the words in dark print. Ask questions such as, *What days is the newspaper talking about? What events or activities are in the paper? (Movies, an international festival, a community fun day, a library birthday party, an Independence Day parade)*

★ Students should read the newspaper and circle all the times and days. Have them compare answers with a partner.

★ Go over the answers with the class. Ask questions such as, *When are the movies playing? On what day?*

ANSWER KEY:

Days: today (Friday), Saturday, Sunday, Independence Day
Times: 7 P.M., 8–10 P.M., 1–3 P.M., 4 P.M., 5 P.M., 9 P.M.

B. Match the events and places.

★ Read the events and places aloud. Pause after each and have students repeat.

★ Go over the example. Ask students where the library birthday party will be. Elicit that it will be at the Main Library.

★ Have students draw a line between the event and the place where it will happen. Walk around to monitor the activity and provide help as needed.

★ Go over the answers with the class. Have them mark the number correct in the self-correct box.

ANSWER KEY:

1. d; 2. e; 3. a; 4. c; 5. b

C. Answer the questions.

★ Have students write the names of the events on the lines. Remind them to look back at the newspaper section to find the answers. Walk around to monitor the activity and provide help as needed.

★ Have them compare answers with a partner and take turns asking and answering the questions.

★ Go over the answers with the class.

ANSWER KEY:

Note: these answers mention the words in the questions, but other answers may be possible.
1. Community Fun Day, Library Birthday Party
2. Community Fun Day, Library Birthday Party, Independence Day Parade
3. Library Birthday Party, Independence Day Parade

D. Complete the sentences.

★ Do the first sentence as an example. Elicit that the students should write 8:00 and 10:00 in the blanks.

★ Instruct students to complete the sentences. They can reread the newspaper to find the information they need. Walk around the room to monitor the activity and provide help as needed.

★ Have students check their answers with a partner.

★ Go over the answers with the class.

ANSWER KEY:

1. 8:00, 10:00; 2. Mexico, China, Japan, France, Colombia; 3. $3; 4. 3215 Caldwell Street; 5. Saturday, 1:00, 3:00; 6. Independence; 7. July 4; 8. Marshall; 9. 100, birthday; 10. K–8

Take It Outside

★ You can assign this exercise as an out-of-class assignment or do it in class. If you do it in class, bring in enough photocopies of an events calendar for the entire class or have each student bring in the events section of a paper.

★ Group students in pairs to list events that might be on an events calendar in your community.

★ Elicit from the class some of the events on their lists: *festivals, art shows, movies, plays, parties, dances, music, parades*. Note that some of this vocabulary will be new to students although they will know about the type of event.

★ Distribute photocopies of the events calendar to each pair of students, or have them work with the one they brought. Have them complete the chart in the book with two events they are interested in.

★ Call on students to tell the class about an event that they might like to go to.

EXPANSION ACTIVITY: Write a Notice

★ Help students brainstorm a list of events that they will be attending soon: *parties, festivals, meetings.*

★ Individually, each student should work to list the information about one event, including *when, where, what day, who will attend*.

★ Write these questions on the board: *What is the event? What day is it? What time is it? Where is it? Who is it for?*

★ Tell students to copy the questions on a piece of paper.

★ Group students in pairs and have them take turns interviewing each other about the event.

★ When they have gathered all the information they need, students should work individually to write a notice about their partner's event. Remind them to use the newspaper articles as models.

★ Ask volunteers to read the notices, or post them in the classroom.

EQUIPPED FOR THE FUTURE ROLE

Work

OBJECTIVE

Planning a Work Schedule

A. Read the story.

★ Ask students to look at the photo. To set the context, ask them, *Is this a man or a woman? Is she a teacher? Is she a doctor?* If possible, give clues to elicit that she is a painter. Cue the students by having them read the first line of the story.

★ Ask students to read the questions below the story, or read the questions to them aloud and have the students repeat. Tell them to pay attention to the information in the questions when they read the story. They may want to underline the answers in the reading.

★ Have students read the story and answer the questions. Walk around the room to monitor the activity and provide help as needed.

★ Have students check their answers with a partner.

★ Go over the answers with the class.

★ Students should also practice asking and answering the questions with a partner.

ANSWER KEY:

1. Lee; 2. at the Alden Community Center;
3. six; 4. two; 5. Monday to Friday;
6. Monday, June 28

B. Look at Isabel's schedule for June.

★ Have students look at the calendar for June. Ask comprehension questions such as, *What day is June 1? How many Wednesdays are in June? What date does Isabel start room 1?*

★ Ask students how many days it takes to paint a room (*two*). Point out that Isabel starts room 1 on June 10 and finishes on June 11, and that is two days. Note that the start and finish dates have been written next to room 1.

★ Have students complete the schedule by writing in the start and finish dates on the lines.

★ Go over the answers.

ANSWER KEY:

Room 1	6/10–6/11
Room 2	6/14–6/15
Room 3	6/16–6/17
Room 4	6/18–6/21
Room 5	6/22–6/23
Room 6	6/24–6/25

C. Write the information on the calendar above.

★ Have students write the information from Activity B on the calendar.

★ Walk around the room to monitor the activity and provide help as needed.

Take It Outside

★ If this is an out-of-class assignment, students can interview a family member, friend, or coworker. For an in-class assignment, have the students interview a partner. Note that although the direction line asks about work tasks, students who don't have jobs can describe other tasks they have to complete, like buying kids' school supplies, buying groceries, mowing the lawn, planting a garden.

★ Have students look at the directions and calendar. Ask them what information they will need to complete the interview. Elicit these questions: *What do you have to do this week (at work)? How long will it take? When will you start _____? When will you finish?* Write the questions on the board.

★ Point out that they will write down information about three tasks that need to be completed during the week.

★ Have students complete the interview and write the information on the calendar.

★ Ask a few students to tell the class about their interviewees' schedules.

EXPANSION ACTIVITY: Group Project

★ Brainstorm ideas for a class event such as a field trip (museum, library, mall), recreational activity (bowling, ice skating, rock climbing, line dancing) or party (holiday, birthday, cultural sharing).

★ Divide the class into pairs or small groups. Make each group responsible for choosing an event that they'd like to organize.

★ Have students work in their pairs or small groups to plan their event. Note that they should make a list of tasks, a schedule for completing the tasks, and assign individual responsibilities.

★ Walk around the room to monitor the activity and provide help as needed.

★ When the groups are finished, ask them to present their plans. With the class, choose one or more events to hold.

Clothing

UNIT OVERVIEW

LESSON	OBJECTIVE	STUDENT BOOK PAGE #
1. Shirts, Skirts, and Sweaters	Identifying Colors and Clothes	p. 68
2. I'm looking for children's clothes.	At a Department Store	p. 70
3. What size is it?	Understanding Sizes and Price Tags	p. 72
4. A Folktale	Reading a Folktale	p. 74
5. It's too short.	Describing Clothes	p. 76
6. Work Clothes	On the Job	p. 78
7. What do you know?	Review and Assessment	p. 80
8. Spotlight	Grammar	p. 82

Big Picture Expansion Activities

FOCUS	TITLE	SUGGESTED USE
Speaking	Find and Match	Lesson 2
Reading	A Story about Berta	Lesson 5
Grammar	What's the object?	Lesson 4
Writing	Writing about Actions	Lesson 7
Speaking	Assessment: Talking about the Picture	Lesson 7

Big Picture Expansion Activity Worksheets

WORKSHEET# /FOCUS	TITLE	TEACHER'S EDITION PAGE #
9. Grammar	What's the Object?	p. 249
10. Reading	A Story about Berta	p. 250

OBJECTIVE

Identifying Colors and Clothes

VOCABULARY

blouse	pants
boots	shirt
briefs	shoes
hat	shorts
coat	skirt
dress	socks
jacket	sweater
necktie	T-shirt
pajamas	undershirt

WINDOW ON GRAMMAR

Present Continuous Statements

THINGS TO DO

1. Learn New Words 🎧

★ Ask students to look at the pictures and listen while you say the words or play the tape or CD.

★ Say the words or play the tape or CD a second time. Pause after each word and ask the students to repeat the word and point to the picture that correctly illustrates the word.

★ Group students in pairs and instruct them to take turns saying each word as their partner points to the correct photo.

★ Ask students to write each word next to the correct picture. Ask about other clothing that they wear (*vest, sweatshirt, jeans*), and have them write other ideas next to the pictures of the light bulbs.

★ Ask students questions about the clothes they're wearing such as, *Who is wearing boots today?*

LISTENING SCRIPT

Lesson 1: Learn New Words

Look at the pictures. Listen to the words. Then listen and repeat.

1.	necktie	What is it? It's a necktie.
2.	undershirt	What is it? It's an undershirt.
3.	briefs	What are they? They're briefs.
4.	shoes	What are they? They're shoes.
5.	boots	What are they? They're boots.
6.	coat	What is it? It's a coat.
7.	shirt	What is it? It's a shirt.
8.	sweater	What is it? It's a sweater.
9.	hat	What is it? It's a hat.
10.	T-shirt	What is it? It's a T-shirt.
11.	jacket	What is it? It's a jacket.
12.	pajamas	What are they? They're pajamas.
13.	socks	What are they? They're socks.
14.	pants	What are they? They're pants.
15.	shorts	What are they? They're shorts.
16.	blouse	What is it? It's a blouse.
17.	skirt	What is it? It's a skirt.
18.	dress	What is it? It's a dress.

Grammar Note:

★ Explain that some of the words in the New Words list are in plural form. Some of these words actually refer to two things (*socks, shoes, boots*). These may be singular or plural (*one sock, two socks*). Others refer to one article of clothing with two legs (*briefs, shorts, pants, pajamas*) and are always plural (*a pair of briefs/shorts/pants/pajamas*).

★ Point out that it seems like *a pair of briefs, etc.* is plural, but *a pair* actually indicates a singular item:

The pants are/The pair of pants is

The shoes are/The pair of shoes is

Pronunciation Notes:

★ This lesson includes words that begin with sibilants (*s, sh*). Consonant clusters that begin with *s* can be hard for students to pronounce.

★ Encourage students to put the tips of their tongues behind the top teeth without the tongue touching the floor of the mouth (to avoid beginning with a vowel sound first). Have them exaggerate the length of the *ssss* sound in *sweater* and *skirt*.

EXPANSION ACTIVITY: Draw the Clothes

★ Divide the class into two teams. Ask a volunteer from each team to come to the board.

★ Whisper the name of a piece of clothing (*socks*) to both students and instruct them to draw the object on the board. The rest of the class should try and guess what it is. The first student to correctly name the article of clothing earns a point for his or her team.

★ Invite new students to the board, and continue playing until all the objects have been illustrated and named.

★ The team with the most points wins.

★ Small prizes for the winning team will probably increase enthusiasm for the game and raise the energy level in the classroom.

2. Learn New Words 🎧

★ Have students look at the colors and listen while you say the words or play the tape or CD.

★ Say the colors or play the tape or CD a second time. Pause after each word and ask the students to repeat the word and point to the color.

LISTENING SCRIPT

Lesson 1: Learn New Words

Look at the squares. Listen to the colors. Then listen and repeat.

1. blue   What color is it? Blue.
2. yellow   What color is it? Yellow.
3. red   What color is it? Red.
4. black   What color is it? Black.
5. brown   What color is it? Brown.
6. green   What color is it? Green.
7. purple   What color is it? Purple.
8. white   What color is it? White.

blue	red
brown	purple
yellow	black
green	white

EXPANSION ACTIVITY: Clothes and Weather

★ Write this sentence starter on the board: *I wear shorts in hot weather*. Point to the *shorts* on the diagram and read the sentence. Point to another item (*sweater*) and elicit a new sentence (*I wear a sweater in cold weather*).

★ Group students in pairs to practice talking about the clothes they wear. Walk around the room to monitor the activity and provide help as needed.

★ Call on a few volunteers to tell the class about their partner: *Maria wears a skirt in hot weather*.

EXPANSION ACTIVITY: Draw What I Say

★ Bring in or have students bring in enough crayons or colored pencils so that each student has a set of the basic colors in this lesson.

★ Draw a square, a triangle, and a circle on the board. Write the name of the shape above each of the shapes. Say each name and have students repeat.

★ Tell students that you are going to give instructions and they should draw what you say. For example, you might say, *Draw a red square at the top of a piece of paper. Draw a yellow circle under the square. Draw a blue triangle next to the yellow circle.*

★ When you are finished, have students compare their drawings with a partner's.

★ Have students work in pairs to practice giving and following instructions about drawing with colors.

3. Practice the Conversation

★ Have students look at the pictures of clothes again. Ask them to find the jacket and ask, *What color is the jacket?*

★ Ask students to read the example question and answer. Play the tape or CD and pause after each sentence to have students repeat.

★ Group students in pairs to practice asking and answering at least six questions about the articles of clothing.

LISTENING SCRIPT

Lesson 1: Practice the Conversation

Listen to the conversation. Then listen and repeat.

A: What color is the jacket?
B: It's brown.

> **Grammar Note:**
> ★ Remind students that we use *is* with singular nouns and *are* with plural nouns: *What color is the jacket? What color are the pants?*

★ ★

📁 **TRY THIS**

★ ★

★ Instruct the students to look at the chart and ask, *What colors are listed in this chart?* Go over the directions and examples.

★ Have students make their own chart. They can write any three colors from this lesson as headings at the top of their chart.

★ Ask students to list five things in the room under each color. Remind them they can use possessives if appropriate (*Ann's shoes*).

★ Students should share with a partner about things on their charts.

★ Call on a few students to tell the class about some things on their charts.

WINDOW ON GRAMMAR: Present Continuous Statements

A. Read the sentences.

★ Read the examples aloud and have students repeat.

★ Ask students to tell you what they need to make the present continuous tense. Identify the pattern *am/is/are* and a verb that ends in *-ing*.

B. Complete the sentences.

★ Look at the first sentence and write it on the board, filling in the blanks with information about yourself.

★ Ask students to complete the remaining sentences. Remind them to look at the examples.

★ Call on a few volunteers to read their sentences to the class. Note that some of the sentences will be different.

EXPANSION ACTIVITY: Describe the Picture

★ Bring in pictures of people and clothes from magazines or have students bring some in from their favorite publications.

★ Ask the students to write 4–6 sentences about the pictures using the present continuous: *The man is wearing black pants. The woman is wearing a green shirt.*

★ Collect all the pictures and descriptions, keeping each description with the photo it describes.

★ Put students in groups of five. Give each group five photos and the corresponding descriptions. Have them put the pictures in the center of the group. Have each student take one of the five descriptions.

★ Have one student in each group read a description while the other students listen and choose the picture that matches. A different student should read each description.

 Students can do Unit 5, Section 1, *Learn New Words* and Section 4, *Fun and Games* on the Interactive CD-ROM.

OBJECTIVE

At a Department Store

VOCABULARY

PEOPLE AND PLACES	ACTIONS
cashier	buying
customer	coming into
customer service	going into
department store	leaving
entrance	running
exit	sleeping
fitting room	talking

THINGS TO DO

1. Learn New Words 🎧

★ Put the "big picture" color overhead transparency for Unit 5, Lesson 2, on the projector or have students look at the "big picture" in their books. Ask questions about the picture: *What is this?* Elicit that the picture shows *a store* or *a department store*.

★ Have students listen and look at the picture while you say the words or play the tape or CD.

★ Say the words or play the tape or CD a second time. Pause after each word and ask the students to repeat and point to each item as it is said.

★ Point to the pictures in random order, and have students say each name.

★ Group students in pairs so that one student can practice saying the item as his or her partner points to the picture. Reverse roles and do the activity again.

LISTENING SCRIPT

Lesson 2: Learn New Words

Look at the picture. Listen to the words. Then listen and repeat.

1. department store	This is Lane's Department Store.
2. fitting room	The fitting room is near the elevator.
3. customer	A customer is near the exit.
4. customer service	There is a woman working at customer service.
5. cashier	The cashier is near the entrance.
6. exit	The exit is across from customer service.
7. entrance	There are people coming in the entrance.
8. coming into	The man is coming into the store.
9. going into	The woman is going into the elevator.
10. talking	The men are talking about the T-shirt.
11. sleeping	The boy is sleeping near the fitting room.
12. leaving	Marc is leaving the store.
13. running	A cashier is running after Tom.
14. buying	The woman is buying many things.

EXPANSION ACTIVITY: Charades

★ Write all the actions from the list of new words on separate slips of paper. Include actions from previous units: *wearing, watching, giving, standing, listening, sitting, driving, dancing, reading, writing, eating, washing dishes.*

★ Tell students that you are going to do one of the actions (*dancing*) and you want them to identify it. After you have elicited the action, rephrase it for the class as a complete sentence using the present continuous (*I am dancing*). Write the sentence on the board.

★ Ask a volunteer to come to the front of the room and give him or her a slip of paper to act out. Help the class identify the action and make a complete sentence. Write the sentence on the board.

★ Continue the activity until all the action words have been demonstrated and named. Instruct students to write down on a piece of paper all the sentences on the board.

2. Practice the Conversation 🎧

★ Have students read the conversation with you. Read each line out loud, pause and have students repeat. Read *A's* lines and have students respond chorally with *B's* answers. Point out that they can use these questions to practice talking about other people in the picture.

★ Model the dialogue with a student. Have the student read *A's* question, but substitute a different person for Marc. Demonstrate how to answer the questions by explaining where the person is and what the person is doing.

★ Group students in pairs to practice asking and answering questions about people in the picture. Walk around the room to monitor their conversations and provide help as needed.

★ Ask volunteers to call on other students and ask questions about the people in the picture.

LISTENING SCRIPT

Lesson 2: Practice the Conversation

Listen to the conversation. Then listen and repeat.

A: Where's Marc?
B: He's near the exit.
A: What's he doing?
B: He's leaving the store.

BIG PICTURE EXPANSION ACTIVITY: SPEAKING—Find and Match

★ On separate slips of paper write three pieces of information about each of six people in the big picture: *their location, their action, a description of what that person is wearing*.

★ Write the headings *location, action,* and *clothes* on the board. Ask students what questions they would ask to find out about each category and write each under the correct heading: *Where are you? What are you doing? What are you wearing?*

★ Distribute the slips of paper to the students and have them make a sentence about the information on the slip and memorize their sentence. For example, if they receive the action *into the fitting room,* they should create the sentence, *I'm going into the fitting room*.

★ Ask students to stand up and walk around the room and group themselves according to corresponding location, action, and description of clothes. For example, the person with the location *near the exit,* the person with the action *leaving the store,* and the person with the description of the clothes *wearing an orange shirt* should all stand together.

★ Walk around the room to monitor the activity and provide help as needed. Make

sure students are asking questions to get the information they need rather than reading each other's slips of paper.

★ When all of the students are standing with their matches, have them tell the class the information on their slips.

3. Practice the Conversation 🎧

★ Repeat the basic procedure from Activity 2.

★ Point to the directory at the bottom of the page and ask a student the location of one of the categories.

★ Demonstrate how to repeat the location as a question in order to confirm the information.

★ Have students work in pairs and practice the conversation using the categories and places on the store directory. Walk around to make sure they understand the activity and provide help if needed.

LISTENING SCRIPT

Lesson 2: Practice the Conversation

Listen to the conversation. Then listen and repeat.

A: Can I help you?
B: Yes, I'm looking for children's clothes.
A: They're on the second floor.
B: Thank you.

EXPANSION ACTIVITY: Beanbag Toss

★ Tell students that you are going to say a category or an item and that they should respond with the location on the store directory.

★ Model the activity. Call on a student and toss him or her the beanbag. (You may certainly substitute a ball or other item.) Name an item (*children's clothes*) and elicit the location (*second floor*). Be sure to include clothing items from Lesson 1 that fit the categories on the directory: *dresses, women's hats, neckties, socks, pajamas, men's caps*.

★ Continue the activity until all the students have had a chance to respond.

 Students can do Unit 5, Section 2, *Listen and Choose* on the Interactive CD-ROM.

OBJECTIVE

Understanding Sizes and Price Tags

VOCABULARY

	Sizes
price tag	small
receipt	medium
size	large
	extra large

WINDOW ON MATH

Multiplying and Dividing

THINGS TO DO

1. Learn New Words 🎧

★ Ask students to look at the pictures and review. Have them identify the names of the clothing they know.

★ Have students look at the pictures while you say the words or play the tape or CD.

★ Say the words or play the tape or CD a second time. Pause after each word and ask the students to repeat and point to each item as it is said.

★ Have students work in pairs and have one student practice saying each item as the other points to the picture. Reverse roles and repeat the activity.

LISTENING SCRIPT

Lesson 3: Learn New Words

Look at the pictures. Listen to the words. Then listen and repeat.

1. price tag	Where's the price tag?
2. receipt	Where's the receipt?
3. size	What size is it?
4. small	What size is it? It's a small.
5. medium	What size is it? It's a medium.
6. large	What size is it? It's a large.
7. extra large	What size is it? It's an extra large.

EXPANSION ACTIVITY: Yard Sale

★ Bring in or have students bring in old clothes. As a variation, bring in pictures of clothing from newspapers or magazines.

★ Give each student some articles of clothing (or pictures). Tell them that they are going to pretend to have a yard sale, and they must determine the size of each article of clothing and set a price. Instruct students to write the sizes and prices in their notes so they can refer to them if necessary.

★ You want to have half the class walk around the room and ask the other half questions about the clothes. Then switch roles. Walk around to monitor the activity and provide help as needed.

2. Practice the Conversation 🎧

★ Have students read the conversation and listen while you read or play the tape or CD.

★ Say the conversation or play the tape or CD a second time. Pause after each line and ask the students to repeat.

★ Note that there are two words in the conversation that are used to express surprise: *Really?* and *Wow!* Say these words with expression and have students repeat. Encourage them to exaggerate the rise in their voices to indicate surprise.

★ Model the conversation with a student.

★ Have students work in pairs and practice the conversation using the things and prices in the pictures shown in the book. Walk around to make sure students understand the activity and provide help if needed.

LISTENING SCRIPT

Lesson 2: Practice the Conversation

Listen to the conversation. Then listen and repeat.

A: What size is the T-shirt?
B: It's a small.
A: Really? Is it on sale?
B: Yes. It's only five dollars.
A: Wow! Five dollars! That's a good price.

EXPANSION ACTIVITY: Memory Game

★ Ask students to look at the pictures and create three questions about items of clothing: *What size is the blouse? How much was the dress before? How much is the dress now?*

★ Have students look at the pictures and try to remember as much about them as they can.

★ With books closed, have students work in pairs to practice asking and answering questions about the items.

★ As a variation, divide the class into teams to create questions. Then, with books closed, have the teams take turns asking and answering each other's questions. Each correct answer earns the team a point.

★ ★

 TRY THIS

★ ★

★ Have students study the receipt from Lane's Department Store. Check comprehension by asking questions such as, *How much is the dress? Which is more money, the T-shirt or the blouse? What is the total?*

★ Ask students to look at the blank receipt. Have them choose three items they want to buy and use them to complete the receipt, including the total amount. Remind them to look at the other receipt as a model.

★ Have students compare their receipts with a partner's.

★ Call on a few students to tell the class what they bought or what their partners bought.

EXPANSION ACTIVITY: Scavenger Hunt

★ Bring in several receipts, or make your own, and enlarge them on a photocopy machine.

★ Tape the receipts to the wall in your classroom.

★ Write on the board or dictate ten questions about your specific receipts and have students write them down. Use these questions as a model:

What costs $13.99?
How much is the total for Big and Small Department Store?

How many dresses are from Martin's Men Shop?

What size are the T-shirts from J-Mart?

How many socks can you buy for $6.00 at Cheap Shoes?

★ Have students walk around with their questions, look at the receipts to find the answers, and write them down on a piece of paper.

WINDOW ON MATH: Multiplying and Dividing

A. Read these sentences. 🎧

★ Have students read the sentences and listen while you read or play the tape or CD.

★ Read the sentences or play the tape or CD a second time. Pause after each line and ask the students to repeat.

★ Make sure students understand the symbols and concepts for multiplying and dividing.

B. Write the missing words.

★ Do the first item together. Ask students to look at item *a* and elicit the correct answer. Have them write it on the line.

★ Ask students to write in the missing words for the other items and check their answers with a partner.

★ Go over the answers with the class.

LISTENING SCRIPT

Lesson 3: Window on Math—Multiplying and Dividing

Listen to the sentences. Then listen and repeat.

1. Six times two equals twelve.
2. Twelve times two equals twenty-four.
3. Six divided by two equals three.
4. Twelve divided by two equals six.

ANSWER KEY:

B. 1. times; 2. times or divided by; 3. divided; 4. times; 5 and 6. Answers will vary.

EXPANSION ACTIVITY: Counting Beans

★ Some students may have difficulty with the concepts of multiplying and dividing, so using concrete objects can be helpful.

★ Bring in a bag of dried beans. Give every student the same number of beans (24).

★ Ask the students to count the beans. Ask them to divide the beans so there are four groups with an equal number of beans in each group. Write this as an equation on the board: $24 \div 4 =$ _____. Elicit the answer: *6*.

★ Continue the activity by having students work with the beans to demonstrate other mathematical principles. For example, you could instruct the class to make four groups that each have three beans. You would then ask, *How many beans are there total in the four groups? How can we write that as an equation?*

 Students can do Unit 5, Section 3, *Read and Write* and Section 4, *Fun and Games* on the Interactive CD-ROM.

OBJECTIVE

Reading a Folktale

VOCABULARY

big hole	scissors
cutting	tailor

WINDOW ON GRAMMAR

Object Pronouns: *me, you, him, her, it, them, us*

1. Learn New Words 🎧

★ Ask students to look at the pictures and identify the objects and actions they know.

★ Have them read the vocabulary words as you say the words or play the tape or CD.

★ Say the words or play the tape or CD a second time. Pause after each word and ask students to repeat. Ask them to point to the picture that illustrates each word.

LISTENING SCRIPT

Lesson 4: Learn New Words

Look at the pictures. Listen to the words. Then Listen and repeat.

1. big hole	3. scissors
2. cutting	4. tailor

2. Read 🎧

★ Ask students to look at the pictures as you read the story aloud or play the tape or CD.

★ For additional literacy practice, read the story and pause after each sentence to have students repeat, or have individual students read each sentence of the story.

★ Have the students read and complete the story chart. Point out the transitions *At the beginning of the story, Next,* and *Five years later*. Make sure students understand their meanings.

★ Have students compare answers with a partner.

★ Go over the answers with the class.

LISTENING SCRIPT

Lesson 4: Read

Look at the pictures. Listen to the story.

Narrator:	1.	This is a story about Simon and Leo. Simon is a tailor. Leo is his friend. One day Leo comes into Simon's store. Leo is wearing a very old coat.
Leo:		Oh, Simon, there is a big hole in my coat. What can I do?
Narrator:	2.	Simon looks at the coat carefully. Then he takes out his scissors.
Leo:		What are you doing, Simon?
Simon:		I'm cutting up your coat.
Narrator:	3.	Simon leaves the room with the pieces of Leo's coat. After an hour, he comes back.
Simon:		Here you are, Leo. Your old coat is now a jacket.
Leo:		Oh, Simon, it's a beautiful jacket. How can I thank you?
Narrator:	4.	It is five years later. Leo comes into Simon's store. He is wearing the jacket.
Leo:		Oh, Simon, there is a big hole in my jacket. What can I do?
Narrator:		Simon looks at the jacket carefully. Then he leaves the room. After an hour, he comes back.
Simon:		Here you are, Leo. Your old jacket is now a vest.
Leo:		Oh, Simon, it's a beautiful vest. How can I thank you?
Narrator:	5.	It is five years later.
Leo:		Oh, Simon, there is a big hole in my vest. What can I do?
Narrator:		Simon looks at the vest carefully. Then he leaves the room. After an hour, he comes back.
Simon:		Here you are, Leo. Your old vest is now a _____.
Leo:		Oh, Simon, it's beautiful. How can I thank you?

ANSWER KEY:

At the beginning of the story, Leo is wearing <u>a coat</u>. Next, Leo is wearing <u>a jacket</u>. Five years later, Leo is wearing <u>a vest</u>.

EXPANSION ACTIVITY: Tell a Story about You

★ Write these sequencing phrases on the board: *At the beginning of this story, Next,* and _____ *years later*.

★ Draw a timeline for yourself on the board and include major life events. Instruct students to draw similar timelines for themselves. Have them share their timelines with partners.

★ Tell students that they are going to share a story about themselves with a partner. Model the activity. (*At the beginning of this story, I am going to school in New York. Next, I am getting married. Fifteen years later, I am living in North Carolina.*) As you add each piece of information, write it next to the appropriate sequencing phrase.

★ Distribute pieces of paper and have the students fold them into thirds. Tell them to write or draw a story about themselves in three parts. Remind them to refer to the timeline they drew earlier.

★ Ask students to share their stories with a partner. Or collect the stories and tell them to the class, encouraging students to guess who the subject of each story is.

3. Predict 🎧

★ Direct students to the last frame of the story. Explain that a word is missing—the word that identifies what the vest will become next.

★ Have students write or draw what they think the vest becomes.

★ Elicit ideas from the class and write them on the board.

★ Read the story or play the tape or CD. Have students listen for the missing word.

LISTENING SCRIPT

Lesson 4: Predict

What is the missing word at the end of the story? Listen and compare.

(Note: This script is the same as in Activity 2, with the blank at the end of the story filled in.)

Simon: Here you are, Leo. Your old vest is now a ___cap___.

Leo: Oh, Simon, it's beautiful. How can I thank you?

ANSWER KEY:

cap

EXPANSION ACTIVITY: Tell a Folktale

★ Put students in small groups according to home countries or parts of the world.

★ Have each group write and illustrate a folktale that they are all familiar with.

★ Walk around to monitor the activity and provide help with vocabulary.

★ When students are finished, have them present the folktale to the class.

WINDOW ON GRAMMAR: Object Pronouns: *me, you, him, her, it, them, us*

★ Read the sentences in the yellow box, pausing after each to have students repeat.

★ Instruct students to look at the object pronouns in bold and elicit the subject pronouns that they correspond to (*I = me, you = you, he = him, she = her, it = it, we = us, they = them*). Explain that object pronouns receive the action in a sentence.

★ Tell students they are going to complete the sentences. Do the first one together. Ask the class, *Why do we write <u>him</u> on the line? Who is "him"?* Elicit that *him* refers to Simon, and Leo is asking Simon the question.

★ Students should complete the sentences with *me, you, him, her, it, them,* or *us*. Remind them to look at the first sentence in each item to figure out which object pronoun to use. Walk around the room to monitor the activity and provide help as needed.

★ Have students check their answers with a partner.

★ Go over the answers with the class.

ANSWER KEY:

1. him; 2. it; 3. it

EXPANSION ACTIVITY: Chain Story

★ Write several sentence starters on the board:

> I am looking at _____
>
> I am talking to _____
>
> I am listening to _____
>
> I am wearing _____
>
> I am opening _____
>
> I am reading _____

★ Tell students that you are going to begin a class story by saying one sentence about yourself. A student will repeat your sentence using an object pronoun, then create a new sentence.

★ Model the activity. Say, *I am looking at my students*. Elicit from the class how they can rephrase your sentence using an object pronoun: *I am looking at them*.

★ Ask a student to create a sentence about him or herself. Remind them that they can use one of the sentences on the board and fill in the blank: *I am wearing pants*. Have a second student rephrase that sentence and add a new one: *He is wearing them. I am listening to the teacher*. Make sure students understand the pattern and answer any questions.

★ Continue the activity until all the students have added to the class story.

BIG PICTURE EXPANSION ACTIVITY: GRAMMAR—What's the object?

★ Make copies of Worksheet #9 (p. 249) and distribute them to students.

★ Put the "big picture" color overhead transparency for Unit 5, Lesson 2, on the projector or have students look at the "big picture" in their books.

★ Tell students to look at the picture for the information needed to complete the sentences in Activity *A*. Go over the example. Have students compare their answers with a partner.

★ Go over the answers with the class.

ANSWER KEY:

1. hats; 2. purple skirt; 3. green pants; 4. hat; 5. door

★ Ask students to read the sentences in Activity B and replace the nouns from Activity A with an object pronoun.

★ Have students check their answers with a partner.

★ Go over the answers with the class.

ANSWER KEY:

1. them; 2. her; 3. them; 4. it; 5. it

 Students can do Unit 5, Section 3, *Read and Write* and Section 4, *Fun and Games* on the Interactive CD-ROM.

OBJECTIVE

Describing Clothes

VOCABULARY

long	too long
loose	too loose
short	too short
tight	too tight

WINDOW ON PRONUNCIATION

Vowel Sounds in *Shoes* and *Should*

1. Learn New Words 🎧

★ Ask students to listen and look at the words and pictures while you say the words or play the tape or CD.

★ Say the words or play the tape or CD a second time. Pause after each word and ask the students to repeat and point to each item as it is said.

★ Group students in pairs and have one student practice saying the item as the other points to the picture. Reverse the roles and repeat the activity.

★ Have students complete items 1–4 using the new words. Remind them to look at the pictures. Point out that the missing word will be the opposite of the word in the first sentence of each item.

★ Have students check their answers with a partner.

★ Go over the answers with the class.

LISTENING SCRIPT

Lesson 5: Learn New Words

Look at the pictures. Listen to the words. Then listen and repeat.

1.	long	The black skirt is long.
2.	short	The green skirt is short.
3.	too long	The black skirt is too long.
4.	too short	The green skirt is too short.
5.	tight	The brown pants are tight.
6.	loose	The black pants are loose.
7.	too tight	The brown pants are too tight.
8.	too loose	The black pants are too loose.

Grammar Note:
★ Point out that we use *too* when something is a problem. Have students look at the pictures with *too* to notice the problem (*slip shows, skirt is dragging on the ground*).

ANSWER KEY:

1. long; 2. too short; 3. tight; 4. too loose

2. Practice the Conversation: Describing Clothes 🎧

★ Set the context for the conversation by having students look at the picture and asking them questions: *Where are they? Who do you see?*

★ Read the conversation or play the tape or CD.

★ Check comprehension: *What kind of clothes are they talking about? What is the problem?*

★ Read or play the conversation again. Pause after each sentence and ask students to repeat.

★ Model with one of the students how to substitute items for those in the script. Cue the student to ask about one of the items listed below the conversation—*sweater* or *jacket*. Demonstrate how to substitute a different problem from the suggestions—*long* or *tight*.

★ Ask students to write in another clothing item and a related problem. They can use these ideas in the conversation.

★ Have them practice the conversation with a partner, with each student taking turns playing each part. Then have them close their books and practice again.

LISTENING SCRIPT

Lesson 5: Practice the Conversation— Describing Clothes

Listen to the conversation. Then listen and repeat.

A: Do you like this dress?
B: It's nice, but I think it's too short.

122 Unit 5

EXPANSION ACTIVITY:
Ask about Your Clothes

★ Distribute pictures from magazines to students grouped in pairs.

★ Instruct them to practice asking and answering questions about the clothes they see in the pictures. Point out that the conversation is for practice only and that the problems don't have to be real ones, so they can be creative.

★ Model the activity by asking the class about your own clothes—*Do you like these pants?*—and elicit ideas: *They're nice, but they're too short/too long/too tight/too loose.*

3. Practice the Conversation: Returning Something 🎧

★ Set the context for the conversation by having students look at the picture and asking them questions: *Where are they? What do you see?*

★ Read the conversation or play the tape or CD.

★ Check comprehension: *What kind of clothes are they talking about? What is the problem?*

★ Read or play the conversation again. Pause after each sentence and ask students to repeat.

★ Choose a more proficient student and model substituting items for those in the script. Have the student read *B's* lines. Demonstrate how to substitute an article of clothing and problem from the suggestions below.

★ Tell students to write in another idea for clothes and another idea for a problem.

LISTENING SCRIPT

Lesson 5: Practice the Conversation— Returning Something

Listen to the conversation. Then listen and repeat.

A: I'd like to return these pants.
B: What's the problem?
A: They're too short.
B: All right. No problem.

BIG PICTURE EXPANSION ACTIVITY:
READING—A Story about Berta

★ Make copies of Worksheet #10 (p. 250) and distribute to students.

★ Put the "big picture" color overhead transparency for Unit 5, Lesson 2, on the projector or have students look at the "big picture" in their books.

★ Have students read the story, or read the story aloud and have students repeat. Help students find Berta in the picture and point to her.

★ Instruct students to circle the correct answers to the questions. Remind them to look at the picture to find some of the answers.

★ Have students check their answers with a partner.

★ Go over the answers with the class.

ANSWER KEY:

1. B; 2. B; 3. B; 4. A; 5. B; 6. A; 7. B; 8. A; 9. A; 10. A

WINDOW ON PRONUNCIATION:
Vowel Sounds in *Shoes* and *Should*

A. Listen to the words. 🎧

★ Tell students that they are going to practice two vowel sounds, the sound in *shoes* and the sound in *should*. Make the sound in *shoes* and have students repeat. Point out that your mouth begins rounded but slightly open and then becomes more closed and rounded, similar to the position for a *w* sound.

★ Then make the vowel sound in *should* and have students repeat. Explain that the mouth is more relaxed and the lips less rounded than in the previous demonstration.

★ Ask students to look at the words in *A*. Read the words or play the tape or CD.

★ Read the words or play the tape or CD a second time. Pause after each and have the students repeat.

★ Tell students that one word in each line has a different vowel sound from the other three words. Read the words or play the tape or CD a third time and have the students circle the word that has a different vowel sound.

★ Have students check their answers with a partner. Go over the answers with the class.

LISTENING SCRIPT

Lesson 5: Window on Pronunciation—Vowel Sounds in *Shoes* and *Should*

A. Listen to the words. Then listen and repeat. Listen again. Circle the word that has a different vowel sound.

1. shoes	should	loose	too
2. look	book	put	two
3. you	noon	woman	loose
4. boots	excuse	good	blue

ANSWER KEY:

1. should; 2. two; 3. woman; 4. good

B. Listen to the words. Then listen and repeat. 🎧

★ Have students look at the words in *B*. Read the words or play the tape or CD.

★ Read the words or play the tape or CD a second time. Pause after each word and have the students repeat.

★ Put each student with a partner and instruct the class to match the words that have the same sound.

★ Point out that each numbered item has the same ending sound as one of the lettered items. Also point out that the words with the same ending sound will have the same vowel sound and same ending consonant.

LISTENING SCRIPT

Lesson 5: Window on Pronunciation—Vowel Sounds in *Shoes* and *Should*

B. Listen to the words. Then listen and repeat.

1. blue	a. book
2. good	b. June
3. cook	c. shoe
4. noon	d. should

ANSWER KEY:

1. c; 2. d; 3. a; 4. b

EXPANSION ACTIVITY: Sort by Sound

★ Group the students in pairs to sort all the words in the Window on Pronunciation into two groups.

★ One group should include words that sound like *shoes*.

★ The other group should include words that sound like *should*.

EQUIPPED FOR THE FUTURE ROLE

Work

OBJECTIVE

On the Job

1. Ask Questions

★ Ask students to look at the pictures and ask them, *Who are the people in the pictures?*

★ Ask the question, *What's Ken wearing?* Have students answer.

★ Have students work in pairs to practice asking and answering questions about the people in the pictures.

★ Call on a few students to talk about some of the people in the pictures.

2. Give Opinions

★ Instruct students to look at the list of occupations. Say each occupation and pause to have students repeat. Remind them that they learned these occupations in Unit 1.

★ Model the activity with a student. Have the student read *A's* lines. Demonstrate how to give opinions: *I think he is a nurse because he's wearing nurse's clothes.*

★ Have students work in pairs to match each person with an occupation. Remind them to practice explaining the reasons for their choices.

EXPANSION ACTIVITY: Who wears what?

★ Have students work in pairs to list the clothes they think people in each occupation would or should wear.

★ Call on students to describe the clothes for one occupation.

3. Read

★ Direct the students' attention to the memo and ask them questions about it: *What is this? Where do you see memos? What is the name of this workplace?*

★ Have students read the memo and underline any words they don't understand. Go over the meanings of those words.

★ Check comprehension by asking questions such as, *What is it about? What is the date of the memo? What clothes are inappropriate?*

★ Tell students to look at the pictures of Leila, Phil, and Rob. Ask the class, *Are these workers wearing the right clothes for work?*

★ Have the students complete the sentences about Leila, Phil, and Rob and then compare answers with a partner.

★ Call on a few students to share their ideas.

ANSWER KEY:

Leila: jeans; Phil: a baseball cap, a T-shirt, shorts, sandals; Rob: a baseball cap, shorts, sneakers

EXPANSION ACTIVITY: What to Wear?

★ Help students brainstorm the places and events where clothes may matter (*work, school, social occasions*) and write them on the board.

★ Put students in small groups to discuss what clothes they think would be appropriate for each place. Have them make a list of appropriate clothing for men and for women in each place.

★ Draw a chart like this one on the board. Include these and/or other headings that students suggest.

	Work	*School*	*Social occasions*
Men			
Women			

★ When students are finished making their lists, have them add their ideas to the chart on the board.

★ Instruct students to use these ideas to write a memo advising classmates on what to wear in a particular situation. Have them use the memo in Activity 3 as a model.

★ Have students share their memos with a partner.

1. Listening Review 🎧

★ Go over the directions with the class.

★ Read the items or play the tape or CD and have the students mark their answers on the Answer Sheet.

★ Walk around to monitor the activity and help students stay on task.

★ Have students check their answers with a partner.

★ Go over the answers with the class.

---**LISTENING SCRIPT**---

Lesson 7: Listening Review

Listen and choose the correct answer. Use the Answer Sheet.

1. What color is his sweater?
2. What's he wearing?
3. Where are the children's clothes?
4. What size is the T-shirt?
5. Is it on sale?
6. What's the price?
7. What's the problem with your shoes?
8. Is it too short?

ANSWER KEY:

1. C; 2. A; 3. A; 4. C; 5. B; 6. C; 7. C; 8. A

2. Dictation 🎧

┌─────────────────────────────────────┐
TESTING FOCUS:
Writing Questions from Dictation

★ All three questions in Activity 2 are *wh-* questions using the verb *be*. Go over the form of these questions: *Question word or phrase + is/am/are + . . .?*

★ Elicit the punctuation and capitalization rules for questions: *begin with a capital letter, end with a question mark*.

★ Point out to students that after they have written their questions from the dictation, they can check to make sure they have the correct form.
└─────────────────────────────────────┘

★ Tell students that they will hear three questions. They should write the questions in the book on the first line next to each number. Make sure they know to leave the second line under each number blank.

★ Read the questions or play the tape or CD. Repeat two more times.

★ Instruct students to write their answers to each question on the lines that follow the question.

★ Have students compare their questions and answers with a partner's.

★ Go over the questions with the class. Call on a few students to answer the questions.

---**LISTENING SCRIPT**---

Lesson 7: Dictation

Listen and write the questions you hear.

1. What are you wearing today?
2. What's your favorite color?
3. Do you like baseball caps?

ANSWER KEY:

Questions: Same questions as Listening Script
Answers: Answers to the questions will vary.

3. Conversation Check: Pair Work

★ Have students work in pairs.

★ Go over the directions. Remind students that each person has some information but that other information is missing. They must ask their partner questions to complete the chart.

★ Walk around to monitor the activity and provide help as needed.

┌─────────────────────────────────────┐
Assessment Note:
★ You can use the Conversation Check Activity as an oral assessment. Ask pairs of students to complete the activity while you note areas of difficulty.
└─────────────────────────────────────┘

LEARNING LOG

★ Point out the four sections of the Learning Log: *I know these words, I can ask, I can say,* and *I can write.*

★ Ask students to check what they know and what they can do.

★ Walk around to note what they don't know or can't do. Use this information to review areas of difficulty.

🖥 BIG PICTURE EXPANSION ACTIVITY: WRITING—Writing about Actions 📁

★ Put the "big picture" color overhead transparency for Unit 5, Lesson 2, on the projector or have students look at the "big picture" in their books.

★ Elicit some ideas about what people are doing and what they are wearing: *Four women are wearing hats. One woman is buying many things.* Write the ideas on the board.

★ Students should work individually to write a description of what the people are doing in the picture. Remind them to use the present continuous tense when writing the description.

★ Walk around the room to monitor the activity and provide help as needed.

★ Have students share their ideas with a partner.

🖥 BIG PICTURE EXPANSION ACTIVITY: SPEAKING Assessment—Talking about the Big Picture

★ You can use the "big picture" to assess the placement of students in open-entry classes, to diagnose difficulties, or to measure progress.

★ Work with one student at a time. Show the "big picture" to the student and ask, *What do you see in the picture?* or, *Tell me about the picture.* Tell the student to speak for as long as possible. Wait a moment for the student to prepare an answer. If the student has difficulty, you can use prompts: *What do you see in the department store? Who do you see? What are they doing?*

★ You can use a rubric like the one below to rate beginning speakers.

3	Uses sentences, although form may be incorrect Can speak for sustained length of time Responds to prompts, but doesn't need them to begin speaking
2	Can use nouns and verbs Uses phrases Answers informational questions
1	Can name objects Uses single words Can answer yes/no questions
0	Cannot say anything independently May be able to point to objects when prompted

TEACHER'S NOTES:

Things that students are doing well:

_____

_____

_____

_____

_____

Things students need additional help with:

_____

_____

_____

_____

_____

_____

Ideas for further practice or for the next class:

_____

_____

_____

_____

_____

 Students can do Unit 5, Section 5, *Practice Test* on the Interactive CD-ROM.

OBJECTIVES

Present Continuous Statements; Information Questions with the Present Continuous

Present Continuous

★ Read the sentences in the grammar paradigm and have students repeat.
★ Call on students and say a personal pronoun (*I*) and a verb (*read*), and have the students create a present continuous sentence (*I am reading*).

1. Write *am, is,* or *are.*

★ Instruct students to look at the directions and go over question 1 as a class.
★ Have students complete the other sentences and check their answers with a partner.
★ Go over the answers with the class.

ANSWER KEY:

1. is; 2. are; 3. is; 4. am; 5. are; 6. am; 7. are; 8. is

2. Write about the people in the pictures.

★ Have students look at the pictures. Ask them to name the action in each picture.
★ Read question 1 together, then have students write sentences about each of the other pictures using the present continuous tense.
★ Students should compare their sentences with a partner's.
★ Go over the answers with the class.

ANSWER KEY:

1. They are running.
2. It is sleeping.
3. He is sitting.
4. They are reading.
5. She is writing.
6. He is talking on the phone.

INFORMATION QUESTIONS WITH THE PRESENT CONTINUOUS

★ Read the questions in the grammar paradigm and have students repeat.
★ Ask students what type of word is first in all the questions (*a question word*), what comes next (*is/are*), what is third (*noun or pronoun*), and what comes last (*verb + ing*). Write this form on the board.
★ Point out that the verbs *is* and *are* agree with the nouns or pronouns that follow them.

3. Match the questions and answers.

★ Have students look at the two columns. Go over question number 1.
★ Instruct students to match the rest of the questions and answers and check their answers with a partner.
★ Go over the answers with the class.
★ Have students work in pairs to practice asking and answering the questions.

ANSWER KEY:

1. He's sleeping; 2. in her room; 3. my teacher; 4. because it's hot; 5. a movie

4. Complete the conversations.

★ Go over the example. Ask students what types of words are written on the blank lines and write the pattern on the board: *question word + be.*
★ Have students complete the conversations.
★ Go over the answers.
★ Have students work in pairs to practice asking and answering the questions.

ANSWER KEY:

A: What are you reading?
A: What is she wearing?
A: Where are they going?
A: What are you listening to?
A: Who is sitting next to you?
B: [Answers will vary.]
A: Who are you sitting next to?
B: [Answers will vary.]

EQUIPPED FOR THE FUTURE ROLE

Community

OBJECTIVE

Making a Return by Mail

VOCABULARY

exchange
gift certificate
refund

A. Read the story.

★ Have students look at the photo and ask them questions to help set the context: *Who do you see in the picture? Where is she? What's wrong?*

★ Ask students to read the questions below the story so they know what information to look for.

★ Have students read the story or, to help with developing literacy skills, read it yourself, pausing after each line to have students repeat.

★ Instruct the students to work individually and answer the questions.

★ Put students in pairs to practice asking and answering the questions.

★ Go over the answers with the class.

ANSWER KEY:

1. Karina; 2. Casual Clothes; 3. blue;
4. they're too big; 5. no

B. Learn new words.

★ Ask students to look at the words in the box. Say each word, pausing after each to have students repeat.

★ Have students look at the form and circle the words. Elicit the meanings of the words or explain them.

C. Look at the form.

★ Have students look at the list of information. Ask the class, *Is the name of the customer on the form in Part B?* Point out that the box next to *name of customer* has a check mark because the customer's name is on the form.

★ Ask the students to read the form and check the boxes to indicate the information they can find on the form. Tell them to leave the box blank if they cannot find the information on the form.

★ Have students check their answers with a partner.

★ Go over the answers with the class.

ANSWER KEY:

☑ name of customer
☑ address of customer
☑ problem with clothes
☑ telephone number of customer
☑ description of clothes
☑ color of clothes
☐ size of clothes
☑ city
☐ school
☑ price
☑ how to handle the return

D. Your brown coat is too small.

★ Read the directions to the students. Have them complete the form with their own personal information and information from the directions.

★ Walk around to monitor the activity and provide help as needed.

★ Have students compare their forms with a partner's.

EXPANSION ACTIVITY: Phone Interview

★ Tell students that they are going to role-play a telephone conversation between a customer and a service representative regarding a merchandise return.

★ Brainstorm the questions the service representative will need to ask the customer to complete the return form. Write the questions on the board: *What is your name/address/city/state/daytime phone? How would you like us to handle your return? What are you returning? Why? What color is it? What is the price?*

★ Make sure students copy the questions on a piece of paper.

★ Have them work in pairs to practice asking and answering the questions. Have them write down their partners' answers. You can also have them work back-to-back to simulate a phone conversation in which they would not be able to see each other's faces.

Take It Outside

★ Have students read the directions for this activity.

★ Brainstorm the types of places that display return policies (*clothing stores, department stores, appliance stores*) and the locations within the store where they are posted (*near the registers, at the customer service desk*).

★ When students have found examples of return policies, elicit the types of information on the policies and write it on the board.

★ If students are unable to get to a store to find return policies, use the examples below.

Bookstore

We'll refund your online purchase if you:

★ Return new books, unopened CDs, cassettes, VHS tapes, DVDs, all textbooks, prints & posters, and software in their **original condition**.

★ Include your **receipt** and completed return form.

★ Return the item **within 30 days** of delivery date.

Camping Store

We believe in offering the very best. If an item you purchase here does not meet your expectations, simply return it to us for a refund or exchange it within 90 days from date of purchase. Please include a copy of the receipt or invoice along with the unused product and original packaging.

Department Store

1. Take the item with all original packaging and accessories plus the invoice to the Customer Service Department.

2. An Associate will issue a credit to the original credit card or provide a store credit for the cost of the item and the sales tax, if applicable.

EQUIPPED FOR THE FUTURE ROLE

Family

OBJECTIVE

Understanding School Dress Codes

A. Circle *yes* or *no* for the sentences about North Park School.

★ Have students look at the photo and ask them, *Who do you see in the picture?* (*a boy*) *What is he wearing?* (*a shirt, pants, a necktie, shoes*)

★ To set the context, ask students to look at the title of the reading and ask them, *What is this reading about?* (*School uniforms*)

★ Students should read the information and the class should go over the first item in Part A together. Have students complete the rest of the items themselves.

★ Make sure students check their answers with a partner.

★ Go over the answers with the class.

ANSWER KEY:

1. yes; 2. no; 3. no; 4. no; 5. no; 6. no

EXPANSION ACTIVITY:
Correct the Errors

★ Have students rewrite the inaccurate sentences from Activity A with the correct information.

★ Go over the rewritten sentences with the class.

B. Write the words in the correct place.

★ Remind students to check the reading to find correct information.

★ Have them write the names of clothes in the correct places on the Venn diagram.

★ Make sure students check their answers with a partner.

★ Go over the answers with the class.

ANSWER KEY:

Blue clothes: pants, slacks, shorts
Blue or white: sweaters, sweatshirts, socks, tights
White: shirts

C. Match the clothes and the problem.

★ Instruct students to look at the section of the reading that says *Do NOT wear to school* to find answers.

★ Go over the example and ask the class, *What kind of shorts are not for school?* Point out that a line is drawn between *shorts* and *too short.*

★ Have students draw a line between the clothes and the problem. Walk around the room to monitor the activity and provide help as needed.

★ Have students check their answers with a partner.

★ Go over the answers with the class.

ANSWER KEY:

1. b; 2. c; 3. d; 4. a

D. Complete the sentences.

★ Tell the students that they will read three conversations. Have them complete the conversations using information from the reading.

★ Go over the answers with the class.

★ Group students in pairs to practice the conversations.

ANSWER KEY:

Sarah's shorts are too short/tight; Are his pants too large? David is wearing a T-shirt.

Take It Outside

★ If this is an out-of-class assignment, have students interview a family member, friend, or coworker. If you assign it in class, they can practice asking and answering the questions with a partner.

★ Read the questions aloud, pausing after each to have students repeat.

★ When students have completed the interview, call on a few volunteers to tell the class about their answers.

EXPANSION ACTIVITY: Your Experience

★ Ask students to list the clothes they used to wear to school, work, church, or as a child or younger person.

★ Have them share their ideas with a partner.

★ Call on a few students to tell the class about their partner's experiences.

UNIT OVERVIEW

LESSON	OBJECTIVE	STUDENT BOOK PAGE #
1. Noodles are delicious.	Identifying Foods	p. 84
2. Do you sell rice?	At the Grocery Store	p. 86
3. How much is it?	Identifying Containers for Food	p. 88
4. Store Flyers	Reading Food Ads	p. 90
5. Is milk on sale?	Asking for Store Information	p. 92
6. The Food Pyramid	Choosing Foods	p. 94
7. What do you know?	Review and Assessment	p. 96
8. Spotlight	Writing	p. 98

Big Picture Expansion Activities

FOCUS	TITLE	SUGGESTED USE
Speaking	*Yes/No* Questions Game	Lesson 2
Reading	Store Signs	Lesson 4
Grammar	Practicing *Yes/No* Questions	Lesson 5
Writing	Describing the Store	Lesson 7
Speaking	Assessment: Talking about the Picture	Lesson 7

Big Picture Expansion Activity Worksheets

WORKSHEET #/FOCUS	TITLE	TEACHER'S EDITION PAGE #
11. Reading	Store Signs	p. 251
12. Grammar	Practicing *Yes/No* Questions	p. 252

OBJECTIVE

Identifying Foods

VOCABULARY

GRAINS	FRUIT	DAIRY
bread	apples	butter
cereal	bananas	cheese
noodles	grapes	milk
rice	oranges	yogurt

VEGETABLES	MEAT, FISH, BEANS, NUTS
carrots	beans
lettuce	chicken
onions	peanuts
tomatoes	shrimp

WINDOW ON GRAMMAR

Questions with *Do you like*

THINGS TO DO

1. Learn New Words 🎧

★ Write on the board the names of the five food categories: Grains; Fruit; Vegetables; Dairy; Meat, Fish, Beans, and Nuts. Have students look at the pictures of foods in their book. Ask them to identify the words they already know. Write those words on the board under the appropriate heading.

★ Have students listen and look at the pictures while you say the words or play the tape or CD.

★ Say the words or play the tape or CD a second time. Pause after each word and ask the students to repeat the word and point to the object in the book.

★ Elicit the remaining words that that aren't yet on the board. Write each word on the board under the correct heading. Check pronunciation as students say the words.

★ Have students practice in pairs. Have one student say the name of a food, and have the other student point to a picture of it.

(**LISTENING SCRIPT**)

Lesson 1: Learn New Words

Look at the pictures. Listen to the words. Then listen and repeat.

1. noodles	11. yogurt
2. bread	12. butter
3. rice	13. peanuts
4. cereal	14. chicken
5. apples	15. shrimp
6. oranges	16. beans
7. grapes	17. onions
8. bananas	18. tomatoes
9. milk	19. lettuce
10. cheese	20. carrots

Pronunciation Notes:

★ The final *s* sound is difficult for students from some language groups. Ask students to stress the "s" on the words that end in "s" as they repeat them. Encourage them to hold the sound longer than necessary. This will help prepare them for Activity 2.

★ Point out that the final *s* can be pronounced in 3 different ways: /s/ /z/ or /iz/. *apples* /z/, *beans* /z/, *onions* /z/, *tomatoes* /z/, *noodles* /z/. But *peanuts* /s/, *carrots* /s/ and *peaches* /iz/ are different.

EXPANSION ACTIVITY: Bingo

★ Have each student make a bingo sheet that consists of 16 squares—four rows with four squares in each row.

★ Have students choose 16 words from the vocabulary list and write one word in each of the squares on the bingo sheet.

★ Explain to students how the game of bingo works and that they should yell out the word "bingo" when they cross off words in a line horizontally, diagonally, or vertically.

★ Randomly say each word from the vocabulary list out loud and have the students cross off the word if they have it on their bingo sheet.

★ Variations on the game can include any other pattern you choose such as an X, a blackout, a diagonal line, and a vertical line, etc.

2. Give Opinions

★ Copy the chart on the board. Underline the *s* at the end of *noodles*. Point out that *bread* has no *s*.

★ Ask students to look at the list of words in Learn New Words. Ask for another word that ends with s (*apples*), and one that doesn't end in s (*rice*), and write them on the chart.

★ Have students complete their own charts on paper.

★ When students are finished, elicit the items that belong in each group and write them on the chart on the board.

ANSWER KEY:

GROUP 1: apples, bananas, beans, grapes, noodles, oranges, peanuts, onions, tomatoes, carrots

GROUP 2: bread, butter, cereal, cheese, chicken, lettuce, milk, rice, shrimp, yogurt

★ Point to the faces that indicate opinions. As you point to each, make a similar face and say the word. Have students imitate the facial expression and repeat the word.

★ Read the two example sentences and have students repeat. Point to an item on the chart on the board and model your opinion (*think apples are good*). Ask volunteers to give their opinions of other items.

★ Group students in pairs and have them practice giving opinions of five foods. Walk around the room to monitor the activity.

Grammar Note:
★ Group 1 represents nouns that can be counted. Such nouns can be preceded by *a/an*, or a number, and can be made plural. When plural, count nouns are used with *are*. Group 2 represents noncount nouns. They are always singular and are used with *is*.

EXPANSION ACTIVITY: Delicious, Good, or Terrible?

★ Draw a chart on the board with three columns with the headings *delicious, good,* and *terrible*. Include the symbols below to represent each word.

★ Have students copy the chart on paper.

★ Ask students to sort the foods from this lesson, and three other foods they know, into one of the three groups, according to their own opinions.

★ Have students talk with a new partner and give their opinions about different foods. Model the structure on the board: *I think apples are delicious.*

3. Write

★ Copy the shopping list on the board.

★ Ask for an example of a food for each category (*What is a fruit you want to buy?* Possible answer: *apples*). Write an example in each square (*apples, milk, bread, chicken*).

★ Have students complete their own shopping lists on paper. Ask them to write down foods they want to buy this week.

★ Call on individual students to copy their lists on the board.

ANSWER KEY:

Answers will vary.

Culture/Civics Note:
★ Students may be surprised to learn that many people in some countries go shopping for food only once or twice a week. You could point out that these people often buy packaged or frozen food that can last a few days or more. People who shop only once or twice a week usually make a list so they will remember everything.

EXPANSION ACTIVITY: Draw the Picture

★ Have the students work in teams of three or four. Explain that a member of each team will draw a picture of a food item on the board and the other students will guess what it is and in which category it belongs.

★ Have the students determine in which order they will draw by identifying each member in the group as A, B, C, etc.

★ Have all A team members go to the board. Show them one vocabulary word. When you say "go" they should all begin to draw a picture of the word on the board.

★ The first student to raise their hand and correctly guess both the object and its category gets a point for their team.

★ You can cycle through as many vocabulary words as you like, each time asking a new student from each team to draw the word.

★ The team that correctly names the most objects and categories wins.

WINDOW ON GRAMMAR
Questions with *Do you like*

★ Have students look at the chart. Point to and say the questions and answers. Have students repeat. Gesture to one student and ask *Do you like rice?* and elicit an answer (*Yes, I do* or *No, I don't*).

★ Now model a question about a different food with a student. Ask, *Do you like chicken?* Elicit a response, either *Yes, I do,* or *No, I don't.* Continue to ask that student about foods until the student answers *Yes, I do* to two questions.

★ Follow the model in the book and write a sentence on the board: *My partner likes _____ and _____.*

★ Have students work in pairs to ask about foods and then write sentences.

★ Call on students to read their sentences to the class. Have each student report back to the class with one sentence about his or her partner.

EXPANSION ACTIVITY: Do you like apples?

★ Have students work in pairs and make a list of things they both like and a list of things they both don't like.

★ If you like, you can extend this activity with a Venn Diagram. Draw two circles like the ones below on the board.

★ Model the activity with a student. Identify one food you like (*I like apples*). Ask the student if he or she likes that food (*Do you like apples?*). If the answer is *yes*, write the item in the area *Things we both like.* Continue the process until you can also write an item only you like in the area *Things I like,* and an item only your partner likes in *Things my partner likes.*

★ You can have students work with a partner to complete the Venn Diagram. Then have more advanced students write summary statements: *I like _____, _____, and _____. My partner likes _____, _____, and _____. We both like _____ and _____.*

Pronunciation Note:

★ Point out the rising intonation in *Yes/No* questions. This will be covered more thoroughly in the Window on Pronunciation in Lesson 5, but students should start to become aware of it now.

OBJECTIVE

At the Grocery Store

VOCABULARY

PLACES	THINGS
Aisle 1	coupons
bakery	frozen foods
checkout counter	ice
produce section	mop
restroom	shopping cart

ACTIONS
cleaning the floor
eating
looking at
pushing a cart
standing in line

THINGS TO DO

1. Talk About the Picture

★ Have students look at the picture of the supermarket. You can display the page or use the color overhead transparency. Ask students to describe the picture, including the foods and number of people they see, the name of the place (elicit *supermarket* or *grocery store*), and the activities taking place.

★ Write a few of the questions about the picture on the board, followed by a few of the responses students give. Ask questions such as *What is Tina doing? Are there oranges in the supermarket? What do you see? How many people are there?*

★ Have students write five sentences about the picture.

★ Ask each student to read one of their sentences to the class.

Grammar Note:
★ Students studied the present continuous in Unit 5. You may want to review how this tense is formed (subject + *be* + verb + *ing*).

EXPANSION ACTIVITY: Telephone Game

★ Have the students work in groups of five or more and arrange their chairs in a circle.

★ Tell students that you will whisper the same sentence to one student in each group. That student will whisper the same sentence in the next student's ear, and so on, until all the students in each group have passed the sentence on. The last student to hear the sentence will say it aloud.

★ Model the activity with one group. (*The bananas are next to the apples.*)

★ Walk around the room and whisper a sentence to one person in each group.

2. Learn New Words 🎧

★ Have students listen and look at the picture while you say the words or play the tape or CD.

★ Say the words or play the tape or CD a second time. Pause after each word and ask students to repeat the word and point to the object in the picture.

LISTENING SCRIPT

Lesson 2: Learn New Words

Look at the picture. Listen to the words. Then listen and repeat.

1. Aisle 1	Where's Aisle 1?
2. restroom	Where's the restroom?
3. ice	Where's the ice?
4. frozen foods	Where are the frozen foods?
5. produce section	Where's the produce section?
6. shopping cart	Where is a shopping cart?
7. mop	Where's the mop?
8. checkout counter	Where's the checkout counter?
9. coupons	Where are the coupons?
10. bakery	Where's the bakery?
11. pushing a cart	Who is pushing a cart?
12. looking at	Who is looking at something?
13. eating	Who is eating something?
14. cleaning the floor	Who is cleaning the floor?
15. standing in line	Who is standing in line?

EXPANSION ACTIVITY:
Name the Category

★ Help students brainstorm foods that belong in different sections of the supermarket: *dairy, meat, bakery, produce, frozen foods, Aisles, etc.* Write the words on the board.

★ Write all the vocabulary words from Lesson 1 on slips of paper, making enough copies so that each student has a slip. Tell students they are going to group themselves by sections in the grocery store.

★ Write on the board: *What food do you have? What section is that in?* Read the questions and have students repeat.

★ Have the students stand up and walk around the room, asking the two questions. When they find other students who have a word in the same section, they should stand with those students.

★ Walk around the classroom to help students with this activity.

★ When all students are in groups, have them read their words aloud to make sure they are in the right sections.

★ For additional practice, you can have students sort themselves by the color of the food, or by the time of day the food is eaten.

3. Practice the Conversation 🎧

★ Have students look at the pictures of the speakers.

★ Read the conversations or play the tape or CD as the students listen.

★ Read or play the conversations again. Pause after each item and ask the students to repeat.

★ Point out that the words ending in *s* are referred to as *they* in the second line, while the words that don't end in *s* are referred to as *it*.

★ Divide the class in two. Have one side read *A's* part, and the other side read *B's* part. If necessary, cue the students by standing in front of the side that is reading, and read with the students. Have the students cover the text in their books and say it again. Switch parts.

★ Model the substitution activity with one of the students. For example, read *A's* first line, but substitute another word from the choices below that doesn't end in s (e.g., *bread*). Have the student read *B's* first line, eliciting *It's in the bakery.* If necessary, cue the student by pointing to the bread in the bakery.

★ In pairs, have the students practice reading the conversations. Circulate to help with pronunciation and intonation.

LISTENING SCRIPT

Lesson 2: Practice the Conversation

Listen to the conversations.
Then listen and repeat.

A: Excuse me. Do you sell rice?
B: Yes, we do. It's in Aisle 1.
A: Thank you.
B: You're welcome.

A: Excuse me. Do you sell bananas?
B: Yes, we do. They're in the produce section.
A: Thank you.
B: You're welcome.

 Students can do Unit 6, Section 1, *Learn New Words* on the Interactive CD-ROM.

Culture/Civics Notes:
★ Point out that many supermarkets have customer service counters. When customers have questions or problems, they can go there for help. The customer service desk takes returns, makes exchanges, and sometimes cashes checks.

★ The man in the produce section in the picture is eating some grapes. Students may come from cultures where customers expect to try something before they buy it. You may want to point out that it is not acceptable to try the food at the supermarket without paying for it unless the food is offered to you by an employee at a special stand, or a sample has been placed near a product for customers to try.

BIG PICTURE EXPANSION ACTIVITY: SPEAKING—*Yes/No* Questions Game

★ Put the "big picture" color overhead transparency for Unit 6, Lesson 2, on the projector or have students look at the "big picture" in their books.

★ As you pass each student, point to one of the people in the picture, giving each student a different character. Don't let other students see which character you point to. Tell the class that they must guess which person each student in the class is by asking *yes/no* questions.

★ Brainstorm questions that students can ask and write them on the board. Your list may include: *Are you a man? Are you a woman? Are you eating grapes? Are you in Aisle 1?*

★ Model this activity by pretending to be one of the people in the picture. Elicit questions and respond with *yes* or *no* until students guess who you are. They can say the name or point to the person when they guess.

OBJECTIVE

Identifying Containers for Food

VOCABULARY

CONTAINERS	OTHER WORDS
a bag of apples	cheap
a bottle of oil	expensive
a box of sugar	
a can of tomatoes	
a carton of milk	
a jar of honey	
a loaf of bread	
a package of cheese	

WINDOW ON MATH

Pounds, Ounces, and Cups

THINGS TO DO

1. Learn New Words 🎧

★ Have students look at the pictures. Ask them, *What foods do you see?* Some words may be new to students (*oil, sugar, honey*).

★ Have students listen and look at the pictures while you say the words or play the tape or CD.

★ Say the words or play the CD a second time. Pause after each word and ask the students to repeat the word and point to the object in the pictures.

★ Have students write the phrases under the appropriate pictures.

★ Draw simple forms on the board to illustrate types of packaging. Ask students for the names of the containers and write them on the board under the container.

★ Play or read the phrases again, pausing after each phrase. As students listen this time, have them point to the object in the picture and repeat the phrase.

★ For additional practice, call out the numbers next to each picture or point to the pictures and have students say the name.

LISTENING SCRIPT

Lesson 3: Learn New Words

Look at the pictures. Listen to the words. Then listen and repeat.

Containers

1. a bag of apples	How much is a bag of apples?
2. a carton of milk	How much is a carton of milk?
3. a loaf of bread	How much is a loaf of bread?
4. a package of cheese	How much is a package of cheese?
5. a jar of honey	How much is a jar of honey?
6. a box of sugar	How much is a box of sugar?
7. a can of tomatoes	How much is a can of tomatoes?
8. a bottle of oil	How much is a bottle of oil?

Other words

9. expensive	It's expensive.
10. cheap	It's cheap.

EXPANSION ACTIVITY: What does it come in?

★ Draw a five-column chart on the board with the headings *bag, box, carton, jar,* and *can* at the top of each column.

★ Have the students work in pairs or small groups. Ask them to copy the chart.

★ Set a time limit of three minutes for each pair or group to put as many food items in the chart as they can. They can use words from this lesson or other words they know.

★ After three minutes, have them count their words and determine which group has the most. Have the group with the most words read theirs aloud and make sure their answers are correct. As the other groups listen, have them check off the words they hear that are also on their lists. Any group with words that weren't called out should read those words.

Culture/Civics Notes:

★ Many foods come in some kind of packaging. You can talk about packaged foods from different countries and foods that don't come in packaging.

★ In many countries, some of this packaging can be recycled (plastic, bottles and cans, newspapers). Talk about what your community does to recycle some of these products.

2. Find Someone Who

★ Make a chart on the board like the one in the book. Include two columns under the headings *Food* and *Person's name,* and include eight rows in each column. Write two phrases from the vocabulary at the beginning of this section under *Food.* Have students copy the chart and fill in the last six lines with any of the phrases from the vocabulary section.

★ Have students look at the example question and possible answers. Read the sentences, pausing so that students can repeat.

★ Model this activity with a student. Ask, *Do you have a loaf of bread at home?* If the student says, *No, I don't,* ask another student. When a student responds *Yes, I do,* write that student's name on the chart under *Person's name* and next to the correct phrase.

★ Ask students to stand up and walk around the room, asking and answering questions about the items on the chart. Have them write a person's name in the blank next to the item only if he or she answers *yes.*

★ At the end of the activity, you can ask questions like, *Who has a loaf of bread at home? Who has a bag of rice?*

★ Have students write sentences with the information in their chart:

_____ *has a loaf of bread.*

_____ *and* _____ *have a loaf of bread.*

★ Call on a few students and have them say one or two of their sentences.

3. Practice the Conversation 🎧

★ Have students look at the picture of a customer asking about prices.

★ Read the conversation or play the tape or CD.

★ Play or read the conversation a second time. Pause after each line and have students repeat.

★ Model the conversation with one of the students. You read *A's* line and demonstrate how to substitute one of the food items.

★ Have students work in pairs to brainstorm typical prices for the foods they buy. Have them write down foods they think are expensive. They can practice the conversation with this information.

LISTENING SCRIPT

Lesson 3: Practice the Conversation

Listen to the conversation. Then listen and repeat.

A: Excuse me. How much is a loaf of bread?
B: Five dollars.
A: Wow! That's expensive.

WINDOW ON MATH
Pounds, Ounces, and Cups

★ Some students will understand these concepts easily, while others may be unfamiliar with multiplying and handling fractions.

★ To introduce the terms and concepts, draw a big circle on the board. Tell the students it is a wheel of cheese or a pizza. Divide it into halves, then fourths, then sixteenths. Tell students that each sixteenth represents one ounce, and the whole thing is a pound.

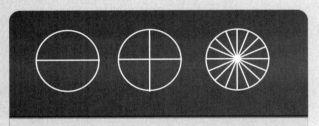

★ Ask questions about the picture in the book: *How many ounces in a pound of cheese? How many ounces in a half pound of cheese? How many ounces in a pound and a half of cheese?* Indicate how much of the circle is a half.

★ Bring in a measuring cup and/or draw one on the board. Show the marks for each ounce on the side of the cup.

★ Have students work in pairs to answer the questions in the book. If appropriate, pair a student who understands the concepts with a student who might not.

ANSWER KEY:

1. 32 ounces; 2. 24 ounces; 3. 4 ounces;
4. 8 ounces; 5. 8 tablespoons

EXPANSION ACTIVITY: What size is it?

★ Have students bring in food containers such as drink cans, bottles, and boxes. Or you can bring the items in yourself. If you have snack machines in your school, students can also collect those containers and wrappers. Have students group containers by type and size and. Ask them questions: *What size can do drinks come in? How many ounces are in a bag of chips?*

OBJECTIVE

Reading Food Ads

WINDOW ON GRAMMAR

Frequency Adverbs

THINGS TO DO

1. Read

★ Have students look at the advertisements in the book. Ask them where they have seen this kind of thing before. Elicit that these flyers are found in supermarkets, in newspapers, and sometimes in the mail. Point out that they advertise sales.

★ Ask students to look at the flyers. Elicit the names of the items they know. They should be able to name most of the foods and most of the containers. Note that *legs* and *fresh* may be unfamiliar to students.

★ Copy the chart on the board. Ask for the price and the size or amount of green beans at Ray's Supermarket. Write the information on the chart.

★ Tell students to complete the chart in their book with information from the flyers.

★ Go over the answers with the class.

ANSWER KEY:

FOOD	RAY'S SUPERMARKET Price	Size/Amount	FORD'S SUPERMARKET Price	Size/Amount
green beans	$1.25	1 lb.	$.99	1 lb.
chicken	$1.20	1 lb.	$.99	1 lb.
orange juice	2/$4	32 oz.	$1.99	64 oz.
vegetable oil	$3.99	96 oz.	$2.99	16 oz.
carrots	2/$6	5 lbs.	$.79	1 lb.

2. Compare

★ Tell students to look at their completed charts. Ask *How much are green beans at Ray's?* ($1.25/pound) *How much are they at Ford's?* ($.99/pound) *Are green beans cheaper (less money) at Ray's or at Ford's?* (Answer: Ford's). Tell students to check the box under *Ford's.*

★ Remind students to look at the price per amount.

★ Have students check the correct boxes for the other items.

★ Have students work in pairs to compare their answers.

★ Go over the answers with the class.

ANSWER KEY:

	Ray's	Ford's
Green beans are cheaper at	☐	☒
Chicken is cheaper at	☐	☒
Orange juice is cheaper at	☒	☐
Vegetable oil is cheaper at	☒	☐
Carrots are cheaper at	☒	☐

EXPANSION ACTIVITY: Comparison Shopping

★ Have students bring in flyers, or you can bring some in from nearby supermarkets.

★ Have students work in small groups and list three things from the flyers that they want to buy. Ask them to compare prices for those items at different stores and tell you where each item is the cheapest and where it is the most expensive.

 Students can do Unit 6, Section 3 *Read and Write* on the Interactive CD-ROM.

★★★★★★★★★★★★★★★★★★★★★★★★★★★★★★★

📁 **TRY THIS**

★★★★★★★★★★★★★★★★★★★★★★★★★★★★★★★

★ Tell students they have $5.00 and have to buy food.

★ Copy the chart on the board.

★ Model the activity by telling students "I have $5. I am going to Ford's. I want to buy orange juice." Write *orange juice* under *Food,* and write *Ford's* under *Store.* Ask students how much the orange juice costs at Ford's ($1.99). Write this under *Price.* Ask how much you have left to spend ($3.01). Tell them that now you will decide how to spend the rest of your money.

★ Have students look at the items and decide which store to go to. Tell them to write down which items they want and can buy for $5 on a piece of paper.

WINDOW ON GRAMMAR
Frequency Adverbs

A. Read the words.

★ Have students look at the frequency adverbs. Say each adverb and have students repeat.

★ Tell students about something you eat every day. (*I always eat cereal in the morning.*) Make sure students understand that you eat it everyday, Sunday through Saturday. Give an example of something you never eat at that time of day. (*I never eat chicken in the morning.*)

B. Complete the sentences with *always*, *usually*, *sometimes*, or *never*.

★ Have students complete the sentences in their books.

★ Elicit examples from students for all of the adverbs by asking questions such as *What do you sometimes eat for dinner?* Restate the students' responses as statements. (*Maria sometimes eats chicken for dinner.*)

★ For more practice, ask students to write two new sentences about their eating habits using frequency adverbs.

EXPANSION ACTIVITY: Forced Choice

★ Write the frequency adverbs on pieces of paper and tape them to the front of the room in a continuum (*always, usually, sometimes, never*).

★ Have a group of students come to the front of the room.

★ Read the items from the Window on Grammar (*eat rice in the morning*) and tell students to move to the adverb that makes the sentence true for them. For example, students who always eat rice in the morning would stand in front of *always*.

★ Repeat with other students and new sentences.

BIG PICTURE EXPANSION ACTIVITY:
READING—Reading Store Signs

★ Make copies of Worksheet #11 (p. 251) and distribute them to the students.

★ Put the color overhead transparency for Unit 6, Lesson 2, on the overhead projector.

★ Read the directions for Activity A aloud.

★ Walk around the room to monitor the activity and provide help as needed.

★ Go over the answers with the class.

★ Do the same for Activity B.

★ For Activity C, have students find Al in the big picture. Ask pre-reading questions, such as *Where is Al? What happened? What is Al doing? How does he feel?*

★ Have students read the paragraph silently and complete the activity.

★ Ask for volunteers to read sentences from the paragraph. Go over the answers.

ANSWER KEY:

A. ☒ customer service   ☒ bakery
    ☒ produce section   ☐ vegetables
    ☒ delicatessen   ☒ open
    ☒ frozen   ☐ closed
    ☐ pizza   ☒ special
    ☐ milk   ☒ meat
    ☒ baking goods   ☒ chicken
    ☒ rice   ☒ entrance

B. 1. ice or entrance; 2. frozen foods, customer service; 3. aisle 1 and aisle 3, or rice, pasta, cereal and canned goods; 4. bakery; 5. Canned goods

C. 1. True; 2. False; 3. False; 4. True; 5. True; 6. False

OBJECTIVE

Asking for Store Information

WINDOW ON PRONUNCIATION

Intonation in *Yes/No* Questions

1. Practice the Conversation: Ordering Food at a Counter 🎧

★ Set the context for the conversation by having students look at the picture and asking them questions: *Where are they? Who do you see? What kind of food is in this section?*

★ Read the conversation or play the tape or CD.

★ Check comprehension: *What number does the customer have? What does the customer want?*

★ Read or play the conversation again. Pause after each sentence and ask students to repeat.

★ Model the activity with a more proficient student. Read *B's* part, and have the student read *A's* part. Cue the student to substitute *28* as the number by pointing to *28* in the first set of choices. Then point to the amount, *A pound,* as you read *B's* second line.

★ Pair students and have them practice the conversation, taking turns playing both parts.

★ Explain that the lightbulb indicates that they have to use their own ideas as substitutions.

LISTENING SCRIPT

Lesson 5: Practice the Conversation—Ordering Food at a Counter

Listen to the conversation. Then listen and repeat.

A: Number 27, please.
B: That's me.
A: What can I get for you?
B: Three pounds of chicken.
A: Anything else?
B: No, that's all.

2. Practice the Conversation: Asking For Help 🎧

★ Repeat the basic procedure from Activity 1.

★ To set the context, ask: *Who is in the picture? Where are they?*

★ To check comprehension, ask: *What does the customer want? How much is it? What size is the bottle? Is that a good price?*

LISTENING SCRIPT

Lesson 5: Practice the Conversation—Asking for Help

Listen to the conversation. Then listen and repeat.

A: Can I help you?
B: Yes. Do you have vegetable oil?
A: Yes, we do. It's on sale this week.
B: How much is it?
A: $1.99 for a 64-ounce bottle.

3. Practice the Conversation: Asking about Sales 🎧

★ Repeat the basic procedure from Activity 1.

★ To set the context, ask: *Who is in the picture? What are they doing?*

★ To check comprehension, ask: *What is on sale? What size is it? How much is it?*

LISTENING SCRIPT

Lesson 5: Practice the Conversation—Asking about Sales

Listen to the conversation. Then listen and repeat.

A: Is milk on sale this week?
B: Yes. It's only 99 cents a carton.
A: What size?
B: 32 ounces.
A: Wow! That's a good price.

 Students can do Unit 6, Section 2, *Listen and Choose* on the Interactive CD-ROM.

WINDOW ON PRONUNCIATION 🎧
Intonation in *Yes/No* Questions

A. Listen to the questions.

★ Tell students that we use our voices and intonation to let the listener know that we are asking a question.

★ Read the directions for Activity A. Read the questions or play the tape or CD.

★ Read or play the questions again and have students repeat.

★ Call on volunteers to read questions. Correct their intonation if necessary.

★ Have students work in pairs and take turns asking and answering the questions. Move around the room and correct intonation problems.

LISTENING SCRIPT

Lesson 5: Window on Pronunciation—Intonation in *Yes/No* Questions

A. Listen to the questions. Then listen and repeat.

1. Can I help you?
2. Do you have grape juice?
3. Is rice on sale this week?
4. Anything else?
5. Do you sell noodles?
6. Do you have a package of cheese at home?
7. Do you like apples?

B. Listen to the sentences.

★ Read the directions for Activity B. Read the items or play the tape or CD.

★ Read or play the items again, pausing to let students repeat.

★ Tell students that they will listen a third time. If they think the sentence or phrase is a statement, they should write a period. If they think the sentence or phrase is a question, they should write a question mark.

★ Go over the answers with the class.

LISTENING SCRIPT

Lesson 5: Window on Pronunciation—Intonation in *Yes/No* Questions

B. Listen to the sentences. Then listen and repeat. Write a period after each statement and a question mark after each question.

1. A. The apples are on sale.
   B. The apples are on sale?
2. A. Okay?
   B. Okay.
3. A. Milk.
   B. Milk?

ANSWER KEY:

1A. period; 1B. question mark; 2A. question mark; 2B. period; 3A. period; 3B. question mark

---

🖼 BIG PICTURE EXPANSION ACTIVITY:
GRAMMAR—Practicing *Yes/No* Questions

★ Make copies of Worksheet #12 (p. 252) and distribute them to the students.

★ Put the color overhead transparency for Unit 6, Lesson 2, on the overhead projector.

★ Read the directions to the students.

★ Note in Activity A that it is possible to answer the questions without looking at the "big picture." But looking at the "big picture" can help.

★ Walk around the room to monitor the activity and provide help as needed.

★ Go over the answers with the class.

ANSWER KEY:

A. 1. b; 2. f; 3. c; 4. e; 5. g; 6. a; 7. d
B. 1. Yes, we do.; 2. Yes, we do.; 3. No, we don't.; 4. Yes, we do.; 5. Yes, we do.; 6. No, we don't.; 7. Yes, we do.; 8. Yes, we do.; 9. Yes, we do.; 10. No, we don't.; 11. Yes, we do.

EQUIPPED FOR THE FUTURE ROLE

Family

OBJECTIVE

Choosing Foods

1. Talk About the Picture

★ To practice pre-reading strategies, ask questions about the visual: *What is this?* (a picture, chart) *What is in the picture?* (types of food)

★ Have students work in small groups to list all the foods they know in the picture. Have them brainstorm additional items for each food group.

★ Ask students to write one additional food next to each group. Call on individual students to say what they added.

> **Culture/Civics Note:**
> ★ Students may not know that the food pyramid illustrates the recommendations of the United States Department of Agriculture (USDA). These are not rules, but suggestions, to help people living in the U.S. eat nutritiously and stay healthy.
> ★ Explain that "use sparingly" means to eat a very small amount.

2. Read

★ Copy the chart on the board.

★ Point to the Bread, Cereal, Rice, and Pasta group. Ask students how many servings people should eat each day. Cue them by pointing to *6 to 11 servings* if necessary.

★ Point to the fruit group. Ask, *How many servings of fruit should we eat?* Elicit the correct response. Write *3 to 5* on the chart on the board.

★ Have students complete the chart individually.

★ Have students check their answers with a partner.

ANSWER KEY:

In any order: Bread, etc: 6 to 11; Fruit: 2 to 4; Vegetable: 3 to 5; Milk, etc: 2 to 3; Meat, etc: 2 to 3; Fats, oils, and sweets: less than 1 serving

3. Write

★ Point to the first picture and ask students to name the food (*bread*). Ask how many slices are in one serving of bread. Point to the information on the chart (*1 slice*).

★ Ask: *How many servings are in the picture?* (*2 servings*). Point out that *2 servings* is written on the line.

★ Point to a serving size for eggs. Elicit the number of servings for 4 eggs.

★ Have students write in the number of servings for the other items (c–g).

ANSWER KEY:

1. 2 servings; 2. 2 servings, 3. 2 servings; 4. 2 servings; 5. 1 serving; 6. 2 servings

★ ★

📁 **TRY THIS**

★ ★

★ Have students read the example sentences.

★ Check comprehension: *How many servings of vegetables does the person eat every day? What does the person eat in the morning?*

★ Model the activity with information about yourself. (*I eat about four servings of fruit every day.*)

★ Brainstorm people that students can write about (*mother, brother, father, sister*). Write sentence stems on the board. (My brother eats _____. My sister usually eats _____.)

★ Have students write four sentences about themselves and their family members.

> ### EXPANSION ACTIVITY:
> ### Create Your Own Pyramid
>
> ★ Group students with other students from the same or a similar culture. Have them create food pyramids that include foods from their cultures.
>
> ★ Circulate to help the groups with new vocabulary from their cultures.
>
> ★ Have groups share pyramids with the class.

1. Listening Review 🎧

★ Go over the directions with the class.
★ Read the items or play the tape or CD.
★ Walk around to monitor the activity and help students stay on task.
★ Have students check their answers with a partner.
★ Go over the answers with the class.

LISTENING SCRIPT

Lesson 7: Listening Review

Listen and choose the word you hear. Use the Answer Sheet.

1. I always eat rice for dinner.
2. I sometimes eat cereal in the morning.
3. She usually eats lunch at noon.
4. They never eat in a restaurant on Sunday.

Listen and choose the best answer. Use the Answer Sheet.

5. Excuse me. Where's the rice?
6. Excuse me. Do you sell ice?
7. How much is a bottle of grape juice?
8. What size bag is it?
9. What's on sale?
10. What can I get for you?

ANSWER KEY:

1. A; 2. B; 3. B; 4. C; 5. C; 6. B; 7. B; 8. A; 9. C; 10. B

2. Dictation 🎧

★ Read or play the paragraph while students complete the activity.
★ Read or play the dictation again if necessary.
★ Copy the dictation on the board. Elicit the missing words and write them in the correct places or have volunteers come to the board and write the words.

LISTENING SCRIPT

Lesson 7: Dictation

Listen and write the missing words.

Attention, shoppers. If you like cereal for breakfast, Corn Crunch is on sale today. It's only $3.95 for a 12-ounce box. With milk and bananas, your breakfast will be delicious and nutritious. The bananas are in the produce section, and the milk is in the dairy section.

ANSWER KEY:

Attention, shoppers. If you like <u>cereal</u> for breakfast, Corn Crunch is on sale today. It's only $3.95 for a <u>12-ounce</u> box. With <u>milk</u> and <u>bananas</u>, your breakfast will be <u>delicious</u> and nutritious. The bananas are in the <u>produce</u> section, and the milk is in the <u>dairy</u> section.

3. Conversation Check: Pair Work

★ Go over the directions. Remind students that each partner has some information, but other information is missing. They must ask their partners questions to complete their charts.
★ Walk around to monitor the activity and provide help as needed.

Assessment Note:
★ You can use the conversation check as an oral assessment. Ask pairs of students to complete the activity while you note areas of difficulty.

LEARNING LOG

★ Point out the four sections of the Learning Log: *I know these words; I can ask; I can say;* and *I can write.*
★ Have students check what they know and what they can do.
★ Walk around to note what they don't know or can't do. Use this information to review areas of difficulty.

Students can do Unit 6, Section 4, *Fun and Games* on the Interactive CD-ROM.

 Students can do Unit 6, Section 5, *Practice Test* on the Interactive CD-ROM.

BIG PICTURE EXPANSION ACTIVITY:
WRITING—Describing the Store

★ Put the transparency for Unit 6, Lesson 2, on the overhead projector.

★ Write the directions on the board: *You work at this supermarket. Describe the supermarket. Tell about the food you sell at the store and where things are. Give the supermarket a name and begin your story with this sentence: I work at (Sunshine) Supermarket. We sell . . . .*

★ Go over the directions.

★ Have them write five sentences.

★ When students are finished, have them read their descriptions to a partner.

BIG PICTURE EXPANSION ACTIVITY:
SPEAKING Assessment—Talking About the Picture

★ You can use the "big picture" as an individual assessment to place new students in open entry classes, to diagnose difficulties, or to measure progress.

★ Work with one student at a time. Show the "big picture" to the student. Ask, *What do you see in the picture?* Or *Tell me about the picture.* Tell the student you want him or her to speak for as long as possible. Wait a moment for the student to prepare to answer.

★ If the student has difficulty, you can use prompts such as *What food do you see? What sections does the store have? What are the people doing?*

★ You can use a rubric like the one below to rate beginning speakers.

3	Uses sentences, although form may be incorrect Can speak for sustained length of time Responds to prompts, but doesn't need them to begin speaking
2	Can use nouns and verbs Uses phrases Answers informational questions
1	Can name objects Uses single words Can answer yes/no questions
0	Cannot say anything independently May be able to point to objects when prompted

TEACHER NOTES:

Things that students are doing well:

_____

_____

_____

_____

_____

_____

Things students need additional help with:

_____

_____

_____

_____

_____

_____

Ideas for further practice or for the next class:

_____

_____

_____

_____

_____

_____

OBJECTIVE

Recipes

FOCUS ON WRITING

Connecting Sentences

1. Read the recipe.

★ Ask students to look at the recipe. Ask, *What is a recipe?* Elicit that a recipe tells us how to make some kind of food. Ask students what they use recipes for.

★ Have students read the recipe, or read the recipe aloud yourself, pausing after each line to have students repeat.

★ Have students underline any unfamiliar words and try to figure out the meanings of the words by context. Go over the meanings.

★ Ask comprehension questions: *What is the recipe for? Whose recipe is it?*

★ Ask the question, *What do you do first to make the soup?* Have students look at the steps on the right side of the page. Point out that the number *1* is written in the circle of the *Wash the vegetables* picture.

★ Have students write the numbers 2–5 next to the pictures to identify their order in the recipe.

★ Have students check their answers with a partner.

★ Go over the answers with the class.

ANSWER KEY:

1. Wash the vegetables; 2. Cut up the potatoes and boil them for 20 minutes; 3. Boil the broccoli for 3 minutes; 4. Blend the vegetables with some water; 5. Add salt and pepper and serve hot.

2. Connect the sentences.

★ Have students look at the box *Focus on Writing.*

★ Go over the examples in the box. Ask students to notice what changes we make when we combine sentences. Point out that we take out the period, add *and,* and don't use a capital letter for the second sentence anymore.

★ Have students look at item *1* and read the sentences.

★ Ask them to use that example in connecting the sentences in items *2–6.*

★ Have them compare their sentences with a partner's.

★ Call on volunteers to read the sentences aloud, or ask volunteers to write them on the board.

ANSWER KEY:

1. Cook it for 30 minutes and serve it hot.
2. Put the vegetables in a blender and blend them.
3. Add the broccoli and boil it for 3 minutes.
4. Cut the potatoes in quarters and boil them.
5. Put water in a large pot and add salt.
6. Cook the vegetables and serve them hot.

3. Choose a favorite recipe.

★ Tell students that they will write a recipe for a food they know how to make. Point out that it can be a very simple recipe (*a fried egg, a cup of coffee*).

★ Have students write a recipe of their choice, completing the recipe form in the book. Have them look at the *My Favorite Soup* recipe for hints.

★ Put students in small groups to talk about their recipes.

EXPANSION ACTIVITY:
Fruit Salad Language Experience

★ Ask students to bring in fruit or bring in a variety of fruit yourself. Bring in the utensils and containers you will need to make fruit salad.

★ List the vocabulary students will need to make the fruit salad. Include the names of all the types of fruits, as well as the verbs (*peel, cut, slice, mix*).

★ Make sure students wash their hands, and then give each a job (*Peel the bananas, wash and separate the grapes, cut the strawberries*).

★ Put all the fruit together.

★ Create a class story or recipe after the activity. Copy the recipe on the board and/or have students copy it in their notebooks.

EQUIPPED FOR THE FUTURE ROLE

Community

OBJECTIVE

Comparing Prices

VOCABULARY

buy/buys	high/highest
compare/compares	low/lowest
cost/costs	shop/shops

A. Learn new words.

★ Say the new words. Have students repeat.

★ Read the story aloud. Ask comprehension questions such as *Who is shopping? When does he go to the supermarket? What stores does he go to?*

★ Read the sentences of the story, pausing to let students repeat.

★ Ask students to circle the new words.

★ Go over the answers.

ANSWER KEY:

Jim is shopping for food today. Jim goes to the supermarket every Saturday. He usually <u>shops</u> in the morning. Jim <u>buys</u> food for his family. Sometimes he goes to Savemor's Supermarket and sometimes he goes to BigMart. He never goes to Fancy Foods. The prices at Savemor's and BigMart are often <u>low</u>. The food at Fancy Foods always <u>costs</u> more. Jim always <u>compares</u> prices. The prices at Fancy Foods are the <u>highest</u>.

Culture/Civics Notes:

★ Some students may come from countries where women do the shopping. Point out that in many cultures, either gender may go grocery shopping.

★ Although students are probably used to shopping for the best price, they may not all be used to the unit pricing that is used in many countries. You may want to point out that in supermarkets, prices are usually given per unit of weight or volume.

B. Complete the sentences.

★ Ask students to name the frequency adverbs.

★ Have them look at the story again and write the correct frequency adverb on the lines.

★ Go over the answers.

ANSWER KEY:

1. sometimes; 2. usually; 3. sometimes;
4. always; 5. always; 6. often

C. Look at the chart.

★ Have students look at the chart. Ask *What are the headings?*

★ Ask students what is being compared (*prices at the three different supermarkets for different products*).

★ Tell students to use the information in the chart to answer the questions.

★ Have students compare their answers with a partner.

★ Go over the answers.

ANSWER KEY:

1. a; 2. c; 3. a; 4. c; 5. b; 6. b.

Take it Outside

★ Have students go to two stores near their homes.

★ Tell them to write the names of the two stores in the headings.

★ Have students find the prices for a pound of bananas and for a pound of green grapes at each store, and write the information on the chart.

★ Go over their answers in class.

EXPANSION ACTIVITY: Write about You

★ Have students work in pairs and tell their partner about their shopping or about the person who shops in their home.

★ Model the activity by telling about yourself. (*I go the supermarket on Monday. I usually go in the evening after work.*)

★ Have students write a paragraph about themselves or the person who shops in their home. Remind students to use the story about Jim as a model for their own writing.

★ Call on volunteers to read their stories to the class.

EQUIPPED FOR THE FUTURE ROLE

Work

OBJECTIVE

Serving Customers

VOCABULARY

deli
sandwich

A. Read the story.

★ Say the new words. Have the students repeat.

★ Read the story aloud. Ask comprehension questions: *Who is the story about?* (Arton), *Where does he work?* (in a deli). Read the story, pausing after each sentence to let students repeat.

★ Point out that we can often find the meaning for new words by looking at the information around the words in the story.

★ Have students look at the story again and complete the sentences.

★ Go over the answers.

ANSWER KEY:

1. A sandwich, meat, cheese, vegetables
2. deli, restaurant, sandwiches

B. Answer the questions about Arton.

★ Tell students they can read the story again if necessary to find the answers.

★ Have them check *yes* or *no* to answer the questions.

ANSWER KEY:

1. no; 2. yes; 3. yes; 4. no

C. Read the sandwich form.

★ Tell students that delis often have an order form that either the customer or the server fills out to order food.

★ Have students look at the completed order form. Point out that the form lists different groups or categories of food. Point out that these are *meat, cheese, bread, condiments,* and *vegetables*.

★ Go over the example. Ask students to point to where that information can be found on the form.

★ Have students answer the questions.

★ Go over the answers.

ANSWER KEY:

1. Lunch for you; 2. Walter Arakaki;
3. American; 4. No; 5. No; 6. Ham

D. Write about you.

★ Bring in pictures of the food items on the order form if you have them. Point out examples of the different items that can go in a sandwich.

★ Tell students to look at the T-chart. Ask them what the headings are (*Food, What I like*).

★ Have them write the type of each food that they like next to the food category. Model this activity by giving information about yourself. (*For meat, I like chicken. For the type of cheese, I like Swiss.*)

★ Have the students complete the chart for themselves and talk about their choices with a partner.

ANSWER KEY:

Answers will vary.

Take It Outside

★ Point to the blank order form. Tell students they can use this form to practice taking an order.

★ Read the questions and have students repeat.

★ Tell them to interview someone outside of class and complete the order form.

★ Ask students about the information on their order forms when they return to class.

EXPANSION ACTIVITY:
Sequencing a Recipe

★ Write these sentences on strips of paper. You will need enough sets to give to each small group.

Take out two pieces of bread.

Spread mustard on one piece of bread and mayonnaise on the other.

Put a piece of ham on top of the mustard.

Lay a piece of Swiss cheese on the ham.

Add a slice of tomato on top of the Swiss cheese.

Put the slice of bread with mayonnaise on top of the sandwich.

Cut the sandwich in half and eat.

★ Put students in small groups of seven. Give each student a sentence strip. Tell them to line up in the correct order to make a sandwich.

★ Have them read their sentences to the class in order.

Families

UNIT OVERVIEW

LESSON	OBJECTIVE	STUDENT BOOK PAGE #
1. What's your brother's name?	Identifying Family Members	p. 100
2. I usually cook dinner.	Identifying Family Responsibilities	p. 102
3. What do you do for fun?	At a Park	p. 104
4. Family Portraits	Describing Families	p. 106
5. Just a minute, please.	Answering the Telephone	p. 108
6. The Garcia Family's Expenses	Making a Family Budget	p. 110
7. What do you know?	Review and Assessment	p. 112
8. Spotlight	Grammar	p. 114

Big Picture Expansion Activities

FOCUS	TITLE	SUGGESTED USE
Speaking	Tell the Story	Lesson 3
Reading	A Family Portrait	Lesson 4
Writing	A Day in the Park	Lesson 7
Grammar	*Do, Does, Don't,* and *Doesn't*	Spotlight
Speaking	Assessment: Talking about the Picture	Lesson 7

Big Picture Expansion Activity Worksheets

WORKSHEET #/FOCUS	TITLE	TEACHER'S EDITION PAGE #
13. Reading	A Family Portrait	p. 253
14. Grammar	*Do, Does, Don't,* and *Doesn't*	p. 254

OBJECTIVE

Identifying Family Members

VOCABULARY

brother	grandson
children	husband
daughter	mother
father	parents
granddaughter	sister
grandfather	son
grandmother	wife

WINDOW ON GRAMMAR

Yes/No Questions + Simple Present

1. Learn New Words 🎧

★ Ask students to look at the pictures and listen while you say the words or play the tape or CD.

★ Say the words or play the tape or CD a second time. Pause after each word and ask the students to repeat the word and point to the photo that correctly illustrates each word.

★ Group students in pairs, and have one student say each word as the other points to the corresponding photo. Reverse roles and repeat the activity.

★ Tell students to look at the headings on the chart. Review the meaning of the words *male* and *female* if necessary.

★ Ask students about the examples: *Is a husband male or female?* Point out that *husband* is written under the heading *male*.

★ Instruct students to write each of the new words in the chart under the appropriate heading.

★ Have students compare their answers with a partner.

★ Go over the answers with the class.

LISTENING SCRIPT

Lesson 1: Learn New Words

Look at the pictures. Listen to the words. Then listen and repeat.

1.	husband	Jack is Mei's husband.
2.	wife	Mei is Jack's wife.
3.	parents	Jack and Mei are parents. They are Ann and Tim's parents.
4.	children	Ann and Tim are children. They are Jack and Mei's children.
5.	mother	Mei is Ann's mother.
6.	daughter	Ann is Mei's daughter.
7.	father	Jack is Tim's father.
8.	son	Tim is Jack's son.
9.	sister	Ann is Tim's sister.
10.	brother	Tim is Ann's brother.
11.	grandmother	Carol is Tim's grandmother.
12.	grandson	Tim is Carol's grandson.
13.	grandfather	Bob is Ann's grandfather.
14.	granddaughter	Ann is Bob's granddaughter.

ANSWER KEY:

MALES	FEMALES	MALES OR FEMALES
husband	wife	parents
father	mother	children
son	daughter	
brother	sister	
grandson	grandmother	
grandfather	granddaughter	

EXPANSION ACTIVITY: What do they do?

★ Ask students to draw a chart like the one in the book, but with the headings *Goes to Work, Goes to School, Goes to School and Work, Other*.

★ Have the students write each word in the appropriate place on the chart to describe the people in their families.

★ Students should share the information on their charts with a partner.

2. Write

★ Some students may be unfamiliar with presenting familial relationships in the form of a tree. Demonstrate how it works by drawing one on the board with your own family's information in it. You can draw a diagram like this:

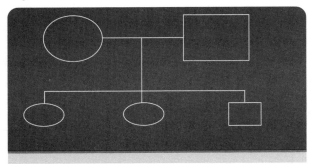

★ Instruct students to add the names of Ann's family to the tree in the book.

★ Have students discuss the tree with a partner.

★ Go over the tree with the class.

ANSWER KEY:

Grandmother: Carol
Grandfather: Bob
Father: Jack
Mother: Mei
Sister: Anne
Brother: Tim

EXPANSION ACTIVITY: Riddles

★ Dictate a riddle to the class: *Carol's son is her mother's* _____. Have students complete the riddle. (*grandson*)

★ Tell students to write their own riddles using Ann's family tree.

★ Have them exchange their riddles with a partner and complete.

★ Call on a few students to read their riddles to the class and elicit from students the correct answers.

★ ★

📁 **TRY THIS**

★ ★

★ Tell students that they are going to make a family tree for a partner. You can ask students to bring in pictures of their family for this activity.

★ Ask students to look at the sample questions. Read the questions aloud, pausing after each to have students repeat.

★ Have students work in pairs to interview each other and complete the activity.

★ Have pairs of students form groups of four people and have each person in the group describe his or her own family tree—the tree his or her partner made based on the interview.

WINDOW ON GRAMMAR: *Yes/No* Questions + Simple Present

A. Read the questions and answers.

★ Read the questions and answers in the grammar paradigm and ask students to repeat. Call on a few students and ask them the questions or variations on those questions.

★ Go over the form of the question. Ask students what word is first in these *yes/no* questions. Point out the form: *Do/does + subject + main verb*

B. Complete the questions with *Do* or *Does*.

★ Ask students to read the directions and complete the questions.

★ Go over the answers with the class.

★ Have students practice asking and answering the questions in pairs.

ANSWER KEY:

1. Do; 2. Does; 3. Do; 4. Do; 5. Does

 Students can do Unit 7, Section 1, *Learn New Words* on the Interactive CD-ROM.

OBJECTIVE

Identifying Family Responsibilities

VOCABULARY

buy the groceries	make the beds
clean the house	pay the bills
cook dinner	take out the trash
do the laundry	wash the dishes
fix things	

WINDOW ON GRAMMAR:

Simple Present Statements

1. Learn New Words 🎧

★ Instruct students to look at the pictures and elicit from them any words they know.

★ Ask them to look at the pictures and listen while you say the words or play the tape or CD.

★ Say the words or play the tape or CD a second time. Pause after each word and ask the students to repeat the word and point to the picture that corresponds to that action.

★ Have students work in pairs, and have one student say the word as his or her partner points to the picture. Reverse roles and repeat the activity.

★ Have students write the correct word under each picture.

LISTENING SCRIPT

Lesson 2: Learn New Words

Look at the pictures. Listen to the words. Then listen and repeat.

1. fix things	Do you fix things at home?
2. make the bed	Do you make the bed at home?
3. wash the dishes	Do you wash the dishes at home?
4. take out the trash	Do you take out the trash at home?
5. buy the groceries	Do you buy the groceries?
6. pay the bills	Do you pay the bills at home?
7. clean the house	Do you clean the house?
8. do the laundry	Do you do the laundry at home?
9. cook dinner	Do you cook dinner at home?

EXPANSION ACTIVITY: Numbered Heads Together

★ Put students in groups of four and give each a number from 1–4.

★ Ask them to discuss how often each activity in the New Words list is done in their home. For example, a family might make beds every day, but fix things only once a month.

★ To go over the answers, ask questions: *How often do you take out the trash?* Then say a number between 1–4. The student in each group with that number needs to report the group's answer to the class.

★ Continue asking questions until every student has reported to the class.

2. Interview

★ Instruct students to look at the questionnaire and explain the headings.

★ Ask the first question: *Do you fix things at home?* Demonstrate how to answer the question with one of the three answer choices.

★ Read each question aloud and have students repeat.

★ Put students in pairs to take turns asking and answering the questions. Point out that they should check their partner's answers.

★ Call on a few students and ask them about their partner: *Does _____ make the beds?*

EXPANSION ACTIVITY: What's your opinion?

★ In this activity, students give their opinion about whether certain chores in the home should be done by a male or a female.

★ Write *Male* on a piece of paper, and *Female* on another piece. Tape each piece of paper on opposite sides of the room.

★ Ask a group of six students to stand at the front of the room. Read a question, beginning with *Who do you think should . . .*, and complete the sentence with one of the activities in the New Word list. For example, ask the group of students, *Who do you think should pay the bills?* Have students move to the signs that express their opinions.

★ When students are standing in the places that represent their opinions, ask them to give a reason. Note that many students will want to stand in the middle. You can decide if that is okay for the activity or if you want to make them choose.

★ Continue the activity with new groups of students. Have the other students ask new questions of the group at the front.

3. Write

★ Read the directions. Then read the example aloud or instruct students to read it silently. Check comprehension: *Does this person usually wash the dishes? Does he or she always make the beds?*

★ Ask the students to underline the words that express how often something is done (*usually, sometimes, never*). Ask students where these words go in the sentence (*before the action word*).

★ Ask students to write about themselves. Remind them to follow the model.

★ Call on a few volunteers to read their stories to the class.

EXPANSION ACTIVITY: Who does what?

★ Have students use the information in Activity 2 to write a story about their partner. They should write about the partner without using names.

★ Collect the stories and redistribute them.

★ Ask students to read the stories aloud while the rest of the class guesses who the subject of each story is.

WINDOW ON GRAMMAR: Simple Present Statements

A. Read the sentences.

★ Read the sentences aloud and pause after each while students repeat. Ask students how the sentences with *he* and *she* are different from the others (*the verbs end in -s or -es*).

B. Complete these sentences.

★ Instruct students to complete the sentences and check their answers with a partner. Go over the answers with the class.

ANSWER KEY:

1. washes; 2. makes; 3. buys; 4. take out; 5. do

C. Write about the people in your family.

★ Have students write five more sentences about the people in their families. Have them read their sentences to a partner.

★ Call on a few students to tell the class about their partners' families.

Grammar Notes:

★ Although students are not expected to be experts at the simple present yet, it may help them to review the spelling rules for forming this tense. Add an *-es* to the verb in the third person (with *he, she* or *it*) if the verb ends in a sibilant (*-s, -ss, -ch, -sh, -z, -zz, -x*). Add an *-s* to verbs in the third person that end in a vowel or that end in a consonant other than a sibilant.

★ Note that words that end in *-es* are pronounced *iz*.

★ *Take out* is a phrasal verb. Students need to know that the *-s* ending is added to the verb *take*, not *out*.

EXPANSION ACTIVITY: Practice -s Endings

★ Ask students to rewrite their stories or the example from Activity 3 using *he* or *she* instead of *I*. They'll have to choose a gender.

★ Have them exchange stories with a partner and make corrections if necessary.

 Students can do Unit 7, Section 2, *Listen and Choose* on the Interactive CD-ROM.

OBJECTIVE

At a Park

VOCABULARY

dance	play soccer
listen to music	read the newspaper
play an instrument	take pictures
play cards	tell stories

1. Talk About the Picture

★ Put the "big picture" color overhead transparency for Unit 7, Lesson 3, on the projector or have students look at the "big picture" in their books.

★ To set the context, ask questions about the picture: *How many people do you see? Where are they? What are they doing? What words do you know?* Write the vocabulary that you have elicited from students on the board.

★ Ask students to write five sentences about the picture. Remind them to use the words on the board if they need help. Walk around the room and provide help as needed.

★ Call on a few students to read their sentences to the class.

EXPANSION ACTIVITY: Memory Challenge

★ Divide the class into teams. Have each team write eight sentences about the picture, half of which are true and half false. Give an example if necessary.

★ When the teams are finished writing their sentences, have everyone close their books. Call on a member of one team to read a sentence, and a member of another team to say if it is *true* or *false*. Each correct answer earns a point.

★ Continue until all the students have both read a sentence and responded with *true* or *false*.

★ The team with the most points wins.

★ Small prizes for the winners will probably increase enthusiasm for the game and raise the energy level in the classroom.

2. Learn New Words 🎧

★ Ask students to look at the picture and listen while you say the words or play the tape or CD.

★ Say the words or play the tape or CD a second time. Pause after each word and ask the students to repeat the word and point to the picture that illustrates that word.

★ Group students in pairs and have one say a word as the other points to the corresponding photo. Reverse roles and do the activity again.

LISTENING SCRIPT

Lesson 3: Learn New Words

Look at the picture. Listen to the words. Then listen and repeat.

1. read the newspaper	Do you read the newspaper?
2. play an instrument	Do you play an instrument?
3. dance	Do you dance?
4. play cards	Do you play cards?
5. take pictures	Do you take pictures?
6. listen to music	Do you listen to music?
7. play soccer	Do you play soccer?
8. tell stories	Do you tell stories?

EXPANSION ACTIVITY: Chain Story

★ Explain that the class is going to tell a chain story. Arrange students in a circle. Begin the story by saying a sentence about the picture. Call on a student who should repeat your sentence and add a new one. A student on either side will then repeat only the previous student's sentence—not yours also—and add a new one.

★ Continue the activity until you've gone around the circle and everyone has added to the story.

★ For a greater challenge, have students repeat all of the sentences that were said to that point, not just the one from the previous student.

3. Interview

★ Tell students to look at the questions and explain the headings.

★ Ask a few students the first question, *Does your family listen to music?* Prompt them to answer with one of the three answer choices.

★ Have students work in pairs to complete the interview. Make sure each student checks the appropriate box for his or her partner.

★ Ask students to complete the sentences about their partners based on the checked boxes.

★ Call on a few students to tell the class about their partners.

EXPANSION ACTIVITY: Rank It

★ Students should work individually and rank each activity according to how often they do it, how much they like it, or how popular it is in their families.

★ Put students in small groups to talk about their rankings.

★ ★

TRY THIS

★ ★

★ Ask students to look at the questions. Read the first two to the class and have a few students give answers.

★ Students should work individually to complete the remaining questions.

★ Have them practice asking and answering questions in pairs.

★ Call on a few volunteers to tell the class about their partners.

BIG PICTURE EXPANSION ACTIVITY: SPEAKING—Tell the Story

★ Put the "big picture" color overhead transparency for Unit 7, Lesson 3, on the projector or have students look at the "big picture" in their books.

★ Invite students to choose someone in the picture that they would like to tell a story about.

★ Model the activity by creating a story about someone in the picture: *Jerry is 23 years old. His family doesn't live with him. He likes to go to the park to play his guitar. Jerry meets a lot of people when he plays his guitar. He has lots of friends.*

★ Have students choose a character. Explain that they are making up a story and need to use imagination. Have them write a list of the details about their character, including information about the person's family and his or her interests.

★ Put the students in pairs and have each person tell the story to his or her partner. Encourage them to say as much as they can about the people in their stories. The partners should point to the person in the picture.

★ Ask a few volunteers to tell their stories to the class.

 Students can do Unit 7, Section 2, *Listen and Choose*, Section 3 *Read and Write,* and Section 4, *Fun and Games* on the Interactive CD-ROM.

OBJECTIVE

Describing Families

WINDOW ON GRAMMAR

Don't and *Doesn't*

1. Read and Take Notes

★ Ask students to look at the pictures. Set the context by asking questions: *Who is in the first picture? How many children does she have? Where do you think she is from?*

★ Ask the students to read the stories or, to promote emerging literacy skills, read the stories aloud, pausing after each sentence to have students repeat. As a variation, have each student read one sentence of each story.

★ Check comprehension by asking questions: *Where is Boris from? How many children does Nhu Trinh have? Who is from China?*

★ Instruct students to look at the chart and go over the headings.

★ Have the students complete the chart. Remind them to read the stories again if they need to.

★ Invite a few different students to tell the class about one of the people in the chart.

ANSWER KEY:

Name	Marital Status	Lives With
Pilar	married	husband and 2 children
Boris	married	wife and daughter
Sonya	single	aunt and uncle
Nhu Trinh	married	husband and son

EXPANSION ACTIVITY: Venn Diagram

★ Ask students to draw a Venn diagram comparing two of the people in the stories.

★ Call on volunteers to draw their Venn diagrams on the board and explain them to the class.

BIG PICTURE EXPANSION ACTIVITY: READING—A Family Portrait

★ Make copies of Worksheet #13 (p. 253) and distribute them to students.

★ Put the "big picture" color overhead transparency for Unit 7, Lesson 3, on the projector or have students look at the "big picture" in their books.

★ Ask students to read the story, or read it aloud, pausing after each line to have students repeat.

★ Have students answer the questions and check their answers with a partner.

★ Go over the answers with the class.

ANSWER KEY:

A: 1. Agnes; 2. Annie; 3. John and Michael; 4. Ivan's daughter; 5. Sophia's husband; 6. Max and Ivan.

B: 1. true; 2. true; 3. false; 4. true

EXPANSION ACTIVITY: Review *Be*

★ If students are still having trouble with the verb *be*, review by having them circle all forms of *be* in the stories.

★ Have students check their answers with a partner.

2. Write

★ Ask students to look at the sentences. Complete the first sentence together.

★ Ask students to complete the sentences by writing about people in their families. Have them read their sentences to partners.

★ Call on a few students to read their sentences to the class.

EXPANSION ACTIVITY: Sentence Match

★ Write the following sentences (or create your own) on separate strips of paper. Mix up the strips and give one to each student. Tell the students to walk around the room until they find their match and then stand together.

My aunt lives in New York.	She is my father's sister.
My uncle is a doctor. He lives in Los Angeles.	He is my aunt's husband. He lives in California.
Cynthia's grandmother lives with her.	She is her father's mother.
Mr. Campos is Tom's uncle. He lives in Boston.	He is his mother's brother.
My sister lives in Florida.	My brother lives in Florida, too.

★ Ask students to read their sentences to the class.

★ ★

 TRY THIS

★ ★

★ Ask students to read the directions. Go over the sentences and give information about yourself.

★ Have students write three sentences about themselves and read them to partners.

EXPANSION ACTIVITY: Role-Play

★ Put students in groups of four. Assign each student in the group one of the four characters in the stories in Lesson 4 as a role-play assignment (Pilar, Boris, Sonya, Nhu Trinh). Make sure they don't tell the others which character they have.

★ Have the students reread the stories silently, remembering as many details about the characters as possible, and then tell them to close their books.

★ Explain that the four characters have just met in a class and are having a conversation to learn more about each other. They're asking lots of questions. Each student in the group should role-play the person he or she was assigned, answering questions as that person might. They cannot give their names, but should answer any other questions asked.

★ At the end of the conversation, the students in the group should guess who was playing each role.

WINDOW ON GRAMMAR: *Don't* and *Doesn't*

A. Read the sentences.

★ Read the sentences aloud, pausing after each to have students repeat. Ask students when we use *doesn't* and when we use *don't*. Make sure they notice that *doesn't* is used with *he* and *she*.

B. Complete these sentences with *don't* or *doesn't*.

★ Have students complete the sentences with *don't* or *doesn't* and check their answers with a partner.

★ Go over the answers with the class.

ANSWER KEY:

1. don't; 2. doesn't; 3. don't; 4. don't;
5. doesn't; 6. don't

 Students can do Unit 7, Section 3, *Read and Write* on the Interactive CD-ROM.

OBJECTIVE

Answering the Telephone

WINDOW ON PRONUNCIATION

Linking Consonant to Vowel

1. Practice the Conversation: Making a Call 🎧

★ Instruct students to look at the picture for Activity 1. To set the context, ask questions: *Who is in the picture? What is their relationship?*

★ Read the conversation aloud or play the tape or CD.

★ Read or play the conversation again. Pause after each sentence and ask students to repeat.

★ Ask comprehension questions about the conversation: *Who does the caller ask for? What number does she want?*

★ Point out that there are two pieces of information in the conversation that may be substituted. Model the conversation with a student. Have the student read *B's* lines.

★ Ask students to write down an additional name and phone number.

★ Have students work in pairs to practice the conversation.

★ Invite volunteers to practice the conversation in front of the class.

LISTENING SCRIPT

Lesson 5: Practice the Conversation— Making a Call

Listen to the conversation. Then listen and repeat.

A: Is Sam there?
B: I think you have the wrong number.
A: Is this 555-1212?
B: No, it isn't.
A: Sorry to bother you.
B: No problem. Bye.

Culture/Civics Notes:

★ If we call a number but think we may have dialed incorrectly, we can confirm by asking, *Is this _____?* and saying the number we want.

★ *Sorry to bother you* is a polite way to apologize for a wrong number. We can also say, *I'm sorry.*

★ A polite way to accept an apology is to say, *No problem.* We can also say, *That's okay.*

2. Practice the Conversation: Answering the Phone. 🎧

★ Repeat the basic procedure from Activity 1.

★ To set the context, ask questions: *Who is in the picture? Are they happy?*

★ Check comprehension by asking additional questions: *Who is calling? Who is Ann?*

★ Have students write in their own ideas. Encourage them to use their own names and their own ways of identifying themselves (*classmate, coworker, brother, sister, student*).

LISTENING SCRIPT

Lesson 5: Practice the Conversation— Answering the Phone

Listen to the conversation. Then listen and repeat.

A: Is Ann there?
B: Who's calling please?
A: This is Pat. I'm her classmate.
B: Just a minute, please. I'll get her.

3. Practice the Conversation: Taking a Message 🎧

★ Repeat the basic procedure from Activity 1.

★ To set the context, ask questions: *Who is in the picture? Do you think she's calling someone or answering the phone?*

★ To check comprehension, ask additional questions: *Who left a message? Who took the message? Who is the message for?*

★ Have students practice the conversation in pairs using their own names and telephone numbers.

LISTENING SCRIPT

Lesson 5: Practice the Conversation— Taking a Message

Listen to the conversation. Then listen and repeat.

A: Can I speak to your father, please?
B: He's not here now. Can I take a message?
A: Can you ask him to call Mr. Rogers? My number is 555-3598.
B: Call Mr. Rogers at 555-3598.
A: Right. Thank you.
B: You're welcome. Good-bye.

Culture/Civics Notes:

★ Students may be uncomfortable asking native English speakers to identify themselves. Assure them that this is a common practice. A polite way to ask for identification is, *May I ask who's calling?*

EXPANSION ACTIVITY: Take a Message

★ Bring in an office telephone message pad and distribute a sheet to each student. Or you can create your own.

★ Go over the information requested on the form: *time, date, who is being called, who is calling, telephone number, message.*

★ Group students in pairs to practice giving and taking telephone messages on the form.

★ To simulate a real phone conversation, and to make the exercise a bit more fun, have pairs of students sit back to back so they can't see each other. Walk around the room to monitor the activity and provide help as needed.

WINDOW ON PRONUNCIATION: Linking Consonant to Vowel

A. Listen to the words. 🎧

★ Ask students to look at the phrases in their books. Write *Sam is* on the board and show a connection between the words by drawing a curved line from the *m* in *Sam* and the *i* in *is*. Say *Sam is* as two clearly distinct words, and then say them again naturally and link the *m* to the *i*.

★ Say the words aloud or play the tape or CD. Pause after each word and have students repeat.

★ Point out that the link between the words occurs when the first word ends in a consonant and the second word begins with a vowel sound. However, *h* is an exception, as in *ask him* and *I'm her*. In these cases the *h* falls silent and the phrase sounds like *askim, I'mer.*

LISTENING SCRIPT

Lesson 5: Window on Pronunciation—Linking Consonant to Vowel

A. Listen to the words. Then listen and repeat.

1. Sam is
2. ask him
3. this is
4. I'm her
5. can I
6. is Ann
7. with Ann
8. just a

B. Listen to the sentences. 🎧

★ Read the sentences or play the tape or CD. Read or play the tape or CD a second time, pausing after each sentence to have students repeat.

★ Put students in pairs to draw a line linking the ending consonants and beginning vowels.

★ Ask volunteers to copy their sentences on the board showing the links.

Lesson 5: Window on Pronunciation—Linking
Consonant to Vowel

***B. Listen to the sentences. Then listen and
repeat.***

1. Can I speak to Mike Elliot, please?
2. Can you ask him to call Pat Adams?
3. My number is 555-1234.
4. Wait a minute.
5. His name is Bob Underwood.

ANSWER KEY:

1. Can I speak to Mike Elliot, please?

2. Can you ask him to call Pat Adams?

3. My number is 555-1234.

4. Wait a minute.

5. His name is Bob Underwood.

**EXPANSION ACTIVITY:
Linking Consonants to Vowels**

★ Ask students to reread one of the stories in
Lesson 4 and mark the *consonant-vowel* links
between words.

★ Have them read the stories (or sentences
from the stories) out loud and help them
connect the consonants and vowels.

EQUIPPED FOR THE FUTURE ROLE

Family

OBJECTIVE

Making a Family Budget

VOCABULARY

child care	rent
clothing	savings
education	transportation
gifts	utilities
groceries	

1. Learn New Words 🎧

★ Instruct the students to look at the photo of the Garcia family and ask questions: *How many children do they have?*

★ Tell students to look at the pictures of the Garcia Family's Expenses and listen while you read the words or play the tape or CD.

★ Read the words or play the tape or CD a second time. Pause after each word and have students repeat and point to the pictures.

★ Have students work in pairs and have one student practice saying the new words as the other points to the pictures. Reverse roles and repeat the activity.

★ Ask students about their own experiences with money and bills. Say each of the new words and have students raise their hands if they also have that expense.

LISTENING SCRIPT

Lesson 6: Learn New Words

Look at the pictures below. Listen to the words. Then listen and repeat.

1. rent	How much do you spend on rent?
2. transportation	How much do you spend on transportation?
3. groceries	How much do you spend on groceries?
4. education	How much do you spend on education?
5. child care	How much do you spend on child care?
6. utilities	How much do you spend on utilities?
7. clothing	How much do you spend on clothing?
8. savings	How much do you save?
9. gifts	How much do you give away?

EXPANSION ACTIVITY: Listening Bingo

★ Explain to students that you are going to tell a story about the Cho family. Use the one below or create your own.

★ Instruct them to mark off a box on the Garcia Family's Expenses every time they hear about that type of expense. Warn students that you may not use the exact word for the particular expense. For example, you may say, *They spend $200 a month on Nicky's school.* In that case, students should mark off *education* on the list of Garcia Family expenses.

The story:
The Cho family lives in a little house. They spend $850 a month on rent. They want to buy a house soon. They have five children and spend a lot of money on food—$600 a month! Mr. Cho drives a red car. They don't make car payments, but they do pay for insurance, gas, and repairs. Those expenses are about $1,500 a year. Mrs. Cho works part-time, but she takes the bus. The youngest Cho is Mary. She is only four, so she goes to day care when Mrs. Cho works. That's about $300 a month. The other four children are all in school. They go to public school, so it's free, but they do have to buy some books and school supplies. The Chos spend about $200 a year on schoolbooks. The heat is included in the rent, but they spend about $60 a month on electricity. The Chos want to save money for their new house, so they put about $400 a month in savings. They also spend $500 a year on gifts.

★ By the end of the story, students should have marked off all the boxes for the Garcia family.

★ You can read the story again and have students take notes about the amount of the expenses.

2. Give Opinions 🎧

★ Tell students to review the amounts of money silently. Then read the amounts aloud, pausing after each to have students repeat.

★ Ask students how much money they think the Garcias spend on rent each month. Remind them to use an amount from the box of examples.

★ Have students work in pairs to guess the amount for each type of expense.

★ Read or play the tape or CD. Have students listen to the amounts and write the notes on the expense sheet above.

★ Go over the answers with the class. Ask them which of the expenses they guessed correctly.

LISTENING SCRIPT

Lesson 6: Give Opinions

Listen to a conversation with Mr. Garcia. Check your answers.

Interviewer: How much do you spend on rent?
Mr. Garcia: The rent on our apartment is $1,000 a month.
Interviewer: And transportation? How much do you spend on transportation?
Mr. Garcia: Well, I take the bus to work, but we also have a car. We spend about $900 a year for car and bus expenses.
Interviewer: What about groceries?
Mr. Garcia: We usually spend about $60 a week or $240 a month on food.
Interviewer: Do you spend money on education?
Mr. Garcia: Yes. My wife is taking a computer course, and my son needs school supplies and books. I think we spend about $800 a year on education.
Interviewer: Do you spend any money on child care?
Mr. Garcia: Yes, for my daughter. She goes to day care three days a week. That costs $300 a month.
Interviewer: What about utilities?
Mr. Garcia: Do you mean heat and electricity?
Interviewer: Yes.
Mr. Garcia: Well, we spend about $75 a month for utilities.
Interviewer: And clothing? Is that a big expense?
Mr. Garcia: I don't know. My wife says we spend about $1,500 a year on clothes.

Interviewer: Can you save any money?
Mr. Garcia: It's difficult with two children, but we try to save $2,000 every year.
Interviewer: That's great. What about gifts? Do you give money away?
Mr. Garcia: Yes, we try to give $200 a year to a local charity.

ANSWER KEY:

1. Rent: $1000/month
2. Car/Bus expenses: $900/year
3. Groceries: $240/month
4. Education: $800/year
5. Childcare: $300/month
6. Utilities: $75
7. Clothing: $1500
8. Savings: $2,000
9. Gifts: $200

3. Answer the Questions

★ Ask students to look at the questions in the box. Instruct them to figure out the Garcia's expenses for the year. This means multiplying monthly expenses by 12.

★ Review the meaning of the phrases *most expensive* and *least expensive*.

★ Have students work in pairs to answer the questions. Go over the answers with the class.

ANSWER KEY:

1.

Rent: $1000/month x 12 =	$ 12,000
Car expenses: $900/year	$ 900
Groceries: $240/month x 12	$ 2,880
Education: $800/year	$ 800
Child care: $300/month x 12	$ 3,600
Utilities: $75/month x 12	$ 900
Clothing: $1500/year	$ 1,500
	$ 22,580

2. rent, child care, groceries, clothing, transportation, utilities, education

3. Answers will vary, but may include entertainment, travel, phone, cable.

4. **Make a Budget**

★ Explain the task to students. Ask them to list their types of expenses in the first column, the amounts per month spent on that expense in the second column, and the yearly amounts in the third.

★ Walk around the room to monitor the activity and provide help as needed.

★ Call on a few volunteers to talk about one of the expenses in their budget.

★ Students can also rank their yearly expenses from the *most expensive* to the *least expensive*. Then they can share which expense is the greatest but they don't have to disclose the amount.

EXPANSION ACTIVITY: Your New Family

★ Put students in groups of three or four to form the "Garcia family." Tell them they have $20,000 per year for their budget. However, their expenses are the same as those listed in Activity 3 above, totaling $22,820, so they must cut their expenses by $2,820.

★ Tell the students they must decide what they need to spend money on, what they will cut back on, and how they will budget their money. They must all agree on their budgets. Walk around to monitor the activity and provide help as needed.

★ Call on a student from each group to share his or her group's ideas with the class.

1. Listening Review 🎧

★ Go over the directions with the class. Have students look at the family tree as they listen to items 1–4.

★ Read the items or play the tape or CD and have the students mark their answers on the Answer Sheet.

★ Walk around to monitor the activity and help students stay on task.

★ Have students check their answers with a partner.

★ Go over the answers with the class.

LISTENING SCRIPT

1. Listening Review

Look at the family tree. Listen and choose the best answer. Use the Answer Sheet.

1. What's Carol's husband's name?
2. Who's Mei?
3. Who's Ann?
4. Who's Tim's grandmother?

Listen and choose the best answer. Use the Answer Sheet.

5. Do you live with your parents?
6. What's your brother's name?
7. Does John have children?
8. Who does the dishes in your family?
9. Where do your parents live?
10. What does she do at home?
11. Do you play an instrument?
12. How often do her children cook dinner?

ANSWER KEY:

1. A; 2. B; 3. C; 4. A; 5. A; 6. A; 7. C; 8. C; 9. B; 10. B; 11. A; 12. B

2. Conversation Check: Pair Work

★ Go over the directions. Put students in pairs to work and remind them that each partner has some information, but that other information is missing. They must each ask their partner questions to complete their chart.

★ Make sure the students check the boxes to show how many questions they asked and answered.

★ Walk around to monitor the activity and provide help as needed.

Assessment Note:

★ You can use the conversation check as an oral assessment. Ask pairs of students to complete the activity while you note areas of difficulty.

LEARNING LOG

★ Point out the four sections of the Learning Log: *I know these words, I can ask, I can say,* and *I can write.*

★ Ask students to check what they know and what they can do.

★ Walk around to note what they don't know or can't do. Use this information to review areas of difficulty.

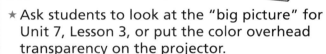

BIG PICTURE EXPANSION ACTIVITY: WRITING—A Day in the Park 📁

★ Ask students to look at the "big picture" for Unit 7, Lesson 3, or put the color overhead transparency on the projector.

★ Ask the students to write a paragraph about the picture. They can describe the weather, the people, and the activities. Remind them to use the present continuous to describe what the people are doing. Walk around to monitor the activity and provide help as needed.

★ Have students read their paragraphs to partners.

★ Invite a few volunteers to read their paragraphs to the class.

BIG PICTURE EXPANSION ACTIVITY: SPEAKING Assessment—Talking about the Picture

★ You can use the "big picture" to assess placement of new students in open-entry classes, to diagnose difficulties, or to measure progress.

★ Work with one student at a time. Show the "big picture" to the student and ask, *What do you see in the picture?* or *Tell me about the picture.* Ask the student to speak for as long as possible. Wait a moment for the student to prepare an answer. If the student has difficulty, you can use prompts: *What do you see in the park? Who do you see in the park? What are the people doing?*

★ You can use a rubric like the one below to rate beginning speakers.

3	Uses sentences, although form may be incorrect Can speak for sustained length of time Responds to prompts, but doesn't need them to begin speaking
2	Can use nouns and verbs Uses phrases Answers informational questions
1	Can name objects Uses single words Can answer yes/no questions
0	Cannot say anything independently May be able to point to objects when prompted

TEACHER'S NOTES:

Things that students are doing well:

Things students need additional help with:

Ideas for further practice or for the next class:

 Students can do Unit 7, Section 5, *Practice Test* on the Interactive CD-ROM.

OBJECTIVE

Simple Present Statements; Information
Questions with the Simple Present

Simple Present Statements

★ Read sentences in the grammar paradigm.
Pause after each to have students repeat.

★ Point out that some verbs are irregular and are
formed in a way that is different from the rule.
Ask students to name the irregular verbs they
know (*be, have, do, go*).

1. Complete the sentences.

★ Make sure students understand that the words
don't/doesn't make a statement negative. Ask
a question to which the answer is *no*: *Do we
live on the moon? No, we don't.*

★ Go over the example. Ask why *doesn't* is
written on the line rather than *don't* (*because
doesn't* agrees with *she*).

★ Have students complete the sentences and
check their answers with a partner.

★ Go over the answers with the class.

ANSWER KEY:

1. doesn't; 2. don't; 3. don't; 4. don't;
5. doesn't; 6. don't; 7. doesn't

EXPANSION ACTIVITY:
Make an Opposite

★ Write item *1* from Activity 1 on the board.
Below it, write the sentence in the negative:
My sister doesn't live with my mother. Ask
students how they should rewrite the second
sentence and write that on the board: *She
lives with me.*

★ Tell students to rewrite all the sentences,
changing the affirmative to negative and the
negative to affirmative.

★ Note that *do/does* is not required in the
positive statements and is usually used for
emphasis.

---

2. Complete the conversations.

★ Go over the example. Point out that the verb
on the second line is the same as in the
question, but that they may have to add an "*s*"
to the verb if the subject is in the third person
(*he, she, it*)

★ Ask students to complete the conversations
and go over the answers with the class.

★ Have students work in pairs to practice the
conversations.

ANSWER KEY:

1. don't/live; 2. do/have; 3. doesn't/lives;
4. don't/cooks

Information Questions with the Simple Present

★ Read the questions in the grammar paradigm
and have students repeat.

★ Call on a few students and ask a question from
the paradigm or a variation: *When do you
usually leave for school? When does she
usually leave for school? What do you need for
school?*

3. Complete the questions.

★ Go over the directions and read the first
question.

★ Ask students to complete the questions with
do or *does* and then write the answers to the
questions on a piece of paper.

★ Go over the correct form of the questions.

★ Call on a few students to answer some of the
questions.

★ Have students work in pairs to practice asking
and answering the questions.

ANSWER KEY:

Questions: 1. does; 2. do; 3. does; 4. do; 5. does;
       6. does
Answers to the questions will vary.

4. Write 4 questions.

★ Instruct students to write four questions they would like to ask a classmate. Tell them that the questions should begin with *Where, When, What, Why, Who, How many.* Walk around to monitor the activity and provide help as needed.

★ Organize students in two concentric circles, facing each other, and have them practice asking and answering their questions. Rotate either the outer or inner circle one person to the right after the questions have been asked and tell students to ask the questions of a new partner. Continue rotating a circle and changing partners a few times.

 BIG PICTURE EXPANSION ACTIVITY: GRAMMAR—*Do, Does, Don't,* and *Doesn't*

★ Make copies of Worksheet #14 and distribute them to students.

★ Put the "big picture" color overhead transparency for Unit 7, Lesson 3, on the projector or have students look at the "big picture" in their books.

★ Direct students to look at the picture for answers to the questions. Have them check their answers with a partner.

★ Go over the answers with the class.

ANSWER KEY:

A. 1. doesn't; 2. does; 3. don't; 4. do; 5. don't; 6. Do; 7. do; 8. does; 9. does; 10. doesn't
B. 1. B; 2. A. 3. B; 4. B; 5. A

EQUIPPED FOR THE FUTURE ROLE

Community

OBJECTIVE

Using Community Resources

A. Read Martin Costa's application to join an organization.

★ Have students look at Martin's application to join an organization. Ask comprehension questions about the application: *What is this? Who is completing the application? What kind of information is on the application?*

★ Have students complete the form that best describes the information in the application.

★ Have students check their answers with a partner.

★ Go over the answers with the class.

ANSWER KEY:

1. 32 Hampstead St.; 2. Thomas; 3. 4/15/65;
4. age depends on today's date—born 4/22/92;
5. (704) 555-9023; 6. Laura

B. List the names, ages, and relationships of the members of the Costa family.

★ Instruct students to complete the chart for all the people in the Costa family.

★ Have them compare answers with a partner.

★ Copy the chart on the board, and ask volunteers to write the information in the chart.

ANSWER KEY:

Name	Age	Relationship
Martin Costa	[depends on	____
Sarah Costa	today's date]	Wife
Thomas Costa		Son
Hannah Costa		Daughter
Laura Costa		Mother

C. Check *Yes* or *No*.

★ Go over the first sentence with the class.

★ Ask students to check the appropriate boxes for sentences 2–6. Remind them to look at the application form if necessary.

★ Have students check their answers with a partner.

★ Go over the answers with the class.

ANSWER KEY:

1. no; 2. no; 3. yes; 4. yes; 5. no; 6. no

D. Complete the application for you.

★ Ask students to complete the application for themselves. Walk around to monitor the activity and provide help as needed.

★ Call on a few students and ask them questions about the information on their forms: *How many males are on your form? Who is the oldest? Do you have a son?*

EXPANSION ACTIVITY: Interview

★ Photocopy the blank application from Activity D and give one to each student.

★ Brainstorm the questions that need to be asked to complete the application, including, *What's your name? What's your address? Who is in your family?* And *What is _____'s birthdate/gender/relationship to you?* Write the questions on the board.

★ Group students in pairs to interview and complete application forms for each other.

📁 Take It Outside

★ Ask students where families might have to fill out application forms (*community center, recreation center, gym, YMCA, swim club, for health insurance*).

★ Have students go to one of these places and pick up an application form, or you can bring in an application form and photocopy it for them. Many applications are available online.

★ Have students work in pairs to list the types of information required on the form.

★ Ask them if there's any information asked for on the real application that they don't see on the applications in the book.

EQUIPPED FOR THE FUTURE ROLE

Work

OBJECTIVE

Understanding Family Leave

A. Read the definition.

★ Have students read the definition. Check comprehension by asking questions about the definition: *What is this? Can a worker take time off from work to care for his or her family? What is the name of the act or law?*

★ Read the phrases in the box and have students repeat each one. Instruct students to write one of the phrases on each of the lines to complete the definitions.

★ Have students check their answers with a partner.

★ Go over the answers with the class.

ANSWER KEY:

1. U. S. Family and Medical Leave Act of 1993; 2. family leave; 3. medical emergency

B. Choose the correct answer.

★ Ask students to read the sentences so they know what information needs to be completed.

★ Have them reread the definition and choose the best answer for each sentence.

★ Go over the answers with the class.

ANSWER KEY:

1. c; 2. b; 3. c; 4. c

C. Read the conversation.

★ Have students read the conversation silently, or you can read it aloud, pausing after each line to have students repeat.

★ Check comprehension by asking questions: *Who is talking in the conversation? What are they talking about?*

★ Ask them to complete the sentences by writing *Rick* or *Tony* on each line. Go over the answers with the class.

★ Have students take turns practicing both parts of the conversation with a partner.

ANSWER KEY:

1. Rick; 2. Tony; 3. Tony; 4. Rick; 5. Tony; 6. Rick

EXPANSION ACTIVITY: Role-Play

★ Put students in pairs to create conversations between a worker and a supervisor. The conversations should include information about the family member who needs care, the specific problem, and the length of time they need to be off work.

★ Walk around to monitor the activity and provide help as needed.

★ Ask volunteers to role-play their conversations in front of the class. As they listen, the other students should take notes on the family member, problem, and length of leave.

D. Answer the questions.

★ Have students answer the questions and then go over the answers with them.

★ Have students practice asking and answering the questions with a partner.

ANSWER KEY:

1. He has to take care of his mother; 2. with Tony; 3. 80; 4. 6 weeks; 5. in one week

Take It Outside

★ To review, ask students to tell you what family leave is.

★ Ask students to bring in a description of the family leave policy at their workplace or a family member or friend's workplace.

★ Have them work in pairs to compare policies.

8 ★ Health

UNIT OVERVIEW

LESSON	OBJECTIVE	STUDENT BOOK PAGE #
1. Head, Shoulders, Knees, and Toes	Identifying Parts of the Body	p. 116
2. I have a bad headache.	At a Clinic	p. 118
3. Put ice on it.	Understanding Doctors' Orders	p. 120
4. Safety Warnings	Reading Warning Labels and Symbols	p. 122
5. I need an ambulance.	Calling for Help	p. 124
6. Places at a Hospital	Finding Places at a Hospital	p. 126
7. What do you know?	Review and Assessment	p. 128
8. Spotlight	Writing	p. 130

Big Picture Expansion Activities

FOCUS	TITLE	SUGGESTED USE
Speaking	Creating a Conversation	Lesson 3
Reading	Maria is Sick	Lesson 4
Grammar	Giving Advice Using *Should*	Lesson 3
Writing	Completing a Patient Information Form	Lesson 7
Speaking	Assessment: Talking about the Picture	Lesson 7

Big Picture Expansion Activity Worksheets

WORKSHEET #/FOCUS	TITLE	TEACHER'S EDITION PAGE #
15. Grammar	Giving Advice Using *Should*	p. 255
16. Reading	Maria is Sick	p. 256
17. Writing	Completing a Patient Information Form	p. 257

OBJECTIVE

Identifying Parts of the Body

VOCABULARY

ankle	finger	neck
arm	foot	nose
back	hand	shoulder
chest	head	stomach
ear	knee	throat
elbow	leg	toe
eye	mouth	wrist

WINDOW ON GRAMMAR

Can for Ability

1. Learn New Words 🎧

★ Have students look at the picture and ask, *What do you see?* Write what they say on the board.

★ Ask students to look at the words and listen while you say them or play the tape or CD.

★ Say the words or play the tape or CD a second time. Pause after each word and ask the students to repeat the word and point to the corresponding photo.

★ Have each student work with a partner and have one student say the word as the partner points to the correct body part in the picture. Reverse roles and do the activity again.

★ Say the words in random order and have the students point to the corresponding part on their own bodies.

LISTENING SCRIPT

Lesson 1: Learn New Words

Look at the picture. Listen to the words. Then listen and repeat.

1. head	8. toe	15. nose
2. neck	9. ankle	16. ear
3. shoulder	10. knee	17. mouth
4. arm	11. stomach	18. chest
5. hand	12. throat	19. back
6. leg	13. eye	20. wrist
7. foot	14. elbow	21. finger

EXPANSION ACTIVITY: Simon Says

★ Tell students that you are going to play a game called *Simon Says.* Students should follow an instruction if the person giving it says *Simon says* before the instruction. They should not follow the instruction if the person does not say *Simon says* before the instruction.

★ Model the activity. Give the instruction, *Simon says, Touch your nose.* Gesture for students to touch their noses. Next, give the instruction *Touch your foot.* If students begin to touch one of their feet, shake your head no. Give a few more instructions with and without saying *Simon says* and make sure students understand the game. If students make a mistake during the actual game, they are out and should sit down.

★ Ask a volunteer to come to the front of the class to give instructions while the rest of the class follows. Continue with additional volunteers.

Grammar Notes:

★ Students may not be familiar with the use of asterisks to note special information. Point out the asterisk next to *foot* in Activity 1 and the note it refers to.

★ Ask students how to make plurals of the other words (*add -s*).

2. Write

★ Direct the students' attention to the chart. Point out the examples written under the appropriate headings in the chart.

★ Have students write all the words from the New Words list in the correct columns on the chart. Remind them to make the words in columns *two* and *ten* plural. Point out that the plural of *foot* is *feet.*

★ Have students check their answers with a partner.

★ Go over the answers with the class.

ANSWER KEY:

I have . . .		
one	**two**	**ten**
head	arms	fingers
neck	hands	toes
back	legs	
chest	feet	
stomach	shoulders	
nose	elbows	
mouth	wrists	
throat	knees	
	ankles	
	eyes	
	ears	

EXPANSION ACTIVITY: Concentration

★ Write ten of the new words on individual sheets of paper in letters large enough to be seen by all the students.

★ Create drawings illustrating the same ten words on separate sheets of paper.

★ Tape the pieces of paper face down to the board or a wall in the classroom. Write numbers from one to twenty on the backs of the pieces of paper.

★ Ask students to call out two numbers to try and match a picture with the correct word. If the numbers match, take them down.

★ Continue playing until all the words and pictures have been matched.

★ As a variation, have students work in pairs to make their own sets of concentration cards and use them to play the game.

3. Practice the Conversation 🎧

★ Read the conversation or play the tape or CD as the students listen.

★ Read or play the conversation again. Pause after each item and ask the students to repeat. Check comprehension by asking them to point to the body part mentioned in the conversation.

★ Have students look at the pictures next to the conversation and name the individual body parts.

★ Repeat the conversation with a student, substituting a body part from those pictured for those scripted in the conversation.

★ Put students in pairs to practice the conversation, substituting other body parts for those in the script. Walk around the room to monitor the activity and provide help as needed.

LISTENING SCRIPT

Lesson 1: Practice the Conversation

Listen to the conversation. Then listen and repeat.

A: What's the problem?
B: My knee hurts.
A: Is it broken?
B: No, I don't think so.

EXPANSION ACTIVITY: Tell Someone New

★ Ask students to memorize the conversation in Activity 3.

★ Have them stand in two lines facing each other. For this exercise, the speakers in one line will be *A* in the conversation, and the speakers in the other line will be *B*. After the students have practiced the conversation, have them switch roles.

★ Move the speaker from the head of one line to the end of that line, and shift everyone up one space. Now each student should be facing someone new. Have them practice the conversation again. Remind them to use different body parts each time.

WINDOW ON GRAMMAR:
Can for Ability

A. Read the questions and answers.

★ Read the questions and answers in the grammar paradigm and prompt students to repeat.

★ Ask questions about students in the class: *Can Jose stand on one foot? Can you speak Spanish?*

B. Complete the sentences with *Yes, I can*, or *No, I can't*.

★ Have students write the answers to the questions and practice asking and answering them with a partner.

ANSWER KEY:

Answers will vary with *Yes, I can*, or *No, I can't*.

 Students can do Unit 8, Section 1, *Learn New Words* and *Fun and Games* on the Interactive CD-ROM.

OBJECTIVE

At a Clinic

VOCABULARY

backache	headache
cough	runny nose
earache	sore throat
fever	stomachache

1. Talk about the Picture

★ Put the "big picture" color overhead transparency for Unit 8, Lesson 2, on the projector or have students look at the "big picture" in their books.

★ Ask questions about the picture: *Where is this? How many people are in the picture? What are they doing? What else do you see?*

★ Direct students' attention to the example sentences and have them write five additional statements about the picture.

★ Ask some students to read their sentences to the class.

EXPANSION ACTIVITY: What's wrong?

★ Say a sentence about the picture that isn't true: *Erik is talking to the nurse.* Ask students to correct the sentence. Possible corrections include, *Tina is talking to the nurse,* or *Erik is sitting in a chair.*

★ Ask students to write five sentences about the picture that are not true. Walk around to monitor the activity and provide help as needed.

★ When the sentences are completed, have individual students or teams read one sentence at a time and ask other students or teams to correct the sentences.

2. Learn New Words 🎧

★ Ask students to look at the pictures and listen while you say the words or play the tape or CD.

★ Say the words or play the tape or CD a second time. Pause after each word and ask the students to repeat the word and point to the person in the picture exhibiting that ailment.

★ Put students in pairs and have one student say the word as their partner points to the correct person in the picture. Reverse roles and repeat the activity.

★ Instruct students to read the two-line exchange. Say it out loud and have students repeat. Students should practice asking and answering questions about other people in the picture using this exchange as a model.

LISTENING SCRIPT

Lesson 2: Learn New Words

Look at the picture. Listen to the words. Then listen and repeat.

1. headache — Tina has a headache.
2. earache — Martin's son has an earache.
3. fever — Louis has a fever.
4. runny nose — Ken has a runny nose.
5. cough — Rose's daughter has a cough.
6. sore throat — Donna has a sore throat.
7. backache — Erik has a backache.
8. stomachache — Tom has a stomachache.

EXPANSION ACTIVITY: How often?

★ Put students in groups of four and assign each a number from one to four.

★ Elicit from students the words they know indicating frequency: *always, sometimes, never.*

★ Ask questions about how often students get the different ailments in the book: *How often do you get headaches?* Give the groups one minute to discuss. Call out a number from one to four. The student in each group with that number must report on the group's answers.

3. Practice the Conversation 🎧

★ Read the conversation or play the tape or CD as the students listen.

★ Read or play the conversation again. Pause after each line and ask the students to repeat. Check comprehension by asking questions: *What's the problem? Does Tina's throat hurt?*

★ Direct students' attention to the pictures below the conversation.

★ Read the conversation with a student and demonstrate how to substitute another health problem for the scripted ailment.

★ Have students practice the conversation in pairs. Walk around to monitor the activity and provide help as needed.

LISTENING SCRIPT

Lesson 2: Practice the Conversation

Listen to the conversation. Then listen and repeat.

Nurse:	What's the problem?
Tina:	I have a bad headache.
Nurse:	Does your throat hurt, too?
Tina:	No, it doesn't.

EXPANSION ACTIVITY: Translator Role-Play

★ Ask students if they have ever needed help with the language when they have gone to the doctor's office.

★ Put students in groups of three and tell each to choose a role: *sick patient, nurse, translator*. Explain to students that they will all speak English, but that one person will repeat the patient's information to the nurse, just as a translator would. They should use the conversation in Activity 3 as a model.

★ Model the activity with two students using the previous Listening Script. You play the role of the translator. Repeat everything that both the nurse and Tina say.

★ Instruct students to practice the role-play in their small groups. You can have them switch roles from time to time. Walk around the room to monitor the activity and provide help as needed.

★ Ask volunteers to perform their role-play in front of the class.

 Students can do Unit 8, Section 1, *Learn New Words* and, Section 2, *Listen and Choose* on the Interactive CD-ROM.

OBJECTIVE

Understanding Doctors' Orders

VOCABULARY

Drink liquids.
Eat soft food.
Bandage it.
Keep it dry.
Put heat on it.
Put ice on it.
Rest.
Take aspirin.
Take cough medicine.
Use eardrops.

WINDOW ON GRAMMAR

Giving Advice with *Should* and *Shouldn't*

1. Learn New Words 🎧

★ Have students look at the pictures and ask them to identify actions or things they know.

★ Say the sentences or play the tape or CD while students look at the sentences and listen.

★ Read the sentences aloud or play the tape or CD a second time. Pause after each sentence and ask the students to repeat and point to the action illustrating each sentence.

★ Group students in pairs and have one student say each sentence as their partner points to the action. Reverse roles and repeat the activity.

★ Students should write the sentences above the pictures.

⌐ LISTENING SCRIPT ⌐

Lesson 3: Learn New Words

Look at the pictures. Listen to the words. Then listen and repeat.

1. A: Drink liquids. B: Drink what? A: Liquids.
2. A: Eat soft food. B: Eat what? A: Soft food.
3. A: Take cough medicine. B: Take what?
   A: Cough medicine.
4. A: Take aspirin. B: Take what? A: Aspirin.
5. A: Use ear drops. B: Use what? A: Ear drops.
6. A: Rest. B: Rest? A: Rest.

7. A: Put heat on it. B: Put what on it? A: Heat.
8. A: Put ice on it. B: Put what on it? A: Ice.
9. A: Bandage it. B: Do what to it? A: Bandage it.
10. A: Keep it dry. B: Keep it what? A: Dry.

EXPANSION ACTIVITY: Find Your Match

★ Write each remedy from Activity 1 on a separate slip of paper. Write a health problem related to each remedy on other slips of paper.

★ Distribute the slips of paper so that each student has either a remedy or a problem.

★ Instruct the students to walk around the room until either their problem or remedy finds its match.

★ Ask each pair of students to read the problem and its remedy. Note that there may be more than one possible remedy for a problem. Discuss other possible remedies and allow students to move to stand with different partners.

2. Interview

★ Write the list of ailments from Lesson 2 on the board.

★ Tell students to look at the chart and ask a question: *What do you do for a stomachache?* Write a few answers on the board.

★ Group students in pairs to ask and answer the questions.

★ Call on students to tell their answers. Write the suggested remedies on the board next to each problem.

EXPANSION ACTIVITY: Compare Your Ideas

★ Draw a cluster diagram on the board like the one below.

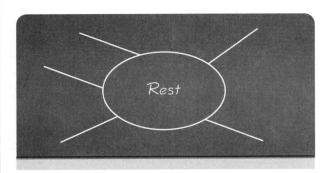

★ Ask students when and why they rest, and write their ideas on the board.

★ Have pairs of students create cluster diagrams with different remedies in the center circle.

★ Call on students to share their ideas with the class.

3. Practice the Conversation 🎧

★ Read the conversation aloud or play the tape or CD as the students listen.

★ Read or play the conversation again. Pause after each sentence and ask the students to repeat. Check comprehension by asking questions: *What's the problem? Is the speaker drinking liquids?*

★ Direct students' attention to the pictures next to the conversation and have them label the ailment in each picture, adding one of their own.

★ Read the conversation with a student and demonstrate how to substitute a different health problem and remedy for the scripted words.

★ Have students work in pairs to practice the conversation. Walk around to monitor the activity and provide help as needed.

LISTENING SCRIPT

Lesson 3: Practice the Conversation

Listen to the conversation. Then listen and repeat.

A: What's the problem?
B: I have a sore throat.
A: Are you drinking liquids?
B: Yes, I am.

Grammar Notes:

★ Direct students to the third line in Activity 3 and point out that the use of the present continuous tense here does not mean that they are doing the activity (*drinking liquids*) at the present moment. Point out that we use the present continuous to talk about things we do during a longer period of time, like the period of time we are sick.

★ Elicit the form of the present continuous for questions (*are + you + verb + ing*). Remind students to use this form in their conversations.

🖼 BIG PICTURE EXPANSION ACTIVITY: SPEAKING—Creating a Conversation

★ Put the "big picture" color overhead transparency for Unit 8, Lesson 2, on the projector or have students look at the "big picture" in their books.

★ Have students work in pairs to create a conversation between one of the patients in the picture and the doctor. Remind them to discuss the physical problem and possible ways to fix the problem.

★ Walk around to monitor the activity and provide help as needed.

★ Ask volunteers to perform the conversation in front of the class, while the class guesses who the patient is.

EXPANSION ACTIVITY: Does it make sense?

★ Write *sore throat* on the board. Under it, write two remedies in the same form as the conversation: *Are you drinking liquids? Are you using ear drops?* Ask students if the remedies make sense or are good for the problem. Write *S* after the first question because it makes sense and *NS* after the second question because it doesn't make sense.

★ Dictate the following problems and remedies to the class. Have students write each sentence. Remember to say each item three times.

Headache: Are you taking aspirin?

Backache: Are you drinking liquids?

Stomachache: Are you keeping it dry?

Cough: Are you keeping a bandage on it?

Fever: Are you resting?

★ Ask students to write *S* after the question if it makes sense and *NS* after the question if it doesn't make sense.

★ Ask volunteers to write the items on the board. Discuss their answers. Note that some students may have different opinions about what remedies make sense. Discuss their ideas, pointing out that there are different approaches to treating health problems.

WINDOW ON GRAMMAR: Giving Advice with *Should* and *Shouldn't*

A. Read these sentences.

★ Read the sentences aloud and have students repeat. Make sure students understand that *should* is used to give sound advice or be critical.

B. Complete the sentences with *should* or *shouldn't*.

★ Ask students a question: *Should you use eardrops for a stomachache?* After the students answer *no*, have them write *shouldn't* on the first line.

★ Students should work individually to complete the sentences in Part B and compare answers with a partner. Go over the answers with the class.

ANSWER KEY:

Part B:
1. You <u>shouldn't</u> use ear drops for a stomachache.
2. You <u>shouldn't</u> take cough medicine for a headache.
3. You <u>should</u> eat soft food for a stomachache.
4. You <u>shouldn't</u> put cough medicine on a sore knee.

C. Write 2 more sentences.

★ Have students write two sentences giving new advice and read them to a partner.

★ Ask some students to read their sentences to the class.

BIG PICTURE EXPANSION ACTIVITY: GRAMMAR—Giving Advice Using *Should*

★ Make copies of Worksheet #15 (p. 255) and distribute them to students.

★ Put the "big picture" color overhead transparency for Unit 8, Lesson 2, on the projector or have students look at the "big picture" in their books.

★ Ask students to complete the sentences. Have them check their answers with a partner.

★ Go over the answers with the class.

★ Put students in pairs to practice the conversations.

ANSWER KEY:

A: 1. backache; 2. stomachache; 3. headache; 4. cough; 5. runny nose; 6. fever; 7. sore throat; 8. earache

B: 1. should; 2. shouldn't/ should; 3. should/shouldn't; 4. shouldn't/should

 Students can do Unit 8, Section 3, *Read and Write* and, Section 4, *Fun and Games* on the Interactive CD-ROM.

OBJECTIVE

Reading Warning Labels and Symbols

VOCABULARY

Do not take internally.
Flammable!
Keep out of reach of children.
Poison!
Pregnant women should not use this.

WINDOW ON MATH

Gallons, Quarts, Pints, Cups, and Ounces

1. Learn New Words 🎧

★ Direct students' attention to the pictures in the boxes under *Warnings* while you say the words or play the tape or CD.

★ Say the words or play the tape or CD a second time. Pause after each warning and ask the students to repeat and point to the picture illustrating the warning.

★ Put each student with a partner and have him or her say each warning as the partner points to the correct picture. Reverse roles and do the activity again.

★ Check comprehension by asking questions: *Should you drink something if it says, "Don't take internally"? Is poison good or bad for you? What can happen to something flammable? If something is on the floor, is it out of the reach of children? What does pregnant mean?*

LISTENING SCRIPT

Lesson 4: Learn New Words

Look at the pictures below. Listen to the words. Then listen and repeat.

1. Flammable!
2. Poison!
3. Do not take internally.
4. Keep out of reach of children.
5. Pregnant women should not use this.

EXPANSION ACTIVITY: Definitions

★ Write these words on the board: *internally, poison, flammable, reach,* and *pregnant.*

★ Put students in pairs to write a definition and a sentence for each word.

★ Call on a few students to read their definitions and sentences to the class. Have the class choose the best definitions and post them in the classroom.

2. Read

★ Instruct students to look at the pictures in the book of common household products and name each one: *paint remover, aspirin, bleach, ammonia.* Ask students what each product is used for.

★ Ask students to read the warning labels in the book and check *True* or *False.* Go over the example. After students have evaluated each label, they should check their answers with a partner.

★ Go over the answers with the class.

ANSWER KEY:

1. false; 2. true; 3. true; 4. true; 5. false

BIG PICTURE EXPANSION ACTIVITY: READING—Maria Is Sick

★ Make copies of Worksheet #16 (p. 256) and distribute them to students.

★ Put the "big picture" color overhead transparency for Unit 8, Lesson 2, on the projector or have students look at the Big Picture in their books.

★ Either have students read the story or read it line by line yourself, pausing after each line to have students repeat.

★ Students should check either *True* or *False* for each sentence and compare answers with a partner. Go over the answers with the class.

★ Instruct students to keep their worksheets because they will need them again for Lesson 7.

ANSWER KEY:

A. Maria is wearing a green shirt.
B. 1. False; 2. False; 3. True; 4. True; 5. False; 6. False; 7. False

EXPANSION ACTIVITY: Other Labels

★ Bring to class enough warning labels for other products that each student has one or a photocopy of one. You can also ask students to bring in labels or products from their homes.

★ Put students in small groups and give each student a label.

★ Write this chart on the board, and make sure students copy it on a piece of paper.

Name of product:	You should:	You shouldn't:

★ Individually, each student will read his or her label and decide what you should and shouldn't do with that product, then share the ideas with the group.

★ Each person in the group should complete the chart for all the product labels in the group.

★ Call on students from each group to talk about one product.

3. Write

★ Ask students to read the directions. Make sure they understand the headings in the chart. Ask them to complete the chart.

★ Put students in pairs or small groups to compare lists.

WINDOW ON MATH:
Gallons, Quarts, Pints, Cups, and Ounces

★ As a class, look at the measurements. Read them out loud and pause after each to have students repeat. Also read the equivalent measurements in the yellow box.

★ Ask questions about the measurements: *How many pints in a quart? How many pints in a gallon?*

★ Have students complete the sentences in Part A and check their answers with a partner.

★ Go over the answers with the class.

★ Also direct students to answer the questions in Part B.

ANSWER KEY:

A. a. 8 cups/64 ounces; b. 8 pints/16 cups; c. 8 quarts/16 pints/256 ounces
B. The gallon is the least expensive.

Culture/Civics Note:

★ Many of your students may come from countries that use the metric system. Help them relate metric measurements to the American system by asking questions comparing the two: *A liter is almost the same size as what?* (a quart) *Is a gallon more or less than a liter?* (more) *Do you buy gasoline in the United States by the gallon or the quart?* (gallon) *How many liters in a gallon?* (about 3.78)

EXPANSION ACTIVITY: Conversion

★ Put students in teams of three.

★ Tell students that you will call out a weight or measure and the form you want it converted to (*quarts/ounces*). Students should raise their hands if they know the answer. The first team with the correct answer gets a point.

★ Call out equivalents from the Window on Math.

★ The team with the most points wins.

OBJECTIVE

Calling for Help

VOCABULARY

bleeding
breathing
choking
having a heart attack

WINDOW ON PRONUNCIATION

Linking Vowel with *Y* or *W*

1. Learn New Words 🎧

★ Ask the students to look at the pictures and listen while you say the sentences or play the tape or CD.

★ Say the sentences or play the tape or CD a second time. Pause after each sentence and ask the students to repeat and point to the picture that correctly illustrates the sentence.

★ Put students in pairs and have one say the sentences as the other points to the picture. Reverse roles and do the activity again.

⌐¡LISTENING SCRIPT ¡⌐

Lesson 5: Learn New Words

Look at the pictures below. Listen to the words. Then listen and repeat.

1. He is choking.	What's the matter? He's choking.
2. He is bleeding.	What's the matter? He's bleeding.
3. She is having a heart attack.	What's the matter? She's having a heart attack.
4. She isn't breathing.	What's the matter? She isn't breathing.

2. Practice the Conversation: Calling 911 🎧

★ Show students the picture in the book for Activity 2. To set the context, ask questions about the picture: *Who is in the picture? What happened?*

★ Question students about what number they should call if there is an emergency (911) and what information they will have to give if they call 911 (*problem, location, maybe name*).

★ Read the conversation or play the tape or CD.

★ Read or play the conversation again. Pause after each sentence and ask students to repeat.

★ To confirm understanding, ask comprehension questions about the conversation: *What number did the person call? What is the problem?*

★ Point out that there are two pieces of scripted information in the conversation that can be substituted for: *the problem and the location.* Model the conversation with a student. Have the student read *A's* lines. Demonstrate how to substitute *My friend is choking* for the scripted problem, and *at 4533 Third Street* for the scripted location.

★ Assign students to create other ideas for the problem and location in the conversation, and put them in pairs to practice the conversation, making substitutions. Walk around to monitor the activity and provide help as needed.

⌐¡LISTENING SCRIPT ¡⌐

Lesson 5: Practice the Conversation— Calling 911

Listen to the conversation. Then listen and repeat.

A: This is 911.
B: We need an ambulance quickly! My friend is bleeding!
A: Where are you?
B: At the corner of Pine and Main.

3. Practice the Conversation: Deciding What to Do

★ Repeat the basic procedure from Activity 2.

★ To set the context, ask questions about the picture: *Who is in the picture? What's wrong?*

★ After students have listened to and repeated the conversation line by line, check comprehension by making additional queries: *What is the problem? Is it an emergency?*

★ Have students create their own ideas for the substitutions in the conversation.

Unit 8   **187**

LISTENING SCRIPT

Lesson 5: Practice the Conversation—Deciding
What to Do

Listen to the conversation. Then listen and repeat.

A: What's the problem?
B: Don has a bad cough. Should I call 911?
A: No. That's not an emergency.

Culture/Civics Note:

★ Some students may be unfamiliar with our
health system. Remind them that emergency
services, including visits to the emergency
room, should be used only in a genuine
emergency—something that is a threat to
life. Emergency services tend to be very
expensive.

EXPANSION ACTIVITY: Call 911?

★ Remind students that they should only call
911 when they're in a true emergency. Tell
students that you are going to say a health
or safety problem and that they should stand
up if they think the problem requires a 911
call. Use the ideas below or create your own.

Someone is bleeding a lot.

Someone has a cough.

Someone drank poison.

Someone has a bad sore throat.

Someone was hit by a car.

Someone is choking.

Someone has a terrible headache.

Someone has a runny nose.

Someone isn't breathing.

Someone is having a heart attack.

★ If there is disagreement (some standing,
some sitting), discuss ideas and opinions.

WINDOW ON PRONUNCIATION: Linking Vowel to Vowel with *Y* or *W*

A. Listen to the words. Then listen and repeat.

★ Point out to students the first phrase in the
list (*he is*) and note that the first word ends
with a vowel sound and the second word
begins with a vowel sound. Say the phrase
exaggerating the *y* sound that connects the
two words.

★ Ask students to look at the phrase *go on*. Say
the phrase, exaggerating the *w* sound that
connects the two words. Point out that
sometimes we connect vowels with a *y* sound
and sometimes with a *w* sound.

★ Have students look at the phrases while you
say the words or play the tape or CD.

★ Say the words or play the tape or CD a
second time, pausing after each word to
have students repeat.

★ Call on a few volunteers to read a phrase
demonstrating the *y* or *w* vowel link.

★ Students should write each phrase in the
correct column in the chart and check their
answers with a partner.

★ Go over the answers with the class. Ask them
when we use each sound. Elicit that when
the word ends in a sound like the letters *E, I*
or *A*, we use a *y* linking sound. When the
word ends in a sound like the letters *O* or *U*,
we use a *w* linking sound.

LISTENING SCRIPT

Lesson 5: Window on Pronunciation
Linking Vowel to Vowel with a *Y* or *W* Sound

A. Listen to the words. Then listen and repeat.

1. he is	9. go on
2. I am	10. play it
3. they are	11. how are
4. go up	12. we own
5. we are	13. you are
6. try another	14 she is
7. who is	15. do it
8. who are	16. day off

ANSWER KEY:

Linking with a *y* sound	Linking with a *w* sound
a. he is	a. go on
b. we are	b. you are
c. I am	c. who is
d. try another	d. how are
e. play it	e. do it
f. she is	f. go up
g. they are	g. who are
h. we own	
i. day off	

B. Listen and complete the conversations. 🎧

★ Direct students to Conversation 1 and have them fill in the blanks. Read the conversation aloud and elicit different endings from the students (*bleeding, choking, having a heart attack*).

★ Have students complete the other conversation and practice them with a partner.

★ Walk around and make sure students are practicing linkages.

★ Ask volunteers to read the conversations aloud.

LISTENING SCRIPT

Lesson 5: Window on Pronunciation
Linking Vowel to Vowel with a *Y* or *W* Sound

B. Listen and complete the conversations.

1.
A: This is 911.
B: My mother is hurt. She is choking.
A: Where are you?
B: We are at 414 Pine Street.

2.
A: Where are you?
B: We are at home.
A: How's Paul?
B: He is resting.

ANSWER KEY:

1.
A: This is 911.
B: My mother is hurt. <u>She is</u> choking.
A: Where are you?
B: <u>I am</u> at 414 Pine Street.

2.
A: Where are you?
B: <u>We are</u> at home.
A: How's Paul?
B: <u>He is</u> resting.

EXPANSION ACTIVITY: Role-Play Practice

★ Distribute one index card to each student. Have them write a physical problem and a location on the card. Note that the problem does not have to be an emergency and that the location can be an address or a place in a building.

★ Model the activity. Write a problem and place on the board: *coughing, kitchen.* Ask students if they would call 911 in this situation and which conversation model they should use (Activity 3). Practice the conversation with a student. Listen for links. Point out that the students can create different conversations if they want to.

★ Collect the cards and redistribute them. Have students work in pairs to practice conversations using the information on the cards.

 Students can do Unit 8, Section 2, *Listen and Choose* and, Section 4, *Fun and Games* on the Interactive CD-ROM.

EQUIPPED FOR THE FUTURE ROLE

Community

OBJECTIVE

Finding Places at a Hospital

VOCABULARY

emergency entrance
lobby
main entrance
visitors' lounge

1. Learn New Words 🎧

★ Direct students' attention to the pictures and ask what kind of place this is.

★ Ask students if they have ever been to a hospital. Elicit the reasons why they went to the hospital and write them on the board.

★ Tell students to look at the pictures and listen as you say the words or play the tape or CD.

★ Play the tape or CD a second time and have students repeat and point to the pictures illustrating the words.

LISTENING SCRIPT

Lesson 6: Learn New Words

Look at the pictures. Listen to the words. Then listen and repeat.

1. Main Entrance	Where's the main entrance?
2. Emergency Entrance	Where's the emergency entrance?
3. Lobby	Where's the lobby?
4. Visitors' Lounge	Where's the visitors' lounge?

2. Talk about the Pictures

★ Ask questions about each picture: *What are the people doing? What do you see? Are there chairs in this picture?*

★ In this exercise, the students should write five sentences about the pictures and read their sentences to a partner.

★ Ask a few students to share their ideas with the class.

EXPANSION ACTIVITY: Memory Game

★ Ask students to look at the pictures and write three questions about the pictures. *How many people are in the visitors' lounge? Are the walls pink in the lobby? Are there stairs in the lounge?*

★ Collect the questions and divide the class into teams.

★ Give students a minute to memorize as much as they can about the pictures and then tell them to close their books.

★ Read a question to each team. Each correct answer earns the team a point.

★ The team with the most points wins.

★ Small prizes for the winners could increase enthusiasm for the game and raise the energy level in the classroom.

3. Read the Map

★ Students should focus their attention on the map. Check comprehension of the map by asking questions about it: *What street is the main entrance on? How many parking areas do you see?*

★ Ask students to look at the questions. Read the questions aloud and pause after each one to have students repeat.

★ Make sure students check either *Yes* or *No* for each question and compare answers with a partner.

★ Go over the answers with the class.

ANSWER KEY:

1. yes; 2. no; 3. no; 4. no; 5. no; 6. no; 7. yes; 8. no; 9. yes; 10. yes

1. Listening Review 🎧

★ Go over the directions with the class.

★ Read the items or play the tape or CD and have the students mark their answers on the Answer Sheet.

★ Walk around to monitor the activity and help students stay on task.

★ Have students check their answers with a partner.

★ Go over the answers with the class.

LISTENING SCRIPT

Lesson 7: Listening Review

Listen to the conversations. Choose the problem you hear. Use the Answer Sheet.

1.
A: What's the matter?
B: My wrist hurts.
A: Can you move it?
B: Yes, a little.

2.
A: What's the matter with Thomas?
B: He has a really bad headache.
A: That's too bad.

3.
A: Can I help you?
B: Yes, I have an appointment with Dr. Jones.
A: What are you here for, Mr. Munro?
B: It's my ear. I have an earache.

4.
A: Hi, I'm Dr. Coffin.
B: Hi, Dr. Coffin. I'm John Fernandez.
A: Nice to meet you. So what's the problem?
B: Oh, I have a sore shoulder.

Listen and choose the best answer. Use the Answer Sheet.

5. What should I do for my backache?
6. What should you do for a stomachache?
7. What number should you call for an ambulance?
8. Should you call 911 for a sore toe?

ANSWER KEY:

1. A; 2. B; 3. B; 4. C; 5. C; 6. B 7. C; 8. C

2. Conversation Check: Pair Work

★ Go over the directions. Have students work in pairs and remind them that each partner has some information, but that other information is missing. They must each ask their partner questions to complete the charts.

★ Make sure students check the boxes to show how many questions they asked and answered.

★ Walk around to monitor the activity and provide help as needed.

Assessment Note:
★ You can use the conversation check as an oral assessment. Ask pairs of students to complete the activity while you note areas of difficulty.

LEARNING LOG

★ Point out the four sections of the Learning Log: *I know these words, I can ask, I can say, and I can write.*

★ Ask students to check what they know and what they can do.

★ Walk around to note what they don't know or can't do. Use this information to review areas of difficulty.

BIG PICTURE EXPANSION ACTIVITY: WRITING—Completing a Patient Information Form

★ Make copies of Worksheet #17 (p. 257) and distribute them to students.

★ Put the "big picture" color overhead transparency for Unit 8, Lesson 2, on the projector or have students look at the "big picture" in their books.

★ Ask students to reread the paragraph about Maria Cordero from the Lesson 4 "big picture" Expansion Activity (Worksheet #16).

★ Instruct students to complete the Patient Information Form for Maria Cordero and compare forms with a partner.

ANSWER KEY:

PATIENT INFORMATION FORM

Patient's Name: _____Maria Cordero_____

Date: _(today's date)_ Time: _(2:45)_

Address: _1220 Central Avenue_

Boston, MA Telephone: _(617) 555-8853_

Birthdate: _10/23/1998_

Reason for visit: _Cough, sore throat, fever_

Check if you have:

☐ headache   ☐ earache

☐ stomachache   ☒ fever

☒ sore throat   ☐ runny nose

☒ cough   ☐ backache

What medicine are you taking now?

none

BIG PICTURE EXPANSION ACTIVITY: SPEAKING Assessment—Talking about the Picture

★ You can use the "big picture" to assess the placement of new students in open-entry classes, to diagnose difficulties, or to measure progress.

★ Work with one student at a time. Show the "big picture" to the student and say, *What do you see in the picture? Tell me about the picture.* Ask the student to speak for as long as possible. Wait a moment for the student to prepare an answer. If the student has difficulty, you can use prompts: *What do you see in the doctor's waiting room? Who do you see? How do they feel?*

★ You can use a rubric like the one below to rate beginning speakers.

3	Uses sentences, although form may be incorrect Can speak for sustained length of time Responds to prompts, but doesn't need them to begin speaking
2	Can use nouns and verbs Uses phrases Answers informational questions
1	Can name objects Uses single words Can answer yes/no questions
0	Cannot say anything independently May be able to point to objects when prompted

TEACHER'S NOTES:

Things that students are doing well:

_____

_____

Things students need additional help with:

_____

_____

Ideas for further practice or for the next class:

_____

_____

 Students can do Unit 8, Section 5, *Practice Test* on the Interactive CD-ROM.

FOCUS ON WRITING

Indent a Paragraph

1. **Read paragraphs A and B.**

★ Ask students to look at the graphs and use them to determine the topics of the paragraphs.

★ Instruct students to read paragraphs A and B or read them aloud yourself, pausing after each line to have students repeat.

★ Direct students' attention to the two columns at the top of the page. Ask them to find all the words in the paragraphs that begin with *s* and *c* and write them in the correct places. Put students in pairs to check their answers. Go over the answers with the class.

★ Students should answer the question at the end of each paragraph by writing a sentence stating their own opinion.

★ Discuss the paragraphs and ask comprehension questions: *What is Story A about? What does the writer think? How many classmates agree with the writer?* Ask similar questions about Story B.

★ Have each student share their opinion with a partner and ask for volunteers to share their opinions with the class.

ANSWER KEY:

S: Should; Six; shouldn't; sick; Seven; sons
C: care; classmates; choose; children; can

2. **Write this paragraph again.**

★ Point students to the *Focus on Writing box*. Read the rules aloud. Make sure students understand that a paragraph is several sentences, all about one topic.

★ Ask students to rewrite the paragraph, indenting the first line. Walk around the room and make sure students are indenting correctly.

3. **Choose 1 opinion question.**

★ Focus the students' attention on the opinion questions. Read the questions aloud, pausing after each to have students repeat.

★ As an activity, each student must choose one of the questions, then ask ten classmates the question and record the results.

★ Instruct students to create a bar graph using the results from the survey. For a model, refer to the graphs in Activity 1.

★ Ask the students to write paragraphs about their results, referring to any of the paragraphs in Spotlight as a model.

★ Call on a few students to share their results with the class.

EXPANSION ACTIVITY: What's Your Opinion?

★ Ask students to write their own opinion questions and collect them, or help them brainstorm other questions and write them on the board.

★ Write *yes* on one side of the board and *no* on the other.

★ Invite volunteers to come to the front of the class. Read a question and have each student move to the answer that expresses his or her opinion. Ask them to give reasons for their choice.

★ Repeat with a new group of volunteers and a different question until everyone in class has had a chance to participate.

EQUIPPED FOR THE FUTURE ROLE

Work

OBJECTIVE

Completing Accident Reports at Work

VOCABULARY

accident
injury
place
supervisor

A. Learn new words.

★ Focus students' attention on the photo and ask questions about it: *Who do you see? What is the problem?*

★ Read the words in the box and have students repeat. Explain the meaning of the words.

★ Ask students to read the story and circle the words. For students with an emerging level of literacy, read the sentences aloud and pause after each to have students repeat; make sure the students go back and circle the new words.

★ Check comprehension by asking questions: *Who is in the story? What is his job? What day is it?*

B. Answer the questions.

★ Read the first question: *What is the problem?* Point out that accident is written on the line.

★ Tell students to write the words from the box that best answer the questions.

★ Have students check their answers with a partner.

★ Go over the answers with the class.

ANSWER KEY:

1. accident; 2. place; 3. injury; 4. supervisor

C. Check *yes* or *no*.

★ Go over the example and point out that *yes* is checked.

★ Instruct students to read the other sentences and check *yes* or *no*. Remind them to reread the story if necessary.

★ Have students check their answers with a partner.

★ Go over the answers with the class.

ANSWER KEY:

1. yes; 2. no; 3. yes; 4. yes; 5. no; 6. yes

D. Complete the form about Peter's accident.

★ After looking over the form in the book, ask them what it is for (*to report accidents*).

★ Do the first item together, and assist students in writing the answer to the question: *What is the name of the employee?*

★ Students should complete the form with information from the story. Walk around to monitor the activity and provide help as needed.

★ Have students compare their answers in pairs.

★ Go over the information on the form.

ANSWER KEY:

Name of Employee ___Peter Banks___ Date of birth ___05/19/68___
Address ___1611 Forest Street___ City ___Stanton___ State ___TN___ zip ___38069___
Sex: ☒ male ☐ female   marital status: ☒ single ☐ married ☐ divorced
Occupation construction worker ___construction worker___
Date of accident: ___7/23/___   Time of the accident: ___1:17 PM___
Place of the accident: ___First Market Bank, 100 Center Street___
Type of injury: ☐ bruise ☐ burn ☒ cut ☐ fracture ☐ sprain
Body part injured: ☐ ankle ☐ arm ☐ back ☐ chest ☐ finger ☒ hand
         ☐ head ☐ ear ☐ eye ☐ leg
Employee signature: _____
Supervisor's signature: _____

E. Write the number of the line in Activity D next to the information.

★ Ask students to look to the right of the form in Activity D. Point out that the lines are numbered.

★ Ask students to write the number of the line where the answer to each question can be found. Go over the example. Walk around to monitor activity and provide help as needed.

★ Have students check their answers with a partner.

★ Go over the answers with the class.

★ Students should practice asking and answering the questions in pairs.

ANSWER KEY:

1. Line 2; 2. Line 3; 3. Line 4; 4. Line 2;
5. Line 1; 6. Line 5

 Take It Outside

★ Assign this activity as an out-of-class exercise or have students do it with a partner in class.

★ Instruct students to interview a family member, friend or coworker.

★ To prepare for the interview, have students look at the form and brainstorm questions as a class that will help them gather information: *What's your date of birth? What's your occupation?* Write the questions on the board.

★ Armed with a list of questions, students will conduct the interview and fill out the form for their interviewee.

★ Call on a few students to share their information with the class.

**EXPANSION ACTIVITY:
Write about an Accident**

★ Assign students to write a story about an accident they had or know about.

★ Remind them to use the story about Peter Banks as a model.

★ Alternatively, have them use the information from the Take It Outside Activity to write a story about the person they interviewed.

★ Call on a few volunteers to read their stories to the class.

EQUIPPED FOR THE FUTURE ROLE

Family

OBJECTIVE

Getting Children Ready for School

VOCABULARY

discount
exam
immunization
income
offer

A. Write the letter of the photo next to the sentence.

★ Have students look at the pictures and ask them questions: *Who is in the picture? Where are they? What are they doing?*

★ Ask students when they take their children to see the doctor (*when they're sick, for a checkup, for vaccinations, before they start school*).

★ Instruct students to read the sentences and write the letter of each picture next to the sentence that correctly describes it.

★ Go over the answers with the class.

ANSWER KEY:

1. a; 2. c; 3. b

B. Answer the questions.

★ Ask students to read the story silently, or read it aloud yourself and pause after each sentence to have students repeat.

★ Tell them to answer the questions and check their answers with a partner.

★ Go over the answers with the class.

★ Put students in pairs to practice asking and answering the questions.

ANSWER KEY:

1. at the doctor's office; 2. her ears and her eyes; 3. to the dentist

C. Learn new words.

★ Direct students' attention to the words in the box. Read the words aloud, pausing after each to have students repeat. Elicit or explain the meanings of the words.

★ Ask students to look at the title and the reading and ask questions about it: *What is it? What is it about?*

★ Have students read the notice and circle the words from the box.

D. Write a word from the box in Activity C next to the meaning.

★ Have students write each of the words from the box next to its meaning. Remind them to reread the article for help in understanding the context. Have students check their answers with a partner.

★ Go over the answers with the class.

ANSWER KEY:

1. income; 2. discount; 3. immunization; 4. offer; 5. exam

E. Match the questions and answers.

★ Read the questions aloud, pausing after each to have students repeat.

★ Ask the first question and elicit an answer. Point out that a line has been drawn from the question to the answer.

★ Instruct students to work individually and match the questions and answers. Go over the answers with the class.

★ Have students work in pairs to practice asking and answering the questions with a partner.

ANSWER KEY:

1. e; 2. a; 3. d; 4. c; 5. b; 6. f

EXPANSION ACTIVITY: Create Questions

★ Ask students to write three other information questions about the newspaper notice.

★ Put students in pairs to ask and answer the new questions.

 Take It Outside

★ Direct students' attention to the chart and have them create questions designed to elicit the information they need.

★ Assign students to interview three people, in or out of class, and make sure they record the information from their interview.

★ Ask a few volunteers to talk about someone they interviewed.

★ Lead a discussion about how often people should get these exams and the reasons why they may not.

House and Home

UNIT OVERVIEW

LESSON	OBJECTIVE	STUDENT BOOK PAGE #
1. Their new house has 3 bedrooms.	Identifying Rooms and Things in a House	p. 132
2. The Lees' old house had a garage.	At Home	p. 134
3. He fell down the stairs.	Understanding a Bar Graph	p. 136
4. Housing Ads	Reading Classified Ads	p. 138
5. I'm calling about the house.	Asking for Housing Information	p. 140
6. Paying bills	Understanding Bills	p. 142
7. What do you know?	Review and Assessment	p. 144
8. Spotlight	Grammar	p. 146

Big Picture Expansion Activities

FOCUS	TITLE	SUGGESTED USE
Speaking	Debating It	Lesson 2
Reading	Where did it happen?	Lesson 3
Grammar	Describing the Lees' Old House	Lesson 4
Writing	Comparing Two Houses	Lesson 7
Speaking	Assessment: Talking about the Picture	Lesson 7

Big Picture Expansion Activity Worksheets

WORKSHEET #/FOCUS	TITLE	TEACHER'S EDITION PAGE #
18. Reading	Where did it happen?	p. 258
19. Writing	Describing the Lees' Old House	p. 259

OBJECTIVE

Identifying Rooms and Things in a House

VOCABULARY

bathroom	kitchen
bathtub	lamp
bed	living room
bedroom	mirror
bookcase	refrigerator
cabinet	shower
carpet	sink
closet	smoke alarm
dining room	sofa
drawer	stove
dresser	toilet

WINDOW ON GRAMMAR

Comparing Past and Present

1. Learn New Words 🎧

★ Have students look at the pictures. Ask them to describe what they see. Write all the words the students know on the board.

★ Say the words or play the tape or CD while students listen and look at the pictures.

★ Say the words or play the tape or CD a second time. Pause after each word and ask the students to repeat the word and point to the object.

★ Group students in pairs and have one student say the word as their partner points to the photo that illustrates it. Reverse roles and do the exercise again.

LISTENING SCRIPT

Lesson 1: Learn New Words

Look at the pictures. Listen to the words. Then listen and repeat.

1. sofa	Where's the sofa?
2. bookcase	Where's the bookcase?
3. lamp	Where's the lamp?
4. smoke alarm	Where's the smoke alarm?
5. carpet	Where's the carpet?
6. mirror	Where's the mirror?
7. sink	Where's the sink?

8. shower	Where's the shower?
9. toilet	Where's the toilet?
10. bathtub	Where's the bathtub?
11. drawer	Where's the drawer?
12. cabinet	Where's the cabinet?
13. closet	Where's the closet?
14. refrigerator	Where's the refrigerator?
15. stove	Where's the stove?
16. dresser	Where's the dresser?
17. bed	Where's the bed?

EXPANSION ACTIVITY: Draw It

★ Divide the class into teams. Ask a member of each team to come to the board.

★ Whisper one of the new words to the "artists" representing each team. Tell them to draw a picture illustrating the word on the board while the rest of the class tries to name it.

★ The first person to correctly name the word earns a point for his or her team.

★ The team with the most points wins.

★ Small prizes for the winners can increase enthusiasm for the game and raise the energy level in the classroom.

2. Write

★ Direct students' attention to the pictures of the kitchen and the bedroom and ask questions: *What do both rooms have?* Write the answers on the board. Read the first sentence and point out that *closets* completes the sentence. Another choice is *drawer*.

★ In this activity, students should work individually to complete the other sentences. Walk around the room to monitor the activity and provide help as needed.

★ Have students compare their answers with a partner.

★ Go over the answers with the class.

ANSWER KEY:

[*answers may vary*] 1. closets, drawers; 2. person/bed or toy/closet; 3. kitchen/stove or kitchen/door; 4. kitchen/bathroom; 5. bedroom/living room

TRY THIS

★ Tell the students that you are going to say some sentences about a room but you will not tell them exactly which room. Talk about one of the rooms in the picture and encourage students to guess the room: *It has a closet but not a bed. There is a cabinet in this room. It has a sink. It doesn't have a mirror.* Answer: *kitchen.*

★ Instruct students to read the directions and go over the example.

★ Ask the students to write down the name of a room and list four things that could be found in it. Then have them write several sentences about that room using the items from their list.

★ Call on a few students to read their sentences as the other students try to guess what room they are describing.

EXPANSION ACTIVITY: Five Questions

★ In this activity, students will ask *yes/no* questions to try and guess a room that another student is thinking about.

★ Model the activity. Begin the game by saying, *I'm thinking of a room in my home.* Students can only ask *yes/no* questions to try and determine the room you're thinking about: *Does it have a closet? Does it have a refrigerator? Is there a mirror?*

★ When a student correctly names the room or if five questions are asked but no one guesses correctly, give the answer and have someone else think of a room.

Grammar Notes:

★ So far, students have been talking about events and situations in the simple present tense. Review the concept of the present by asking what time we are talking about when using this tense (*daily, everyday*).

★ Introduce the concept of the past by writing some of these words on the board: *yesterday, last year, last month, last November, two years ago, in 1990.* You can also write today's

date on the board and a date from a few years ago. Elicit that today is the present and the other date is in the past.

WINDOW ON GRAMMAR: Comparing Past and Present

A. Read the sentences.

★ Read the sentences, pausing after each to have students repeat. Point out the present and past tenses of *have* and *be*.

B. Complete the sentences with *has* or *had*.

★ Tell students to complete the sentences with *has* or *had*. Go over the answers with the class.

★ You can offer a bit of help by pointing out the words that refer to the present (*new, this year*) and the words that refer to the past (*old, last year*).

C. Complete the sentences with *is* or *was*.

★ Have students complete the sentences with *is* or *was* and go over the answers.

ANSWER KEY:

B. 1. has; 2. had; 3. had; 4. has
C. 1. was; 2. is

EXPANSION ACTIVITY: Then and Now

★ Write today's date and a date from five years ago on the board. Tell students about yourself five years ago: *I was 25. I had no children. I was single.* Write this information under the old date. Do the same with the current date and present tense: *I am 30. I have 2 children. I am married.*

★ Ask students to write five sentences about themselves five years ago and five sentences about themselves now. Put students in pairs to share their information with a partner.

 Students can do Unit 9, Section 1, *Learn New Words*, Section 2, *Listen and Choose,* and Section 4, *Fun and Games* on the Interactive CD-ROM.

OBJECTIVE

At Home

VOCABULARY

carport	patio
driveway	pool
fireplace	stairs
garage	yard
garden	

1. Learn New Words 🎧

★ Have students look at the pictures and identify what they see. Write what they say on the board.

★ Say the words or play the tape or CD, making sure the students are listening and looking at the words.

★ Say the words or play the tape or CD a second time. Pause after each word and ask the students to repeat the word and point to the picture representing that word.

★ Group students in pairs and have one say the name as their partner points to the object. Reverse roles and repeat the activity.

★ Ask the class more detailed questions about the words and the pictures: *Which house has a pool? Which house has a garden?*

EXPANSION ACTIVITY: Draw Your House

★ Have students draw the floor plan of their house or apartment, including the yard, garage, etc. Have them draw the rooms and furniture and label everything. They can use the vocabulary from this lesson and from lesson 1.

★ Walk around the room and provide additional vocabulary, if necessary, for items students want to label.

★ Have students work with a partner to describe his or her home.

LISTENING SCRIPT

Lesson 2: Learn New Words

Look at the pictures. Listen to the words. Then listen and repeat.

1. pool — Does your house have a pool?
2. patio — Does your house have a patio?
3. front yard — Does your house have a front yard?
4. carport — Does your house have a carport?
5. driveway — Does your house have a driveway?
6. garage — Does your house have a garage?
7. porch — Does your house have a porch?
8. backyard — Does your house have a backyard?
9. garden — Does your house have a garden?

2. Talk about the Pictures

★ Direct students' attention to the picture of the houses and ask questions: *Who are the people in the pictures? How old are they in each picture? Do they look different?* Point out that the children look older in the picture of the new house.

★ Have students write 5 sentences about each picture. Have them share their sentences with a partner.

EXPANSION ACTIVITY: Dictation

★ Tell students you are going to dictate six sentences about the two houses. After each sentence, the students should write *new* or *old* on a piece of paper to identify which house the sentence is about.

★ Dictate the sentences below or create your own. Read each sentence three times.

1. *It has a garden.* (old)
2. *There is a garage.* (old)
3. *There is a swimming pool behind the house.* (new)
4. *It has a patio.* (old)
5. *The car is in the driveway, not in the carport.* (old)
6. *The children are playing basketball.* (new)

★ After the dictation, students should compare answers with a partner.

★ Go over the answers with the class.

★ *Variation:* Ask students to look at the pictures and remember as much as they can about them. Write *new* and *old* on either side of the board and invite volunteers to come to the front of the room. As you read each sentence, the volunteers should stand in front of the correct word.

3. Compare

★ Instruct students to look at the objects under each heading and write additional objects that are in the houses.

★ Call on students to share ideas with the class.

★ Ask students which house they like better. Have them give a reason: *I like the new house better because it has a swimming pool and I like swimming pools.*

BIG PICTURE EXPANSION ACTIVITY: SPEAKING—Debating It

★ Put the "big picture" color overhead transparency for Unit 9, Lesson 2, on the projector or have students look at the "big picture" in their books.

★ Put students in groups of four. In each group, two students will list reasons why the new house is better and the other two will list reasons why the old house is better. The reasons should not include personal opinions with phrases such as *I like* or *I want.* Instead, the reasons should be persuasive: *The new house is better because you can exercise in the backyard.*

★ Instruct students to discuss their ideas in the groups and try to come to an agreement on which house is better. Walk around to monitor the activity and provide help as needed.

★ Call on students to share their ideas.

★ ★

 TRY THIS

★ ★

★ Give students the assignment of describing their *dream house.* Tell them to write sentences beginning with, *My dream house has . . .* and *It doesn't have . . . .* Give them an example. Think big and be creative so the students will too!

★ After they've written their sentences, group students in pairs and have them take turns describing their dream house. Make sure each pair writes down anything they have in common and shares it with the class.

Students can do Unit 9, Section 2, *Listen and Choose* and Section 3, *Read and Write* on the Interactive CD-ROM.

OBJECTIVE

Understanding a Bar Graph

VOCABULARY

cut his hand with a knife
fell down the stairs
fell off a chair
fell off a ladder
slipped in the shower
tripped on the carpet

WINDOW ON GRAMMAR

Simple Past: Regular and Irregular Verbs

1. Learn New Words 🎧

★ Direct students' attention to each picture and ask questions: *What do you see?* Elicit all the words the students know and write them on the board.

★ Ask students to look at the phrases and listen while you say them or play the tape or CD.

★ Say the phrases or play the tape or CD a second time. Pause after each phrase and ask the students to repeat and point to the correct picture.

★ Group students in pairs and have one say each phrase as the other points to the corresponding picture. Reverse roles and repeat the activity.

★ Have students write the correct phrase under each picture. Go over the answers with the class.

LISTENING SCRIPT

Lesson 3: Learn New Words

Look at the pictures. Listen to the words. Then listen and repeat.

1. fell down the stairs
   A: What happened to Joe?
   B: He fell down the stairs.
2. fell off a ladder
   A: What happened to Sylvia?
   B: She fell off a ladder.
3. fell off a chair
   A: What happened to Carol?
   B: She fell off a chair.
4. slipped in the shower
   A: What happened to Mike?
   B: He slipped in the shower.
5. cut his hand with a knife
   A: What happened to Nick?
   B: He cut his hand with a knife.
6. tripped on the carpet
   A: What happened to Donna?
   B: She tripped on the carpet.

EXPANSION ACTIVITY: Write the Story 📁

★ Write these question words on the board: *who, what, where, when, why*.

★ Tell a story about a time when you or someone you know had an accident. Make sure to include information that will provide answers to sentences that begin with the question words. When you are finished, ask students to give the *who, what, where, when,* and *why* about your story. Write the information on the board.

★ Assign students to tell a partner about a time they or someone they know had an accident. As they listen to their partners' stories, the students should take notes about *who, what, where, when* and *why*.

★ Have the students work individually to write their partners' stories.

★ Call on a few volunteers to read the story to the class.

2. Practice the Conversation 🎧

★ Read the conversation or play the tape or CD as the students listen.

★ Read or play the conversation again. Pause after each item and ask the students to repeat. Check comprehension by asking questions: *Who is the conversation about? What happened?*

★ Model the conversation with a student. Have the student read *A's* lines and substitute a different name for the scripted information. You should substitute the relevant accident for that person.

★ Group students in pairs to practice the conversation. Make sure they ask about the other people in the pictures. Walk around the room to monitor the activity and provide help as needed.

LISTENING SCRIPT

Lesson 3: Practice the Conversation

Listen to the conversation. Then listen and repeat.

A: What happened to Joe?
B: He fell down the stairs.
A: Is he okay now?
B: Yes, I think so.

EXPANSION ACTIVITY:
Review Health Problems

★ Write the conversation from Unit 9, Activity 2, on the board, substituting the last line with, *No, he hurt his back.* Students can review vocabulary from Unit 8 by substituting that vocabulary in that last line.

★ Instruct students to look at the pictures and predict a health problem as a result of each accident.

★ Have students work in pairs to practice the new conversation. Walk around to monitor the activity and provide help as needed.

3. Read

★ Direct students' attention to the graph in the center of the page. Point out that this is a bar graph. Ask students what the bar graph is about: *Accidents people have at home.* Explain the causes of injuries.

★ Check comprehension by asking questions about the graph: *What causes the most injuries each year? (stairs) What causes the smallest number of injuries? (carpets)*

★ Tell students to look at the questions. Go over the first one together. Have students work individually to finish matching the questions and answers.

★ Students should check their answers with a partner.

★ Go over the answers with the class.

ANSWER KEY:

1. 1,050,000; 2. 450,000; 3. 275,000; 4. 80,000

EXPANSION ACTIVITY:
Class Bar Graph

★ Ask students what kinds of accidents they have had in their homes in the past five years and write them on the board.

★ Point to each type of accident on the board and ask students to raise their hands if they had such an accident in the last five years. Put tally marks next to each accident type according to the number of raised hands.

★ Assign students to create a bar graph like the one in the book using the accident types and numbers of injuries listed on the board.

★ Walk around to monitor the activity and provide help as needed.

BIG PICTURE EXPANSION ACTIVITY:
READING—Where did it happen?

★ Make copies of Worksheet #18 (p. 258) and distribute them to students.

★ Put the "big picture" color overhead transparency for Unit 9, Lesson 2, on the projector or have students look at the "big picture" in their books.

★ Have students read the story, or read the story line by line, pausing after each to have students repeat. Check comprehension by asking questions about the story: *Who is this story about? What accidents has Norman had? How many times did he go to the hospital?*

★ Make sure students check the box that correctly indicates where the accident happened. Remind them to look at the picture and reread the story to find the answers. Have them check their answers with a partner.

★ Go over the answers with the class.

ANSWER KEY:

B. 1. old; 2. old; 3. new; 4. new; 5. old

WINDOW ON GRAMMAR: Simple Past—Regular and Irregular Verbs

A. Read the sentences.

★ Have students look at the sentences. Read the sentences aloud, pausing after each to have students repeat.

★ Remind students that the past tense is formed by adding -ed to the end of regular verbs. Contrast this with irregular verbs, which do not follow a pattern. Explain that students must learn and memorize the past tense forms of irregular verbs.

B. Complete the sentences with the past form of the verb.

★ Read aloud the first sentence in Part B. Point out that the verb is shown underneath the line. Ask students if *like* is a regular or an irregular verb and what the past tense of *like* is.

★ Instruct students to work individually and complete the sentences before checking their answers with a partner.

★ Go over the answers with the class.

ANSWER KEY:

B. 1. liked; 2. fell; 3. worked; 4. went; 5. got

Grammar Notes:
★ Although regular verbs end in -ed, we do not add -ed to verbs that end in -e already. Point out that we only add -d to words such as *like* (*liked*).

★ Point out that in one-syllable words that end in a *consonant-vowel-consonant* pattern, we double the final consonant and then add -ed: *slipped, tripped*.

Pronunciation Notes:
★ There are different pronunciation rules for verbs ending in -ed.

★ The -ed ending is pronounced as a separate syllable for verbs ending in a *d* or *t* sound, as in *needed* and *wanted*.

★ The *d* is pronounced as a *t* sound after the unvoiced consonant sounds *f, soft g/j, k, p, s, ch, sh, x* as in *worked, liked* and *slipped*.

★ The *d* is pronounced as a *d* sound after voiced consonants such as *b, hard g, l, m, n, r, v, z* as in *called* and *named* or vowel sounds like *played* and *showed*.

EXPANSION ACTIVITY: Beanbag Toss

★ This activity will help reinforce regular past tense verbs and the irregular verbs *fall, get, go,* and *cut* learned in Unit 9, Lesson 3.

★ Call out a verb (*work*) and toss a ball or a beanbag to a student. The student will respond with the past tense form of that verb (*worked*). The student should throw the ball or beanbag back to you.

★ Throw the beanbag or ball to different students until all have participated. The following is a list of regular verbs you can use: *slip, trip, ask, circle, close, listen, open, practice, raise, repeat, like, look, talk, cook, clean, fix, play, wash, rest, work*.

 Students can do Unit 9, Section 4, *Fun and Games* on the Interactive CD-ROM.

OBJECTIVE

Reading Classified Ads

VOCABULARY

apartment
condo
mobile home

WINDOW ON GRAMMAR

Simple Past Statements: Negative and Affirmative

1. Learn New Words 🎧

★ Have students look at the pictures and listen while you say the words or play the tape or CD.

★ Say the words or play the tape or CD a second time. Pause after each word and ask the students to repeat the word and point to the picture correctly illustrating that word.

★ Say each word in random order and have the students point to the correct picture.

★ Ask the class who has lived in an apartment, a condo, or a mobile home. Elicit the differences between these types of housing. Point out that a condo may be like an apartment, but people can rent or own a condo, whereas they can only rent apartments.

LISTENING SCRIPT

Lesson 4: Learn New Words

Look at the pictures. Listen to the words. Then listen and repeat.

1. apartment   Do you live in an apartment?
2. condo   Do you live in a condo?
3. mobile home Do you live in a mobile home?

2. Write 🎧

★ Write some examples of abbreviations on the board: *St., Mrs., Mr.* Ask what each stands for and write out the full word for each abbreviation on the board. Encourage students to name other abbreviations. Explain that an abbreviation is a shortened form of a word, one in which letters have usually been removed.

★ Assign students to look at the first ad and identify some abbreviations (*bed, bath, nr, mo*) and the full words they replace (*bedroom, bathroom, near, month*).

★ Read each ad aloud or listen to the tape or CD as students follow along in their books.

★ Look at the list of words. Point out that *apt* is an abbreviation for *apartment* (see ad *d*) and has been written on the line next to *apartment*.

★ Read or play the ads again and have students listen and write the other abbreviations for the words.

★ Go over the answers with the class.

LISTENING SCRIPT

Lesson 4: What's the Abbreviation?

Read and listen to the classified ads. Find the abbreviations for these words. Some words have more than one abbreviation.

a. House for rent. Three bedrooms, two bathrooms. Near schools. Patio and pool. $1350 per month. Call Eileen at 555-4000.
b. For rent. Mobile home. One bedroom, one bathroom. Near public pool. $795 per month. Call Joe, 555-1928.
c. House for sale. Three bedrooms, two bathrooms, big kitchen, two fireplaces, patio, garage. $210,000. Call Marlene, 555-1200, ext. 15.
d. For rent. Two bedroom, two bathroom apartment. Pool and patio. $950. Call John, 555-4583.
e. For sale. Two bedroom, one-and-a-half bathroom condo. Near stores. $175,000. Call Smith Realty, 555-6767.
f. Apartment for rent. One bedroom, one bathroom. $825 per month. Call 555-9904.
g. Condo for rent. Two bedrooms, one bathroom, garage, near schools, $1100 per month. Call Bev, 555-4954.
h. Mobile home for rent. Two bedroom, one bathroom, patio, no pets, $875 per month. Call 555-9948.

ANSWER KEY:

1. apt; 2. bath/bth/BA; 3. bed/BR/Br; 4. nr; 5. mo; 6. gar

EXPANSION ACTIVITY: Write It Out

★ Tell students to write out two of the ads—one for a place they would really like to live in and one for a place they wouldn't like to live in. Make sure they substitute full words for abbreviations.

★ Ask students to give three reasons why they would like to have each place, making up reasons for not wanting the undesirable place.

★ Put students in groups of three to read their ads to each other. The group should guess which place the student really wants.

3. Read

★ Direct students' attention to question *1*. Read it aloud and tell the class they must read the ads to find the answer.

★ Have students read the ads to answer questions *2-5*.

★ Students should check their answers with a partner.

★ Go over the answers with the class.

ANSWER KEY:

1. a, g; 2. b, f, h; 3. c; 4. a, c, d, h;
5. Answers will vary.

EXPANSION ACTIVITY: Newspaper Ad Scavenger Hunt

★ Put students in pairs. Bring in enough newspapers or photocopy enough pages of classified ads for housing so that each pair of students has something to work with.

★ Instruct the students to read the ads and prepare to complete a scavenger hunt. Use the list below for ideas, but be sure to adapt it to your local housing ads.

Write the contact information for the place that:

Has a garden and swimming pool _____

Has 2 bedrooms _____

Has 3 bedrooms and 1 bath _____

Is less than $950 a month _____

Is a condo with 2 bedrooms _____

★ Call on students to tell the class about the ads they found.

★★★★★★★★★★★★★★★★★★★★★★★★★★★★★★★★

 TRY THIS

★★★★★★★★★★★★★★★★★★★★★★★★★★★★★★★★

★ Encourage students to imagine their dream houses and brainstorm what they would include.

★ Working individually, ask each student to write a classified ad for their dream house. Then have them read their ad to a partner.

★ Call on students to share their ads with the class.

EXPANSION ACTIVITY: Whose Dream is it?

★ Collect the classified ads that each student created in the Try This activity. Shuffle and redistribute them so that each student has an ad that someone else wrote.

★ Call on students to read the ads aloud as the rest of the class tries to guess who wrote it.

WINDOW ON GRAMMAR: Simple Past Statements—Negative and Affirmative

A. Read the sentences.

★ Direct students' attention to the sentences in the yellow box. Read the sentences aloud, pausing after each to have students repeat.

★ Ask students which words or phrases indicate the past tense: *last year, in 2001, yesterday, last week*, and all of the verbs because they are in the past tense.

★ Point out the pattern in each pair of sentences: the first sentence is negative; the second affirmative. Make sure students understand how to form the negative (*didn't + verb*).

B. Complete the sentences.

★ Go over the first sentence.

★ Tell students to complete the rest of the sentences, following the pattern in Part A.

★ Go over the answers with the class.

ANSWER KEY:

B. 1. didn't rent; 2. didn't fall; 3. didn't like; 4. didn't hurt

BIG PICTURE EXPANSION ACTIVITY: GRAMMAR—Describing the Lees' Old House

★ Make copies of Worksheet #19 (p. 259) and distribute them to students.

★ Put the "big picture" color overhead transparency for Unit 9, Lesson 2, on the projector or have students look at the "big picture" in their books.

★ Assign students to complete the sentences using the simple past tense and check their answers with a partner.

★ Go over the answers with the class.

ANSWER KEY:

1. a; 2. a; 3. b; 4. b; 5. a; 6. a; 7. a; 8. b

EXPANSION ACTIVITY: Pass It On

★ Students are going to listen to a negative statement and then add new information using a positive statement, following the pattern shown in Window on Grammar.

★ Say a negative statement: *I didn't buy a car last year.* Then add new information by making a positive but incomplete statement: *I bought _____.* Prompt students to give possible responses: *a bicycle, a truck, an airplane.* Write their answers on the board.

★ Point to one student and repeat with a different sentence that is relevant to your school, class, or city, if possible: *They didn't paint this classroom blue.* The student should respond with new and positive information: *They painted it yellow.* Then that student should create a new negative sentence and call on another student.

★ Continue until all students have had a chance to participate.

OBJECTIVE

Asking for Housing Information

WINDOW ON PRONUNCIATION

Stress in Compound Nouns

1. Practice the Conversation: Calling about a House 🎧

* Direct students' attention to the picture in Conversation 1. To set the context, ask questions about the picture: *Who is in the picture? What are they doing?*
* Read the conversation or play the tape or CD.
* Read or play the conversation again. Pause after each sentence and ask students to repeat.
* Ask comprehension questions about the conversation: *What is he calling about? What does he want it to have?*
* Point out that there are two pieces of scripted information in the conversation that can be substituted for: *the type of housing and the feature.* Model the conversation with a student. Have the student read *B's* lines. Demonstrate how to substitute different types of housing and housing features.
* Ask students to write other ideas next to the lightbulb.
* Put students in pairs to practice the conversation. Walk around to monitor the activity and provide help as needed.

LISTENING SCRIPT

Lesson 5: Practice the Conversation—Calling about a House

Listen to the conversation. Then listen and repeat.

A: I'm calling about the house for rent. Is it still available?
B: Yes, it is.
A: Can you tell me, does it have a front yard?
B: Yes, it does.

2. Practice the Conversation: Asking about Rooms 🎧

* Repeat the basic procedure from Activity 1.
* To set the context, ask the class some questions about where they live: *How many bedrooms are in your home? How many bathrooms do you have?*
* To check comprehension, ask questions about the conversation: *What did the caller find out about the house?*

LISTENING SCRIPT

Lesson 5: Practice the Conversation—Asking about Rooms

Listen to the conversation. Then listen and repeat.

A: How many bedrooms does it have?
B: Three.
A: And how many bathrooms?
B: Two.

3. Practice the Conversation: Asking about Rent 🎧

* Repeat the basic procedure from Activity 1.
* To set the context, ask students if their rent covers any utilities.
* To check comprehension, ask questions about the conversation: *Does the rent include electricity?*

Culture/Civics Note:

* Most utilities are usually not included in the rent; however, the water bill can be an exception. Renters should always clarify which, if any, utilities are included in the rent.

LISTENING SCRIPT

Lesson 5: Practice the Conversation—Asking about Rent

Listen to the conversation. Then listen and repeat.

A: How much is the rent?
B: One thousand two hundred dollars a month.
A: Does it include utilities?
B: No, it doesn't.

EXPANSION ACTIVITY: Reading Big Numbers

★ There are different ways to say numbers above one hundred.

★ Write these numbers on the board: *900; 1,100; 4,200; 8,700*. Say the numbers aloud, pausing after each to have students repeat. Because these are three- and four-digit numbers ending in two zeroes, they are often said as the *first one or two numbers + hundred*: 900 is *nine hundred*; 1,100 is *eleven hundred*; 4,200 is *forty-two hundred*; 8,700 is *eighty-seven hundred*. We can also say these numbers as *thousands + hundreds: one thousand, one hundred; four thousand, two hundred; eight thousand seven hundred*.

★ Write the numbers *825, 950, 6,320, and 9,444* on the board. Explain that those that don't end in two zeros are often said as one- and two-digit numbers, or as two, two-digit numbers: 825 is *eight twenty-five*, and 950 is *nine-fifty*; 6,320 is *sixty-three twenty*, and 9,444 is *ninety-four forty-four*. We can also say these numbers in a manner that recognizes the sequential value of each numeral in the larger number: *eight hundred twenty-five; nine hundred fifty; six thousand three hundred and twenty; nine thousand four hundred and forty four*.

★ Assign students to look at the Housing Ads in Lesson 4 and write down the rent and sale prices.

★ Have them in pairs to practice saying the prices with a partner.

★ Go over the pronunciation with the class.

WINDOW ON PRONUNCIATION: Stress in Compound Nouns

A. Listen to the words. Then listen and repeat. 🎧

★ Remind students that compound nouns are formed from two or more nouns. Direct students' attention to the first item and ask them to name the two nouns that form the compound noun.

★ Make sure students are looking at the words. Say the words or play the tape or CD.

★ Say the words or play the tape or CD a second time. Pause after each and have students repeat.

★ Assign students to work individually and underline the part of the word that is stressed. They should also check their answers with a partner.

★ Go over the answers with the class. The first part of each compound noun should be underlined.

LISTENING SCRIPT

Lesson 5: Window on Pronunciation
Stress in Compound Nouns

Listen to the words. Then listen and repeat.

1. bookcase	6. grandson
2. carport	7. bathtub
3. bedroom	8. drugstore
4. fireplace	9. mailbox
5. bathroom	10. headache

B. Work with a partner. Ask and answer the questions.

★ Do the first question with the class. Point out that all of the answers to the questions are compound nouns from Activity A.

★ Have students practice asking and answering the questions in pairs.

★ Call on students to answer each question.

ANSWER KEY:

B. 1. mailbox; 2. drugstore; 3. bedroom; 4. bathroom; 5. bookcase; 6. grandson; 7. headache; 8. carport; 9. bathtub; 10. fireplace

EXPANSION ACTIVITY:
Making Compound Nouns

★ Instruct students to draw a vertical line separating the two nouns in each compound noun in Activity A. Tell them that they are going to create new compound nouns using some of these nouns.

★ Below are two columns of nouns that, when combined, will create twelve new compound nouns. Each compound noun includes one of the nouns from Activity A. Write the two columns of nouns on the board, but be sure to change the order of the words in the columns so the compound noun is not obvious.

book	mobile
book	end
bed	time
bed	sore
board	room
fire	man
fire	arm
grand	daughter
bath	robe
mail	man
ear	ache
stomach	ache

★ Put each student with a partner to create new compound nouns using a word from each column.

★ Check the answers by having a student draw a line on the board connecting the two words that make up each compound noun as other students read the words: *bookmobile, bookend, bedtime, bedsore, boardroom, fireman, firearm, granddaughter, bathrobe, mailman, earache, stomachache*

EQUIPPED FOR THE FUTURE ROLE

Family

OBJECTIVE

Understanding Bills

VOCABULARY

account number
amount due
amount enclosed
new charges

1. Learn New Words 🎧

★ Direct students' attention to the photo and ask, *What do you think the man is doing?* Have students look at the bills and ask, *What are these?* Ask students what bills they pay each month and write them on the board.

★ Tell students to look at the bills and listen while you say the words or play the tape or CD.

★ Say the words or play the tape or CD a second time. Pause after each phrase and ask the students to repeat and point to that phrase on the bills in their books.

★ Check comprehension by asking questions about the bills : *What is the first bill for? How much is the telephone bill? What's the account number on the telephone bill?*

LISTENING SCRIPT

Lesson 6: Learn New Words

Look at the bills below. Listen to the words. Then listen and repeat.

1. account number	The account number is 6464560483-0.
2. amount due	The amount due is $133.19.
3. amount enclosed	The amount enclosed is $133.19.
4. new charges	The amount of new charges is $56.29.

EXPANSION ACTIVITY: Take Notes

★ Write the chart below on the board and ask students to copy it on a piece of paper.

Information on the bill	Gas and Electric Company	Telephone Company
Address of company		
Account number		
Bill period		
New charges		
Amount due		
Due date		

★ Put students in pairs to complete the chart. One student should look at the Gas and Electric bill while the other student closes the book and asks questions about the bill to complete the chart. Then have the partners switch roles and do the same for the telephone bill. Go over the answers with the class.

ANSWER KEY:

Information on the bill	Gas and Electric Company	Telephone Company
Address of company	P.O. Box 4157 Long Beach, CA	P.O. Box 330 Long Beach, CA
Account number	6464560483-0	000-493-384 4979 004
Bill period	not listed	Dec. 15- Jan. 15
New charges	$133.19	$56.29
Amount due	$133.19	$56.29
Due date	02/07/05	02/02/05

2. Read

★ Assign students to read the sentences and check *True* or *False* after each sentence. Tell them they can look at the bills in Activity 1 to find the information they need.

★ Have students check their answers with a partner.

★ Go over the answers with the class.

ANSWER KEY:

1. False; 2. True; 3. True; 4. True; 5. False

3. Write

★ Direct students' attention to the checks and ask them whose checking account the checks come from. Tell them they are going to help John Alvarez pay his bills this month by completing the checks.

★ Ask students to write the missing information on the checks. Walk around to monitor the activity and provide help as needed.

★ Have students compare their checks with a partner's and go over the answers with the class.

ANSWER KEY:

Check 1129: Date—any date before the due date of 02/07/05; $133.19; One hundred thirty-three and 19/100

Check 1130: Date—any date before the due date of 02/05/05; T&T Telephone Company; $56.29; Fifty-six and 29/100

1. Listening Review 🎧

TESTING FOCUS: Discrete Listening Tasks
* ★ Ask the students to name the objects in each picture for items 1–4. For example, for Item 1 they should say *sink, closet, dresser*.
* ★ Read the directions for items 1–4. Point out that students will listen to a whole conversation and must pick out one of the three words.
* ★ Remind them that they do not need to pay attention to everything in the conversation for this type of task; they are to focus on listening for one of those three words only.
---

* ★ Go over the directions with the class. Tell them to answer on the Answer Sheet.
* ★ Instruct students to look at the pictures and answer questions 1–4.
* ★ Read the items or play the tape or CD. Walk around to monitor the activity and help students stay on task.

LISTENING SCRIPT

Lesson 7: Listening Review

Listen to the conversations. Choose the correct picture. Use the Answer Sheet.

1. A: Where's my blue sweater?
   B: It's in your dresser.
   A: Oh, thanks.
2. A: Where's Joe?
   B: He's in the kitchen
   A: What's he doing there?
   B: He's cleaning the stove.
3. A: I'm calling about the apartment for rent.
   B: Yes. What do you want to know?
   A: Can you tell me, does it have a garden?
   B: Yes, it does. It has a beautiful garden.
4. A: What happened to your brother?
   B: He fell off a ladder.
   A: That's too bad. Is he okay now?
   B: Yes, he's fine.

ANSWER KEY:

1. C; 2. B; 3. B; 4. A

* ★ Have students read the possible answers for questions 5–8.
* ★ Read the items or play the tape or CD.
* ★ Walk around to monitor the activity and help students stay on task.
* ★ Students should check their answers with a partner.
* ★ Go over the answers with the class.

LISTENING SCRIPT

Lesson 7: Listening Review

Listen and choose the best answer. Use the Answer Sheet.

5. Where's the smoke alarm?
6. Does the apartment have a shower?
7. Do you live in an apartment?
8. How many bedrooms does it have?

ANSWER KEY:

5. B; 6. C; 7. B; 8. C

2. Conversation Check: Pair Work

* ★ Go over the directions. Put students in pairs and remind them that each partner has some information, but that other information is missing. They must each ask their partner questions to complete the chart.
* ★ Walk around to monitor the activity and provide help as needed.

Assessment Note:
* ★ You can use the conversation check as an oral assessment. Ask pairs of students to complete the activity while you note areas of difficulty.

LEARNING LOG

* ★ Point out the four sections of the Learning Log: *I know these words, I can ask, I can say,* and *I can write*.
* ★ Ask students to check what they know and what they can do.
* ★ Walk around to note what they don't know or can't do. Use this information to review areas of difficulty.

BIG PICTURE EXPANSION ACTIVITY: WRITING—Comparing Two Houses

★ Put the "big picture" color overhead transparency for Unit 9, Lesson 2, on the projector or have students look at the "big picture" in their books.

★ Have students write a paragraph comparing the two houses. You can begin by brainstorming with the class ideas for ways in which the two houses differ. Write the ideas on the board.

★ Have the students write their paragraphs. They can write about one house in one paragraph and about the other house in a separate paragraph. Or they can compare the houses in one paragraph sentence by sentence.

★ Call on individual students to share their paragraphs with the class.

BIG PICTURE EXPANSION ACTIVITY: SPEAKING Assessment—Talking about the Picture

★ You can use the "big picture" to assess the placement of new students in open-entry classes, to diagnose difficulties, or to measure progress.

★ Work with one student at a time. Show the "big picture" to the student and say, *What do you see in the picture?* or, *Tell me about the picture.* Tell the student to speak for as long as possible. Wait a moment for the student to prepare an answer. If the student has difficulty, you can use prompts: *What is different in these two pictures? What is the same? What are the people doing in each picture?*

★ You can use a rubric like the one below to rate beginning speakers.

3	Uses sentences, although form may be incorrect Can speak for sustained length of time Responds to prompts, but doesn't need them to begin speaking
2	Can use nouns and verbs Uses phrases Answers informational questions
1	Can name objects Uses single words Can answer yes/no questions
0	Cannot say anything independently May be able to point to objects when prompted

TEACHER'S NOTES:

Things that students are doing well:

_____

_____

_____

_____

_____

Things students need additional help with:

_____

_____

_____

_____

_____

Ideas for further practice or for the next class:

_____

_____

_____

_____

 Students can do Unit 9 *Practice Test* on the Interactive CD-ROM.

OBJECTIVE

Simple Past Statements; Information Questions with the Simple Past

Simple Past Statements

★ Read the sentences in the grammar paradigm and have students repeat.

★ Ask questions that will lead to responses similar to the examples: *How did you go to class yesterday? Where were you yesterday at 1 P.M.?* Prompt students to answer with information about themselves: *I walked to class yesterday. I was at home.*

★ Direct students' attention to the irregular verbs in the yellow box. Say the words, pausing after each to have students repeat.

★ Call on students and say one of the irregular verbs in the present tense form. Ask them to respond with the simple past.

1. Write about yesterday. 🗀

★ Go over the example. Point out that the verb changed from *has* to *had* in the sentence about *yesterday.*

★ Working individually, instruct students to rewrite the sentences using the simple past and compare their sentences with a partner.

★ Go over the answers with the class.

ANSWER KEY:

1. She had shrimp for dinner yesterday.
2. He bought a pint of milk yesterday.
3. I made the beds yesterday.
4. My friends were here yesterday.
5. The weather was terrible yesterday.
6. He ate six servings of vegetables yesterday.
7. I got up before 7:00 yesterday.
8. I ran to the bus stop yesterday.

2. Write 5 sentences about what you did yesterday.

★ Go over the directions. Read the words in the box, pausing after each to have students repeat.

★ Ask students to write about what they did yesterday.

★ Put students in pairs to share their sentences with each other and tell them to read each sentence two times. The first time, the partner should just listen for general understanding. The second time, the partner should listen discretely for words in the box and circle them when they hear them.

★ Call on a few students to read sentences aloud.

Information Questions with the Simple Past

★ Read the information questions in the grammar paradigm and have students repeat.

★ Ask questions similar to the ones in the paradigm that relate to your students' life experiences: *When did you leave for class yesterday? Why did you leave class early? How many apples did you eat yesterday?*

★ Point out that the past tense is shown by using *did*. The verb remains in the base form.

3. Match the questions and answers.

★ Read each of the questions, pausing to have students repeat. Read question a second time and elicit the correct answer from the column on the right.

★ Have students finish matching the questions with correct answers.

★ Go over the answers with the class.

★ Put students in pairs to take turns asking and answering the questions.

ANSWER KEY:

1. e; 2. d; 3. f; 4. c; 5. g; 6. h; 7. a; 8. b

EXPANSION ACTIVITY:
Talk about Your Day

★ As a class, brainstorm *wh-* questions the students would like to use to ask their classmates about what they did yesterday. Write them all on the board.

★ Put students in pairs to take turns asking and answering some of the questions.

★ Call on students to tell the class a few things about what their partner did yesterday: *Tito ate two bananas and some chicken yesterday. He didn't drink water, but he drank three Cokes.*

4. Complete the conversations.

★ Go over the example.

★ Students should work individually to complete the conversations.

★ Review the answers with the class.

★ Have the students practice the conversations with a partner.

ANSWER KEY:

1. did/went
2. did/saw
3. liked
4. did/ate
5. Did/didn't
6. bought
7. did/cost

EQUIPPED FOR THE FUTURE ROLE

Work

OBJECTIVE

Following Safety Rules

VOCABULARY

harness	protective equipment
ear plugs	machinery
hard hat	coveralls
safety glasses	gloves

A. Learn new words.

★ Direct students' attention to the photo and ask questions about it: *Who do you see? Where is he? What is he wearing? What kind of work does he do?*

★ Say the words in the box, pausing after each to have students repeat.

★ Ask students to read the safety rules or read the sentences aloud, pausing to have students repeat. Then circle the words from the box.

B. Match the protective equipment and the body part.

★ Read each item under *Protective Equipment* and under *Body Parts* and have students repeat.

★ Go over the first item, pointing out that a line is drawn between *safety glasses* and *eyes*. Ask the class why this is so.

★ Have students work individually to match the equipment to the body part and then check their answers with a partner.

★ Go over the answers with the class.

ANSWER KEY:

1. c; 2. f; 3. b; 4. e; 5. d; 6. a

C. Complete the sentences.

★ Go over the meanings of the words in the box.

★ Ask students to complete the sentences with one of these words and then check their answers with a partner.

★ Go over the answers with the class.

ANSWER KEY:

1. slip; 2. leave; 3. fall; 4. hurt; 5. cut

EXPANSION ACTIVITY:
Create Questions about the Reading

★ Ask students to create five questions about the safety rules like the following: *Can you wear loose clothing around machinery? Should you put boxes in the aisles?*

★ Group students in pairs to take turns asking and answering the questions they wrote.

★ Call on a few students to ask questions of the class.

D. Circle the correct word.

★ Tell students to read the story about Rita and circle the correct words. Sometimes they will have to choose between the present and past form of the same verb and sometimes they will choose between two different words.

★ Have students check their answers with a partner.

★ Go over the answers with the class.

ANSWER KEY:

slipped; was; hurt; is; is; had; is; clean up

E. Write about you.

★ Read the questions and have students repeat.

★ Ask them to think about an incident they want to write about, and then practice asking and answering questions about the incident with a partner.

★ Assign students to write a story about the incident they told their partner about. They should include what happened, when and where it happened, and what they did about it.

★ Call on a few students to read their stories to the class.

📁 Take It Outside

★ Read the question and have students repeat.

★ Ask students to interview someone outside of class about a safety rule and write down that rule.

★ Discuss the rules as a class and make sure everyone understands them.

EQUIPPED FOR THE FUTURE ROLE

Community

OBJECTIVE

Understanding Housing Rights

VOCABULARY

family status
housing discrimination
nationality
religion

A. Read the information below.

★ Direct students' attention to the photo. Set the context by asking questions about it: *Who do you see? Where are they? What do you think they are doing? What is the relationship among the people?*

★ Remind students that they can use the context to understand the meaning of new words or phrases. Instruct them to read the information and write a definition of housing discrimination on the line.

★ Make sure students check their answers with a partner.

★ Go over the definition with the class.

ANSWER KEY:

Housing discrimination: treating people unfairly when they are buying or renting a home because of things like nationality, race, gender, and religion. (Specific language will vary.)

B. Circle the correct answer.

★ Ask students to circle the answer that best completes the sentence.

★ Have them check their answers with a partner.

★ Go over the answers with the class.

ANSWER KEY:

1. a; 2. b; 3. b; 4. c

C. Answer the questions about you.

★ Go over the questions and ask students to work individually to answer them. Remind them to use complete sentences.

★ Group students in pairs to practice asking and answering the questions.

★ Call on a few students to answer the questions. Write on the board a list of problems that students have had with houses or apartments.

D. Look at the phone book.

★ Ask students to look at the list of problems. Make sure they understand the terms.

★ Instruct them to read the information in the phone book and find an appropriate phone number to call for each problem.

★ Do the first one as an example. Ask students which place they would call about housing discrimination. Elicit that they should call the Fair Housing Office. Make sure they draw a line between the problem and the correct phone number.

★ Have students check their answers with a partner.

★ Go over the answers with the class.

ANSWER KEY:

1. c; 2. a; 3. b; 4. e; 5. d

📁 Take It Outside

★ Assign students to look through the phone book to find local phone numbers for the six services in the box. Have them make a list of the local service organizations and phone numbers.

EXPANSION ACTIVITY: Welcome to the Community

★ Brainstorm things that new residents in a community might need. Put students in small groups to create a new resident brochure that provides information about community services and organizations. Each group can determine for themselves what to include.

★ Ask the groups to present their brochures to the rest of the class, highlighting the things they thought it important to include.

UNIT
10 ★ Work

UNIT OVERVIEW

LESSON	OBJECTIVE	STUDENT BOOK PAGE #
1. Can you use a computer?	Identifying Occupations and Skills	p. 148
2. Do you have experience?	Talking about Help Wanted Ads	p. 150
3. Tell me about yourself.	At a Job Interview	p. 152
4. The Amazing Story of Mr. Kazi	Reading a Success Story	p. 154
5. Why did you leave your last job?	Answering Job Interview Questions	p. 156
6. Job Applications	Completing a Job Application	p. 158
7. What do you know?	Review and Assessment	p. 160
8. Spotlight	Writing	p. 162

Big Picture Expansions Activities

FOCUS	TITLE	SUGGESTED USE
Speaking	Creating a Conversation	Lesson 3
Reading	James Needs a New Job	Lesson 6
Grammar	*Yes/No* Simple Past Tense	Lesson 5
Writing	Writing About your Work Experience	Lesson 7
Speaking	Assessment: Talking About the Picture	Lesson 7

Big Picture Expansion Activity Worksheets

WORKSHEET#/FOCUS	TITLE	TEACHER'S EDITION PAGE #
20. Grammar	*Yes/No* Questions in the Simple Past Tense	p. 260
21. Reading	James Needs a New Job	p. 261

OBJECTIVE

Identifying Occupations and Skills

VOCABULARY

chef	mover
child care worker	office manager
construction worker	plumber
landscaper	stylist
mechanic	truck driver

WINDOW ON GRAMMAR

Yes/No Questions + Simple Past

1. Learn New Words 🎧

★ Have students look at the pictures and ask them to name everything they can. Write all of the words on the board.

★ Direct students' attention to the pictures and make sure they listen while you say the words or play the tape or CD.

★ Say the words or play the tape or CD a second time. Pause after each word and ask the students to repeat the word and point to the photo of a person with that job.

★ Put students in pairs and have one say an occupation as the other points to the correct photo. Reverse roles and repeat the activity.

★ Instruct students to write the correct occupation above each picture to complete each sentence. Call on students and ask questions about the jobs: *Who cooks food? Who lifts heavy things?* Make sure they correctly name the occupation.

★ Ask students which of the jobs pictured are *indoor jobs*. Make sure students notice the Venn diagram and see the indoor jobs listed on the left. Ask students which are the *outdoor jobs*, and *indoor/outdoor jobs*.

LISTENING SCRIPT

Lesson 1: Learn New Words

Look at the pictures. Listen to the words. Then listen and repeat.

1. chef	A chef cooks food.
2. office manager	An office manager uses a computer.
3. plumber	A plumber repairs sinks and toilets.
4. stylist	A stylist cuts hair.
5. child care worker	A child care worker takes care of children.
6. mechanic	A mechanic fixes cars.
7. mover	A mover lifts heavy things.
8. construction worker	A construction worker builds buildings.
9. truck driver	A truck driver drives a truck.
10. landscaper	A landscaper takes care of plants.

EXPANSION ACTIVITY: Act It Out

★ Write each occupation on an index card or piece of paper.

★ Group students in pairs and give each pair a card. Explain that they are going to act out the occupation on the card for the class to guess.

★ Model the activity by acting out an occupation while the class guesses what you are. For example, if you are a stylist, ask a student to sit in a chair while you pretend to cut his or her hair. Ask the class questions while you act: *What is my occupation? What do I do?* Elicit the correct answer.

★ After students have prepared their mimes, ask each pair to come one at a time to the front of the room. Give them time to mime their occupation and ask the class questions: What's his/her occupation? *What does he/she do?*

2. Write

★ Instruct students to read the example sentences. Ask them if they know people who can perform the tasks listed under each of the jobs: *Who do you know that can lift heavy things?* Write a few answers on the board in complete sentences. *Tatiana's husband can lift heavy things.*

★ Ask students to write five sentences about their friends and family and read their sentences to a partner.

★ Call on students to read their sentences to the class.

EXPANSION ACTIVITY: You Should Be a . . .

★ Write the conversation on the board:

A: What can you do?

B: I can ____.

A: You should be a ____.

★ Model the activity with a student by asking, *What can you do?* Prompt the student to respond with, *I can ____.* The student should complete the sentence with a skill listed in this lesson: *I can take care of children.* Based on the student's skill, then make a suggestion for an occupation: *You should be a child care worker.*

★ Put each student with a partner and have them take turns making suggestions following the model. Walk around the room to monitor the activity and provide help as needed.

3. Find Someone Who

★ Have students look at the example. Call on a student and ask, *Can you drive a car?* Elicit either a positive or a negative response: *Yes, I can*, or *No, I can't*.

★ Ask students to look at the box and determine the question form for each item: *Can you cook rice? Can you lift 50 pounds? Can you use a computer?* Have them create one more idea and the appropriate question.

★ Have students stand up and walk around the room asking the questions. Remind them to write a person's name next to an item only if that person answers *Yes, I can*.

★ Call on students to tell the class about their classmates: *Antonio can lift 50 pounds*.

EXPANSION ACTIVITY: Category Sort

★ Invite a group of students to stand at the front of the room. Explain that one side of the room is *yes* and the other side is *no*, and make sure they know which is which.

★ Ask questions about skills: *Can you drive a car?* Students who answer *yes* should move to the *yes* side of the room. Students who answer *no* should move to the other side of the room.

★ This is a fast-paced activity. Keep asking questions quickly, giving students just enough time to move.

★ For a lively variation, arrange enough chairs or pieces of paper in a circle so that all but one student have a designated place to stand or sit. If using paper, tape it to the floor.

★ Have the extra person stand in the center of the circle and ask the class a question: *Can you cook food?* Everyone who can answer *yes* must stand up and quickly move to a new chair or piece of paper. The person in the center also takes this opportunity to find a free spot. The person left without a spot must ask the next question.

WINDOW ON GRAMMAR:
Yes/No Questions + Simple Past

A. Read the questions and answers.

★ Have students look at the sentences in the yellow box. Read the questions and answers, pausing after each to have students repeat.

★ Call on students and ask the two questions.

★ Point out the form of the question—*did + subject + verb*—and the short answers: *Yes/No + subject + did/didn't.*

B. Ask a partner these questions.

★ Read the questions, pausing after each to have students repeat.

★ Put students in pairs to practice asking and answering the questions.

★ Call on students and ask them the questions.

C. Write your own question.

★ Tell students to write their own questions and then take turns asking and answering them with a partner.

★ Call on students to ask their questions of someone else in the class.

 Students can do Unit 10, Section 1, *Learn New Words* and Section 4, *Fun and Games* on the Interactive CD-ROM.

OBJECTIVE

Talking about Help Wanted Ads

WINDOW ON MATH

Word Problems

1. Read

★ Have students look at the ads and ask them questions: *What are these? Where can you see them? What jobs are in the ads?*

★ Have students look at the chart. Make sure they understand the headings. Ask about the office manager job: *Is the office manager position full-time or part-time? Does it offer benefits?*

★ Ask students to read the ads and take notes in the chart about the other jobs.

★ Have them compare answers with a partner.

★ Go over the answers with the class.

ANSWER KEY:

Job	Part-Time or Full-Time?	Benefits?
Office manager	full-time	yes
construction worker	full-time	yes
Chef	information not in the ad	information not in the ad
Child care worker	part-time	no
Landscaper	full-time	yes
Pharmacist's Assistant	full-time	yes

EXPANSION ACTIVITY: What's the job?

★ In this activity, students can ask five *yes/no* questions to try and guess the job being described in the ad. Students cannot guess the job until they have asked five questions.

★ Model the activity. Select one of the ads to answer questions about and make statements that indicate you are the employer: *I'm looking for workers.* The students' responsibility is to ask *yes/no* questions about the job: *Is it full-time? Do you need experience? Do I call Judy Eno?* Answer their questions based on the information in the ad.

★ Continue the activity with different students in the role of the employer.

2. Write

★ Read the questions in the directions and have students look at the example.

★ Tell students to write two sentences answering the questions and then read their sentences to a partner.

★ Call on students to read their sentences to the class.

EXPANSION ACTIVITY: Interview

★ Write the chart below on the board and make sure students copy it on a piece of paper. Go over the headings with the class.

Name	Which job do you like the best?	Why?	Which job do you like the least?	Why?

★ Students must interview three classmates to complete the chart. They can discuss the job listings in the book, look at job listings in a newspaper, or think of other jobs.

★ Call on a few students to tell the class about one of their classmates.

3. Practice the Conversation

★ Read the conversation or play the tape or CD as the students listen.

★ Read or play the conversation again. Pause after each line and ask the students to repeat. Check comprehension by asking questions: *What job is the conversation about? How much experience does the person have?*

★ Model the conversation with a student. Have the student read *B's* lines. Demonstrate how to substitute a different job for the scripted position of *office manager*.

★ Have students work in pairs to practice the conversation and ask about the jobs in the ads. Walk around the room to monitor the activity and provide help as needed.

LISTENING SCRIPT

Lesson 2: Practice the Conversation

Listen to the conversation. Then listen and repeat.

A: I'm calling about the ad for an office manager.
B: Do you have experience?
A: Yes, I do. I have two years of experience.
B: Good! Can you come in for an interview tomorrow at 3:00?
A: Yes. I'll be there.

**EXPANSION ACTIVITY:
Your Work Experience**

★ Write the conversation from Activity 3 on the board. Underline the phrases *an office manager, 2 years of experience,* and *at 3.*

★ Tell students to practice the conversation again. They should substitute for the underlined sections in the interview with a different job they really want, the amount of experience they have in that job, and a possible interview time. Walk around the room to monitor the activity and provide help as needed.

★★★★★★★★★★★★★★★★★★★★★★★★★★★★★★★

📁 **TRY THIS**

★★★★★★★★★★★★★★★★★★★★★★★★★★★★★★★

★ Draw a cluster diagram on the board with *Dream Job* in the center. Encourage students to name their ideal jobs and aspects of an ideal job and write their ideas on the diagram.

★ Ask students to decide exactly what their own dream job is. Have them write a job ad for their dream job. Remind them to look at the ads for ideas of how to structure their ad.

★ When completed, have students read their ads to a partner.

★ Call on a few students to read their ads to the class.

**EXPANSION ACTIVITY:
Aspects of Your Dream Job**

★ Brainstorm questions that focus on specific aspects of a job: *Do you want a full-time or part-time job? Are benefits important to you? Do you want to work outside or inside? Do you want to work in an office? A store? Do you like to work alone? Do you like to work with people? Do you like to work in a quiet or a loud place? Do you like computers? Can you lift heavy things? Do you like math? Do you like writing?*

★ Tell the students to write the answers to these questions on a piece of paper and then work with a partner, taking turns asking and answering the questions.

★ Ask students to look at the dream job they selected in the Try This activity and determine if their dream job includes the aspects of a job that are important to them.

WINDOW ON MATH: Word Problems

★ Explain that these word problems tell a story, but require math to answer the final question.

★ Read the first problem as an example. Help students create an equation by asking questions: *How many hours did Sam work each week? How much did he earn an hour? How much did he earn in one week? How much did he earn in four weeks?* Write the equation on the board: *40 hours × $20/hour = $800/week / $800/week × 4 weeks = $3,200/month.* Then erase the words and leave just the numbers.

★ Tell the students to write equations for the word problems and then answer them. Walk around the room to monitor students' progress and provide help as needed.

★ Go over the answers with the class.

ANSWER KEY:

1. $4 (40 \times 20) = \$3,200$
2. $3 \times 12 \times 9 = \$324$
3. $(5 \times 6 \times 10) + (2 \times 7 \times 15) = 300 + 210 = \$510$

EXPANSION ACTIVITY: Write a Math Word Problem

★ Assign students to write a word problem following the models in the Window on Math. Make sure they include the equation and, on a separate piece of paper, the solution.

★ Have students exchange problems with a partner and solve the problem. Compare the solution with that of the student who created the problem.

★ After you have checked the problems, have a volunteer dictate a problem to the class for listening practice. Correct the dictation and have the class solve the problem.

 Students can do Unit 10, Section 2, *Listen and Choose* and, Section 4, *Fun and Games* on the Interactive CD-ROM.

OBJECTIVE

At a Job Interview

1. Talk about the Picture

★ Put the overhead color transparency for Unit 10, Lesson 3, on the overhead projector or have students look at the picture in their books. Ask them to name the things and actions they see in the picture. Write the words on the board.

★ Group students in pairs and have them talk about the picture with a partner using the vocabulary on the board.

★ Tell them to look at the examples and write five sentences of their own about the picture. Ask a few volunteers to read their sentences to the class.

BIG PICTURE EXPANSION ACTIVITY: SPEAKING—Creating a Conversation

★ Put the "big picture" color overhead transparency for Unit 10, Lesson 3, on the projector or have students look at the "big picture" in their book.

★ Set the context for this activity by asking questions: *What do you think the people are talking about?* Help students brainstorm ideas and write them on the board: *dream jobs, hours, work experience, money, location.*

★ Put each student with a partner to create conversations or interviews that include two people in the picture.

★ Explain that students must write at least three lines for each speaker. Remind them to use the ideas on the board and the conversation from Lesson 2. Walk around to monitor the activity and provide help as needed.

★ Ask volunteers to act out their conversations in front of the class. Have the class guess which people in the picture are speaking.

---

2. Listen and Take Notes 🎧

★ Tell students they are going to listen to a job interview. Make sure they look at the notes in the chart so they know what to listen for.

★ Read the interview or play the tape or CD while students listen and write in the missing information.

★ Read the interview or play the tape or CD a second time and have students check their notes.

★ Go over the answers with the class.

LISTENING SCRIPT

Lesson 3: Listen and Take Notes

Listen to Rosa's job interview. Write the missing information.

Manager:	So, Rosa, tell me about yourself.
Rosa:	Well, I'm really interested in retail. Right now I'm the store manager at Lane's. I got the job in 2000.
Manager:	That's very interesting. Do you like your job?
Rosa:	Yes, very much. I'm really sad Lane's is closing soon.
Manager:	Yes, that is too bad. And what did you do before that?
Rosa:	Well, I was a salesclerk at Lane's for almost two years, from 1998 to 2000. Then I got promoted to store manager.
Manager:	Yes, I see.
Rosa:	And before that, I worked as a salesclerk at a store called The Elephant's Trunk.
Manager:	When was that?
Rosa:	I worked there from 1996 to 1998. I learned a lot there.

ANSWER KEY:

Store manager/salesclerk/1996–1998

3. Give Opinions

★ Direct students' attention to the pictures. Read the phrases under the pictures aloud, pausing after each to have students repeat.

★ Ask the class, *Do you think it's OK to be late for a job interview?* Elicit a *no* answer and ask why not. Possible answers include the following: *It's rude. They'll think you're not a good worker. Americans like people to be on time.*

★ Ask students to look at the example chart in the book of what you should and shouldn't do at a job interview.

★ Have students make a new chart on a piece of paper like the one in the book. Have them complete the chart, writing down their ideas about what someone should and shouldn't do at a job interview. Remind them to use the phrases in the pictures and add other ideas if they want. Have students compare answers with a partner when finished.

★ Call on students to share their ideas with the class.

EXPANSION ACTIVITY:
Agree or Disagree?

★ Write *agree* on one side of the board and *disagree* on the other. Invite a group of 4–6 students to come to the front of the room. As you say a statement, motion for students to move to the word that accurately expresses their opinions. Ask each student to explain his or her position: *I agree. You shouldn't chew gum at an interview. I disagree. It's okay to chew gum at an interview.* Repeat the activity with other volunteers until all students have participated.

★ Use the statements below for the activity or create your own.

You should come early to a job interview.

You shouldn't call the interviewer by his or her first name.

You should wear a suit.

It's OK to smoke.

You should talk a lot.

It's OK to ask for something to drink.

You should use your hands a lot.

 Students can do Unit 10, Section 2, *Listen and Choose* on the Interactive CD-ROM.

OBJECTIVE

Reading a Success Story

WINDOW ON GRAMMAR

Future with *Be going to*

1. Talk about the Pictures

★ Instruct students to look at the pictures in order from numbers 1 to 4. Ask about each picture: *What do you see? What are they doing? Where are they?*

★ Go over the example regarding the first picture. Have students write one sentence about each picture and read their sentences to a partner.

★ Call on students to share their ideas with the class.

EXPANSION ACTIVITY:
Tell a Story from the Pictures

★ Tell students to either cover the writing above each picture or close their books. Review the words from Unit 5 that helped organize the order of a story: *At the beginning of the story, next, _____ years later.*

★ Explain to students that they are to write a story about Mr. Kazi using only the information in the pictures. Encourage them to be creative—there are no right or wrong stories.

★ Have students read their stories to a partner.

★ Call on a few students to read stories aloud to the class.

---

2. Read

★ Ask students to read the story silently. Then read the story aloud, pausing after each line to have students repeat, or call on students to take turns reading one line each from the story.

★ Tell the students to underline all the words related to time you are reading. Answers should include the following: *when he was 23 years old, first job, On weekends, Soon, for the next three years, A few years later, seven days a week, soon, A year later, Today, in the future.*

★ Ask students when the story takes place—the past, present, or future. Point out that it is written in the past tense except for Part 6.

★ Have the students read the sentences in Activity 2 and note the event that happened first. Have the students put the other events in order.

★ Make sure students check their answers with a partner.

★ Go over the answers with the class.

ANSWER KEY:

1. Mr. Kazi worked at a car rental agency.
2. He worked as a chef's assistant.
3. He managed a fast-food restaurant.
4. He bought a fast-food restaurant.
5. He bought three restaurants.
6. He owns 168 restaurants.

3. Check True or False

★ Ask students to read the sentences and check *True* or *False*.

★ Have them check their answers with a partner.

★ Go over the answers with the class.

ANSWER KEY:

1. False; 2. False; 3. True; 4. True; 5. False;
6. True

★ ★

TRY THIS

★ ★

★ Go over the directions. Then tell a story about yourself. As you talk about five events, write a list on the board: *went to college, studied English literature, went to Brazil, got married, moved to Florida.* After that, provide a detail or two about each event: *I lived in a small apartment in New York.*

★ Assign students to write their own stories and include five events in the order that they occurred. Remind them to use words like *first, next, then* to show sequence and to write in the simple past tense. Encourage them to include some details about the events.

★ When complete, have students read their stories to a partner.

EXPANSION ACTIVITY:
Guess the Order of Events

★ In this activity, students will write three events from their lives in random order and other students will guess the correct order in which they occurred. Example: *I went to Japan. I had a dog named Snickers. I bought a house.* Suggest to students that they choose events that don't have an obvious order.

★ Put students in small groups to share their events. As each student reads the sentences, the other members of the group should try to guess the order in which they actually happened.

★ Call on students from each group to talk about their events.

WINDOW ON GRAMMAR:
Future with *Be going to*

A. Read the sentences.

★ Ask students to look at the examples. Read the sentences aloud, pausing after each to have students repeat. Explain this form of the future tense—*am/is/are going to + verb*—and write it on the board.

B. Complete the sentences.

★ Go over the first sentence and have students complete the other sentences.

★ Make sure students check their answers with a partner.

★ Go over the answers with the class.

ANSWER KEY:

B. 1. is going to buy; 2. am going to go; 3. are going to study; 4. is going to manage; 5. are going to work

 Students can do Unit 10, Section 3, *Read and Write* on the Interactive CD-ROM.

OBJECTIVE

Answering Job Interview Questions

WINDOW ON PRONUNCIATION

Stressing Important Words in Sentences

1. Practice the Conversation: Talking About Work Experience 🎧

★ Direct students' attention to the picture in Activity 1. To set the context, ask questions about the picture: *Who is in the picture? What are they doing? Who is being interviewed?*

★ Read the conversation or play the tape or CD.

★ Read or play the conversation again. Pause after each sentence and ask students to repeat.

★ Ask comprehension questions about the conversation: *What was his last job? What does he like to do?*

★ Point out that there are three pieces of information in the scripted conversation that can be substituted for—the place, the job, and what the person liked to do. Model the conversation with a student. Have the student read *A's* lines. Demonstrate how to substitute *restaurant* for the scripted place, *chef's assistant* for the job, and *cooking good food* for what was liked.

★ Assign students to write other ideas for place, job, and what was liked. Put them in pairs to practice the conversation, making substitutions. Walk around to monitor the activity and provide help as needed.

LISTENING SCRIPT

Lesson 5: Practice the Conversation: Talking about Work Experience

Listen to the conversation. Then listen and repeat.

A: Tell me about your last job.
B: Well, I worked at a department store. I was a salesclerk.
A: Did you like the job?
B: Yes. I liked helping people. And there was always something to do.

2. Practice the Conversation: Talking about Changing Jobs

★ Repeat the basic procedure from Activity 1.

★ To set the context, ask questions about the conversation: *How do you think the interview is going?*

★ After students have listened to and repeated the conversation, check comprehension by asking questions: *Why did he leave his last job? Why does he want to work there?*

LISTENING SCRIPT

Lesson 5: Practice the Conversation: Talking about Changing Jobs

Listen to the conversation. Then listen and repeat.

A: Why did you leave your last job?
B: I went back to school.
A: I see. And why do you want to work here?
B: I think it's a very good company.

3. Practice the Conversation: Answering Job Interview Questions

★ Repeat the basic procedure from Activity 1.

★ To set the context, ask questions about the conversation: *How do you think the interviewee is feeling now? Is it a good interview?*

★ After students have listened to and repeated the conversation, check comprehension by asking, *Why should the company hire him?*

LISTENING SCRIPT

Lesson 5: Practice the Conversation: Answering Job Interview Questions

Listen to the conversation. Then listen and repeat.

A: Why should I hire you?
B: I'm good with people.
A: That's good. We like our employees to be good with people.
B: I'm glad to hear that.

Culture/Civics Notes:

★ Students may be unfamiliar with the messages of body language. Discuss the body language of the interviewee in each picture. Point out that his arms are crossed in the first picture and this often implies reservation or shyness. In picture two the interviewee is more expressive, his hands are open wide as he is explaining. He looks more animated and engaged. In the third picture, his finger is pointing upwards. This indicates that he is making a point.

★ Explain that we often use our hands as we talk. Point out that too much gesturing with the hands could be distracting, but keeping them motionless or too close to the body can also indicate a lack of energy or interest.

WINDOW ON PRONUNCIATION: Stressing Important Words in Sentences

A. Listen to the sentences. Then listen and repeat.

★ Ask students to look at the sentences. Read the sentences or play the tape or CD.

★ Say the words or play the tape or CD a second time. Pause after each sentence and have students repeat.

★ Tell students to underline the stressed words in each sentence and check their answers with a partner.

★ Go over the answers with the class. Ask students what types of words are stressed: *nouns, verbs, adjectives*. Point out that little words—*about, at, a, your*—are not usually stressed.

★ Call on a few volunteers to read sentences, stressing the important words.

LISTENING SCRIPT

Lesson 5: Window on Pronunciation
Stressing Important Words in Sentences

A. Listen to the sentences. Then listen and repeat.

1. Tell me about your last job.
2. I worked at a department store.
3. Why did you leave your last job?
4. Why should I hire you?

ANSWER KEY:

<u>Tell</u> me about your <u>last job</u>.
I <u>worked</u> at a <u>department</u> store.
<u>Why</u> did you <u>leave</u> your last <u>job</u>?
<u>Why</u> should <u>I</u> hire <u>you</u>?

B. Listen to the questions.

★ Ask students to look at the questions. Say the words or play the tape or CD, pausing after each question to have students repeat.

★ Say the words and play the tape or CD a second time. Tell the students to underline the stressed words and check their answers with a partner.

★ Go over the answers with the class.

★ Assign students to write answers to the questions. Put students in pairs to practice asking and answering the questions.

LISTENING SCRIPT

Lesson 5: Window on Pronunciation
Stressing Important Words in Sentences

B. Listen to the questions. Underline the stressed words.

1. What did you do in your last job?
2. Did you like the job?
3. Why should I hire you?
4. Why do you want to work here?

ANSWER KEY:

1. <u>What</u> did you <u>do</u> in your <u>last</u> job?
2. Did you <u>like</u> the <u>job</u>?
3. <u>Why</u> should <u>I</u> hire <u>you</u>?
4. <u>Why</u> do you want to work <u>here</u>?

BIG PICTURE EXPANSION ACTIVITY: GRAMMAR—*Yes/No* Questions in the Simple Past Tense

★ Make copies of Worksheet #20 (p. 260) and distribute them to students.

★ Put the "big picture" color overhead transparency for Unit 10, Lesson 3, on the projector or have students look at the "big picture" in their books.

★ Instruct students to look at the companies' names and, as a class, brainstorm ideas about what these companies might do.

★ Look at the worksheet and have students identify the company that would require the work experience listed in the column on the left. Go over the answers.

★ Tell students to complete the interviews with *Yes, I did,* or *No, I didn't*. Remind them to look at the statements again for help. Have students check their answers with a partner. Go over the answers with the class.

★ Students should practice the interviews with a partner.

ANSWER KEY:

A. 1. Data or The Insurance Group; 2. The Solar Group; 3. Big Top Clowns; 4. World Engineering

B. 1. Yes, I did; 2. No, I didn't; 3. No, I didn't; 4. Yes, I did.

Students can do Unit 10, Section 2, *Listen and Choose* on the Interactive CD-ROM.

EQUIPPED FOR THE FUTURE ROLE

Work

OBJECTIVE

Completing a Job Application

1. Read

★ Direct students' attention to the photo as you read about Francis Yasine. Check comprehension by asking questions: *What did Francis do in his home country? Does he want a full-time or part-time job?*

★ Tell students to look at the application form and ask questions about the items that are filled out: *When was he born? Does Francis have a valid driver's license? What days is Francis available to work? What information is missing?*

★ Ask students to read the paragraph and complete the job application form.

★ Have students compare their forms with a partner's.

★ Go over the answers with the class.

ANSWER KEY:

Job Application
Personal Information

First Name: ___Francis___

Middle Initial: ___M___

Last Name: ___Yasine___

Birth Date: _6_/_23_/_70_

Present Address: ___2435 Melford Avenue___

City: ___Sacramento___

State: ___CA___

Zip Code: ___95652___

Phone Number: (916) 555-4938

★ Are you currently employed?　　☐ Yes ☒ No

★ Do you have a valid driver's license?　☒ Yes ☐ No

★ Do you have access to an automobile?　☒ Yes ☐ No

★ Number of hours/week desired: ___40–full-time___

★ Days and A.M./P.M. Hours Available:

Mon.	Tues.	Wed.	Thurs.	Fri.	Sat.
☒ A.M.	☒ A.M.	☒ A.M.	☒ A.M..	☒ A.M.	☒ A.M.
☒ P.M.	☒ P.M.	☒ P.M.	☒ P.M.	☒ P.M.	☐ P.M.

EXPANSION ACTIVITY: Dictation—*True* or *False*

★ Make sure students close their books for dictation.

★ Dictate five sentences, some true and some false, about Francis Yasine. Use the sentences below or create your own.

　1. *His middle name is Edward.* (False)
　2. *He was a cook in his country.* (False)
　3. *He liked his job a lot.* (True)
　4. *He wants to work part-time.* (False)
　5. *He lives in the United States now.* (True)

★ When you're through dictating, have students check their sentences with a partner.

★ Instruct students to write *true* or *false* after each sentence, and then rewrite the false statements to make them true.

★ Go over the sentences and the answers with the class.

2. Write

★ Have students complete the job application with information about themselves. Walk around to monitor the activity and provide help as needed.

★ Call on a few students to answer questions about the information on their forms: *What is your middle initial? Are you currently employed? What days are you available to work?*

3. Interview

★ Help students brainstorm questions that they could ask about the information on the application form in Activity 2 and write the questions on the board.

★ Have students work in pairs to practice asking and answering questions about the forms.

📺 BIG PICTURE EXPANSION ACTIVITY: READING—James Needs a New Job

★ Make copies of Worksheet #21 (p. 261) and distribute them to students.

★ Put the "big picture" color overhead transparency for Unit 10, Lesson 3, on the projector or have students look at the "big picture" in their books.

★ Read the story aloud, pausing after each line to have students repeat, or give students a few minutes to read the story to themselves. Check comprehension by asking questions: *Where is James from? What jobs did he have in the Ivory Coast?*

★ Students should then answer the questions independently but check their answers with a partner.

★ Tell students to look at the "big picture," guess who James is and give reasons for their answer.

★ Ask students to complete the application form for James. Walk around to monitor the activity and provide help as needed.

ANSWER KEY:

A. 1. Office manager; 2. pharmacist; 3. chef's assistant; 4. in front of the World Engineering desk. He's the man in wheelchair.

B.

Job Application

Personal Information

First Name: _James_
Middle Initial: _M._
Last Name: _Mannah_
Birth Date: _02 / 01 / 1970_
Present Address: _2919 8th Street_
City: _Arlington_
State: _VA_
Zip Code: _22413_
Phone Number: (703)-555-8620

WORK EXPERIENCE (start with the most recent)

WHEN	COMPANY	OCCUPATION
2001–now	Tony's Restaurant	Chef's assistant
1993–1998	Pharmacie Premier	Pharmacist
1990–1992	West Africa Engineering	Office Manager

 Students can do Unit 10, Section 3 *Read and Write* on the Interactive CD-ROM.

1. Listening Review 🎧

TESTING FOCUS: Taking Notes while Listening
★ Students may need to take notes as they listen to questions 7 and 8 in Activity 1. Point out that these questions are word problems, and they may want to write down numerical information.

★ Go over the directions with the class. Read the items or play the tape or CD and have the students mark their answers on the Answer Sheet.

★ Walk around to monitor the activity and help students stay on task.

★ Have students check their answers with a partner.

★ Go over the answers with the class.

LISTENING SCRIPT

Lesson 7: Listening Review

Listen and choose the best answer. Use the Answer Sheet.

1. What do stylists do?
2. Can he lift heavy things?
3. Did she work last week?
4. Is it a part-time job?
5. Why did you leave your last job?
6. Why should I hire you?
7. Sam worked 10 hours last week. He earns $20 an hour. How much did he earn last week?
8. Mei worked 40 hours last week. She earns $20 an hour. How much did she earn last week?

ANSWER KEY:

1. B; 2. A; 3. C; 4. A; 5. B; 6. A; 7. B; 8. B

2. Dictation 🎧

★ Go over the directions with the class. Read the items or play the tape or CD and instruct the students to write the questions they hear.

★ Walk around to monitor the activity and help students stay on task.

★ Ask three students to write the sentences on the board.

★ Tell students to answer the questions on paper and then work with a partner to practice asking and answering the questions.

★ Call on a few students and ask them the questions.

LISTENING SCRIPT

Lesson 7: Dictation

Listen and write the questions you hear.

1. Did you work last year?
2. Can you drive a car?
3. Do you have a job now?

3. Conversation Check: Pair Work

★ Go over the directions. Group students in pairs and remind them that each partner has some information, but that other information is missing. They must each ask their partner questions to complete the chart.

★ Walk around to monitor the activity and provide help as needed.

Assessment Note:
★ You can use the conversation check as an oral assessment. Ask pairs of students to complete the activity while you note areas of difficulty.

LEARNING LOG

★ Point out the four sections of the Learning Log: *I know these words, I can ask, I can say,* and *I can write.*

★ Ask students to check what they know and what they can do.

★ Walk around to note what they don't know or can't do. Use this information to review areas of difficulty.

BIG PICTURE EXPANSION ACTIVITY: WRITING—Writing about Your Work Experience 📁

★ Put the "big picture" color overhead transparency for Unit 10, Lesson 3, on the projector or have students look at the "big picture" in their books. Help students imagine that they are going to talk to one of the companies at this job fair.

★ Tell students to write a description of their past experience that might help them get a job.

★ Model the activity. Tell the students you are applying for a job with *Big Top Clowns*. Write your experience on the board: *I worked at a day care center in college. I am an actor and was a clown in a play. I have children now, so I can take care of children. I'm funny. I work well with people.* Point out that they can use sentences with the simple past or present tense.

★ Walk around to monitor the activity and provide help as needed.

★ Put students in pairs to share their experience.

BIG PICTURE EXPANSION ACTIVITY:
SPEAKING Assessment—Talking about the Picture

★ You can use the "big picture" to assess the placement of new students in open-entry classes, to diagnose difficulties, or to measure progress.

★ Work with one student at a time. Show the "big picture" from Unit 10, Lesson 3, to the student and say, *What do you see in the picture?* or, *Tell me about the picture.* Tell the student to speak for as long as possible. Wait a moment for the student to prepare an answer. If the student has difficulty, you can use prompts: *What do you see in the room? Who do you see in the room? What are they doing?*

★ You can use a rubric like the one below to rate beginning speakers.

3	Uses sentences, although form may be incorrect Can speak for sustained length of time Responds to prompts, but doesn't need them to begin speaking
2	Can use nouns and verbs Uses phrases Answers informational questions
1	Can name objects Uses single words Can answer yes/no questions
0	Cannot say anything independently May be able to point to objects when prompted

TEACHER'S NOTES:

Things that students are doing well:

Things students need additional help with:

Ideas for further practice or for the next class:

 Students can do Unit 10, Section 5 *Practice Test* on the Interactive CD-ROM.

FOCUS ON WRITING

Idea Lists

1. Read the stories below.

★ Ask students to look at the pictures and identify the names of things they know. Write them on the board.

★ Tell students to read paragraphs A, B, and C. Alternatively, read them aloud, pausing after each line to have students repeat.

★ Direct students' attention to the two columns at the top of the page. Ask students to find all the words in the paragraphs that begin with *H* and *M* and write them in the correct column. Make sure students check their answers with a partner. Go over the answers with the class.

★ Discuss the paragraphs and ask comprehension questions about them: *Did the person in story A have a good week? (yes). Did anything bad happen? (Yes, her daughter cut her hand.)* Ask similar questions about stories *B* and *C*.

ANSWER KEY:

Words with H: happened, her, hand, husband, he's, hospital, house, helped
Words with M: me, My, movie, mother, Miami

2. Complete the paragraph below.

★ Direct students' attention to the *Focus on Writing* box. Read the advice in the box aloud.

★ Ask students to read the Idea List and then ask them comprehension questions: *What are some good things in the list? What are some bad things?*

★ Have students look at the story frame with the blanks in the sentences. Read the first two sentences and ask if they should write the good things or the bad things next. Point out that one good thing is written on the first line. Instruct the students to write the other two good things on the next two lines.

★ Read the statement, *Three bad things happened.* Ask the students what should come next in the paragraph. Tell them to finish the paragraph with the three bad things from the list.

★ Call on students to read the paragraph aloud.

3. What happened to you last week?

★ Tell students to list the good things and bad things that happened to them last week in the *Idea List.*

★ Call on students to tell you about some of the things on their lists.

★ After making the list, students should write a paragraph about last week. Remind them to follow the models in Activities 1 and 2.

★ Put students in pairs and have them take turns reading their stories with a partner. Instruct each student to write down one good thing and one bad thing that happened to his or her partner last week.

★ Call on students to tell the class a good and a bad thing about their partner's week.

EXPANSION ACTIVITY:
What about next week?

★ Ask students to make an idea list about good and bad things that they have to do next week and share their idea lists with a partner.

★ Call on students to share their ideas with the class.

★ Review the use of *be going to* to talk about the future and tell students to write their ideas in that form: *I'm going to go to a party. I'm going to see the dentist.*

★ Students should then turn their idea lists into paragraphs about next week and read their stories to a partner.

★ Call on students to read their stories to the class or to explain one good thing and one bad thing about their partner's upcoming week.

EQUIPPED FOR THE FUTURE ROLE

Family

OBJECTIVE

Setting Goals

A. Take the quiz.

★ Direct students' attention to the quiz and ask, *What is this? Where do you see quizzes (or questionnaires) like this?*

★ Have students read the quiz or read it aloud, pausing after each item to have students repeat. Ask students to check the things they would like to do in the next five years.

★ Call on a few students to tell the class about their goals.

B. Read the story.

★ To set the context for the story, have students look at the picture. Ask then, *Who do you see? Where are they? What do you think their relationship is?*

★ Have students read about Tatiana, or read the story aloud, pausing after each sentence to have students repeat.

★ Check comprehension by asking questions: *Where is Tatiana from? What is her job now? What does she like to do?*

★ Instruct students to underline Tatiana's goals and check their answers with a partner.

★ Go over the answers with the class.

ANSWER KEY:

Tatiana is from Peru. She came to the United States in 1999 with her daughter, Claudia. Tatiana is working in a clothing store now and Claudia goes to school. Tatiana loves to cook and <u>wants to be a chef</u>. She wants to work in a nice restaurant, so she is going to start classes at the community college in September. She is going to study how to be a chef. Tatiana <u>is saving money for her classes</u>. She needs $1,000. Tatiana is going to work some extra hours at the store, but she <u>wants Claudia to have child care after school</u>. Tatiana is going to ask her sister to take care of Claudia after school.

EXPANSION ACTIVITY: Create Questions

★ Ask students to create three information questions about Tatiana's story. Put them in pairs to practice asking and answering questions.

C. Complete the chart.

★ Ask students what goals Tatiana has. Point out that the goals should be written in the column on the left, and how she is going to reach the goals in the column on the right.

★ Ask students to reread the paragraph to find three goals and the three ways Tatiana is going to reach them.

★ After completing the chart, students should compare theirs with a partner's.

★ Go over the answers with the class.

ANSWER KEY:

Tatiana's goal	What Tatiana is going to do to reach her goal.
Be a chef	Go to school
Save money for classes	Work extra hours at the store
Have childcare for Claudia	Ask her sister to take care of Claudia

D. Choose three of your goals from Exercise A.

★ Ask students to write three of their goals in the chart. Remind them to look at Exercise A. Remind them to write how much each goal will cost and how they are planning to reach each goal.

★ Have students share their ideas with a partner.

★ Call on a few students to share their ideas with the class.

Take It Outside

★ Direct students' attention to the chart. Read the questions at the top of each column, pausing to have students repeat.

★ Assign students to interview someone and write the information they get in the chart.

★ Call on a few students to tell the class about the person they interviewed.

EQUIPPED FOR THE FUTURE ROLE

Community

OBJECTIVE

Understanding Website Information

A. Predict the answers to the questions below.

★ Read each question and pause to have students repeat.

★ Ask them to guess the answer to the first question ($5.15). Point out that this is information they don't know, but trying to predict what a reading is about can help them to better understand it. Tell students to draw a line from each question to the correct answer.

★ When students finish matching the questions and answers, have them compare answers with a partner.

B. Read the Frequently Asked Questions (FAQs).

★ Direct students' attention to the reading and ask what it's about. Explain that this information is an employment law that tells people about work, wages, and hours in the U.S. The information is available on a U.S. government Website. Point out that many websites have a section called *Frequently Asked Questions.*

★ Ask students to read the information, or read the information aloud and pause to have students repeat.

★ Tell students to check their predictions in Exercise A. Go over the answers with the class.

★ Put students in pairs to practice asking and answering the questions.

ANSWER KEY:

1. b; 2. c. 3. d. 4. a

C. Write the number of the question in Activity B where you can find the answer.

★ Have students read the questions, or read each question aloud and pause to have students repeat. Ask the first question and have students look at Question 5 in the *FAQs* in

Exercise B. That's where they will find out if a 12-year-old can baby sit.

★ Have students complete the rest of the questions, and make sure they include where to find the relevant information.

★ Have students check their answers with a partner. Go over the answers with the class.

ANSWER KEY:

1. Question 5; 2. Question 4; 3. Question 3; 4. Question 2; 5. Question 4; 6. Question 5

EXPANSION ACTIVITY: Get the Answer

★ Ask students to look at questions 1–6 in Exercise C and identify where in the *FAQs* they can find the answers to the questions. Have them read those sections of the *FAQs* and write the answers to questions 1–6.

★ Put students in pairs to practice asking and answering questions.

★ Go over the answers with the class.

D. Check *true* or *false*.

★ Ask students to read the statements and check *true* or *false*. Remind them to reread the information if necessary to find the answers.

★ Have students check their answers with a partner. Go over the answers with the class.

ANSWER KEY:

1. true; 2. true; 3. false; 4. false; 5. true; 6. true

Take It Outside

★ Go over the directions. Make sure students understand how to write the Website address. Take them to a computer lab at school or to a public library.

★ Have them write 2 FAQs from the Website. Have them also write the answers to those 2 questions. Encourage them to summarize, using language they understand.

★ Have students work in groups of four. Ask each student to explain the information they found.

★ Discuss some of their answers with the whole class.

Name: _____   Date: _____

Grammar: Practicing *Is* and *Are*

Directions: Look at the "big picture" in Unit 1, Lesson 2. Complete the sentences with *is* or *are*.

In the Classroom

1. Four students are at one table. The students _____ in chairs.

2. The teacher is a man. He _____ in the classroom.

3. The map _____ on the wall.

4. The notebooks _____ on the table.

5. You _____ not in the class.

6. The computer _____ on the table.

7. Jane _____ a student in the class.

8. We _____ in our class.

9. The door _____ open.

10. The chairs _____ green.

Name: _____   Date: _____

Reading: Who is Jane?

A. Directions: Look at the "big picture" in Unit 1, Lesson 2. Locate Jane in the picture. Read the story and add the correct punctuation marks.

Jane is a Student

Jane is a student   She is from Salzburg   Austria   Her last name is Thiede   Her birthplace is Innsbruck   Austria   Jane is in the United States now   She is in Seattle Washington   Her address is 23 High Street   Jane is single

B. Directions: Read the questions about Jane. Write the answers.

1. What is Jane's last name?   _____
2. What is her birthplace?   _____
3. What is her address?   _____
4. What is her marital status?   _____
5. Is Jane a student?   _____

Name: _____   Date: _____

Reading: A Story about Janet

A. Directions: Look at the "big picture" in Unit 2, Lesson 3. Read the story below.

Janet the Police Officer

Janet Miller is a police officer. She works at the Westville Police Station. The police station is across the street from the post office and near the Westville Library. The post office is also across the street from the community center. Janet is a student in a class at the community center. Janet's home is not near the police station. She takes the bus to work.

B. Directions: Read the statements about Janet Miller and check (✓) *yes* or *no*.

1. Is Janet a bus driver?   ☐ yes   ☐ no
2. Is Janet a student?   ☐ yes   ☐ no
3. Is her class across the street from the post office?   ☐ yes   ☐ no
4. Is her work near the library?   ☐ yes   ☐ no
5. Is Janet's home near the police station?   ☐ yes   ☐ no

Name: _____   Date: _____

Grammar: *There is / There are*

A. Directions: Look at the "big picture" in Unit 2, Lesson 3. Read the questions below and circle the correct answer.

1. Is there a hospital near the drugstore?

   A. Yes, there is.   B. No, there isn't.

2. Is there a community center in Westville?

   A. Yes, there is.   B. No, there isn't

3. Is there a restaurant across from the police station?

   A. Yes, there is.   B. No, there isn't

4. Is there a pay phone in front of the drugstore?

   A. Yes, there is.   B. No, there isn't.

5. Is there a bookmobile behind the hospital?

   A. Yes, there is.   B. No, there isn't.

B. Directions: Write *is* or *are* in the blanks to complete the sentences below.

1. There _____ a library near the fire station.
2. There _____ a taxi next to the drugstore.
3. There _____ two cars next to the post office.
4. There _____ people in the restaurant.
5. There _____ cars in the parking lot.

Name: _____   Date: _____

Reading: Pablo and His Son

Directions: Look at the "big picture" in Unit 3, Lesson 2. Read the story. Then look at the sentences and check *yes* or *no*.

At the Library

Pablo Martinez is at the library today. He is at school every day from 2:00 P.M. to 5:00 P.M. He is at work from 6:00 P.M. to 2:00 A.M. But today is Tuesday. Pablo goes to the library every Tuesday with Tomas. Tomas is 4 years old. He goes to Story Hour. The librarian reads books. Tomas listens. Pablo looks at books and videos and uses the computer.

1. It is 3:00 P.M. Is Pablo at the library?   ❏ yes   ❏ no

2. It is Tuesday.   ❏ yes   ❏ no

3. Tomas is at Story Hour.   ❏ yes   ❏ no

4. Pablo is at Story Hour.   ❏ yes   ❏ no

5. Pablo is at work.   ❏ yes   ❏ no

6. It is 8:00 P.M.   ❏ yes   ❏ no

7. Tomas is 4 years old.   ❏ yes   ❏ no

8. Pablo uses the computer.   ❏ yes   ❏ no

9. It is morning.   ❏ yes   ❏ no

10. Pablo's family name is Tomas.   ❏ yes   ❏ no

Name: _____   Date: _____

Grammar: Questions and Answers about the Library

A. Directions: Look at the "big picture" in Unit 3, Lesson 2. Answer the questions about the library's hours. Answers with *Yes, it is.* or *No, it isn't.*

1. A: Is the library open on Thursday?

   B: _____

2. A: Is the library open at 10:00 A.M. on Monday?

   B: _____

3. A: Is it open on Saturday at noon?

   B: _____

4. A: Is it open on Friday at 3:00 P.M.?

   B: _____

5. A: Is the library closed on Sunday?

   B: _____

6. A: Is Story Hour on Wednesday?

   B: _____

B. Directions: Look at the "big picture" and read the signs. Answer the questions.

1. A: I have three videos for one week. How much is it?

   B: _____

2. A: How much is it for one video for two weeks?

   B: _____

3. A: There are three books. They are one day late. How much is it?

   B: _____

4. A: One book is five days late. How much is it?

   B: _____

Name: _____   Date: _____

Reading: A Story about Alice

A. Directions: Read about Alice. Then look at the "big picture" in Unit 4, Lesson 2.
Add her activities to the calendar.

Alice's Busy Month

Alice has many things on her calendar for May. But there are many more things to do in May. She is very busy. In the first week, she has English class on Wednesday and Friday. In the second week of May, Alice has lunch with her friend on the day between her job interview and her basketball game. She has a meeting at the library on the Sunday after the game. Alice likes to go dancing every Saturday.

B. Directions: Answer the questions.

1. What does *busy* mean?
   A. have nothing to do
   B. have a rainy month
   C. have a lot to do

2. What dates are Alice's English class?
   A. May 2nd and May 10th
   B. May 2nd and May 4th
   C. May 7th and May 10th

3. What day does Alice have lunch with her friend?
   A. Monday
   B. Wednesday
   C. Thursday

Name: _____   Date: _____

Grammar: Singular and Plural Nouns

A. Directions: Look at the "big picture" in Unit 4, Lesson 2. Then write the plural forms of the words below.

Singular	Plural
1. basketball	_____
2. parent	_____
3. dentist	_____
4. doctor	_____
5. computer	_____
6. hour	_____

B. Directions: Complete the sentences. Write the plural forms of one of the words from Part A in the blanks below.

1. There are usually 23 _____ at the hospital on Tuesdays.

2. In Alice's class on Thursday, there are 15 _____ at the tables.

3. More than 150 _____ went to the PTO meeting.

4. It is 4:00 P.M. now. We have two _____ until the meeting at 6:00.

5. We need five _____ for the game on Friday.

6. There are three _____ at the office I go to. I have to get my teeth cleaned.

Name: _____   Date: _____

Grammar: What's the Object?

A. Directions: Look at the "big picture" in Unit 5, Lesson 2. Complete the sentences with words from the box below.

green pants   hats   purple skirt   door   hat

1. Some women near the entrance are wearing _____*hats*_____.

2. A man is running near a woman in a _____.

3. A woman is at the customer service counter. She wants to return her _____.
   They are too long.

4. A woman is wearing a big red _____.

5. A man in an orange shirt and blue pants is walking through the _____.

B. Directions: Rewrite the sentences in Activity A by writing an object pronoun in each blank (*me, you, him, her, it, them, us*).

1. Some women near the entrance are wearing _____.

2. A man is running near _____.

3. She wants to return _____.

4. A woman is wearing _____.

5. A man in an orange shirt and blue pants is walking through _____.

Name: _____   Date: _____

Reading: A Story about Berta

Directions: Read the story. Look at the "big picture" in Unit 5, Lesson 2. Then circle the correct answers to the questions.

What's the problem?

Berta is shopping at Lane's Department store today. She is at the customer service counter. She wants to return some pants. They're too long. Berta is not happy. The salesclerk's name is Georgia. She is working hard today. Georgia asks Berta "What's the problem?"

1. What is Berta doing today?
   A. working   B. shopping

2. What is the salesclerk's name?
   A. Berta   B. Georgia

3. What does Berta want to return?
   A. a dress   B. some pants

4. Where is Berta?
   A. at the customer service counter B. at the checkout counter

5. What is the problem with the pants?
   A. They're too short.   B. They're too long.

6. What color are the pants Berta wants to return?
   A. green   B. blue

7. What is Berta wearing?
   A. green pants   B. a blue suit

8. Is Berta wearing a hat?
   A. No   B. Yes

9. What size are the pants?
   A. small   B. large

10. Is the salesclerk wearing glasses?
    A. No   B. Yes

Name: _____   Date: _____

Reading: Store Signs

A. Directions: Look at the "big picture" in Unit 6, Lesson 2. Check the words you see on signs in the store.

- ☐ customer service
- ☐ produce section
- ☐ delicatessen
- ☐ frozen
- ☐ pizza
- ☐ milk
- ☐ baking goods
- ☐ rice

- ☐ bakery
- ☐ vegetables
- ☐ open
- ☐ closed
- ☐ special
- ☐ meat
- ☐ chicken
- ☐ entrance

B. Directions: Look at the "big picture" and read the signs. Complete the sentences.

1. Frozen foods are next to the _____.
2. The entrance is between the _____ and _____.
3. Baking goods are between _____ and _____.
4. Erik is in the _____.
5. _____ are in Aisle 3.

C. Directions: Read the paragraph. Then check (✓) *True* or *False* for each sentence.

Al is cleaning the floor. He cleans the floor every day. Customers always drop food in the produce section. Sometimes they step on it, too. Al wants to work in the bakery or at the checkout counter. He likes to talk to people and help them. He doesn't like to clean the floor.

	TRUE	FALSE
1. Al cleans the floor every day.	☐	☐
2. Al drops food every day.	☐	☐
3. Al likes to clean the floor.	☐	☐
4. Customers drop food in the produce section.	☐	☐
5. Al likes talking to people.	☐	☐
6. Al works at the checkout counter.	☐	☐

Name: _____   Date: _____

Grammar: Practicing *Yes/No* Questions

A. Directions: Match the questions and answers.

CUSTOMER	STORE CLERK
1. Can I pay with a check?	A. Yes, there is. It's near Aisle 1.
2. Do you have canned tomatoes?	B. Sure. We take cash, checks, or credit cards.
3. Do you work here?	C. Yes, I do. Can I help you?
4. Are grapes on sale this week?	D. Yes, we do. It's in the bakery.
5. Is vegetable oil on sale?	E. No, they aren't.
6. Is there a meat department?	F. Yes, we do. Aisle 3.
7. Do you have fresh bread?	G. Yes, it is. Two bottles for $3.

B. Directions: Look at the "big picture" in Unit 6, Lesson 2. You work in the store. Answer the customer's questions.

1. Do you sell oranges?   *Yes, we do.*

2. Do you sell bananas? _____

3. Do you sell shoes? _____

4. Do you have milk? _____

5. Do you sell ice? _____

6. Do you have an Aisle 8? _____

7. Do you have a customer service desk? _____

8. Do you have a bakery? _____

9. Do you have frozen foods? _____

10. Do you sell clothes? _____

11. Do you have bags for the vegetables? _____

Name: _____   Date: _____

Reading: A Family Portrait

A. Directions: Look at the "big picture" in Unit 7, Lesson 3. Read the story below.
Then answer the questions.

My name is Ivan Wasowski. I am from Poland. I live with my wife, Agnes, and her
brother, Max. Our daughter, Sophia, lives near us. Sophia is married to Jack. They have
three children, Annie, John, and Michael. We often go to the park. I usually play cards
with Max. John likes to take pictures. Michael likes to play with John. Our granddaughter
Annie is only four years old. She likes to play and walk with her mother. She loves her
grandmother very much. Agnes tells Annie stories about Poland. We are happy here.

1. Who is Ivan's wife?   _____

2. Who is Ivan's granddaughter?   _____

3. What are his grandsons' names?   _____

4. Who is Sophia?   _____

5. Who is Jack?   _____

6. Who likes to play cards?   _____

B. Directions: Look at "big picture" to identify the people described in the story.
Read the sentences below. Check *true* or *false* for each sentence.

1. John is taking a picture.   ☐ true   ☐ false

2. Michael is wearing a yellow shirt.   ☐ true   ☐ false

3. Max and Jack are playing cards.   ☐ true   ☐ false

4. John has yellow shorts.   ☐ true   ☐ false

Name: _____   Date: _____

Grammar: *Do, Does, Don't,* and *Doesn't*

A. Directions: Look at the "big picture" in Unit 7, Lesson 3. Write *do, does, don't,* or *doesn't* on the lines.

1. The boy has a camera to take pictures. He _____ have a hat.

2. The girl is riding her bike home. Where _____ she live?

3. The family is eating lunch at the table. They have chicken. They _____ have fish.

4. Where _____ the men play cards?

5. People play cards and soccer in the park. They _____ watch TV in the park.

6. The boys are playing soccer. _____ they have a soccer ball?

7. Where _____ the kids play?

8. How many cameras _____ the boy have?

9. What _____ the dog like to do?

10. The boy has a guitar. He _____ have a piano.

B. Directions: Look at the "big picture." Circle the correct answers.

1. The family at the table _____ rice.

   A. has   B. doesn't have

2. The men are playing cards. They always _____ at a table.

   A. sit   B. don't sit

3. The boys never play basketball. They _____ it.

   A. like   B. don't like

4. The park has lots of grass and trees. It _____ a store.

   A. has   B. doesn't have

5. The woman is holding her daughter's hand. She _____ a sweater, but she

   _____ shoes and a purse.

   A. doesn't have/has   B. has/doesn't have

Name: _____   Date: _____

Grammar: Giving Advice Using *Should*

A. Directions: Look at the "big picture" in Unit 8, Lesson 2. Look at the people.
Complete the sentences with a problem from Lesson 2, Learn New Words.

1. Erik has a _____.   5. Ken has a _____.

2. Tom has a _____.   6. Louis has a _____.

3. Tina has a _____.   7. Donna has a _____.

4. Rose's daughter has a _____.   8. Martin's son has an _____.

B. Directions: Complete the conversations below. Use *should* or *shouldn't.*

1. Erik: What should I do?

   Dr. Lambert: You _____ put heat on it. Heat is good for it.

2. Ken: Should I put ice on it?

   Dr. Lambert: No, you _____. You _____ use ear drops.

3. Louis: I feel terrible. What should I do?

   Dr. Lambert: You _____ rest and drink liquids. You _____ go to
   work.

4. Rose: Maria is very sick, Dr. Lambert. What should we do?

   Dr. Lambert: Well, Maria _____ go to school. She _____ rest, drink

   liquids, and take cough medicine.

Name: _____   Date: _____

Reading: Maria is Sick

A. Directions: Look at the "big picture" in Unit 8, Lesson 2. Read the story and identify Maria in the "big picture."

    Maria Cordero is sick today. She has a terrible cough. She also has a fever and a sore throat. Her mother, Rose, is at the doctor's office with Maria. Maria's birthdate is 10/23/1998. She is almost never sick. She never has stomachaches or headaches. Today, she has a sore throat, a cough, and a fever! Maria and Rose live at 1220 Central Avenue in Boston, MA. Their telephone number is (617) 555-8853. Maria is not taking medicine. Rose is thinking about giving Maria aspirin. She wants to ask the doctor first.

Question: Look at the picture. What is Maria wearing? _____

B. Directions: Read the sentences and check (✓) *True* or *False*.

	TRUE	FALSE
1. Maria is 30 years old.	☐	☐
2. It is lunchtime at the doctor's office.	☐	☐
3. Maria is coughing.	☐	☐
4. Rose and Maria are waiting to see the doctor.	☐	☐
5. Maria gets headaches often.	☐	☐
6. Maria is taking medicine now.	☐	☐
7. The doctor says it's OK to give Maria aspirin.	☐	☐

Name: _____   Date: _____

Writing: Completing a Patient Information Form

Directions: Look at the "big picture" in Unit 8, Lesson 2. Then reread the story about Maria in Lesson 4 Big Picture Expansion (Worksheet 16) to complete the form below. Use today's date and the current time.

Patient Information Form

Patient's Name: _____

Date: _____   Time: _____

Address: _____

_____

Birthdate: _____

Reason for visit: _____

Check if you have:

- ☐ headache   ☐ earache

- ☐ stomachache   ☐ fever

- ☐ sore throat   ☐ runny nose

- ☐ cough   ☐ backache

What medicine are you taking now? _____

_____

Name: _____   Date: _____

Reading: Where did it happen?

A. Directions: Look at the "big picture" in Unit 9, Lesson 2. Then read the story.

Poor Norman Lee

    Norman Lee has many accidents. He went to the hospital three times when the Lees lived in their old house. Norman went to the hospital two times last year. One time he slipped in the garage and cut his chin. Another time he fell off a chair on the porch and broke his arm. Last month, Norman slipped on the patio by the pool and cut his head. Last week, Norman played basketball with a friend. The basketball went up on the roof. Norman went up to get it. He fell off the ladder and hurt his hand. He was really hurt when he closed his finger in the red car's door. Poor Norman Lee.

B. Directions: Check the box that shows where the accident happened.

	OLD HOUSE	NEW HOUSE
1. Norman slipped in the garage and cut his chin.	❑	❑
2. He fell off a chair and broke his arm.	❑	❑
3. He slipped and cut his head.	❑	❑
4. He fell off the ladder and hurt his hand.	❑	❑
5. He hurt his finger in the car door.	❑	❑

Name: _____   Date: _____

Grammar: Describing the Lees' Old House

Directions: Look at the "big picture" in Unit 9, Lesson 2. Complete the sentences below using the affirmative or the negative form of the simple past. Choose A or B for each sentence.

1. The Lees' old house _____ a garden.
   A. had   B. didn't have

2. It _____ a garage.
   A. had   B. didn't have

3. The Lees _____ a pool at their old house.
   A. had   B. didn't have

4. The Lees _____ basketball at their old house.
   A. played   B. didn't play

5. Their old house _____ a blue door.
   A. had   B. didn't have

6. The Lees _____ a dog at their old house.
   A. owned   B. didn't own

7. The Lees don't rent their new house, but they _____ their old one.
   A. rented   B. didn't rent

8. In their old house, the Lees _____ a blue car.
   A. drove   B. didn't drive

Name: _____   Date: _____

Grammar: *Yes/No* Questions in the Simple Past Tense

A. Directions: Look at the "big picture" in Unit 10, Lesson 3. Write the name of the company in the picture that would value the work experience listed.

WORK EXPERIENCE	COMPANY
1. I type very fast. At my last job I entered a lot of information in the computer.	
2. I'm an engineer. I worked on making a solar-powered car at my last job.	
3. I'm a comedian. At my last job I went to birthday parties and made children laugh.	
4. I'm an engineer. I worked in construction and I traveled a lot at my last job.	

B. Directions: Complete the interviews. Use the information above to answer the questions with *Yes, I did,* or *No, I didn't.*

1. A: I see you want to be an engineer. Did you travel in your last job?

   B: _____

2. A: When you worked for the engineering company, did you take care of children?

   B: _____

3. A: When you worked as a comedian, did you cook food?

   B: _____

4. A: I see you can type very fast. Did you use a computer in your last job?

   B: _____

Name: _____   Date: _____

Reading: James Needs a New Job

A. Directions: Look at the "big picture" in Unit 10, Lesson 3. Read the story about James Mannah. Then answer the questions.

James Michael Mannah is from Ivory Coast in Africa. He moved to the United States a few years ago. James was a pharmacist in Africa from 1993–1998 at Pharmacie Premier. Before that, he was an office manager for West Africa Engineering, an engineering company, from 1990–1992. When he moved to the United States, James went to school to learn English. He is working as a chef's assistant in a Tony's Restaurant. He wants to work as an office manager again, so he is at the job fair. He wore his blue suit and red tie.

1. What was James' first job?   _____

2. What was James' second job?   _____

3. What is his current job?   _____

4. Where is James in the picture?   _____

B. Read the paragraph above. Complete the application for James Mannah.

Job Application
Personal Information

First Name: _____   Middle Initial: _____

Last Name: _____

Birth Date: ___02/01/1970___

Present Address: ___2919 8th Street___

City: ___Arlington___

State: ___VA___

Zip Code: ___22413___

Phone Number: ___(703) 555-8620___

Work Experience (start with the most recent)

When	Company	Occupation
2001–now		Chef's assistant
1990–1992		

Unit 1

Lesson 1

A.
1. Colombia
2. Somalia
3. Haiti
4. Canada
5. China
6. Brazil
7. France
8. Mexico
9. Vietnam
10. Morocco

B.
1. is
2. are
3. is
4. am
5. are
6. is
7. are
8. are
9. are
10. are
11. is

C.
1. They are from Mexico.
2. You are from Brazil.
3. She is from Haiti.
4. We are from Colombia.
5. He is from China.
6. They are from Canada.
7. It is in South America.

D.
1. b
2. f
3. e
4. c
5. a
6. d

E.
1. he's
2. I'm
3. they're
4. she's
5. we're
6. you're

Lesson 2

A.
1. chair
2. table
3. book
4. clock
5. map
6. computer

B.
1. b
2. a
3. c
4. b
5. c

C.
Answers may vary, but may include: table, desk, chair, book, sofa, television, etc.

D.
1. b
2. e
3. f
4. d
5. c
6. a

E.
Answers may vary.

Lesson 3

A.
Sit down. 5
Take out a piece of paper and a pencil. 1
Open your book to page 9. 4
Write your name on the piece of paper. 2
Listen to the words I say. 3
Write the words on the piece of paper. 6

B.
1, 4, 6, 7, 10

C.
1. book, 2. pen, 3. pencil, 5. piece of paper, 7. notebook

D.
Answers may vary.

E.
2 two
7 seven
9 nine
0 zero
8 eight
6 six
4 four
3 three
1 one
5 five

F.
1. three
2. five
3. ten
4. eight
5. six

G.
1. a
2. b
3. a
4. b

Lesson 4

A.
1. gender
2. female
3. street
4. single
5. address

B.
Answers may vary.

C.
1. c
2. e
3. d
4. f
5. b
6. a

D.
1. Where are you from?
2. I am from Hanoi, Vietnam.
3. What's the teacher's name?
4. Her name is Susan Foster.
5. What is his birthplace?
6. His birthplace is Guadalajara, Mexico.

E.
Questions
1. Where are you from.
3. What's the teacher's name?
5. What is his birthplace?

COPY FOR MONDAY

Answers

2. I am from Hanoi, Vietnam.

4. Her name is Susan Foster.

6. His birthplace is Guadalajara, Mexico.

F.

1. Rosa Lynch

2. Houston, Texas

3. Charlotte

4. 28204

5. 122 4th Street

Application Lesson: Family

A.

1. West Elementary

2. North High

3. South Middle

C.

1. 3	4. 10
2. 2	5. 2
3. 4	6. 1

D.

1. South Middle School

2. 58 Elm Street

3. Charlotte

4. 9–12

5. West Elementary School

E.

1. 3	4. 9
2. 2	5. 3
3. 4	

Take It Outside

Answers may vary.

Application Lesson: Community

B.

1. Keiko

2. Rosa Lynch

3. Ishikawa

4. Rosa

5. 44 Market Street; Charlotte, North Carolina, 28205

C.

1. yes	4. yes
2. no	5. no
3. yes	6. yes

D.

Answers may vary.

Take It Outside

Answers may vary.

Review

1. a	6. a
2. c	7. b
3. a	8. c
4. b	9. c
5. d	10. a

Spotlight: Grammar

A.

My name <u>is</u> Patricia. I <u>am</u> from Ghana. My teacher <u>is</u> from the United States. Her name <u>is</u> Monica Timmons. <u>I'm</u> married. There <u>are</u> 22 students in my class. Five students <u>are</u> from Somalia, and ten <u>are</u> from Mexico. Six students <u>are</u> Chinese. They <u>are</u> from Beijing. <u>I'm</u> the only student from Ghana. We <u>are</u> all in English class.

B.

1. is	4. are
2. is	5. isn't
3. is	6. isn't

C.

1. I'm	8. you're not; you aren't
2. you're	9. he isn't
3. we're	10. I'm not
4. he's	11. they aren't; they're not
5. it's	12. she isn't; she's not
6. she's	13. it isn't; it's not
7. they're	14. we aren't; we're not

D.

I: my	he: his
you: your	we: our
she: her	they: their

E.

1. a	4. b
2. b	5. c
3. c	

Unit 2

Lesson 1

A.

1. school

2. supermarket

3. gas station

4. park

B.

1. police station

2. library

3. community center

4. fire station

5. school

C.

1. b	4. d
2. a	5. f
3. e	6. c

D.

1. There are seven restaurants in Marshville.
2. There is one drugstore on Main Street.
3. There is one library on Baxter Street.
4. There are ten gas stations in my city.
5. There are two police stations in town.
6. There are three laundromats in my city.

E.

1. a	3. a
2. a	4. b

F.

Answers may vary.

G.

Answers may vary.

Lesson 2

A.

1. next to
2. across from
3. in back of; next to
4. between
5. on the corner of

B.

1. Yes, there is.
2. No, there isn't.
3. Yes, there is.
4. No, there isn't.
5. No, there isn't.

C.

1. police station
2. hospital
3. restaurant
4. Third, State
5. gas station

D.

1. It's next to the restaurant. / It's across from the bank.
2. Yes, it is.
3. You're welcome.

E.

schools, supermarkets, restaurants, community center, post office, laundromat

F.

Near Ballenbrook Estates: schools, supermarkets, restaurants

In Ballenbrook Estates: community center, post office, laundromat

G.

1. A: Is there a movie theater near your home?

   B: Answers may vary.
2. A: Are there any drugstores in your town?

   B: Answers may vary.

H.

Answers may vary.

Lesson 3

A.

1. parking
2. bus stop
3. mailbox
4. pay phone
5. car
6. a stop light
7. ATM
8. police
9. laundromat

B.

4, 1, 2, 3

C.

1. No, there isn't./No, there's not.
2. Yes, there is.
3. Yes, there is.

D.

1. e	4. c
2. b	5. a
3. d	

E.

1. There is one
2. There are two
3. There are three
4. There is one
5. There is one
6. There is one

F.

Answers may vary.

Lesson 4

A.

1. b	4. a
2. b	5. b
3. a	6. b

B.

1. Locke
2. Washington, Locke
3. Washington, Oakton
4. Mashburn
5. Washington

C.

1. 5	4. 6
2. 8	5. 5
3. 12	6. 8

D.

1. 5 + 5 = 10
2. 5 + 8 = 13
3. 12 + 6 = 18
4. 5 < 8
5. 6 + 6 = 12
6. 12 − 2 = 10

E.

Answers may vary.

F.

Answers may vary.

Application Lesson: Family

B.

1. near/in front of
2. next to
3. in front of/next to
4. across from
5. between

C.

1. f   4. c
2. b   5. d
3. e   6. a

D.

Actual answers may vary.
Suggested answers:

1. It's near the gym.
2. It's across from the cafeteria.
3. It's next to the main office.
4. It's next to the nurse's office.
5. It's across from the gym.
6. It's next to the library.

F.

1. yes   4. no
2. no   5. no
3. yes

Take It Outside

Answers may vary.

Application Lesson: Work

B.

1. bus driver
2. Hoover Elementary School
3. mileage log
4. cities, gas station
5. Highway 321

C.

1. Marco is a bus driver.
2. He works at Hoover Elementary School.
3. It's 1.5 miles from the school to the gas station.
4. It's 10 miles from the school to the town of Locke and back.
5. His last name is Santori.
6. The school is on Highway 321.

D, E, F, Take It Outside

Answers may vary.

Review

1. c   6. a
2. b   7. c
3. a   8. b
4. a   9. d
5. c   10. c

Unit 3

Lesson 1

A.

1. 2:00
2. 8:10
3. 9:45
4. 10:15
5. 11:00
6. 4:30
7. 1:45
8. 7:30
9. 3:15
10. 6:20

B.

1. fifteen
2. 46
3. seventeen
4. thirty-two
5. 29
6. 33
7. fifty-two
8. thirty-five
9. 55
10. eighteen

C.

1. It's one o'clock.
2. It's nine-thirty.
3. No, it isn't. It's ten o'clock.
4. Yes, it is.

D.

Answers may vary.

E.

1. in the morning
2. minutes
3. noon
4. A.M.
5. after
6. before
7. at night

F.

1. Is   4. Are
2. Is   5. Is
3. Are

Lesson 2

A.

B.

1. Wednesday
2. Thursday
3. Monday
4. morning, night
5. closed

C.

1. from 7:00 A.M. to 5:30 P.M.
2. from 8:00 A.M. to noon
3. No. It is closed.
4. from 7:00 A.M. to 4:30 P.M.
5. from 7:00 A.M. to 5:30 P.M.
6. from 7:00 A.M. to 5:30 P.M.

D.

1. yes
2. yes
3. no
4. yes
5. yes

E.

1. When is the library open on Tuesday?
2. Is the supermarket open at midnight?
3. The gas station is closed at 5:00 A.M.
4. The hospital is open Sunday to Saturday.
5. The park is closed at 6:00 P.M.

Lesson 3

A.

1. penny
2. nickel
3. dime
4. quarter
5. dollar

B.

1. 25¢
2. $1.00
3. five dollars
4. 5¢
5. $20.00
6. fifty dollars
7. a dime
8. $1,000.00

C.

1. $11.00
2. 30¢
3. $53.00
4. 35¢
5. 65¢
6. 71¢
7. 20¢
8. 65¢
9. 6¢
10. 15¢

D.

1. b
2. e
3. c
4. d
5. a

E.

Answers may vary.

Lesson 4

A.

1. no
2. yes
3. yes
4. yes
5. yes
6. no
7. no
8. no
9. no
10. yes

B.

1. a
2. a
3. b
4. a
5. b

C.

1. $13.50
2. $7.90
3. $30.00
4. $4.95
5. $14.95
6. $5.00
7. $4.50
8. 75¢
9. $43.00
10. $8.00

D.

$100.00 − $7.90 = $92.10
$92.10 − $22.10 = $70.00
$70.00 − $20.00 = $50.00
$50.00 − $10.00 = $40.00
$40.00 − $15.00 = $25.00
$25.00 − $15.00 = $10.00

Application Lesson: Work

B.

1. a
2. b
3. b
4. a
5. b

C.

1. full-time
2. salary
3. vacation
4. vacation leave

D.

1. b
2. a
3. d
4. e
5. f
6. c

E.

1. $10.00
2. 40
3. $400.00
4. 6

Take It Outside

Answers may vary.

Application Lesson: Family

B.

1. hotel
2. $69
3. $30
4. car
5. 1300 South Street
6. 1-800-555-3211

C.

Sand Castle Beach Hotel: telephone number, amount of money for a room, name of the hotel

Martin Autos: address, amount of money for a car, name of car company, days of the week

D.

1. $198
2. $426
3. $129
4. $237

Take It Outside

Answers may vary.

Review

1. a
2. a
3. a
4. b
5. d
6. d
7. b
8. c
9. a
10. b

Spotlight: Grammar

A.

1. f
2. c
3. d
4. e
5. b
6. a

B.

1. No, she isn't.
2. Yes, they are.
3. No, they aren't.
4. No, they aren't.

C.

Charles: Ivory Coast, salesclerk, married

Bernadette: Ivory Coast, nurse, married

D.

1. It's a book.
2. Tracy Edwards
3. It's $10.95.
4. They're on the desk.
5. from 9:00 A.M. to 4:00 P.M.

E.

A: Who is _____?
B: Terry Winter.
A: Where is _____?
B: It's on Main Street.
A: Where is _____?/
   What's the address _____?
B: 3215 Park Street.
A: Where are they from _____?
B: They're from Russia.

Unit 4

Lesson 1

A.

1. January
2. February
3. March
4. April
5. May
6. June
7. July
8. August
9. September
10. October
11. November
12. December

B.

Answers may vary.

C.

1. 2
2. 5
3. 0
4. 4
5. 0
6. 3

D.

1. a
2. c
3. b
4. c
5. b
6. b

E.

Answers may vary.

Lesson 2

A.

1. birthday party
2. job interview
3. PTO meeting
4. basketball game
5. dentist appointment
6. doctor's appointment

B.

1. first
2. seventh
3. fifteenth
4. third
5. ninth
6. eighth
7. thirteenth
8. second
9. fifth
10. twelfth

C.

2—What day is that?
4—Oh, sorry. I have a job interview on Thursday.
3—It's Thursday.
1—Do you want to meet on the 2nd?
5—Some other time, then.

D.

1. b
2. e
3. c
4. a
5. d
6. f

E.

Answers may vary.

Lesson 3

A.

1. 17th
2. twenty-second
3. twentieth
4. 23rd
5. twenty-eighth

B.

1. Thursday
2. 2:30 P.M.
3. Sarah Parker
4. May 13

C.

1. a	4. b
2. b	5. a
3. a	6. b

D.

1. February 9, 2005
2. July 15, 1999
3. 8/1/02
4. May 31, 1960
5. 3/3/91
6. January 1, 2003
7. 4/9/01
8. December 25, 1972
9. September 12, 2006
10. 6/8/95

E.

1. A: What day is the basketball game?
   B: It's on Friday.
2. A: When is the PTO meeting?
   B: It's on March 13th.
3. A: What day is that?
   B: It's Tuesday.

F.

Michiko Jones

has a dentist's appointment on: 12/8/04 at 10:30 A.M.

(M) T W TH F

Lesson 4

A.

Across:

1. Valentine's
3. Independence
4. Thanksgiving
6. New Year's

Down:

2. Election Day
5. Day

B.

C.

1. New Year's Day
2. Valentine's Day
3. Independence Day
4. Labor Day
5. Election Day
6. Thanksgiving

D.

Singular: book, teacher, hour, week, city

Plural: desks, students, holidays, words, libraries

E.

1. drugstores	6. minutes
2. days	7. notebooks
3. stoplights	8. telephones
4. pennies	9. dollars
5. restaurants	10. families

F.

Answers may vary.

G.

Answers may vary.

Application Lesson: Community

A.

Days: today (Friday), Saturday, Sunday

Times: 7:00 P.M., 8:00–10:00 P.M.; 1:00–3:00 P.M., 4:00 P.M., 5:00 P.M., 9:00 P.M., 9:00 P.M.

B.

1. d	4. c
2. e	5. b
3. a	

C.

1. Community Fun Day, Library Birthday Party
2. Community Fun Day, Library Birthday Party, Independence Day Parade and Fireworks
3. Library Birthday Party, Independence Day Parade

D.

1. 8:00 to 10:00 P.M.
2. Mexico, China, Japan, France, Colombia
3. $3
4. 3215 Caldwell Street
5. Saturday, 1:00 to 3:00 P.M.
6. Independence
7. July 4
8. Marshall
9. 100; birthday
10. K–8

Take It Outside

Answers may vary.

Application Lesson: Work

A.

1. Lee
2. the Alden Community Center
3. 6
4. 2
5. Monday to Friday
6. Monday, June 28

B.

Room 1: 6/10–6/11
Room 2: 6/14–6/15
Room 3: 6/16–6/17
Room 4: 6/18–6/21
Room 5: 6/22–6/23
Room 6: 6/24–6/25

C.

14: Start room 2
15: Finish room 2
16: Start room 3
17: Finish room 3
18: Start room 4
21: Finish room 4
22: Start room 5
23: Finish room 5
24: Start room 6
25: Finish room 6

Take It Outside

Answers may vary.

Review

1. b
2. b
3. c
4. c
5. b
6. b
7. d
8. b
9. c
10. c

Unit 5

Lesson 1

A.

Singular: necktie, undershirt, coat, shirt, sweater, hat, T-shirt, jacket, blouse, skirt, dress

Plural: briefs, shoes, boots, pajamas, socks, pants, shorts

B.

1. is
2. are
3. are
4. is
5. are
6. is
7. are
8. are
9. is
10. are
11. is

C.

1. A: What <u>is</u> John wearing?
   B: He <u>is</u> wearing a blue sweater.
2. A: Where <u>is</u> my green dress?
   B: I <u>am</u> wearing it.
3. A: I <u>am</u> wearing a red blouse.
   B: No, you <u>are</u> not. Your blouse <u>is</u> pink.
4. A: <u>Is</u> Lana wearing a dress?
   B: No, she <u>is</u> not. She <u>is</u> wearing a skirt.
5. A: What <u>are</u> Sara and Tom wearing?
   B: They <u>are</u> wearing orange shirts.

D.

1. no
2. yes
3. no
4. no
5. yes
6. no

E.

Answers may vary.

Lesson 2

A.

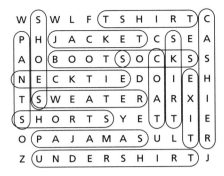

B.

4—The third floor?
1—Can I help you?
3—They're on the third floor.
5—That's right.
2—Yes, I'm looking for children's clothes.
6—Thanks.

C.

1. a
2. a
3. b
4. a
5. a
6. b

D.

1. am
2. are
3. are
4. is
5. are
6. is

E.

Answers may vary.

Lesson 3

A.

small < medium < large < extra large

B.

S—small
M—medium
L—large
XL—extra large

C.

1. b	4. c
2. a	5. a
3. a	6. b

D.

1. $5 \times 3 = 15$
2. $6 \times 3 = 18$
3. $20 \div 5 = 4$
4. $2 \times 4 = 8$
5. $30 \div 3 = 10$
6. $24 \div 8 = 3$

E.

1. three blouses = $30.00
2. two pairs of socks = $4.00
3. one pair of shoes = $20.00
4. two neckties = $24.00
5. one pair of pants = $15
   Total = $93.00

F.

Answers may vary.

Lesson 4

B.

9. Hans buys soap at the store.
4. Hans bumps into an old woman.
10. Hans's mother washes his dirty clothes.
2. Hans steps in a hole.
5. Hans helps the woman. She stands up.
1. Hans's mother asks Hans to go to the store.
6. Hans sees an old man.
3. A man tells Hans the street is slippery.
7. An old man tells Hans to wash.
8. Hans goes into the store.

C.

1. Hans buys <u>it</u> at the store.
2. Hans bumps into <u>her</u>.
3. Hans's mother washes <u>them</u>.
4. Hans steps in <u>it</u>.
5. Hans helps <u>her</u>. She stands up.
6. Hans's mother asks <u>him</u> to go to the store.
7. Hans sees <u>him</u>.
8. A man tells <u>him</u> the street is slippery.
9. An old man tells <u>him</u> to wash.
10. Hans goes into <u>it</u>.

D.

1. cold	3. yes
2. hot	4. small

Application Lesson: Community

A.

1. Karina
2. Casual Clothes
3. blue
4. The pants are too big.
5. No

C.

Information includes: name of customer, address of customer, problem with clothes, telephone number of customer, description of clothes, color of clothes, city, price, how to handle the return

Information does not include: size of clothes, school

D.

Answers may vary.

Take It Outside

Answers may vary.

Application Lesson: Family

A.

1. yes	4. no
2. no	5. no
3. no	6. no

B.

Blue clothes: pants, slacks, shorts, skirts

Blue or white: sweaters, socks, tights

White clothes: shirts

C.

1. b	3. d
2. c	4. a

D.

1. short/tight
2. large
3. T-shirt

Take It Outside

Answers may vary.

Review

1. a	6. d
2. b	7. d
3. c	8. a
4. d	9. c
5. c	10. a

Spotlight: Grammar

A.

1. is	4. am
2. are	5. is not
3. are	6. are not

B.

1. I am going to the store now.
2. I am studying English.
3. She is reading her book.
4. The library is opening at 10:00 A.M.
5. We are listening to the radio.
6. They are sleeping.

C.

1. Their class is over.
2. Mr. and Mrs. Zinberg
3. a black sweater
4. next to Darren

D.

1. Who is standing by the board?
2. What are you wearing today?
3. Where are your parents living?
4. Why are you learning English?
5. Who is listening in the class?

Answers to the questions above may vary.

Unit 6

Lesson 1
A.

Yellow: bananas, butter

Green: beans, grapes, apples, lettuce

Orange: oranges, carrots

B.

1. are	5. are
2. are	6. Is
3. is	7. are
4. is	8. is

C.

1. chicken
2. noodles
3. yes
4. Saturday
5. Thursday
6. Tuesday

D.

Answers may vary.

E.

1. no	4. yes
2. no	5. yes
3. yes	

F.

Answers may vary.

G.

Answers may vary.

Lesson 2
A.

1. fruit
2. bakery
3. frozen food
4. vegetables
5. canned goods
6. dairy

B.

1. bakery
2. fruit; vegetables
3. dairy

C.

1. b	4. a
2. a	5. b
3. b	6. a

D.

1. b
2. a
3. c

E.

1. yes	4. no
2. yes	5. no
3. no	6. no

Lesson 3
A.

1. h	6. a
2. c, e	7. c, g
3. d,f	8. e
4. c	9. c
5. b	10. d

B.

bottle: oil, milk

jar: honey, jelly

carton: milk

box: cereal, sugar

Actual food answers may vary.

C.

1. 32 tablespoons
2. 32 ounces
3. 16 fluid ounces
4. 1.5 pounds
5. 4 fluid ounces
6. 1.5 cups

D.

1. $6.99
2. $13.98
3. 5.0 pounds
4. ½, .5
5. $6.99
6. $3.00

Lesson 4
A.

Milk: $3, (2/$5 =) $2.50, 50¢

Honey: $2, $1.50, 50¢

Carrots: $3.00, $1.99, $1.01

B.

1. 64 fluid ounces
2. 8 ounces
3. 3 pounds

C.

1. c	4. e
2. b	5. d
3. f	6. a

D.

Answers may vary.

E.
1. 2
2. 3
3. $2.00
4. $4.99
5. $2.99
6. $2.00

Application Lesson: Community
B.
1. sometimes
2. usually
3. sometimes
4. always
5. always
6. often

C.
Milk: $2.99
Bananas: $ .59
Shrimp: $5.99
Butter: $3.35

D.
1. a   4. c
2. c   5. b
3. a   6. b

Take It Outside
Answers may vary.

Application Lesson: Work
A.
1. meat, cheese, vegetables
2. restaurant, sandwiches

B.
1. no   3. yes
2. no   4. no
   (He *circles* the kind of bread
   the *customer* wants.)

C.
1. Lunch for You
2. Walter Arakaki
3. American
4. No
5. No
6. Ham

D.
Answers may vary.

Take It Outside
Answers may vary.

Review
1. a   6. c
2. b   7. a
3. d   8. d
4. b   9. a
5. c   10. b

Unit 7

Lesson 1
A.
From left to right:
brother
niece
father
mother
daughter
Elizabeth
husband

B.
1. false   4. false
2. true   5. false
3. true   6. false

C.
1. Does   4. Do
2. Do   5. Does
3. Does   6. Does

D.
1. Do you live with your parents?
2. Does your brother live near you?
3. Do you have children?
4. Does your grandfather play cards?
5. Do they live alone?
6. Does he have brothers?

E.
Answers may vary.

Lesson 2
A.
1. c   5. g
2. e   6. d
3. b   7. a
4. f

B.
1. Madeline   4. Yes
2. Charmaine 5. No
3. Madeline   6. No

C.
+ S: cook, take, tell, make, buy, work, read, clean, live, play
+ ES: watch, go, do, wash, fix

D.
Everyone in my family helps at home. I cook dinner on Monday and Wednesday. My mother always does the laundry. My father washes the dishes after dinner. My sisters take out the trash. My brothers clean the house. We all make our beds in the morning. My mother usually pays the bills, but sometimes my father does. Do you help at home?

E.
Answers may vary.

F.
Answers may vary.

Lesson 3

A.

1. a   4. b
2. b   5. a
3. b   6. b

B.

1. play soccer
2. listen to music
3. play cards
4. read the newspaper

C.

Answers may vary.

D.

play: soccer, music, cards, an instrument

listen to: music, the story, the teacher, an instrument

read: the book, music, the newspaper, the story

Lesson 4

A.

Across:

1. granddaughter
4. mother
5. father
6. husband

Down:

1. grandfather
2. aunt
3. nephew

B.

C.

1. cards   4. son
2. dishes   5. cards
3. story   6. wash

D.

1. don't   7. don't
2. doesn't   8. doesn't
3. don't   9. don't
4. doesn't   10. doesn't
5. don't   11. don't
6. don't

E.

My mother <u>cleans</u> our house. She <u>doesn't clean/does not</u> every day because she <u>works</u> too. My father <u>drives</u> a bus. He <u>goes</u> to work Monday through Friday. I <u>take</u> out the trash. My brother <u>cooks</u> dinner. My sister <u>doesn't do/does not do</u> anything. She is a baby. My grandmother and grandfather <u>live</u> with us. They <u>don't go/do not go</u> to school or to work. My grandmother <u>listens</u> to music. My grandfather <u>reads</u> the newspaper. We <u>don't play/do not play</u> cards, but we <u>play</u> soccer.

F.

Answers may vary.

Application Lesson: Family

A.

1. 32 Hampstead Street
2. Thomas
3. April 15, 1965
4. (depends on today's date)
5. (704) 555-9023
6. Laura Costa

B.

Martin Costa, ____, -----
Sarah Costa, ____, wife
Thomas, ____, son
Hannah, ____, daughter
Laura, ____, mother

C.

1. no   4. yes
2. no   5. no
3. yes   6. no

D.

Answers may vary.

Take It Outside

Answers may vary.

Application Lesson: Work

A.

1. U.S. Family and Medical Leave Act of 1993
2. family leave
3. medical emergency

B.

1. c   3. c
2. b   4. c

C.

1. Rick   4. Rick
2. Tony   5. Tony
3. Tony   6. Rick

D.

1. His mother hurt her back. He has to take care of her.
2. Tony's mother lives with him.
3. She is 80 years old.
4. Tony needs 6 weeks leave.
5. The leave starts next week.

Take It Outside
Answers may vary.

Review
1. d	6. b
2. a	7. a
3. c	8. c
4. d	9. b
5. c	10. a

Spotlight: Grammar
A.
1. doesn't	4. don't
2. don't	5. don't
3. don't	6. doesn't

B.
1. like, don't like
2. has, doesn't have
3. go, don't go
4. pays, doesn't pay

C.
1. I want fish.
2. She lives in Omaha.
3. at 7:00 A.M.
4. Yes, I do.
5. Mac Everland

D.
1. How many hours <u>do</u> you work?
2. Who <u>does</u> your teacher live with?
3. Where <u>do</u> your parents live?
4. When <u>does</u> the class start?
5. What <u>does</u> your family eat for breakfast?
6. How much <u>does</u> a shirt cost?

Answers to the questions above may vary.

Unit 8

Lesson 1
A.
From top center line, moving clockwise: arm, head, shoulder, elbow, back, knee, foot, ankle, leg, hand

B.
1. finger	5. mouth
2. throat	6. chest
3. wrist	7. nose
4. stomach	

C.
1. no	4. yes
2. no	5. no
3. yes	6. yes

D.
Answers may vary.

E.
1. Can you touch your toes?
2. I can read a book in English.
3. They can drive to school.
4. We can go to the store.
5. Can he cook dinner?
6. Can Giovanna go to school?

Lesson 2
A.
1. b	3. a
2. d	4. c

B.
1. b	4. b
2. a	5. a
3. a	

C.
1. earache
2. backache
3. stomachache
4. sore throat

D.
1. Barbara Ann Peppers
2. October 17, 1978
3. headaches, earaches
4. Health Plus
5. a terrible cough

E.
Answers may vary.

Lesson 3
A.
1. heat	4. food
2. medicine	5. liquids
3. dry	6. ear drops

B
headaches; headache; backache; fever; cough; runny nose; fever.

C.
1. a
2. c
3. b

D.
Answers may vary.

E.
Should: see a doctor every year, do your homework, read to your children, play with your children, eat healthy food

Shouldn't: watch TV every day, sleep in class, drive a car without a driver's license, use ear drops for a headache, eat ice cream for every meal

F.
1. You shouldn't go to bed.
2. You shouldn't see a doctor.
3. We shouldn't have a party.
4. They shouldn't pay the bill.
5. She shouldn't be late.
6. I shouldn't eat dinner.

Lesson 4

B.
1. ammonia
2. bleach
3. heat
4. Clear Glass, Ants Out, and Chlor-Up
5. flush
6. clothes

C.
1. false
2. false
3. true
4. true
5. true
6. false

D.
1. ½
2. 16
3. 5
4. 4
5. 2

E.
Clear Glass Cleaner: 64 oz, 4 pints
Ants Out: 24 oz., 1.5 pt.
Chlor-Up Cleaner: 32 oz., 2 pt.

Application Lesson: Work

B.
1. accident
2. place
3. injury
4. supervisor

C.
1. yes
2. no
3. yes
4. yes
5. no
6. yes

D.
Peter Barks; single; construction worker; 7/23; 1:17 P.M.; First Market Bank - 100 Center Street; cut; hand

E.
1. Line 2
2. Line 3
3. Line 4
4. Line 2
5. Line 1
6. Line 5

Take It Outside
Answers may vary.

Application Lesson: Family

A.
1. a
2. c
3. b

B.
1. the doctor's office
2. Lin's ears and eyes
3. the dentist

D.
1. income
2. discount
3. immunization
4. offer
5. exam

E.
1. e
2. a
3. d
4. c
5. b
6. f

Take It Outside
Answers may vary.

Review
1. a
2. b
3. c
4. d
5. c
6. d
7. c
8. b
9. b
10. a

Unit 9

Lesson 1

A.
Answers may vary. Possibilities include:

Bathroom—bathtub, cabinet, shower, toilet

Bedroom—bookcase, lamp, bed, dresser, table, carpet, closet, chair

Dining room—lamp, smoke alarm, table, carpet, chair

Kitchen—lamp, cabinet, stove, smoke alarm, table, refrigerator, closet, chair

Living room—bookcase, lamp, cabinet, smoke alarm, table, carpet, sofa, chair

B.
1. true
2. false
3. false
4. true
5. false
6. false

C.
Answers may vary.

D.
1. have, had
2. had
3. has
4. has
5. has
6. had

E.
1. was
2. is
3. was
4. were
5. are
6. was

F.
1. There is a cabinet in his kitchen.
2. My bathroom has a shower.
3. The bed is in Mandy's bedroom.
4. There are four smoke detectors in my house.

Lesson 2

A.

pool, garden, yard, patio

B.

1. e	4. c
2. a	5. b
3. f	6. d

C.

1. car	4. chairs
2. flowers	5. fire
3. grass	6. water

D.

1. a	4. b
2. b	5. b
3. a	6. a

E.

Answers may vary.

F.

1. yes	4. yes
2. no	5. yes
3. yes	

Lesson 3

A.

1. fell	6. needed
2. slipped	7. worked
3. cut	8. hurt
4. liked	9. wanted
5. got	10. tripped

B.

Regular: slipped, liked, needed, worked, wanted, tripped

Irregular: fell, cut, got, hurt

C.

1. hurt	4. worked
2. cut	5. fell
3. got	6. slipped

D.

1. e	4. d
2. b	5. c
3. a	

F.

Picture A: Step 5

Picture B: Step 4

G.

1. no	4. no
2. yes	5. yes
3. yes	

H.

Answers may vary.

Lesson 4

A.

B.

1. b	4. c
2. d	5. e
3. f	6. a

C.

1. bought	4. was
2. needed	5. called
3. had	6. liked

D.

1. Tamara didn't like the party.
2. Sammy didn't want a banana.
3. We didn't work very hard yesterday.
4. They didn't need books for class.
5. You didn't get hurt in the game.
6. I didn't fall off the ladder.

E.

Answers may vary.

Application Lesson: Work

B.

1. c	4. e
2. f	5. d
3. b	6. a

C.

1. slip	4. hurt
2. leave	5. cut
3. fall	

D.

Last week, Rita slipped on the floor at work. There was some oil on the floor. She hurt her back. Rita is better now. She is back at work. Her supervisor had a meeting yesterday with all the workers. Now everyone is careful. All the workers clean up water on the floor.

E.

Answers may vary.

Take It Outside

Answers may vary.

Application Lesson: Community

A.

Housing discrimination is not being able to get housing based on race, color, nationality, religion, sex, family status, or disability. (Specific language will vary.)

B.

1. a	3. b
2. b	4. c

C.

Answers may vary.

D.

1. c	4. e
2. a	5. d
3. b	

Take It Outside

Answers may vary.

Review

1. c	6. d
2. a	7. b
3. d	8. b
4. b	9. b
5. d	10. c

Spotlight: Grammar

A.

1. I cooked rice yesterday.
2. My sister cleaned the house yesterday.
3. My teacher ran 40 minutes yesterday.
4. The Hermans washed their car yesterday.
5. He drank apple juice yesterday.

B.

1. walked, didn't drive
2. got up, didn't sleep
3. didn't go, was
4. didn't work, spent
5. ate, didn't drink

C.

_2_ They were on sale.
_1_ I went to school and to work.
_6_ We ate at home.
_7_ I watched about 2 hours.
_4_ I went to bed at 10:00 P.M.
_3_ I bought 12.
_5_ I wrote to my parents.

D.

Answers may vary.

Unit 10

Lesson 1

A.

1. i	6. g
2. a	7. e
3. f	8. c
4. j	9. h
5. b	10. d

B.

1. Claire can drive a car, take care of children, and use a computer.
2. No, Claire wants a part-time job for after school.
3. Claire can be a child care worker, a receptionist, or an office worker. Other answers may vary.

C.

Answers may vary.

D.

Answers may vary.

E.

1. a	4. b
2. a	5. a
3. b	6. a

Lesson 2

A.

1. req'd	4. FT
2. hr.	5. exp.
3. eves.	6. PT

B.

1. office manager
2. office manager, landscaper
3. stylist
4. stylist
5. stylist
6. $18
7. office manager
8. driver's license
9. landscaper
10. stylist
11. office manager

C.

Office manager: Full-time; $400/week; experience, computer and office skills; fax resume

Landscaper: Full-time; $18; Driver's license; In person

Stylist: Part-time; $8.50/hour, nothing is required; Call

D.

1. $720
2. $216
3. $10
4. $85
5. $115

E.

_2_ Do you have experience?

_4_ Can you come in for an interview tomorrow at 10?

_3_ Yes, I do. I was a mechanic for 3 years in Mexico.

_1_ I'm calling about the ad for a mechanic.

_5_ Yes. I'll be there at 10.

Lesson 3
A.

1. c	4. f
2. b	5. d
3. e	6. a

B.

Answers may vary.

C.

1. truck driver
2. child care worker
3. chef
4. landscaper
5. mover

D.

1. false	4. true
2. false	5. true
3. true	6. false

Lesson 4
B.

_6_ Douglas Nichols died.

_2_ Doug got his first job.

_1_ He was born.

_3_ He married Sophia.

_4_ Doug became the owner of Nichols Motorcycle Company.

_5_ He finished college.

C.

1939 was born

1958 got his first job

1964 married Sophia

1966 became owner

1989 decided to go back to school

1994 finished college

1995 started teaching

2004 died

D.

Answers may vary.

E.

1. am	4. are
2. is	5. is
3. Is	6. Are

F.

Answers may vary.

Application Lesson: Family
A.

Answers may vary.

B.

wants to be a chef; wants to work in a nice restaurant; start classes at the community college in September; wants Claudia to have child care after school

C.

Be a chef: Start classes at the community college to study how to be a chef

Save money for classes: Work extra hours at the store

Have child care for Claudia: Ask her sister to take care of Claudia

D.

Answers may vary.

Take It Outside

Answers may vary.

Application Lesson: Community
A.

1. b	3. d
2. c	4. a

C.

1. Question 5
2. Question 4
3. Question 3
4. Question 2
5. Question 4
6. Question 5

D.

1. true	4. false
2. true	5. true
3. false	6. true

Take It Outside

Answers may vary.

Review

1. a	6. a
2. b	7. c
3. c	8. d
4. d	9. d
5. a	10. b

Name _____ Date _____ Score _____

LISTENING: Listen to the conversations. Then choose the correct answer for each question.

Conversation 1 🎧

1. What is the man's name?
   A. Victor
   B. Paolo
   C. Ben

2. Where is he from?
   A. Mary
   B. Somalia
   C. Mexico

Conversation 2 🎧

3. The woman's name is _____.
   A. Ms. Jones
   B. Mr. Campos
   C. Mrs. Helen

4. The man's first name is _____.
   A. Campos
   B. Martin
   C. Jones

5. In this conversation, the 2 people are _____.
   A. meeting for the first time
   B. introducing a friend
   C. saying goodbye

GRAMMAR: Choose the word or punctuation mark that correctly completes each sentence.

6. We _____ from Japan.
   A. am
   B. is
   C. are

7. I _____ a teacher.
   A. am
   B. is
   C. are

8. They _____ students.
   A. am
   B. is
   C. are

9. Where _____ you from?
   A. am
   B. is
   C. are

10. This _____ my friend.
    A. am
    B. is
    C. are

11. What is your last name___
    A. .
    B. ?
    C. ,

12. I am a student___
    A. .
    B. ?
    C. ,

13. He is from Paris___ France.
    A. .
    B. ?
    C. ,

READING/VOCABULARY: Read the following ads. Then choose the answer that correctly completes each sentence.

Immediate Openings for Nurses **Call (603) 555-7000 for an interview. Experience necessary.** **Mercy Hospital** **3299 Porter Ave.**	**Bus Driver Wanted** Earn $16/hour Call for an interview: (405) 555-1276	**SALESCLERK** Evenings and weekends. Apply in person: Andrew's Men Shop 949 South St.

14. Mercy Hospital has jobs for _____.
    A. bus drivers
    B. nurses
    C. doctors

15. For the sales clerk job, _____.
    A. go to 3299 Porter Avenue
    B. call (405) 555-1276
    C. go to 949 South Street

16. The telephone number for the bus driver job is _____.
    A. (603) 555-7000
    B. (405) 555-1276
    C. $16/hour

17. Is there is an ad for a pharmacist?
    A. yes
    B. no

18. Is the telephone number for Mercy Hospital (603) 555-1276?
    A. yes
    B. no

19–20. WRITING: Complete the following form with your personal information.

Application Form

Name: _____
      First   Middle   Last

Address: _____
        Street   City   State   Zip Code

Name _____ Date _____ Score _____

LISTENING: Listen to the conversations. Then choose the correct answer for each question.

Conversation 1 🎧

1. What does the man want?

   A. a school

   B. a post office

   C. a police station

2. Where is it?

   A. on Pine Street

   B. next to the police station

   C. on College Street

3. Where is the police station?

   A. in back of the post office

   B. across from the post office

   C. between the post office and the college

Conversation 2 🎧

4. Does the woman want to find a gas station?

   A. yes

   B. no

5. Is the ATM across from the bank?

   A. yes

   B. no

6. Are the man and the woman friends?

   A. yes

   B. no

GRAMMAR: Choose the word or phrase that correctly completes each sentence.

7. There _____ 2 restaurants in town.

   A. is

   B. are

   C. am

8. There _____ a hospital near the school.

   A. is

   B. are

   C. am

9. Excuse me, _____ 2 gas stations on Pine Street?

   A. are there

   B. is there

   C. there is

10. Mr. Sutton, _____ a library near here?

    A. is there

    B. there are

    C. are there

11. I think _____ 4 banks in town.

    A. are there

    B. is there

    C. there are

READING/VOCABULARY: Read the following library information. Then choose the correct answer for each question below.

Get a library card today!

With a PLFC library card, you can check out books, audio books, and videotapes at libraries in Fairfax County. You can use the computers. You can bring your children to story hour.

- **Ask for an application at a library checkout desk or sign up online – www.plfc.org.**
- **Fairfax County residents get a free library card.**
- **Non-Fairfax County residents pay $25 for a library card.**
- **Your library card will be mailed to your home address.**
- **You can take out books, audio books, and videotapes for 3 weeks.**
- **Story hour is Saturday morning at 10:00.**

---

12. Where can you find this information?

    A. at a bank

    B. at a library

    C. at a hospital

13. What can you check out?

    A. books, videotapes, audio books

    B. computers, books, videotapes

    C. cards, audio books, books

14. I live in Fairfax County. Is the card free?

    A. yes

    B. no

15. I live in Sussex County. Is the card $15?

    A. yes

    B. no

16. Can we check out the computers?

    A. yes

    B. no

17. Is the library open Saturday morning?

    A. yes

    B. no

18. Are there books for children?

    A. yes

    B. no

19–20. WRITING: Write 2 sentences about the places on the map. Use words like *next to, between,* or *across from* to show location.

1. _____

2. _____

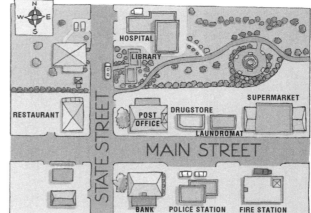

Name _____ **Date** _____ **Score** _____

LISTENING: Listen to the conversations. Then choose the correct answer for each item.

Conversation 1 🎧

1. The man asks a question to someone at _____.

   A. a library

   B. a restaurant

   C. a pharmacy

2. When is this place open on Sunday?

   A. 10:00 to 6:00

   B. 10:00 to 5:00

   C. 6:00 to 10:00

3. The man and the woman are _____.

   A. students at school

   B. a customer and a pharmacist

   C. a teacher and a nurse

Conversation 2 🎧

4. What is this conversation about?

   A. an address

   B. a zip code

   C. a telephone number

5. What kind of place is the listing for?

   A. a hospital

   B. a gas station

   C. a restaurant

6. What city is it in?

   A. Chicago

   B. Seattle

   C. Illinois

GRAMMAR: Choose the correct answer for each question.

7. How much is a penny and a quarter?

   A. six cents

   B. eleven cents

   C. twenty-six cents

8. How much is a quarter and two dimes?

   A. twenty-one cents

   B. forty-five cents

   C. fifty-five cents

9. How much is a nickel and a half-dollar?

   A. $1.05

   B. $.55

   C. $.35

10. Is the bank open on Saturday at noon?

   A. Yes, it is.

   B. No, he isn't.

   C. Yes, they are.

11. Are schools open at 3:00 A.M.?

   A. Yes, it is.

   B. No, it isn't.

   C. No, they aren't.

12. Is the post office open on Sunday?

   A. Yes, they are.

   B. No, they aren't.

   C. No, it isn't.

READING/VOCABULARY: Read the following information. Then choose the answer that correctly completes each sentence.

> ## Mama Green's Restaurant
>
> | | | | |
> |---|---|---|---|
> | Sunday | 11 A.M. – 11 P.M. | Thursday | 11 A.M. - midnight |
> | Monday | closed | Friday | 11 A.M. – 1 A.M. |
> | Tuesday | 11 A.M. – midnight | Saturday | 11 A.M. – 1 A.M. |
> | Wednesday | 11 A.M. – midnight | | |

13. The restaurant is open for _____ hours on Sunday.
    A. 10
    B. 12
    C. 14

14. It is open for _____ hours on Friday.
    A. 10
    B. 12
    C. 14

15. The restaurant is closed on _____.
    A. Sunday
    B. Monday
    C. Tuesday

16. It opens _____.
    A. in the morning
    B. in the afternoon
    C. at night

17. The restaurant is open for _____ hours total on Tuesday and Wednesday.
    A. 12
    B. 26
    C. 36

18. It closes at 11 P.M. on _____.
    A. Friday
    B. Saturday
    C. Sunday

19–20. WRITING: Write a check to Mama Green's Restaurant for lunch today. Lunch cost $15.49.

DAVID CAMPOS
35 Hay St., Apt. 3C
Coral Beach, FL 33915   127

DATE_____

PAY TO THE
ORDER OF_____ $ _____

_____ DOLLARS

TRUE BANK
Florida

MEMO_____   _____

⑈012345678⑈:   123ᴵᴵᴵ456 7ᴵᴵᵔ 0127

Name _____   Date _____   Score _____

LISTENING: Listen to the conversations. Then choose the correct answer for each question.

Conversation 1 🎧

1. What kind of appointment are they talking about?

    A. job

    B. dentist's

    C. doctor's

2. What date is the appointment?

    A. June 3rd

    B. June 13th

    C. June 30th

3. What day is the appointment?

    A. Tuesday

    B. Wednesday

    C. Thursday

Conversation 2 🎧

4. The 2 men are talking _____.

    A. on the telephone

    B. at work

    C. at the doctor's office

5. What does Mr. Brown want to do?

    A. make an appointment

    B. reschedule an appointment

    C. cancel an appointment

6. There is an opening on _____.

    A. November 4

    B. November 9

    C. November 14

GRAMMAR: Choose the correct answer to complete each sentence.

7. How many _____ are in a week?

    A. days

    B. months

    C. day

8. How many hours are in a _____?

    A. years

    B. weeks

    C. day

9. _____ weeks are in a year?

    A. How much

    B. How many

    C. How are

10. There are 30 _____ in November.

    A. day

    B. months

    C. days

11. There are 20 _____ in my class.

    A. student

    B. students

    C. teacher

12. There is 1 _____ in September.

    A. week

    B. holiday

    C. holidays

READING/VOCABULARY: Look over the calendar. Then read the questions, and choose the correct answer for each question.

JANUARY 2005				
MON	**TUES**	**WED**	**THURS**	**FRI**
5 Classes begin—start 2nd semester **Parents Teachers Organization Meeting** When: 7:15 P.M. Where: Room 105	**6** **Spelling Bee** When: 10:30 A.M. Where: Room 113 **Girls Basketball Practice** When: 4:00 P.M. Where: Gymnasium **Boys Basketball Practice** When: 6:30 P.M. Where: Gymnasium	**7** **Boys Basketball Practice** When: 6:00 P.M. Where: Field **Mexico Sister School Meeting** When: 7:30 P.M. Where: Media Center	**8** **Girls Basketball Practice** When: 6:00 P.M. Where: Gymnasium **Rising Grade 9 Parent Orientation** • Middle School When: 6:15 P.M. Where: Room 225	**9** **Admissions Interviews** **9th Grade Dance** When: 8:00 P.M. Where: Gymnasium **1st Semester report cards issued**

13. In what month is this calendar?

    A. 2005

    B. January

    C. September

14. What is this calendar for?

    A. a doctor's office

    B. a school

    C. a gas station

15. When are the admissions interviews?

    A. the fifth

    B. the seventh

    C. the ninth

16. When do boys have basketball practice?

    A. on Tuesday and Wednesday

    B. on Tuesday and Thursday

    C. on Tuesday and Friday

17. When does the second semester begin?

    A. 2/5

    B. 5/1

    C. 1/5

18. What time is the PTO meeting?

    A. 7:15 P.M.

    B. 7:00 A.M.

    C. 8:15 P.M.

19–20. WRITING: Write 2 sentences about your favorite holiday.

_____

_____

Name _____ Date _____ Score _____

LISTENING: Listen to the conversations. Then choose the correct answer for each sentence.

Conversation 1 🎧

1. These 2 men are _____.

   A. students

   B. a customer and a salesclerk

   C. a pharmacist and a cashier

2. The man is looking for _____.

   A. men's clothes

   B. men's coats

   C. men's sweaters

3. The coats are _____.

   A. on the second floor

   B. near the children's clothes

   C. next to the sweaters

Conversation 2 🎧

4. What are these women talking about?

   A. a t-shirt

   B. a coat

   C. a dress

5. Which size is too long?

   A. small

   B. medium

   C. large

6. Which size is not too long?

   A. small

   B. medium

   C. large

GRAMMAR: Choose the correct word to complete each sentence.

7. She _____ wearing a red shirt.

   A. am

   B. is

   C. are

8. They _____ talking on the telephone.

   A. are

   B. is

   C. am

9. We _____ buying books.

   A. am

   B. is

   C. are

10. Ann is my friend. I talk to _____ on the phone.

    A. me

    B. her

    C. she

11. She asks the students questions. She asks _____ about class.

    A. it

    B. us

    C. them

12. A salesclerk sells shoes. The customer buys _____.

    A. them

    B. him

    C. it

READING/VOCABULARY: Read the following information. Then choose the correct answer for each sentence.

HOW TO DRESS FOR A JOB INTERVIEW

MEN
- Wear a suit or a jacket and pants. Wear a neutral color or a dark color—blue, black, or gray is good.
- Wear a tie and a belt.
- Wear socks that are the same color as the pants.
- Wear black or brown shoes.
- Don't wear clothes that are too tight or too short.

WOMEN
- Wear a suit, a dress with a jacket, or pants and a jacket. Some appropriate colors are navy blue, black, dark green, dark red, or gray.
- Wear a white shirt or a color that looks good with the suit or pants.
- Wear black or brown shoes.
- Don't wear clothes that are too tight or too short.

---

13. This information is for someone who is going to _____.

    A. work

    B. interview for a new job

    C. school

14. Bob is wearing brown pants to an interview. It is a good idea for him to wear _____.

    A. brown socks

    B. a blue jacket

    C. red shoes

15. Which dress is good for a job interview?

    A. a pink dress

    B. a yellow dress

    C. a black dress

16. Both men and women can wear _____ to job interviews.

    A. tight clothes

    B. suits

    C. dresses

17. It is not a good idea to wear something _____ to a job interview.

    A. too short

    B. too dark

    C. too clean

18. Barbara doesn't have a suit, so she can wear _____.

    A. a tie and a jacket

    B. a dress and a jacket

    C. shorts and a t-shirt

19–20. WRITING: Write 2 sentences about what you are wearing today.

_____

_____

Name _____ Date _____ Score _____

LISTENING: Listen to the conversations. Then choose the correct answer for each question.

Conversation 1 🎧

1. What does the woman want?
   - A. tomatoes
   - B. orange juice
   - C. tomato juice

2. Where is the product the woman wants?
   - A. aisle one
   - B. fruit section
   - C. aisle nine

Conversation 2 🎧

3. Corn Crunchies are a type of _____.
   - A. cereal
   - B. vegetable
   - C. meat

4. How much are the Corn Crunchies?
   - A. $10.99 a box
   - B. $2.99 a box
   - C. $2.19 a box

5. In the conversations, the people are _____.
   - A. at home
   - B. at a supermarket
   - C. at school

6. Corn Crunchies usually cost $2.99.
   - A. true
   - B. false

GRAMMAR: Choose the correct word or phrase to complete the sentence.

7. A: Linda, do you like tomatoes?

   B: Yes, _____.
   - A. I do
   - B. I don't

8. A: Mike, do you and Tina eat fish?

   B: No, _____.
   - A. I don't
   - B. we don't

9. A: Mr. Campos, do we need our books tomorrow?

   B: Yes, _____.
   - A. you do
   - B. they do

10. A: Do you sell notebooks?

    B: _____.
    - A. Yes, we do.
    - B. Yes, they do.

11. A: Do you have a box of Corn Crunchies?

    B: _____.
    - A. No, you don't.
    - B. No, we don't.

12. Tom eats dinner every day at 6 o'clock. Tom _____ eats at 6.
    - A. always
    - B. sometimes
    - C. never

13. Wendy eats rice 2 or 3 days a month. Wendy _____ eats rice.
    - A. always
    - B. sometimes
    - C. never

READING/VOCABULARY: Read the following paragraph. Then choose the correct word or phrase to complete each sentence below.

> ## Back to School
>
> School is starting on Monday, and it's time to make school lunches. It's important to include nutritious food in your children's lunches. We have some ideas for you. Cut fruit, vegetables, bread, and cheese into small pieces so kids can pick them up easily. Slice apples or bananas to put in a peanut butter sandwich. These lunches are nutritious and delicious!

14. School starts on _____.

    A. Sunday

    B. Monday

    C. Tuesday

15. Another word for *kids* is _____.

    A. parents

    B. lunches

    C. children

16. Children _____ like fruit, bread, cheese, and peanut butter sandwiches.

    A. don't

    B. usually

    C. never

17. In the reading, it says you can slice _____ to put in a sandwich.

    A. bananas and apples

    B. apples and oranges

    C. fruit, vegetables, bread, and cheese

18. A *sandwich* is a kind of food that children often eat _____.

    A. for lunch

    B. in the morning

    C. at midnight

19–20. WRITING: Write 2 sentences about what you and your family eat at different times of the day. Use *always*, *usually*, *sometimes*, or *never*.

_____

_____

_____

_____

Name _____ Date _____ Score _____

LISTENING: Listen to the conversation. Then choose the correct answer for each question.

Conversation 1 🎧

1. What are the man and woman talking about?

    A. cleaning the house

    B. family responsibilities

    C. family expenses

2. Who does the man live with?

    A. his brother

    B. his parents

    C. his sister and brother

3. Who cooks dinner in his house?

    A. his sister

    B. his brother

    C. he does

Conversation 2 🎧

4. The man on the telephone is the girl's father.

    A. true

    B. false

5. The girl's mother is home.

    A. true

    B. false

6. The girl's mother works with Tom Lawson.

    A. true

    B. false

GRAMMAR: Choose the correct word or phrase to complete each sentence.

7. A: Does he listen to music?

  B: Yes, he _____.

    A. does   B. do

8. A: Do you wash the dishes?

  B: No, I _____.

    A. does   B. don't

9. A: What does she do?

  B: She _____.

    A. pays the bills   B. cook dinner

10. A: Who in your family plays an instrument?

  B: We all _____.

    A. does   B. do

11. _____ your parents live with you?

    A. Do   B. Does

12. Where _____ you buy groceries?

    A. do   B. does

READING/VOCABULARY: Read the following paragraph. Then choose the correct answer to complete each sentence.

My name is Mei. My husband's name is Jack. We have two children, Ann and Tim. I live in California now. Jack's parents live near us. We see them every week. I like my mother-in-law and father-in-law very much, but I miss my parents. My parents live in New York. Every year we go to New York to see them. My children love New York. My mother and I cook a lot of Chinese food. We buy presents for Jack's family. My mother tells stories about her life in China. My father plays an instrument and Ann dances.

13. Mei's mother is Tim's _____.

   A. sister

   B. wife

   C. grandmother

14. Ann's father is Mei's _____.

   A. father

   B. husband

   C. grandfather

15. Jack's mother is Mei's _____.

   A. grandmother

   B. sister

   C. mother-in-law

16. Who plays an instrument?

   A. Mei's father

   B. Ann's father

   C. Jack's grandfather

17. Mei likes Jack's parents.

   A. true

   B. false

18. We know Mei's parents are probably from China because _____.

   A. they live in New York

   B. her mother tells stories about China

   C. her father plays an instrument

19–20. WRITING: Write 2 sentences about the people in your family. Write about the responsibilities they have at home or about the things they do for fun.

_____

_____

_____

_____

Name _____ Date _____ Score _____

LISTENING: Listen to the conversations. Then choose the correct answer for each question.

Conversation 1 🎧

1. Where do you think these people are?

    A. at school

    B. at the doctor's office

    C. at the pharmacy

2. Who has the problem?

    A. the man

    B. the woman

    C. the doctor

3. What is the problem?

    A. a fever

    B. a fever and a sore throat

    C. a fever, a headache, and a sore throat

Conversation 2 🎧

4. Who is the man calling?

    A. the hospital

    B. the doctor

    C. 911

5 What's wrong with the man's friend?

    A. He isn't breathing.

    B. He is choking.

    C. He is bleeding.

6. Where are they?

    A. in a supermarket

    B. in a parking lot

    C. at the corner of Jackson and Pine

GRAMMAR: Choose the correct answer for each sentence.

7. He can _____ an instrument.

    A. play

    B. plays

    C. to play

8. A: Can you touch your toes?

    B: Yes, I _____.

    A. can't

    B. touch

    C. can

9. Can they play soccer?

    A. No, they don't.

    B. No, they can't.

    C. No, they aren't.

10. Should children drink alcohol?

    A. Yes, he should.

    B. No, she shouldn't.

    C. No, they shouldn't.

11. I'm tired. I should _____ the dishes.

    A. not wash

    B. should wash

    C. not washing

12. "It's a good idea for her to play basketball," means _____.

    A. She can play basketball.

    B. She is playing basketball.

    C. She should play basketball.

READING/VOCABULARY: Read the following information. Then choose the correct answer for each sentence.

```
See-Clear

                Window Cleaner
                  With ammonia

CAUTION: Keep out of reach of children. Do not
take internally. If swallowed, drink a lot of water.
If product gets in eyes, wash eyes with water for
15 minutes.
        16 fluid ounces (1 pint) 473 milliliters
```

13. You can use this product _____.

    A. for a headache

    B. for cooking

    C. for windows

14. You should drink See-Clear.

    A. true

    B. false

15. You should not give See-Clear to children.

    A. true

    B. false

16. If you have See-Clear in your eyes, you should _____.

    A. drink water

    B. wash your eyes with water

    C. call 911

17. This information is on _____.

    A. a wall

    B. some medicine

    C. a bottle of cleaner

18. Why does a person need this information?

    A. for safety

    B. to save money

    C. to know how much to use

19–20. WRITING: Read the letter from a mother below. Write 2 sentences giving her advice. Use *should* and *shouldn't*.

My son is very sick. He has a fever, a headache, and a sore throat. He isn't breathing very well because he has a cold. What should I do?

_____

_____

Name _____ Date _____ Score _____

LISTENING: Listen to the conversation. Then choose the correct answer for each sentence.

Conversation 1 🎧

1. Henry is talking to a friend.

   A. true

   B. false

2. Henry tripped on the carpet.

   A. true

   B. false

3. Henry hurt his foot and his back.

   A. true

   B. false

Conversation 2 🎧

4. The man is calling about _____.

   A. a house

   B. an apartment

   C. a mobile home

5. It has _____ bedrooms.

   A. 1

   B. 2

   C. 3

6. The rent is _____.

   A. $825 a month

   B. $525 a month

   C. $835 a month

GRAMMAR: Choose the correct answer to complete each sentence.

7. They didn't _____ the house last year.

   A. rented

   B. rent

   C. renting

8. Mario rented an apartment. He didn't _____ a condo.

   A. buy

   B. buys

   C. bought

9. Jack _____ down the stairs yesterday.

   A. fall

   B. falls

   C. fell

10. We _____ at the housing ads every day. We want a new house.

    A. look

    B. looked

    C. don't look

11. Cynthia _____ to Kansas last month.

    A. not go

    B. went

    C. goes

12. Our old house _____ a garden, but our new apartment _____.

    A. didn't have/didn't have

    B. had/doesn't

    C. had/didn't have

READING/VOCABULARY: Read the following ads. Then choose the correct answer for each sentence.

House for Rent	For Rent
4BR, 2BA, big kitchen, fireplace, garage $1250/mo Call Martin Realty 555-4035	3 bed, 2 bath apt. pool and patio, nr schools $1000/mo. Call Tina at 555-8092

13. Where can you find this information?

    A. on a map

    B. on a label

    C. in a newspaper

14. The house has four bathrooms.

    A. true

    B. false

15. The apartment has a fireplace.

    A. true

    B. false

16. The house has a small kitchen.

    A. true

    B. false

17. The apartment is near schools.

    A. true

    B. false

18. The rent for the apartment is more expensive than the house.

    A. true

    B. false

19–20. WRITING: Write 2 sentences about where you lived in 1995. Use the simple past tense.

_____

_____

_____

_____

Name _____ Date _____ Score _____

LISTENING: Listen to the conversation. Then choose the correct answer for each sentence.

Conversation 1 🎧

1. The 2 people on the phone are _____.
   A. a mover and a customer
   B. a pharmacist and a person looking for a job
   C. a farmer and a chef

2. The man wants to be _____.
   A. a pharmacist's assistant
   B. a mechanic
   C. a chef's assistant

3. The meeting is at _____.
   A. 9:00 on Tuesday
   B. 10:30 tomorrow
   C. 9:30 on Thursday

Conversation 2 🎧

4. The two men are in a restaurant.
   A. true
   B. false

5. The man wants to be a landscaper.
   A. true
   B. false

6. He worked as a chef in his last job.
   A. true
   B. false

GRAMMAR: Choose the best answer for each sentence.

7. Did he work as a mechanic?
   A. Yes, he worked.
   B. Yes, he does.
   C. Yes, he did.

8. Did you go to the store yesterday?
   A. No, I didn't.
   B. No, I went.
   C. No, I don't.

9. Did she _____ the dishes?
   A. wash
   B. washes
   C. washed

10. We _____ buy a house next year.
    A. go to
    B. are going to
    C. is going to

11. She _____ eat at a restaurant tonight.
    A. going to
    B. is going to
    C. goes to

12. What are you going to do next Saturday?
    A. I go shopping.
    B. She's going to meet her teacher.
    C. We're going to see some friends.

READING/VOCABULARY: Read the following ad. Then choose the correct answer for each sentence.

City General Hospital

Nurses
Pharmacists
Pharmacist Assistants
Nurse Assistants

City General is looking for experienced workers for all positions. Full-time or part-time available. Great benefits. $12–$40 an hour. Call (618) 555-2000 to apply.

---

13. The jobs in the ad are at _____.

    A. a hospital

    B. a drugstore

    C. the General Market

14. You need experience for all the jobs.

    A. true

    B. false

15. All the jobs are for 40 hours a week.

    A. true

    B. false

16. You need to apply for the jobs in person.

    A. true

    B. false

17. Nurse assistants might earn $45 an hour.

    A. true

    B. false

18. Pharmacists might earn $35 an hour.

    A. true

    B. false

19–20. WRITING: Write 2 sentences about your skills or work experience.

_____

_____

_____

_____

UNIT 1 TEST

Conversation 1

Female: Hi, I'm Mary.
Male: Hi Mary. I'm Victor.
Female: Where are you from?
Male: Mexico.

Conversation 2

Male: Hello, I'm Martin Campos.
Female: Nice to meet you, Mr. Campos. I'm Helen Jones.
Male: Nice to meet you, Ms. Jones.

UNIT 2 TEST

Conversation 1

Male: Excuse me. Is there a post office near here?
Female: Yes, there is. There's one on College Street.
Male: On College Street?
Female: Yes, across from the police station.

Conversation 2

Female: Excuse me. Is there a bank near here?
Male: Sorry, I don't know.
Female: Is there an ATM near here?
Male: Yes, there's one next to the gas station.

UNIT 3 TEST

Conversation 1

Female: Mercy Hospital Pharmacy. Can I help you?
Male: Are you open on Sunday?
Female: Yes, we're open from 10 to 6.
Male: Thanks.

Conversation 2

Male: Visioncom. What city and state?
Female: Chicago, Illinois.
Male: What listing?
Female: Mama Green's Restaurant.
Male: The number is area code (312) 555-3381.

UNIT 4 TEST

Conversation 1 #s 1,2,3

Male: When is your doctor's appointment?
Female: It's on June 13th.
Male: What day is that?
Female: It's a Thursday.

Conversation 2 #s 4,5,6

Male 1: Dr. Lambert's office.
Male 2: This is Robert Brown. I need to reschedule my appointment.
Male 1: Okay. I have an opening on November 4th at 9:00.
Male 2: Great. I'll take it. Thanks.

UNIT 5 TEST

Conversation 1

Male 1:	Can I help you?
Male 2:	Yes, I'm looking for men's coats.
Male 1:	They're on the first floor.
Male 2:	The first floor?
Male 1:	Yes, they're next to the sweaters.

Conversation 2

Female 1:	What size is this dress?
Female 2:	It's a medium.
Female 1:	Really? I think it's too long. Do you have a small?
Female 2:	Yes. Here you go.
Female 1:	Thank you! This is not too long.

UNIT 6 TEST

Conversation 1

Female:	Excuse me. Do you sell tomato juice?
Male:	Yes, we do. It's in aisle nine.
Female:	Do you sell apple-banana juice?
Male:	No, I'm sorry. We don't.

Conversation 2

Male 1:	Do you have cereal on sale this week?
Male 2:	Yes, we do. Corn Crunchies are $2.99 a box.
Male 1:	What size?
Male 2:	10 ounces.

UNIT 7 TEST

Conversation 1

Female:	Do your parents live with you?
Male:	No, they don't. They live in Panama. I live with my brother and sister.
Female:	Who does the laundry in your family?
Male:	I do. My sister cooks dinner, and my brother buys the groceries.

Conversation 2

Male:	Can I speak to your mother please?
Female:	She's not here now. Can I take a message?
Male:	Can you ask her to call Tom Lawson? I work with her.
Female:	Okay.
Male:	Thank you.
Female:	You're welcome.

UNIT 8 TEST

Conversation 1

Female:	What's the problem?
Male:	I have a fever.
Female:	Does your head hurt, too?
Male:	Yes, it does. And I have a sore throat.

Conversation 2

Female:	This is 911.
Male:	We need an ambulance quickly! My friend isn't breathing!
Female:	Where are you?
Male:	In the parking lot of Giant Supermarket. It's on Jackson Street.

UNIT 9 TEST

Conversation 1

Female: What happened to Henry?

Male: He slipped in the shower.

Female: Is he okay?

Male: No, he hurt his foot and his back.

Conversation 2

Male: I'm calling about the apartment for rent. Is it still available?

Female: Yes, it is.

Male: How many bedrooms does it have?

Female: Three.

Male: And how many bathrooms?

Female: One.

Male: How much is the rent?

Female: $825 a month.

UNIT 10 TEST

Conversation 1

Male: I'm calling about the ad for a pharmacist's assistant.

Female: Do you have experience?

Male: Yes, I do. I have three years experience in my country.

Female: Can you come in for an interview on Thursday at 9:30?

Male: Yes, I'll be there.

Conversation 2

Male 1: Tell me about your last job.

Male 2: I worked at an apartment building. I was a landscaper.

Male 1: Did you like the job?

Male 2: Yes. I liked taking care of plants. And I like to work with my hands.

Male 1: Why did you leave your last job?

Male 2: I went back to school. I studied to be a chef. Now I want to work in this restaurant.

Unit Test Answer Key

UNIT 1 TEST

Answer Key:

1. a; 2. c; 3. a; 4. b; 5. a; 6. c; 7. a; 8. c; 9. c; 10. b;
11. b; 12. a ; 13. c; 14. b; 15. c; 16. b; 17. b; 18. b
19 and 20. Answers will vary according to individual student's information.

> **Application Form**
>
> Name: <u>Paul   Richard   Bridges</u>
>   First   Middle   Last
> Address: <u>8517 Alvardo St. Los Angeles CA 91012</u>
>   Street   City   State Zip Code

UNIT 2 TEST

Answer Key:

1. b; 2. c; 3. b; 4. b; 5. b; 6. b; 7. b; 8. a; 9. a; 10. a;
11. c; 12. b; 13. a; 14. a; 15. b; 16. b; 17. a; 18. a
19 and 20. Answers will vary. Possible answers may include the following sentences:

> The post office is next to the drugstore.
> The laundromat is between the drugstore and the supermarket.
> The bank is across from the post office.
> There's a park in front of the library.
> There's a restaurant on the corner of State Street and Main Street.

UNIT 3 TEST

Answer Key:

1. c; 2. a; 3. b; 4. c; 5. c; 6. a; 7. c; 8. b; 9. b; 10. a;
11. c; 12. c; 13. b; 14. c; 15. b; 16. a; 17. b; 18. c
19 and 20.

UNIT 4 TEST

Answer Key:

1. c; 2. b; 3. c; 4. a; 5. b; 6. a; 7. a; 8. c; 9. b ; 10. c;
11. b; 12. b ; 13. b; 14. b; 15. c; 16. a; 17. c; 18. a
19 and 20. Answers will vary. Possible answers may include similar sentences:

> My favorite holiday is Thanksgiving. It's in November.
> My favorite holiday is Valentine's Day. I like this holiday because I give my girlfriend flowers and she gives me chocolate.

UNIT 5 TEST

Answer Key:

1. b; 2. b; 3. c; 4. c; 5. b; 6. a; 7. b; 8. a; 9. c; 10. b;
11. c; 12. a; 13. b; 14. a; 15. c; 16. b; 17. a; 18. b
19 and 20. Answers will vary. Possible answers may include similar sentences:

> I'm wearing blue pants and a white sweater. My pants are too long.
> I'm wearing a dress. The dress is green and yellow.
> I'm wearing a big coat because it's cold today. I'm wearing brown boots.

UNIT 6 TEST

Answer Key:

1. c; 2. c; 3. a; 4. b; 5. b; 6. b; 7. a; 8. b; 9. a; 10: a;
11. b; 12. a; 13. b; 14. b; 15. c; 16. b; 17. a ; 18. a
19 and 20. Answers will vary. Possible answers may include similar sentences:

> I usually eat cereal for breakfast. My father always eats rice.
> My family often eats chicken for dinner. We usually eat fruits and vegetables, too.
> We never eat pizza for breakfast. My parents always drink coffee in the morning.

UNIT 7 TEST

Answer Key:

1. b; 2. c; 3. a; 4. b; 5. b; 6. a; 7. a; 8. b; 9. a; 10. b; 11. a; 12. a; 13. c; 14. b; 15. c ; 16. a; 17. a; 18. b

19 and 20. Answers will vary. Possible answers may include similar sentences:

> My father pays the bills and my mother often fixes things. They like to listen to music.

> I live with my husband and daughter. I usually cook dinner and my husband washes the dishes.

> I live with my sister and my parents. My sister likes to take pictures and my parents sometimes play cards.

UNIT 8 TEST

Answer Key:

1. b; 2. a; 3. c; 4. c; 5. a; 6. b; 7. a; 8. c; 9. b; 10. c; 11. a; 12. c; 13. c; 14. b; 15. a; 16. b; 17. c; 18. a

19 and 20. Answers will vary. Possible answers may include the following sentences:

> He should take aspirin.

> He should drink liquids.

> He shouldn't call 911.

> He should rest.

UNIT 9 TEST

Answer Key:

1. b; 2. b; 3. a; 4. b; 5. c; 6. a; 7. b; 8. a; 9. c; 10. a; 11. b; 12. b; 13. c; 14. b; 15. b; 16. b; 17. a; 18. b

19 and 20. Answers will vary. All answers should be in the past tense. Possible answers may include similar sentences:

> Our house was small. It had one bedroom and one bathroom.

> I lived in a beautiful apartment in 1995. It had two big bedrooms and one bathroom.

UNIT 10 TEST

Answer Key:

1. b; 2. a; 3. c; 4. b; 5. b; 6. b; 7. c; 8. a; 9. a; 10. b; 11. b; 12. c; 13. a; 14. a; 15. b; 16. b; 17. b; 18. a

19 and 20. Answers will vary. Possible answers may include similar sentences:

> I was a teacher for five years. I like children and I'm creative.

> I can drive a truck. I was a mechanic for two years.